A Million Miles from Broadway
Musical Theatre Beyond New York and London

Friendlysong Books
Vancouver ● London

Published by The Friendlysong Company, Inc.
4827 Georgia Street, Delta, British Columbia, Canada V4K 2T1

Cataloguing:

Atkey, Mel (1958-)

A Million Miles from Broadway – Musical Theatre Beyond New York and London
Includes bibliographic references and index
ISBN 978-0-9916957-0-6

1 – Musicals – International – History and criticism.

Cover photo credits, clockwise from top left:
Athanaeum Theatre, Melbourne, photo by author
Royal AlexandraTheatre, Toronto, photo by author
NovelloTheatre, London, 2007, photo by author
Dracula, Buenos Aires,1991, courtesy of Angel Mahler
Anne of Green Gables, Theatre Under The Stars, Vancouver, 2003, photo courtesy of Roger Smith
Forbidden City, photo courtesy of Singapore Repertory Theatre

Books by Mel Atkey

When We Both Got to Heaven: James Atkey Among the Anishnabek at Colpoy's Bay

Broadway North: The Dream of a Canadian Musical Theatre

Running Away with the Circus (or, "Now is the Winter of our Missing Tent") (forthcoming)

Table of Contents

Dedication: "Normandy Lane"..5
Acknowledgements..6

OVERTURE

Preface: A Search for Signs of Life..8

ACT I: THE PARENTS

European Musical Comedy (Oops, I Mean Operetta)........................18
Musicals for the Masses: Emanuel Schikaneder and the Theater an der Wien..............26
Cabaret: From "le Chat Noir" to the Algonquin Room..........................35
Give My Regards to Friedrichstrasse..50
Paris: Where Musicals Were Born, and Where they Go to Die.............56
Declaration of Independence..79

ENTR'ACTE: A NEW WORLD ORDER

The New World(s) 86
The Rock 'n' Roll Syndrome 88
Universality Part 1: "Do They Understand This Show in America? It's So Japanese!".....96
Universality Part 2: A Sense of Time and Place............................109

ACT II: THE OFFSPRING

"Who Will Buy?" Lionel Bart and the Post-war British Musical...............117
Europopera...124
Canada – "Still Deciding What it Will Be"..................................132
Larrikins and Sentimental Blokes: Musicals Down Under.....................153
South Africa: "Freedom is Coming"..179
"Down South American Way" – Musical Theatre in Latin America..............191
"The Theatre Is Alive" – Musical Theatre in Asia...........................199
New Musicals: "You Have to Kiss a Lot of Frogs"...........................222

FINALE

Are We Up For It?..235

Bibliography...240
List of interviewees...252
Author's biography...253

Norman and Elaine Campbell

Dedication: "Normandy Lane"

A few years ago, Norman and Elaine Campbell, composer and co-lyricist of *Anne of Green Gables - The Musical™*, applied to the local authorities to change the name of the road leading to their farm house in Covehead, Prince Edward Island. They asked for it to be renamed "Normandy Lane". Eventually the word came back from a jubilant official, "Mr. Campbell, we've agreed to your request to rename it 'Normandy Road'". "No! You don't understand!"

For those of us struggling to create new musical theatre, (especially those of us who do not live in New York) it seems we are always struggling against those in the majority who just don't "get it". Norman and Elaine were my mentors. Both professionally and personally, they were role models. As Canadian musical writers, we were all swimming against the current, but it was great comfort to know that at least we were swimming together. So this book is dedicated, not just to Norm and Elaine, but to all those in "Normandy Lane" – swimming uphill together.

Thanks to Cliff Jones for telling me this story.

Acknowledgements

A book like this cannot be written without the invaluable assistance of others. (Especially when it is done without the help of government grants.) I have consulted many experts in the field, including those with experience and expertise far beyond my own.

In Australia, I "dips me lid" to Ray Kolle, a musical book writer who introduced me to Tony Sheldon, Peter Pinne and Frank Van Straten, who have each written and published their own accounts of Australian musical theatre. Will Conyers and P.J. Buchanan had me as a guest on their show *Broadway at Bedtime*, and through Will I met Aaron Joyner of Magnormos and Dr. Peter Wyllie Johnston, whose doctoral thesis was on Australian musicals. Col Macdonald, the current owner of Collits' Inn, provided me with a copy of the original recording of his home's namesake musical, while Jonathan Harvey gave me a video of the more recent concert production of that work that he produced. From Kookaburra I want to thank Peter Cousens and Peter Ross. Thanks also to Jill Perryman, Jenny Benjamin and Peter Stannard.

In Singapore, I would like to thank Dr. Kenneth Lyen, Stella Kon and Desmond Moey of Musical Theatre Limited for their hospitality and information, and Veronica Goh of the Esplanade Theatres on the Bay. Dick Lee met up with me in London, and Ken Low corresponded by email. Aaron Hales in Perth, Western Australia also supplied helpful leads. Charlotte Nors of Singapore Repertory Theatre provided photographs.

In Japan, very special thanks to Amon Miyamoto (and to his interpreter, Yuriri Naka).

Dr. Leonie Rae Stickland in Perth supplied invaluable information on the TakarazukaRevue, and Julian Forsyth provided background information on the German cabaret composer Mischa Spoliansky.

For South Africa, I would like to acknowledge Percy Tucker and Prof. Michael Simpson for their background information.

For Argentina, I want to thank Elena Roger, who put me in touch with Pablo Gorlero, who has written the definitive history of Argentine musical comedy, and to Guillermo Masutti, who represents the team of Angel Mahler and Pepe Cibrian . I would also like to thank Peter Pinne, who lived in Santiago in the late 1990s and shared his experience of Latin American musicals.

For the Netherlands, I would like to thank René Driessen and Hugh Ross, and Rosalie Mohr and Paul Eenens of Stage Entertainment.

Bob Martin, Don McKellar and Lisa Lambert provided invaluable information on the development of *The Drowsy Chaperone*.

Thanks to Stephen Cole for sharing his experiences in Qatar.

For help with *Irma la Douce*, thanks to Greg MacKellan of 42nd Street Moon, San Francisco.

From Broadway Asia International, thanks to Damon Brooks and Simone Genatt.

For information on the development process of new musicals, I want to thank Georgina Bexon of Mercury Musical Developments, Chris Gradyof Musical Theatre Matters, John Sparks of Theatre Building Chicago, Søren Møller of Uterus and Kerry Michael of Theatre Royal Stratford East.

For their general support, I want to thank Mark Fox, archivist for Really Useful Theatres; Charles Gilbert of the Musical Theatre Educators AllianceInternational; Virginia Reh of Lyric Canada; Michael Owen, Archivist, Ira and Leonore Gershwin Trusts; Scott Ashton Swan of Applause Musicals Society, Vancouver; Raymond Padua of White Rabbit Productions, Winnipeg; Lawrence Westlake; Tedde Moore; Teng Ky-gan; Martin Taylor; Jeremy Sams; Prof. David Overton, Dr. Michael Kunze, Gyles Brandreth, Tony Castro, Dr. Andrew Killick, Ian Fenwick, Athena Stanley, Leslie (Hoban) Blake, Kurt Gänzl (the author of many highly authoritative books on musical theatre, some of which are listed in my bibliography), and the staff of the Victoria and Albert Museum's Theatre Collection (formerly the Theatre Museum). Thanks also to Barry Penhale and Jane Gibson of Natural Heritage Books. And special thanks to the late Cheryl Hutcherson for being such a tireless theatre supporter.

Above all, I would like to thank my family – my parents, Ken and Marion Atkey, my sisters Marilyn Atkey and Beverley Atkey Beese and my brother-in-law Bill Beese for their continued support.

Within the text, I have indicated the dates of birth and death (where applicable) of the major players where this information is available.

Preface: A Search for Signs of Life

The notion that the musical theatre is, primarily, an American art form has been, for many generations, a given. Like jazz, it is said to be America's gift to the world. However, while it is undeniable that the modern musical reached its zenith on Broadway in the 1940s and 50s, "the history of the musical theatre", in the words of historian Kurt Gänzl, "is no one-nation or one-center affair."[1]   American composer-lyricist Maury Yeston (1945-) says, "Broadway is now a very long street running from the Kartnerstrasse in Vienna through Hamburg and Amsterdam, across to the West End, New York, Chicago, Minneapolis, L.A., to the Ginza and beyond."[2] Musical comedy wasn't born in America, and I do not believe that Broadway is its "end destination".

I grew up in Vancouver, British Columbia, where my early exposure to musicals came through local amateur productions, movies and the odd touring show. Like *The Drowsy Chaperone*'s "Man in Chair" character, I saw them from a remote distance, and they were therefore filtered through local perceptions. New York may have been literally about 3,000 miles away, but it might as well have been a million.

Of course, we know that the American musical was the child of a European parent. What is not so widely understood is that the parent had other offspring as well, and therefore the American musical has siblings. So why did the late Peter Stone, a former president of the Dramatists Guild and a noted Broadway librettist, once claim that no musical theatre existed outside of New York City?[3] This seemed to be a slightly perverse assertion since, at the time, Broadway was dominated by *Cats*, *Phantom of the Opera* and *Les Misérables*, with barely an American-written musical to be seen (or heard).

With all due respect to the late Mr. Stone, musical theatre does indeed exist outside of New York. I'm not talking about the many franchised versions of *Cats* and *Phantom of the Opera* that have played everywhere from Tel Aviv to Abu Dabi. I'm referring to indigenous musical theatre created in places other than New York by people other than New Yorkers and drawing on traditions other than those of Broadway. We are now in the world of what Canadian academic Marshall McLuhan (1911-80) called the "global village".[4]

Music is, after all, a universal language. I believe that it is hardwired into us. Some say that it stems from the beating of the heart, our natural metronome. "Singing is as essential for humans as it is for our fellow musical creatures", says David Rothenberg, author of *Why Birds Sing: A Journey into the History of Bird Song*. "Birds, whales and humans all sing because we must, because it is of our very essence."[5] Since prehistoric times, music and dance and storytelling have formed a part of religious rites of all kinds. The first Greek dramas were sung (although the music has long since been lost). Why? What makes us sing?

The noted Indian classical musician Hazrat Inayat Khan says that "the human body was made in tone and rhythm."[6] Sarah Schlesinger, chair of the Tisch School of the Arts' Graduate Musical Theatre Writing Program adds, "To my mind, the merging of words and music is the most powerful mode of expression available to us. When this power is used in the service of storytelling, there is no limit to what is possible."[7]

Perhaps the question we should really be asking is what *stops* us from singing? Diana Deutsch, a psychologist at the University of California at San Diego has discovered an interesting phenomenon. When a recording of a short, spoken phrase is played back several times in succession, it begins to sound like music. "It brings to the fore a real mystery – why don't we hear speech as song all the time?" The answer, she believes, is that the human brain suppresses our recognition of pitch, and that the exact repetition of a sound we've already processed over-rides this. "It stops the inhibition of the pitch region of the brain so we hear song, which is really what we ought to have been hearing in the first place."[8]

When composer Howard Goodall related a story in his book *Big Bangs* of how a particular piece of music came to him in a somewhat mystical way, somebody suggested to him that it was the most convincing proof he had yet heard of the existence of God. "There are no easy answers to account for being moved to tears by notes on a page, or of being stirred to anger and action, or being comforted in our loneliness", he says. "It's a mystery how Rachmaninoff's flowing melodies and ripe harmonies make people feel romantic and amorous, or how Ravel's Boléro conjures up sexiness."[9] Certain harmonies have an emotional effect on an audience – so much so that, at some points in our dark and distant past, authorities have actually tried to ban augmented fourths on the pretext that they were intrinsically evil.

It also seems that music is an innate talent. Whether the product of nature or nurture, it defies scientific analysis. It's what I call the *je ne sais quoi* factor – you can have a PhD in composition, and not have the "talent" of some kid with a guitar who plays by ear. "Songwriters are a breed apart", says composer and conductor André Previn. "Application of musical sophistication has very little to do with basic melodic genius. It isn't an inflammatory opinion to say that Irving Berlin's songs are better than Leonard Bernstein's, nor is the fact that Bernstein had more musical knowledge in his eyelashes than Berlin had in his whole persona up for debate."[10]

Music also has regional characteristics. Edward Elgar is thought to be quintessentially English, while Sergei Prokofiev is unmistakably Russian and George Gershwin uniquely American. Musical styles can evoke a sense of place and time. It hardly matters that the music may not actually be indigenous to that place. American music is, for the most part, a fusion of European and African forms. What gives it that unique imprint? Dr. Aniruddh Patel of the Neuroscience Institute in San Diego argues that even instrumental music is influenced by language in its rhythm and accent.

"Composers, like every other person in their culture, learn the patterns of their language and it's latent in their minds, so when they compose, they have those patterns to draw on."[11] This can make translation very difficult. "It seems to me that the music of any country is a reflection of its language", says American composer and lyricist Stephen Sondheim, "and that the rhythms of that particular country's language are what is appropriate. As soon as you translate it, it's very very hard to make it sound as if it is really wedded to the music."[12]

If music and theatre are primal and have existed since the beginning of civilisation, it should follow that musical theatre is also universal. That is the premise of this book. Each country that I discuss in the ensuing chapters is struggling to find its own unique voice. For some it has been a greater struggle than for others: some have to deal with oppressive political regimes, some with domestic indifference, and many are shouting to be heard over louder and more prosperous voices. Some countries have been turning out artists of international stature for many years, while others are embryonic.

I have, for the most part, excluded the thoroughly-explored history of the Broadway or West End musical, except to place the development of American and British musicals in a "universal" context. This is not in any sense anti-New York or anti-London. It's just that the lights of Broadway are so bright that it's often difficult to see anything else. Sometimes, just as a ship travelling at night must dim its own lights in order to maintain visibility, so we have to block out those bright lights of Broadway so that we can see (hear) ourselves think.

The fact is that the world is changing, and its centre of gravity is shifting. "At the military and political level, we still live in a unipolar [i.e. US dominated] world," says Fareed Zakaria, author of *The Post-American World*. "But along every other dimension – industrial, financial, social, cultural – the distribution of power is shifting, moving away from American dominance. In terms of war and peace, economics and business, ideas and art, this will produce a landscape that is quite different from the one we have lived in until now – one defined and directed from many places and by many peoples."[13]

Until the Second World War, there were not two centres for musical theatre, but at least four. Alan Jay Lerner, the librettist behind *My Fair Lady* said, "Broadway cannot live without the musical theatre, but the musical theatre can live without Broadway. After all, its first home was Paris and then Vienna and then London and then New York. So changes of address are not uncommon."[14] I believe that musical theatre is evolving back toward being this kind of an international form again. "Writers and composers in other countries have made serious attempts to rival the creative spirits of the American musical theatre", wrote the late Broadway conductor Lehman Engel in 1981. "There seems to be no reason why they should not succeed."[15] In addition to his BMI musical theatre workshops in New York, Los Angeles and Nashville, Engel also taught them in Toronto.

Even within the United States, musical theatre is shifting away from Broadway and the West End. Maury Yeston and Arthur Kopit's *Phantom* is an example of a show that has been produced very profitably in the regions without ever playing in New York. "Of course, people dream of having their shows discovered and raised to the Tony Award or Olivier Award winning level in a commercial production in New York or London", says John Sparks, the artistic director of the Academy for New Musical Theatre in Los Angeles. "But this is no longer the primary focus. Writers, producers, non-profit theatres and others involved in the form are focusing on more local audiences."

In this book's first "Act", I tell the story of the musical's origins in France, Britain, central Europe, and its migration to (and partial reinvention in) America. This is not just an academic exercise or a history lesson; it is to point out the foundations both of our existing musical theatre and of potential future developments. I believe that in order to understand where musical theatre is going, you need to know something about where it came from. According to Lerner, it all started in Paris – a city now known ironically as the graveyard of musicals. I recently went there in search of its actual birthplace. Just around the corner from the Quatre Septembre Métro station, up the Rue Monsigny, lies the Théâtre des Bouffes-Parisiens. Originally dating from 1826, it was opened by Louis Comte (1783-1859), a ventriloquist and director of the École de Comédiens, a theatre for children. However, it was the man with whom, almost thirty years later, Comte's son Charles would go into business that would make this place special. His name was Jacques Offenbach. The year was 1858 and the show that would change the face of musical theatre forever (and have people dancing the can-can in the aisles) was called *Orphée aux Enfers* – "Orpheus in the Underworld".

Paris was, at the time, the cultural capital of the Western world, and as the Belle Epoque approached, things would only get better. The people who invented champagne also invented the cabarets where audiences could sip it. And of course, the Folies-Bergère and the Moulin Rouge. And "comédie-musicale" – musical comedy. A revolution was in the air – and it spread from Paris to Vienna, Berlin, Budapest, London, New York and the world.

Yes, musical theatre is revolutionary. As I began my research for this book, one of my most startling discoveries was the extent to which the development of popular musical theatre coincided with the development of democracy. Sometimes it was part of the democratic struggle, but more often it was a by-product of that evolution. John Gay's *The Beggars' Opera* was a political satire. Although it was later appropriated by the elite, Mozart's *The Magic Flute* (which premiered only two years after the French Revolution), was written for the masses. Gilbert and Sullivan poked fun at the upper classes and those in authority. It is hardly surprising that the Americans embraced the form so enthusiastically – but they were not the only ones. Musical comedy and cabaret flourished in Weimar Berlin (but not under the Nazis, who were not noted for their sense of fun), and in late 19th century Paris. Musicals – as opposed to most opera – are written and composed in the vernacular, and are accessible to the masses. What Mozart (and after him, Kurt Weill, Leonard Bernstein and, more recently, Maury Yeston and Howard Goodall) sought to do was to educate those masses, and to bring sophisticated musical and dramatic forms to as wide an audience as possible.

So, if it's true that musical theatre developed alongside democracy, then why has it lost its leading role in Western culture? In the 1950s, rock and roll usurped the musical as the "vernacular" form. It became the music of the streets, the voice of protest. (It was an uneasy coalition between the kids who bought the records and made the music, and the businessmen who saw a market niche and exploited it.) On the other hand, the musical sought a rapprochement with opera. Some say that the musical failed to keep up with the times. "As a creative musical force, the contemporary West End musical is dead," says Neil Tennant of the 80s pop duo The Pet Shop Boys. "It contains the sort of music you only find in musicals; it has no relevance to contemporary music; it exists in a creative ghetto… The music and lyrics have one foot in the past and the other in parody."[16] Others will argue that popular music has declined in craftsmanship. Rock and roll has seldom fulfilled Mozart's aim to elevate the tastes of the masses. A few shows have attempted to combine contemporary pop music with sophistication, but all too often the one defeated the other. (Tennant produced Liza Minelli's 1989 technopop disco version of Sondheim's "Losing My Mind", sandblasting away any trace of sophistication or subtlety, then goring it of whatever harmony or texture may have lain within.)

Still, musicals remain by far the most popular form of live theatre, and they've found support from some unlikely sources. "The musicals I've seen recently knocked spots off any modern drama", says British playwright Steven Berkoff. "*Chicago* is unbelievably clever. Most new plays bore me to death."[17]

Music is a direct conduit to the human heart, and there is no more potent force and nothing bolder or more radical than splashing that across a stage. The American theatre critic Brooks Atkinson said, "I have sometimes wondered whether it is not a more genuine and comprehensive form of theater than the spoken drama… It is the one element of poetry left in a form of entertainment that was all poetry originally".[18] It has a great tradition, yet it continues to break new ground. Like jazz, it has a devout following of highly literate enthusiasts. Of course, like any art form, there are camp and tacky elements, to be sure. Sometimes it descends into kitsch, but at its core, it is the most demanding of performing art forms.

As we move into this new global musical world, it is important to understand its heritage. I talk to all too many young actors and actresses, straight out of stage school, who seem to think that musical theatre began with *Les Misérables* or even *Rent*. When I was a participant in Toronto's Guild of Canadian Musical Theatre Writers' workshops – based on the teachings of Lehman Engel – I was told to study the works that came before me. This, it was assumed, meant the great Broadway songwriters.

12

What I learned was that, while Jerome Kern and George Gershwin had studied and been influenced by the great European operettas and musical comedies, they yearned to create something that was more identifiably American. It was, for them, part of the long process of overcoming a cultural inferiority complex. (Even today, many American artists, deep down, fear they may be "Rome" to Britain's "Greece".) As a Canadian, and a musical theatre writer, this was something I could relate to. I also longed to hear my own culture represented. Therefore I studied the craft of the great Broadway writers in order to learn from them, but not to copy their worldview. Inspired by the late composer Norman Campbell (*Anne of Green Gables - The Musical*), I began to study the history of musical theatre in my own country. The result was *Broadway North: The Dream of a Canadian Musical Theatre*, published in 2006.

Then a curious thing happened. That book seemed to strike a chord in other countries. I was featured on a Melbourne radio show called *Broadway at Bedtime*, and found that the situations for Canadians and Australians were uncannily similar. Australian actors longed to play in their own accents. Singaporeans wanted to see theatre that reflected their East-meets-West experience. South Africans sang for their freedom, and still burst into song at the drop of a hat.

I began to think about how the principle of (metaphorically) putting the audience "on stage" – might apply in a broader context. I could see that "universality" is an idea that has two parts – establishing an individual (or national) identity, then sharing it with the world. The Irish playwright John Coulter, who immigrated to Canada in 1936 said, "What virtue is there in becoming specifically Canadian? Why not aim at the idea of internationalism in the theatre at least? I should reply that in my belief the way to internationalism in the theatre as in all else lies through the prior achievement of the greatest degree of nationalism. It is an organic growth outward from a core which is the individual himself, in this case, the individual playwright."[19] Howard Panter, creative director of London's Ambassador Theatre Group has said, "A lot of the musicals that hit my desk are transatlantic. But I believe if you can be very local and very specific, you can actually have universal resonance."[20]

To me, "globalisation" does not have to mean "world conquest". On the contrary, it can mean that we engage with the world as equals. If a show has universal appeal, it does not mean that one culture has spread its tentacles to its neighbours and subjugated them, but rather that the neighbours are able to feel some sense of ownership or involvement in the work. I want to explore what that word "universal" does (and does not) mean. To me, it can suggest a single show such as *Fiddler on the Roof* that finds broad appeal in many different countries. It can also imply a place where we are able to experience work from other cultures and thereby broaden our own horizons. I believe that great cultures can take root anywhere, so long as they are nurtured. The seeds are there, but they haven't always been watered.

For the purposes of this book, I define a musical as a theatrical entertainment that is aimed at a popular audience (as opposed to a social, economic or intellectual elite), and in which music and drama (or at least theatricality) work together to create a whole that is greater than the sum of its parts. This embraces musical comedy, operetta and revue, as well as certain operas (*Carmen*, *The Magic Flute*) and some of the more theatrical cabaret acts. This notion antedates *The Black Crook* and other American musicals. (In fact, antedating such terms is a commonly accepted practice. After all, Sir Isaac Newton predated the term "scientist"[21] by some two centuries.) It is this democratisation – the musical as a common man's opera – which leads me to the belief that it can be adapted to other cultures.

This book does not set out to be a comprehensive history of the musical. Rather, it is a manifesto with an agenda. Where I give the background of European and American musicals, it is to put it into a modern context. I'm concerned with how we can learn from our heritage and what roots we have to draw from. I should explain that I make a distinction between "heritage" and "history". Because I am a creator of musicals myself, my view is toward the future. I'm interested in both the actual roots of the musical and the potential roots.

Therefore, when I talk about the relationship between musical theatre and cabaret, for instance, I am not just talking about its historic impact, but also its potential future influence. For example, if I were a French writer looking to write Parisian musicals, I would be studying everyone from Christiné to Monnot and Legrand as well as the songs of Brel, Aznavour and Trenet, and the cabaret and café-concert. Since the 1930s, French musical comedy has failed to keep pace with Broadway, yet I feel that there were ways they could have. Similarly, if I were writing musicals in Germany, I would want to learn about Weill, Holländer and Spoliansky, as well as the great director/impresario Max Reinhardt. When I talk about how the American musical found its own voice, it is to point the way for other cultures who also want to assert their own identities. We know that the American musical is a confluence of European operetta, jazz and vaudeville. When Lionel Bart wrote *Oliver!*, he created an equivalent cocktail of English music hall and folk traditions. Therefore, when I look at musicals in other countries, I consider the allied forms – e.g. Irish drama with Celtic dance and music – that could potentially be combined, even if this has not yet happened.

In some cases, such as Canada and Australia, the musicals fall broadly within the European and American traditions – although they have arrived at their own variances. On the other hand, in South Africa, they have their own indigenous musical story telling tradition. Many of the cultures that I discuss in this book have yet to reach maturity in their theatrical development, and so I touch on avenues that might have future significance.

In recent years, Broadway has played host to *Sarafina!* (from Johannesburg), *The Drowsy Chaperone* (from Toronto) and *Priscilla -- Queen of the Dessert* (from Sydney).

We now have something called World Music. Why not World Musical Theatre? After all, nineteenth century New York — in what the Europeans derisively referred to as "the colonies" — was a pretty unlikely place for anything of cultural importance to prosper. What the musical theatre requires is people with talent and the need to express themselves in drama and in song, and an atmosphere in which that talent can be nurtured. It also requires skill — which can be learned. When you live and work away from the centres of New York and London, this means that you study both the great international works *and* the forms that come out of your own environment.

We should be aware of the works of the past, in order to create better works in the future. My objective with this book is practical. I want the musicals of the future to be well-crafted, and for their creators and performers to be well versed in their own heritage. If one writes musicals in Canada, you should be familiar with the works of Rodgers and Hammerstein, but also with *Spring Thaw* and *Anne of Green Gables*. If you're an Australian, you may want to know about *Collits' Inn* and *The Sentimental Bloke*. It is also helpful, for example, for First Nations people in Canada to understand how Australian aborigines are developing their own musical theatre forms. In Japan, how are the anime and manga traditions put to use in musicals? And the "chanchada"s of Brazil? And what about Korean "Ch'angguk", South African "Mbaqanga", India's "Bollywood" and the new work coming out of Singapore and Argentina? If you truly believe that musical theatre is an international form, without boundaries, you'll want to learn about all of them.

ACT I: The Parents

European Musical Comedy (Oops, I Mean Operetta)

According to musicologist Wilfred Mellers, "Musical comedy – a Plain Man's popular art – had its origins in the impact of democracy on opera, which had been initially an aristocratic art"[1]. Perhaps it's not a co-incidence that Mozart wrote *Die Zauberflöte* ("The Magic Flute") shortly after the French revolution, a time when the writing was on the wall for any autocrat with despotic tendencies. It's not so much that the early musicals were overtly political. (And, yes, I *am* calling *The Magic Flute* a musical.) It's more that demo*cratic* change begets demo*graphic* change. John and the Missus were now attending the theatre, and it was their lives and their values that would be represented on stage.

I intend, in later chapters, to look at how Paris, Vienna and Berlin developed as centres for musical theatre, and at how London and New York first adapted the continental European forms and then ultimately created the English-speaking musical theatre that would predominate. I will also discuss the unique contribution that cabaret – in its many forms – has made. Then, in "Act II", I will look at how other centres in other parts of the world are trying to follow their examples and create their own unique forms.

In the Viennese theatre of the late eighteenth century, there was no such thing as a "non-musical". This was especially true of the Volkskomödie, the popular theatre. A few decades earlier Emperor Charles VI had required the Kärntnertortheater (officially the "Imperial and Royal Court Theatre of Vienna", although its mandate specified that it was to appeal to all classes) to combine German comedy with its repertoire of Italian opera in order to reach a wider audience. The result was a higher level of composition in their Singspiel – a popular form of opera that featured spoken dialogue. The aristocracy, who had developed a taste for French comedy, showed little or no interest in a German national theatre. While the theatre of the court had bizarre regulations – such as one prohibiting the intermingling of comedic and serious elements – the popular theatre had no such restrictions, and offered far greater scope for innovation. We know that Mozart attended the Kärntnertortheater with his father Leopold in 1768, when the prodigy was twelve years old. Mozart the elder didn't approve. He wrote to a friend, "That the Viennese, generally speaking, do not care to see serious and sensible performances, have little or no idea of them, and only want to see foolish stuff, devils, ghosts, magic... witches and apparitions is well known, and their theatres prove it every day."[2] The son apparently disagreed. Twenty-three years later, in what was clearly an act of rebellion, he would write a show that would include all that and more.

Wolfgang Amadeus Mozart

The book – sorry, "libretto" – of *The Magic Flute* was furnished by Schikaneder (played by Simon Callow in the film *Amadeus*), the actor-manager of Vienna's Freihaus-Theater auf der Wieden where it premiered on September 30, 1791 with Schikaneder in the comic role of Papageno. In the Viennese popular theatre, the librettist was king, and the composer's name appeared in small print – if he was lucky. Since Schikaneder was the producer and director as well as the comic lead – and it was his name on the (sometimes rubber) cheques – he was effectively in control, and had some considerable influence over all aspects of the production, including the music.

All of this apparently didn't bother Mozart. He had anonymously contributed songs to previous Schikaneder productions, and for some time, he had been trying to reach beyond the stuffy confines of the state theatres and into "vaudeville" (or *vaux de ville*, street songs). "He approved Schikaneder's aims and methods for developing a style of people's opera", says author and lecturer George Collerick. "Mozart saw such ventures as a means to raise standards of popular taste."[3] Eleven years earlier, his father had counselled him, "I recommend you in your work not to think only of the musicians in the audience, but also those who are not musicians. You should know that there are always 100 ignoramuses as against 10 true connoisseurs. Therefore, don't forget the so-called popular style which will tickle also the long ears." Mozart replied, "Don't worry about the so-called popular style, for in my opera there's music for all kinds of people – except for the long ears."[4]

According to Eva Badura-Skoda, professor of music at the University of Wisconsin-Madison, "Mozart broke the boundaries of the Viennese Singspiel and created a full-sized German opera... The high quality of popular music in Vienna in the time of Haydn and Mozart, and the affinity of these great composers to folk music... caused most probably the extraordinary world success of Viennese classical music, unbroken, valid, and alive even today."[5]

It wasn't just "classical" music that he was influencing. These were some of the first rumblings of what would later be called operetta, then finally emerge as musical comedy, although *The Magic Flute* soon gained stature as a piece of grand opera, and in doing so its "vaudeville" origins were played down. (If I were being churlish, I might suggest that it has been hijacked by the very establishment that it was rebelling against.)

Although Vienna would eventually claim its place as a centre for operetta, the form first took root in Paris in the mid-nineteenth century. It was an actor-conductor-composer-organist (and, no doubt, usher and ticket seller) named Florimond Ronger

(1825-92) who is credited with advancing the form known as opéra-bouffe. Using the stage name Hervé, his hits included *Don Quixote et Sancho Pança* (1848). But it was a German-Jewish immigrant from Cologne who was to create what many consider to be the first modern musical.

Jacques Offenbach

Born in 1819 in Cologne-Deutz, Jacob, whose original family name had, at various times, been Eberst, Wiener or Levy, was the son of the cantor of Cologne's synagogue. When, as a fourteen-year-old, he arrived in Paris to study at the Conservatoire, he changed his first name to the more French sounding Jacques, and his surname was derived from his family's hometown of Offenbach-am-Main. Jacques Offenbach (1819-80) supported himself by playing cello in the orchestra of the Opéra-Comique, and quit the Conservatoire without ever receiving a diploma. In 1853, he began writing short comic operas, but was limited by law to only four actors and one act – an attempt to protect the hegemony of Paris' "legitimate" opera houses. Once this restriction was lifted, he was able to spread his wings, moving on from the burlesques and vaudevilles that were popular at the time. His somewhat subversive take on the Orpheus myth – in which the hero is forced to rescue his wife Euridyce from Hades – opened at his own Théàtre des Bouffes-Parisiens on 21 October 1858. The libretto was by Ludovic Halévy (1834-1908), the nephew of Offenbach's mentor and teacher Fromental Halévy (1799-1862), the composer of *La Juive*.

Orphée aux Enfers was what, in modern terms, we would call a "sleeper". The review in *Journal des Débats* was so antipathetic that an open feud erupted in the media, the publicity from which ironically resulted in a respectable run of 228 performances. All of this was good news for Offenbach's many creditors.

In creating this new form, Offenbach was, in fact, rebelling against what he believed to be the heavy handed and pompous tendency of Italian opera, then prevalent in Paris. Believing that opera's true French heritage was being discarded, according to biographer Peter Grammond, he "assimilated every kind of traditional and popular song so that his music was always close to the tastes of the ordinary French citizen."[6] Grammond explains, "Composers like Irving Berlin and Richard Rodgers would be disgruntled not to find people singing and whistling their works for they are written expressly for that purpose, and they, rather than the serious composers, who depend as greatly on official patronage to get their works produced as the early composers did on the nobility, are the real heirs to Mozart, Lully, Rossini, Donizetti and Offenbach."[7]

Orphée's fame beyond France grew slowly, as German language productions played in Vienna, Berlin and even New York. English playwright John Robinson Planché (1796-1880) admired Offenbach's music but loathed the libretto by Hector Crémieux (1828-92) and Ludovic Halévy (1834-1908), which included infidelity and suggestions of sadomasochism. On top of this, the then-risqué can-can was judged too racy for Victorian London, so Planché adapted their work into a pastiche called *Orpheus in the Haymarket*, which opened in 1865. One reviewer complained of the "washed-out and colourless result."[8] Not until twenty years later did it finally reach Broadway in English under the now famous title *Orpheus in the Underworld*, although his *La Grande-Duchesse de Gérolstein* had already been well received there. Grammond concludes, "Offenbach was unquestionably the key figure and the most powerful catalyst in the establishment of our popular musical theatre… a task which he achieved by having one ear bent to operatic developments from Mozart to Donizetti and one to the earthier music of the cafés and music halls."[9] While Offenbach certainly affected the work that followed, his real influence might be summed up in an expression used by modern political pundits – by reaching out to a new audience, he "changed the weather". "Offenbach possessed all the qualities essential to the successful composition of musicals;" wrote British light music composer and conductor Mark Lubbock (1898-1986) in 1957, "apparently inexhaustible fertility and musical invention, a predominantly personal idiom… together with range and variety."[10] "In the musical theatre", says Alan Jay Lerner, "he was indeed the father of us all."[11]

Even *Carmen*, one of the greatest and most popular of operas, is arguably really a musical – in structure, if not in vocal style. In fact, it is probably the only opera in the world whose melodies are as familiar to the man in the street as are the songs from *Oklahoma!*. Written for Paris' Opéra-Comique, a more "middlebrow" establishment than the elitist Paris Opéra, it contained (in its original form) large tracts of spoken dialogue. The music was by Offenbach's friend and protégé Georges Bizet (1838-75), and the libretto was co-written by frequent Offenbach collaborator Halévy with Henri Meilhac (1831-97), based on a novel by Prosper Mérimée. Like Offenbach, Bizet was a student of Halévy's uncle Fromental Halévy, who was also his father-in-law.

Its premiere in 1875 received only mixed reviews. If he wanted his work to be accepted by the major opera houses of the world, then Bizet had to conform. Although he was contracted to write the necessary recitative for the Viennese premiere, he suffered a heart attack and died (at the age of only thirty-seven) before work was begun, and so the job was left to his friend Ernest Guiraud, who would also later complete Offenbach's *Tales of Hoffman*. Performing Arts critic and musicologist David Foil says, "As in a classic American musical comedy, the dialogue between musical numbers in an opéra-comique tends to underscore the characters' humanity, to reveal subtleties and interesting contradictions in their personalities. Instead of the alluring, vampish prima donna that reigns supreme in Guiraud's version, the Carmen of Bizet's opéra-comique is raunchy, sometimes wickedly funny, petty, tantalizingly remote, and unpredictable. Likewise, Bizet's Don José is not the bellowing overgrown boy he can sometimes seem in the Guiraud version, but a deeply conflicted young man full of repressed rage. He is teetering on the brink of insanity, an obsessive-compulsive who becomes a homicidal stalker. In the case of Don José, the opéra-comique version does not make the character lighter, but much, much darker."[12] When Leonard Bernstein – one of the first modern conductors to champion the restoration of the original opéra-comique version – presented excerpts from *Carmen* on Japanese television in the early 1960s, he did the spoken dialogue alongside the recitative for comparison, using Broadway actors for the former and singers from the Metropolitan Opera for the latter.[13] Perhaps this structural similitude to the musical explains why Oscar Hammerstein II was so successful in adapting it as *Carmen Jones* in 1943. Although the Guiraud version remained the dominant one for a century or so after its premiere, the original opéra-comique version has now regained popularity.

Meilhac and Halévy would also between them provide the source material for two of the most popular operettas of all time – *Die Fledermaus* ("The Bat") (1874), with music by Johann Strauss Jr. (1825-99) and *Die Lustige Witwe* ("The Merry Widow", 1905) with music by Franz Lehár (1870-1948). While the former was based on a Meilhac and Halévy's play *Le Réveillon* (which also formed the basis for Offenbach's *La Vie Parisienne*), they did not provide the libretto – Richard Genée did.

At this point, I feel that I should say something about this term "operetta". It has been used to describe everything from Strauss to Vincent Scotto. The *Oxford Concise Dictionary of Music* defines it as "Little opera. Strictly a play with [overture], songs, entr'actes and dances, but the term has become synonymous with 'light opera', e.g. Offenbach's *La Belle Hélène* and Strauss's *Die Fledermaus*, and 'musical comedy', e.g. Coward's *Bitter-Sweet*."[14] I tend to compare it to terms like "Victorolla" and "gramophone", which are simply archaic terms for a record player. While "operetta" may imply the quasi-operatic world of Strauss, it is also applied to the works of Gilbert and Sullivan, who often employed actors who sing, rather than opera singers. George Colerick describes operetta as "a variety of opera, just as demanding artistically, and with special features, such as the dependence on clearly enunciated speech and the combination of song with movement in set pieces which at the high moments bring audiences to a state of excitement relieved by synchronised clapping."[15] According to Stephen Sondheim, "'Opera' implies endless stentorian singing; 'operetta' implies gleeful choirs of peasants dancing in the town square; 'opéra-bouffe' implies hilarious (in intent, at least) complications of mistaken identity; 'musical comedy' implies showbiz pizzazz and blindingly bright energy; 'musical play' implies musical comedy that isn't funny. For me, an opera is something that is performed in an opera house in front of an opera audience. The ambience, along with the audience's expectation, is what flavors the evening… Opera is defined by the eye and ear of the beholder."[16]

The world of the nineteenth century was not as clear-cut in separating "classical" versus "popular" as we are in the twenty-first century. Looking at it from a modern standpoint, works that are not performed in opera houses and that do not use operatic voice production would be classed as musicals. I will go further, and say that a show that aims for a popular audience is a musical, as is one in which the libretto is of equal importance to the music. Broadway conductor Lehman Engel writes that Offenbach, Strauss and Arthur Sullivan together "represented a synthesis, a fruition and a culmination. Though alike in intention, their respective works were totally dissimilar in style. In a narrow sense, despite their enormous popularity, these men produced no direct musical heirs of quality. Indirectly, however, the tradition they created was to be found most vitally developed in contemporary American musical theater."[17] "What most impressed its admirers?" Professor Richard Kislan asks. "Two qualities. The serious artistic approach to the elements of the libretto (especially plot and characterization), and the music of composers of international stature. The European librettists introduced a frankness in dialogue and situation hitherto avoided in English-language musicals. The European composers set much of these lyrics to attractive and entertaining music that responded to valid dramatic considerations as well as the composer's need for a free musical imagination."[18]

Operetta finally took root on English soil with the fourth collaboration between playwright William Schwenk Gilbert (1836-1911) and composer Arthur Seymour Sullivan (1842-1900), the first theatrical song writing team to receive equal credit for music and lyrics. Gilbert aimed his barbed wit at virtually anybody of higher social status than himself when *H.M.S. Pinafore – or – The Lass that Loved a Sailor* opened at London's Opéra Comique on 25 May 1878. In fact, their partnership began rather inauspiciously seven years earlier with *Thespis*, which ran for only sixty-three performances at the Gaiety Theatre. Only fragments of Sullivan's score survive from this early work. It took one more modest success – *Trial By Jury* (1875) – and one more failure – *The Sorcerer* (1877) before that all-important breakthrough came.

This was not the beginning of musical comedy in Britain – that is usually dated to John Gay (1685-1732)'s *The Beggars' Opera* in 1728. However, Gilbert and Sullivan created the first English works with original music (*Beggars' Opera* borrowed established arias and folk tunes) to capture the imagination of the world. Their contribution to the development of the modern musical theatre is well documented, and I feel no need to duplicate what others have already told in detail. Many Americans – Alan Jay Lerner and Ira Gershwin among them – cite Gilbert as a master lyricist, which of course he was. But his work was always quintessentially English. It is also of its time, yet much of it is relevant today to a modern, non-British audience.

The Theatre Committee of the Writers Guild of Great Britain, in a submission to the UK Parliament's Culture, Media and Sport Committee in November 2003 said, "While Britain historically produced a fair number of musicals, these were the works of unique individuals (Noël Coward, Ivor Novello, Noel Gay, etc) rather than the product of a musical theatre culture."[19] What is a musical theatre culture, if not a collection of such "unique individuals"? Unlike the Americans, they never coalesced into an identifiable "British school" because there was no imperative for them to do so.

Britannia ruled the waves. The very fact that they spoke English defined them. (Only by rebelling against this hegemony did the Americans put their own unique stamp on the form.)

And so they plodded along. Vivian Ellis (1903-96) (*Mr. Cinders*, *Bless the Bride*) wrote a number of pleasantly comfortable shows that were as English as warm beer and cold toast, and that had scarcely any impact beyond Britain's borders. Even Ivor Novello (1893-1951)'s success was, for the most part, confined to Britain – or at most, the British Empire. Only Noël Coward (1899-1973) seemed to catch the fancy of American audiences – and that was largely because this polymath not only wrote the book, music and lyrics, but also produced, directed and starred in such shows as *Bittersweet* (1929) and *Conversation Piece* (1934). Even so, he is better remembered for his many plays and his speciality songs ("Mad Dogs and Englishmen", "Mad About the Boy") than for his book musicals.

In the period after World War II, the English musicals began to look staid and quaint next to the brash American shows that began to dominate the West End – *Annie Get Your Gun*, *Oklahoma!* and even *My Fair Lady*. Only later did Lionel Bart, David Heneker and others begin to bring it back to life. (But that's another chapter.)

Other European countries developed their own musical theatre traditions, although these didn't travel as widely as the French, German and English ones. Spain (and the Spanish-speaking world) developed a form of its own. The term "Zarzuela" literally means "bramble bush", but refers to a form of (usually) light opera with spoken dialogue. The name actually refers to the royal palace near Madrid where these masque-like pieces were first performed. Although the form dates to the seventeenth century, it was revived in the 1850s with an aim of presenting opera with a Spanish accent by Francisco Asenjo Barbieri (1823-94) whose works included *El barberillo de Lavapiés*, *Jugar con fuego*, *Pan y toros*, *Don Quijote*, *Los diamantes de la corona*, and *El Diablo en el poder*. It reached its apotheosis in the first half of the twentieth century with works by Jacinto Guerrero (1895-1951), José Serrano (1873-1941) and Amadeu Vives (1871-1932) whose *Doña Francisquita* (1923) is considered by some to be the pinnacle of the genre. Christopher Webber, author of *The Zarzuela Companion* (Scarecrow Press, 2002) calls this "one of the few zarzuelas which has 'travelled' abroad. With its easy lyricism, fluent orchestration and colourful evocation of 19th Century Madrid – not to mention its memorable vocal and choral writing – it certainly encapsulates Vives' sweetly potent charm, and his love for the city where he worked and died".[20]

Although their popularity never reached the English speaking world, the Zarzuelas did spread to Latin America, especially Cuba and Mexico, as well as the Philippines, and were performed in Catalan and Basque as well as Castilian Spanish. The Mexican opera singer Placido Domingo was the son of Zarzuela singers, and the song "El

Cóndor Pasa", made popular by Simon and Garfunkel, is from a 1913 Zarzuela of the same name by Peruvian composer Daniel Alomía Robles (1871-1942).

Even Stalinist Russia produced musical comedies. Since 1929, the Leningrad State Musical Comedy Theatre had been the home of Russian operetta and musical comedy, and during the Second World War was the only theatre to remain open during the entire siege of Leningrad. From the land of Mussorgsky and Rimsky-Korsakov sprang Isaak Osipovich Dunayevsky (1900-55), who wrote some fourteen operettas, including *The Golden Valley* (1937) and *The Free Wind* (1947), and forty-two musical films, mostly for the director Grigorii Aleksandrov (1903-83), a former collaborator of Sergei Eisenstein. Rimgaila Salys, Professor of Russian studies at the University of Colorado says, "Aleksandrov recognized that Russia was a singing country with a rich tradition of folk and urban melodies."[21] Their film musicals together included *Happy Guys* (1934) and *Circus* (1936).

As one might expect from a two-time winner of the Stalin Prize, Dunayevsky's works often contained political messages, such as his cantata *Glory of the Railwaymen* and his *Rhapsody on Songs of the People of the Soviet Union*. Whereas I have argued that the musical grew up alongside democracy, in this case the genre came under the purview of the Peoples' Commissar of Enlightenment. Comedy films were given a mandate to "become a medium of Communist enlightenment and agitation, an instrument of the Party in educating and organizing the masses around the basic task of the period of socialist construction."[22] Needless to say, their work did not transfer to the West End and Broadway, although Dunayevsky's stage and film musicals were popular within the Soviet Bloc.

All of this would soon grind to a crashing halt. Beginning in the 1920s, the European musical theatre faced a challenge from the New World – and a holocaust in its own back yard.

Musicals for the Masses: Emanuel Schikaneder and the Theater an der Wien

In the last chapter, I gave an overview of how the musical began in Paris, and migrated to Vienna, London and the world. But what of the unique character of the city whose very name implies music and dancing?

Whereas New York is known as a centre for commerce and Paris for its fashion and art, Vienna is all about music – especially waltzes and operettas. More than any of the other historic capitals of musical theatre, Vienna is rooted in the classical world – of Mozart and Beethoven. "One of the oldest and richest traditions in world theatre"[1], says musical historian Kurt Gänzl. Yet, in the modern era of megamusicals, its significance is in danger of being forgotten.

Since the fourteenth century, Vienna has been a centre for the study of music, existing at a cross-roads of French. German, Dutch and Italian trains of thought. "Creativity is often the result of reconciling opposing ideas or influences"[2], says Michael Cherlin, professor of music theory at University of Minnesota. "Although every culture derives its own personality in part through being affected by the impact of other cultures, the musical life of Vienna is particularly remarkable in this regard... Ideals of clarity and grace, derived in large part from the French Enlightenment, intermingle with the conceptualization of music as drama derived in large part from the ascendancy of Italian opera." Like New York in the nineteenth and twentieth centuries, Vienna was a cultural melting pot. Yet, it is only since the late eighteenth century that important works began to be written in German – the language of the masses.

Vienna's time of musical prosperity roughly coincided with its period as the capital of the Austro-Hungarian empire, and consequently it attracted the best musical talents – classical and popular – of not only Austria, but also Hungary and Bohemia (now the Czech Republic). Emperor Joseph's 1782 "Decrees of Tolerance" made it possible for Jews, Lutherans, Calvinists and others to enter areas of business previously denied them. "Vienna's many-sided musical culture, throughout the 19th century and beyond, had interesting racial implications, beyond the other important social ones", says George Colerick. "The Habsburg Empire offered for a long time an unusual kind of multi-racial stability. It stimulated an incomparable variety of musical achievements."[3] (The same was also then true of Berlin – how things would change in a few short years!) In fact, it has been a series of contradictions – a culturally conservative city that pioneered many social democratic policies, and a multi-cultural society that waffled between tolerance and anti-Semitism.

In the late eighteenth century, political change was sweeping across Europe. The French revolution put Europe's ruling classes on notice, and the theatrical tastes of the general populace began to be felt in the development of singspiele, which would eventually become operetta and musical comedy.

It is not within the remit of this book to duplicate what others have already written about the city's immense contribution to musical history, which is comprehensively documented elsewhere. However, I think it's important to place Viennese musical theatre within the context of the other places and works discussed. The American musical theatre, after all, defined itself by first of all imitating the Viennese operetta and then later moving on from it.

As a musical writer, I've learned that when writing a musical biography, it is best to focus on a specific event or aspect of the subject's life. The cultural life of a city is no different. In the case of Vienna, I've narrowed in on one particular theatre, and the man who built it. In it you will find the story of the Viennese musical in a microcosm.

Emanuel Schikaneder

Although his name is seldom heard in the same sentence as those of Florenz Ziegfeld, Max Reinhardt or Cameron Mackintosh, Emanuel Schikaneder (1751-1812) is, for me, one of the great (pardon the expression) unsung heroes of the musical. The friendship that he struck up with Leopold Mozart – and, more significantly with his son Wolfgang Amadeus (1756-91) – would change musical and theatrical history, and add immeasurably to the development of popular musical theatre. His biographer Kurt Honolka says, "Schikaneder's universality and creative fantasy could be compared to Max Reinhardt's; to a certain extent he managed to achieve a thoroughly 'modern' form of theater presentation. His Singspiele and comic operas… anticipate the later Viennese operetta, while his extravagant spectaculars point toward the revue and the musical."[4] Most significantly, although he is credited with co-creating one of the grandest of all operas, his intended audience was largely working class.

Schikaneder was born in Straubing, Bavaria in 1751 to a poor family, and was educated by Jesuits in Regensburg, where he sang in the cathedral. He joined the acting company of Andreas Schopf at the age of 22, where he performed in opera, farce and singspiele. He began to write and act in his own musical pieces, creating both the libretti and scores. By the time he was twenty-seven, he had triumphed as *Hamlet*, and was running his own company. It was two years later, during an extended stay in Salzburg, that he met the Mozarts. The young composer became enthralled with the populist entertainments that Schikaneder produced, making anonymous musical contributions to a number of them. It was eleven years later that they created the work that would lay new foundations for both musical comedy and opera.

27

"No one would dispute that Mozart's music is responsible for the stature of the opera and that his librettist's contribution is of lesser importance", says Honolka. "But Schikaneder was author, producer and director, controlling casting and the magnificence or sparseness of the scenery, all of which means his contribution to the success of the evening can hardly be overestimated."[5] I would go even further than that. *The Magic Flute* wouldn't have happened without both its composer and its librettist. It appears to have been Schikaneder's idea in the first place; it was the librettist who hired Mozart, and not the reverse, as was often the case. In writing a show of this nature, Mozart was enthusiastically entering into Schikaneder's world of populist entertainment, and eschewing the snootiness of court-based Italian opera. It appears to have been a true collaboration: when Schikaneder suggested that Papageno should stammer when first meeting Papagena, it is reported that Mozart obligingly rewrote the scene. Over the past two centuries, scholars and critics have debated the merits of Schikaneder's libretto. Only in the world of opera would it be suggested that a masterpiece could be created on the strength of the music alone, without first having a strong "book". Although Mozart himself dictated that the libretto must be the servant of the music, in a Broadway musical – at least in the post *Oklahoma!* period – the book writer is paramount.

The Magic Flute opened on 30 September 1791 at the Theater auf der Wieden and ran for an initial 223 performances there in repertory. Emboldened by its success, Schikaneder determined to eventually build his own theatre, and secured an imperial privilege from the then-Emperor Joseph, which was, fourteen years later, confirmed by Emperor Franz, his successor.   With the backing of a wealthy merchant named Bartholomäus Zitterbarth, he opened the Theater an der Wien, designed in the Empire style by Franz Jäger, on 13 June 1801. A theatre-going journalist named Adolf Bäuerle wrote, "If Schikaneder and Zitterbarth had had the idea… to charge admission simply for looking at the glories of their Theater an der Wien, Schikaneder would certainly have been able to take in vast sums of money without giving one single performance."[6]

A year after opening his new theatre, he presented a revival of *The Magic Flute* with some revisions to the libretto, and a new scenic design that took full advantage of the expanded stage facilities. Unfortunately, by this time Mozart had been dead for a decade. Even though, as the capital of the Austrian Empire the city would soon emerge into its greatest era of political and cultural importance, the musical theatre revolution they had started together had stalled, and Schikaneder's greatest artistic achievements were behind him. Within two years, he and Zitterbarth had parted company, and they were forced to sell the theatre to Gesellschaft der Cavaliere ("Society of Cavaliers"), a consortium of court nobles, including Count Ferdinand Palffy von Erdöd, who acquired full ownership in 1813. Schikaneder's imperial privilege allowed him to retain some influence as Artistic Director, and he was able to appoint no less than Ludwig von Beethoven as his director of music, presenting the premiere of the latter's opera *Fidelio* in 1805. He made his final appearance on the stage of the theatre he built on 23

December 1806, and would die in poverty six years later. Honolka says that "his greatest contribution is found in his concept of popular theater of higher quality".[7] It would be some seven decades before the theatre he built would make its next great mark on history.

Palffy attempted to court popularity with pantomime and variety, in addition to opera and ballet, but failed financially, and he was forced to sell the theatre in 1825. Under Carl Carl – who also ran the Carltheater in Leopoldstadt – it became Vienna's leading popular theatre, premiering many of Johann Nestroy's (1801-62) plays. (While Nestroy's comedies remain staples of the German-speaking theatre, few have ever been translated into English, although one became the basis for Thornton Wilder's *The Matchmaker*, which later became the musical *Hello, Dolly!*)

In 1845, Franz Pokorny acquired the theatre after a benefactor paid its debts, and Carl was forced out. Pokorny updated the facilities, intending to produce operas, but in spite of several guest performances by the "Swedish nightingale" Jenny Lind, he quickly went bankrupt and in 1848 his son Alois took over.

In 1858, Offenbach's *Le Mariage aux lanternes* was presented for the first time in German in Vienna – the first of over sixty such presentations in his lifetime – and within a year, German-language writers began knocking off their own "opéra-bouffe"s. Franz von Suppé (1819-95), a pupil of Donizetti's, soon emerged as a leading light when his *Das Pensionat* ("The Girl's Finishing School") opened at the Theater an der Wien in 1860.

From 1862, under Friedrich Strampfer, the theatre continued on its new course, presenting the operettas of Offenbach. Marie Geistinger and Maximilian Steiner (1839-80) took over in 1869, and five years later would present the show that would herald the so-called "Golden Age" of Viennese operetta.

It was a long time coming. For sixteen years, audiences had shown a decided preference for the French opéra-bouffe, despite the best efforts of Suppé and others. The city had been in an economic slump following a stock market crash that devastated the commercial theatres. Then from out of this gloom a French comedy, *Le Réveillon* ("The Midnight Supper") by frequent Offenbach collaborators Henri Meilhac and Ludovic Halévy (in turn based on *Das Gefängnis* ("The Prison") by Roderich Benedix) would give birth to what would become the touchstone of Viennese Operetta.

The original plan was simply to present the play but Steiner, unhappy with the translation he had commissioned, decided that it needed to be set to music. He approached the "waltz king" Johann Strauss Jr. to provide the score, and the libretto was by Richard Genée (1823-95), a composer in his own right. (Several of the great Broadway lyricists were also composers, or were at least musically trained, including Sheldon Harnick and Alan Jay Lerner; Frank Loesser and Stephen Sondheim began their careers as lyricists, and like Genée, graduated to writing the score as well.) The result would translate a Parisian comedy into something very Viennese. *Die Fledermaus*[8] ("The Bat") opened at the Theater and der Wien on 5 April 1874, starring the theatre's co-director Marie Geistinger as Rosalinde. It did not however immediately set the theatrical world alight, enjoying a very modest run in Vienna, but gaining more acceptance in Berlin, and spreading throughout the Germanic world. Only much later would it become popular in English and other languages. In 1950, New York's Metropolitan Opera commissioned new English lyrics by Broadway and Hollywood legend Howard Dietz (1896-1983) for a production adapted and directed by Garson Kanin (1912-99).

By the end of the nineteenth century, the generation behind the "Golden Age" had almost all passed away, and the lights of Vienna appeared ready to dim. But then a new generation began to emerge, and with them, a lighter, breezier, less "classical" form. Although largely centred in Vienna, this new generation of writers would be drawn from throughout central Europe, especially from within the Austro-Hungarian Empire, where the talent pool was mobile.

After a 1900 renovation by theatre architects Ferdinand Fellner Jr. and Hermann Helmer, Wilhelm Karczag took over the management of the Theater an der Wien, as the operetta entered its so-called "Silver Age". (Why it is called that is curious, since the "Silver Age" seemed to produce more enduring works than the "Golden Age" did.)

Die Lustige Witwe ("The Merry Widow", 1905) was originally offered to composer Richard Heuberger (1850-1914), who had enjoyed some success in 1898 with *Opera Ball*, but he failed to provide a satisfactory score. The commission was then offered to a young Hungarian musical director, Franz Lehár (1870-1948), who had already enjoyed some success with *Wiener Frauen* and *Der Rastelbinder*, both in 1901. The book by Victor Léon (1858-1940) and Leo Stein (1861-1921) was, like that of *Die Fledermaus* a generation earlier, based on an 1862 play by Henri Meilhac, *L'Attaché d'ambassade* ("The Embassy Attaché"). In fact, Léon and Stein were a bit of a holdover from that previous age: Léon had worked with Strauss on *Simplicius* in 1887.

The setting for *The Merry Widow* was the Paris embassy of "Pontevedro", a thinly disguised Montenegro. For Lehár, this was an opportunity to add some Balkan musical colour, although some Montenegrin students were less than thrilled to have their homeland made the object of fun.

The Merry Widow's success was immediate. A London production opened in 1907, and it soon spread across Europe and North America. (Its influence on the later American musical is unmistakable: listen to the "Maxime's" sequence, then listen to the verse leading into "Shall We Dance?" from *The King and I*.) With some of the money he was now earning, Lehár bought a baroque mansion in the suburb of Nussdorf that had once belonged to Emanuel Schikaneder. He was to be one of the few composers to stay behind – and prosper – under the Nazis.

In 1901, writer and drama critic Felix Salten presented a short-lived cabaret season – Austria's first – in the theatre's cellar. A more permanent cabaret known as Die Hölle ("Hell") was opened by Sigmund and Leopold Natzler in 1906 with art nouveau décor designed by Heinrich Lefler and Joseph Urban. With Fritz Grünbaum (1880-1941) as its Master of Ceremonies, it presented songs, comedies and even small operettas, including Franz Lehàr's *Frühling* ("Spring"), as well as works by future operetta composers Leo Fall, Edmund Eysler, Robert Stolz and Ralph Benatzky. In one incident in 1910, Grünbaum – who was to become one of Austria's greatest cabaret artists and actors – was injured in a duel after he slapped an Imperial officer for shouting out anti-Semitic remarks. Die Hölle closed in 1928 (although the space remains as one of the theatre's bars), and Grünbaum would eventually die in the Dachau concentration camp.

In the same year as Die Hölle opened, Grünbaum would also establish himself as a librettist in the main theatre upstairs. With co-author A. M. Willner (1859 - 1929) and composer Leo Fall (1873-1925), he wrote *Die Dollarprinzessin* ("The Dollar Princess"), based on a comedy by Gatti-Trotha with a contemporary American setting.

It travelled first to London, with a new book by Basil Hood and lyrics by Adrian Ross where it played successfully for over a year at Daly's Theatre. In New York it was given a new libretto by George Grossmith Jr., (the son of a Gilbert and Sullivan veteran) and some additional music by Jerome Kern. The *New York Times* complained that it had been rather too anglicised. "If you care for the charm and grace of English musical comedy you are quite sure to enjoy *The Dollar Princess*. If you are looking for Austrian fire and dash you are quite likely to be disappointed."[9] Not for the last time, German-language musical theatre would indulge its fascination with the culture that would soon overtake it.

Like Fall, Oscar Straus (1870-1954) had also written for the cabarets, including some presented by Max Reinhardt. Alan Jay Lerner says, "He was the only one of them all with an appreciation of comedy."[10] In 1908, Straus's *Der tapfere Soldat* ("The Courageous Soldier") opened with a libretto by Rudolf Bernauer (1880-1953) and Leopold Jacobson based on George Bernard Shaw's *Arms and the Man*. While its success in Vienna was modest, an English translation by Stan Stange, *The Chocolate Soldier* was loved by everybody – except Shaw, who forbade any further musical adaptations from his works. (Lerner and Loewe would have to wait for him to die before they could turn *Pygmalion* into *My Fair Lady*.)

In 1909, another Hungarian composer with a cabaret background made his debut at the Theater an der Wien with a show that had premiered in Budapest the previous year. *Tatárjárás* ("Tatar Campaign"), with a score by Emmerich Kálmán (1882-1953) was translated into German as *Herbstmanöver*, and was the beginning of a long Viennese career.

Many of his best known works premiered at the theatre's rivals, including *Die Csárdásfürstin* ("The Csárdás Princess") which opened at the Johann-Strauss-Theater in 1915. Kálmán would make good use here of both his Hungarian and cabaret roots. The libretto by Leo Stein and Bela Jenbach is set in Budapest's Orpheum cabaret, and concerns a star making her farewell appearance before embarking on a tour of the U.S. A hit throughout Europe, it missed out on English (*The Gipsy Princess*) and American (*The Riviera Girl*) success because of an apparent inability to come up with a decent adaptation. Kálmán also spent some time in New York, contributing to the score of *Golden Dawn* with a libretto by Oscar Hammerstein II (1895-1960) and Otto Harbach (1873-1963). He was collaborating with Lorenz Hart on a show when the latter passed away in 1943. He died in Paris in 1953.

World War I adversely affected the operetta in two ways. During the war, nothing was exported to Britain or France. And after the war, the Habsburg Empire – and the glamour that went with it – was a distant memory. In a country that had thrown off its monarchy, people lost interest in stories about princes and counts. At the same time, New York was beginning to assert itself. Elegance and gentility were usurped by the rhythms of jazz. The centre of gravity was slowly shifting, but while it may have been the beginning of the end for European operetta, it wasn't quite done yet.

The stereotyped image we have of a Viennese operetta is an old-world vision of counts and baronesses sipping champaign as they waltz at a grand ball, an image derived from *Die Fledermaus* and *The Merry Widow*. In reality, the Viennese may not have kept pace with Broadway, but just as the Parisians moved on from Offenbach and Messager, so the Viennese moved on after Strauss and Lehár. The trouble was, English speaking audiences by and large were only interested in the stereotype, and so the jazzier "operettas" with contemporary – sometimes even American – settings tended to stay home.

Karczag's son-in-law Hubert Marischka (1882-1959) took over the Theater an der Wien in 1923, continuing the policy of post-classical operetta that would come to an end with the rise of Hitler. Its swan song was Ralph Benatzky (1884 - 1957)'s 1936 jazzy Hollywood satire *Axel an der Himmelstür* ("Axel at the Gates of Heaven"). With a book by Paul Morgan and Adolph Schütz and lyrics by Hans Weigl, it starred the Swedish actress-singer Zarah Leander (1907-81) as a Hollywood diva, and Danish actor Max Hansen (1897-1961) in the title role. One need only examine the fates of these collaborators to understand what happened to Viennese musical theatre. Benatzky escaped to the U.S., whereas Morgan died in a concentration camp. Leander, on the other hand, became a star of Nazi films.

Benatzky had earlier secured an international reputation with *Im Weissen Rössl* in 1930 at Berlin's Grosse Schauspielhaus for director/choreographer Erik Charell (1894-1974), which travelled to London the following year as *The White Horse Inn*.

Productions in Paris, Vienna, Budapest and eventually New York followed. In each case, the book was localised and songs by other composers interpolated, although Charell remained at the helm. It remains the most popular musical export from 1930s Berlin.

During the Second World War the theatre was requisitioned by Kraft Durch Freude ("Strength Through Joy"), providing Nazi propaganda. From 1945, for ten years, it was home to the Vienna State Opera. In 1960, it was rescued from demolition by the municipality of Vienna, and became a venue for modern musicals, including *Cats*, which ran from 1983-88. In 1992, it hosted the massively successful German-language musical *Elisabeth*, with book and lyrics by Dr. Michael Kunze (1943-) and music by Sylvester Levay (1945-), which ran for six years. Although it has, since then, become a full-time opera house, I like to think that its builder would be proud of the fact that throughout most of its two hundred plus years' history it has catered to a wide audience with popular tastes.

Of course, the Theater an der Wien was not the only venue for operettas in Vienna. The Carltheater, home of many of Suppé's works, began its life as the Leopoldstädter Theater, and was comprehensively rebuilt in 1847. It closed in 1929, and having suffered bomb damage during the war, was demolished in 1951. The Raimund Theater, named for the playwright Ferdinand Raimund, opened in 1893 as a playhouse, and became a home for musicals and operettas from 1908. It survives as a commercial house and in recent years has hosted *A Chorus Line*, *Les Misérables*, *Kiss of the Spider Woman* and *Beauty and the Beast*, as well as German musicals *Dance of the Vampires* (with music by Jim Steinman (1947 -) and lyrics by Michael Kunze) and *Rebecca* (with music by Levay and lyrics by Kunze). The Volksoper was built in 1898 as the Kaiser-Jubiläums-Stadttheater and has for most of its history housed plays, operas and musicals. In its early years it was Vienna's second opera house, behind the State Opera, but after 1929 focused on operettas. The Wiener Bürgertheater (not to be confused with the Burgtheater) was built in 1905 under the management of actor and writer Oskar Fronz, with Edmund Eysler (1874-1949) as house composer, also presenting hits by Lehár, Fall and Kálmán. It was demolished in 1960 as part of what seems to have been a "let's-destroy-our-cultural-heritage" campaign. The Johann-Strauss-Theater, built in 1908, and the Wiener Stadttheater of 1914 suffered a similar fortune – one which the Theater an der Wien only narrowly escaped. The fate of the "bricks and mortar" seems to echo that of the Viennese musical itself. What need would they have for theatres if the operetta is dead?

Of course, the traumatic events of the Nazi occupation are not the only reason for the decline of Viennese musicals. The writing was on the wall long before that. While revivals of the classic operettas sated the appetites of tourists, there was little interest in new work. (A warning to us all.) For whatever reason, the generation of writers and composers who eventually followed after Kálmán, Lehár and Benatzky chose to largely ignore their examples and to follow instead the leads of American and British writers. Yet American composers such as Leonard Bernstein (1918-90) (*Candide*) and

Stephen Sondheim (1930 -   ) (*A Little Night Music*) managed to create works that brought a late twentieth century sensibility to the Viennese operetta form.

Cabaret: From "Le Chat Noir" to the Algonquin Room

Before I continue to tell the story of how operetta morphed into the modern musical comedy, I am going to take you on a little side excursion. It is generally acknowledged that the musical has benefited from many ancillary art forms, such as vaudeville, burlesque, ballet and opera. But there is one that is close to my heart, because for both writers and performers, it has often acted as their proving ground.

While cabaret exists as a separate form in and of itself, it is inextricably linked – aesthetically, commercially and historically – with the worlds of theatre and music, and thereby with the musical theatre. This is especially true of the French and German cabarets of the early twentieth century. Weimar Kabarett was a theatrical form, which borrowed from Broadway and operetta. Mischa Spoliansky and Friedrich Holländer were cabaret writers who wrote musicals. Same with Vincent Scotto and Leo Fall. In many of its incarnations, it seems that cabaret and revue have been a development ground where writers honed their skills, to be later applied to larger canvases. This is as true in New York as it was in Berlin and Paris.

Of the contribution of "café-concert", music hall and cabaret to the musical theatre, opera historian Richard Traubner says, "Both the music halls and the *bal*s [dance halls] had a direct influence on the infant operetta, requiring songs (for the most part) to be accessible to untrained ears. They had to be catchy and, if possible, eminently danceable... Offenbach and his librettists were hardly unaware of the *café-concert*. Many of their stars... were groomed there, and the valuable training in diction, comic values and 'putting across' songs were unmistakable facets of the very first and greatest operettas."[1]

The relationship between cabaret and musical theatre varies widely in different places. In New York, the cabaret repertoire tends to be dominated by show tunes, and many of the performers are Broadway actors. In Europe, the cabaret has stood as a separate – yet still related – art form, and as often as not is cast as the mother rather than the child.

Yet according to Maximillien de Lafayette, the self-proclaimed "world authority on cabaret" (not to mention UFOs) who claims to have written more than 1200 books, eleven dictionaries and nine encyclopaedias, "The overwhelming majority of cabaret goers in the United States misunderstand the real meaning of the world [sic] Cabaret ... It disturbs me to see and hear well-established American singers... associating Broadway with cabaret."[2] Surely, if the majority of people "misunderstand" the meaning of something, it is because the meaning has changed. This sort of "puritanism" only muddies the already murky waters, for those who want to treat the word as an "appellation of origin" will have a difficult time. In fact, "cabaret" has taken on a different form in each one of the many countries it has taken root in. In Paris, it was a place where the bohemian avant-garde met. In Berlin, it was a showcase for political satire and alternative sexuality. In New York, it is a venue for hearing the Great American Songbook. In my native Canada, it sometimes even refers to taverns where Country and Western music is heard, but is also synonymous with small-scale musical theatre.

The word "cabaret" is derived from the Latin "camera", meaning chamber or room, originally the Greek "kamárã", meaning "vault" or "arch". At first, the term was used in French to refer to wine cellars and taverns, which, as early as the fifteenth century, often included entertainment. The modern sense of the word "camera" comes from "camera obscura", a darkened room in which a reflected image of the world outside is projected. This came to be used for an optically similar device for recording pictures on emulsion.

As a term for the entertainment on offer – as opposed to the venue itself – most histories of the cabaret begin in 1881[3] with the Chat Noir, a lair for bohemian artists in Montmartre. Paris was, at the time, the cultural capital of the Western world, and people from the visual and performing arts formed an unofficial alliance of Impressionists, Dadaists, etc. The Chat Noir was the headquarters of the Hydropathes, a group of artists, intellectuals and musicians led by Rodolphe Salis (1851-97), an entrepreneur and would-be artist and poet, the son of a brewer, whom history professor Jeffrey Jackson describes as "something of a publicity genius."[4] He was the master of the promotional stunt. When Chat Noir moved to larger premises, he staged a funeral procession to the new venue. He also published his own newspaper. "To many observers," Jackson says, "this kind of crass commercialism betrayed the neighborhood's reputation for placing a higher value on artistic expression." Salis had chosen Montmartre because the rent was lower than in the Latin Quarter, but soon the mixture of criminals, prostitutes, poor workers and eccentric artists made it a focal point for modernism. Among its early patron/performers was the composer Claude Debussy (1862-1918), who became friendly with a number of Impressionist painters.

Musically, the cabaret was a bastion of the traditional chansons, mixed with a touch of political satire and anything else the avant-garde of the "fin-de-siècle" and "belle époque" could come up with. "It is difficult to imagine now the full importance of the song as a medium of public communication in those radio and television free days", says Lisa Appignanesi, author of *The Cabaret*. "Not only was the chanson a love lyric or mood piece which entertained, but it could function as a reporting vehicle – a performed alternative to the newspaper, which because of its dependence on machinery and finance, was largely controlled by the ruling class… Thus it came to serve as a democratic tool, a satirical weapon for criticism and protest."[5]

36

The entertainment was, in the beginning, spontaneous and unstructured, with Salis himself as compere. Some of the songs were pastiches of popular arias by Offenbach and others, with satirical lyrics. One might have heard the black humour of Maurice Mac-Nab (1856-89) or the songs of Aristide Bruant (1851-1925), the chansonnier who would eventually open his own cabaret, Le Merliton in the Chat Noir's original site when the latter moved to larger premises in 1885. Bruant would also come to own the nearby Lapin Agile.

In Jean Renoir's 1954 musical comedy film *French Can-Can*, Jean Gabin – a chansonnier in real life – plays a fictionalised character representing the founder of the Moulin Rouge who overhears a serving girl singing what he supposes to be a song of the streets. This is in fact "Complainte de la Butte", written for the film by Georges Van Parys (1902-71), with lyrics by Renoir. Van Parys began his own career as a cabaret pianist at Chez Fischer.

Looking at the list of musical contributors to the early cabarets, you might be forgiven for supposing that this was a hotbed of the esoteric, but you would be only partly right. The idea of drawing on so-called street songs was central to the Parisian cabaret ethos. The group of French composers known as Les Six – a name given in 1920 by music critic Henri Collet of the trade paper *Comœdia* to Georges Auric (1899-1983), Louis Durey (1888-1979), Arthur Honneger (1892-1955), Darius Milhaud (1892-1974), Francis Poulenc (1899-1963) and Germaine Taillefere (1892-1983), all followers of Eric Satie (1866-1925) and the playwright Jean Cocteau – drew inspiration from Parisian folklore, music hall and circus. They also frequented the cabarets (although Satie later renounced this). Milhaud and the others incorporated American jazz rhythms into their work. "Les Six wanted to unite jazz techniques with their own French compositions," writes Jeffrey Jackson in *Making Jazz French*. "American jazz (ironically, since it was an imported form) became a way of articulating a seemingly lost vitality within the French musical tradition that [Milhaud] hoped to reconstruct with a more muscular sound."[6]

Early in his career Satie had, through economic necessity, become a cabaret accompanist to singers such as Albert Tinchant (1860-92) and Charles de Sivry. Steven Moore Whiting describes him as "the composer whose music bore the most distinctive impression of the Montmartre cabarets… Satie transferred the techniques of parodic quotation and distortion learned in the cabaret to whimsical but disconcerting piano suites, to songs by turn medieval and madcap, and eventually to avant-garde ballets like *Parade* (1917), *Mercure* (1924) and *Relâche* (1924) – leaving it to enraged critics and engaged supporters to argue whether his music was *fumisterie* or motivated by serious artistic intentions or both at once."[7]

Soon, the cabarets developed a bourgeois clientele who would "slum it" in a sort of radical-chic sense, taking Bruant's verbal abuse on the chin, or listening to the radical polemics of Jules Jouy (1855-97), or even an elaborate shadow play. Indeed the Prince of Wales managed, on occasion, to slip in anonymously.

Other cabarets of the same period included the still-surviving Lapin Agile, which in its previous guise as Cabaret des Assassins, had been open as a tavern since 1860 (in a building dating to 1795). People like Pablo Picasso and André Gill lived a bohemian existence there, playing pranks and somehow avoiding Paris' rather draconian censors. In fact, the Lapin Agile takes its name from the sign that Gill painted for the entrance: a rabbit jumping out of a sauce-pan – "Lapin à Gill", or "Gill's Rabbit". This later became corrupted to "Lapin Agile", or "The Nimble Rabbit".

One of the most infamous pranks was instigated by the writer Roland Dorgelès, who expressed his disdain for the Cubists – fellow Lapin patrons – whom he deemed to be pretentious. He took particular aim at Guillaume Apollinaire, a poet, chansonnier and spokesman for the avant garde. Dorgelès invented a fictitious artist called Joachim-Raphael Boronali, and submitted a painting called "Le soleil se couche sur l'Adriatique" under that name to the Salon des Indépendants, where "Boronali", who was proclaimed to be the leader of a new artistic school called "Excessivisim", became the toast of the critics.

Of course, there was no such artist as Boronali. So who was responsible for the painting? Lolo, that's who – the donkey who belonged to the Lapin's proprietor, Frédéric "Frédé" Gerard. Witnessed by an officer of the court, Dorgelès tied a paintbrush to Lolo's tail, and submitted the resulting masterpiece.

When I visited the Lapin Agile in June 2008, I found an audience that included Japanese tourists, but the repertoire was all in French. It included standards such as "La Vie en Rose" as well as older songs dating to the Belle Époque. One assumes that the paintings on the dimly lit walls are mostly reproductions. Gone are the days when Picasso paid his bar tab in canvases – his painting "At the Lapin Agile" has been valued at more than $8 million. The cabaret's fame has been revived in recent years by the Steve Martin play *Picasso at the Lapin Agile*, which concerns a fictional meeting between the artist and Albert Einstein. Now, it's a sort-of living museum of cabaret, where the audiences are encouraged to sing along.

The original Chat Noir closed when Salis died in 1897. After World War I, American jazz became a greater influence, and vied with the more traditional chanson for public acceptance, until the Hot Jazz Club of France promoted a French form of jazz, with musicians like Stéphane Grappelli and Django Reinhardt and the American expatriate singer Josephine Baker. "For some, Josephine Baker's *La Revue Nègre* embodied a transfusion of new blood and energy for a France stultified by tradition and sorely in need of renewal", say African-American author and lecturer Henry Louis Gates Jr. and his colleague Karen C. C. Dalton in their introduction to *Josephine Baker and La Revue Nègre*. "For others, who held that the future of civilization itself lay in protecting an untainted French culture from invaders from the jungle, *La Revue Nègre* foretold the disintegration of centuries of classical cultural attainment, achievements of the mind over the body."[8] The centre for cabaret began to move across the Seine to Montparnesse in the Latin Quarter. The world of the cabaret also meshed with the world of the café-concert and the music hall with the emergence of artists such as Edith Piaf, Charles Trenet, Léo Ferré and Jacques Brel.

At the end of the nineteenth century, the concept of cabaret began to spread – both through foreign visitors to Paris, and foreign sojourns by Parisians. By the early years of the twentieth century, Berlin had become the world's third largest city, behind London and New York. Peter Jelavich of Johns Hopkins University says, "Germany was a fertile ground for cabaret because it had a very strong theatrical culture going back to the eighteenth century. I also think that imperial Germany [was] not a repressive society but it certainly was not democratic either. And so you had enough freedom to be able to voice criticism but enough structural constraints, both politically and socially, so that there was a lot of aggravation and tension. That's a very fertile mix for cabaret, which flourishes best when people are discontented and yet they have enough freedom to voice that discontent."[9]

Contrary to English prejudices, Berliners did indeed possess a sense of humour – something called "Berliner Witz" – developed in the furnace of a highly cosmopolitan city. (Two centuries earlier, Berlin had welcomed Jewish refugees expelled from Vienna, as well as French Huguenots – ironic, given the holocaust that was to come.) When Marlene Dietrich returned to Berlin for a concert in 1960, she told her audience that "no matter what madness affects the world, Berliners will keep their sense of humour".[10]

Unlike the Chat Noir and Lapin Agile, Berlin's first cabaret was in a legitimate theatre space. Ernst Von Wolzogen (1855-1934)'s Buntes ("Motley") Theatre – sometimes known as the "Überbrettl" ("superior club"), possibly an ironic play on Nietsche's word Übermensch ("superman") – opened on January 18, 1901 in the Alexanderplatz. His musical collaborators included Oscar Straus, the Viennese composer who would later gain fame for his operettas and musical comedies. Wolzogen, a poet and dramatist with aristocratic breeding who had written the libretto for Richard Strauss's *Feuersnot*, started out with lofty ambitions of finding a middle ground between the avant-garde and the banality of popular entertainment, but soon found himself pandering, out of economic pragmatism, to the erotic tastes of his middle class audience. Due to the initial success of this venture, the Überbrettl soon had many imitators, and Wolzogen took his own show on tour.

In many ways, Wolzogen became a victim of his own success. With all the new interest in cabarets, he was forced out of his original premises, and built a spectacular new 800 seat auditorium designed by August Endell. Unfortunately, he had fallen out with some of his artistes, including Oscar Straus, who were lured away by his rivals. Consequently, the quality of his entertainment – which had never found wide favour with the critics – declined. He had also failed to develop a stable of Berliner writers – much of his material was imported from Munich and other places. The Motley theatre never lived up to its lofty artistic ambitions, and soon folded. According to Peter Jelavich, "both press and public realized that they often could find much better entertainment at the more established vaudeville halls."[11]

Almost concurrent with Wolzogen's enterprise was a literary parody called Schall und Rauch (Sound and Smoke), established by a man who would become one of the world's most respected theatrical innovators: Max Reinhardt. Like Wolzogen's, this first incarnation was short lived, but it set Reinhardt on his future course, one that included the production of many revues, (and Sound and Smoke would be revived in 1919). At the same time, Munich's Eleven Executioners, founded by *Spring Awakening* playwright Frank Wedekind and others, began as a theatrical club in open rebellion against censorship.

In his novel *Goodbye to Berlin* (which formed the basis for both the play *I Am a Camera* and the musical *Cabaret*), Christopher Isherwood (1904-86) describes the character of cabaret singer Sally Bowles: "She had a surprisingly deep husky voice. She sang badly, without any expression, her hands hanging down at her sides – yet her performance was, in its own way, effective because of her startling appearance and her air of not caring a curse what people thought of her."[12] He could easily have been describing Marlene Dietrich or Lotte Lenya.

The composer Rudolph Nelson (1878-1960) helped to move cabaret in the direction of topical revue, both before and after the First World War. In 1907 he opened a cabaret on the Friedrichstrasse that borrowed its name from Paris's Chat Noir, and its entertainment was patronised by the Kaiser himself. Nelson frequently collaborated with Kurt Tucholsky who wrote in 1913, "If you analyse these cabaret songs, then you find that the bottom line confirms the existence of extra-marital relations."[13] According to Lisa Appignanesi, "[Nelson's] revues had that mixture of the capricious, the racy, erotic and sentimental which Tucholsky was always drawn to."[14]

Suffice to say that cabaret (or kabarett) gained a reputation for Weimar decadence. Whether this was an expression of artistic freedom or commercial pragmatism is hard to say. Did the cabarets really resist Nazism, or did they – albeit accidentally – help bring it about? There is a theory that the cabaret decadence pushed tolerance to the breaking point. Others say that the cabarets failed to actively support the fragile democracy of the republic. When somebody said to English comedian Peter

Cook that the Berlin kabaretts were the most powerful satire in history, he replied "Yeah, they really showed Hitler, didn't they?"[15]

The history of Weimar kabarett and its defiance of censorship and moral strictures has been told many times, and there is no need to repeat it in detail here. What I am interested in exploring is its relationship with musical theatre, and especially the development of songwriters.

Perhaps the best known composer was the London-born Friedrich Holländer (1896-1976), who became internationally famous for his score for the 1930 film *The Blue Angel*, including the now-standard "Falling in Love Again" with English lyrics by Sammy Lerner. (The fact that Berlin was also home to the Ufa film studios no doubt helped to create a large talent pool.) Hollander was the son of Victor Holländer, the composer of the pre-war Metropol Theater revues, and the nephew of Felix Holländer, a member of Max Reinhardt's production staff. Educated at the Berlin Conservatory, by the age of eighteen he had become associate conductor of the Prague Opera House. However, it was lighter music that would prove to be his forté. Having already made a name for himself with songs for Sound and Smoke, Friedrich wrote both songs and scripts for cabaret star Rosa Valetti (1878-1937)'s Cabaret Grössenwahn ("Cabaret Megalomania", modelled on Aristide Bruant's Le Merliton) in the early 1920s, as well as for his eventual wife Blandine Ebinger (1899-1993). (Valetti would later play Celia Peachum in the original production of *Threepenny Opera*.)

Hoping to emulate the success of Weill and Brecht's *Threepenny Opera*, he also wrote at least one book musical: an adaptation of the *Bourgeoise Gentilhomme* called *Bourgeois Bleibt Bourgois* ("Bourgeois Remains Bourgeois") with book by Ernst Toller (1893 – 1939) and Walter Hasenclever (1890-1940), lyrics by Hermann Kesten (1900-96) and directed by Andrew Granowsky. It opened on 2 February 1929 at the Lessing Theatre and lasted only eight performances. "Critics were divided between those who primarily blamed Granowsky and those who blamed the authors... But the text was severely criticised, especially the second part, which one critic called 'shallow repetition'. Holländer thought the text departed too far from Molière. Kesten, writing nearly thirty years after the event, was unkindly dismissive of his former colleagues."[16]

It was Rosa Valetti who first introduced Holländer to the *Blue Angel*'s future star Marlene Dietrich (1901-92). Following that film's success, Holländer left for Hollywood. There he became "Frederick Hollander" and wrote scores for well over a hundred films, as well as a number of songs in collaboration with future Broadway tunesmith Frank Loesser (1910-69). Some of these were sung by Dietrich in films like *Destry Rides Again* ("The Boys in the Back Room"). He tried to revive Berlin's Tingel-Tangel cabaret on Santa Monica Boulevard, but it was a dismal failure, even when sung in English. He even tried his hand at film directing, with *The Only Girl* (1934), starring Charles Boyer, for which he also wrote the score. In the 1950s, and 60s, he returned to Germany, mounting revues in Munich.

Another important composer for the Weimar cabaret was Mischa Spoliansky (1898-1985), who worked on both *Sound and Smoke* and Trude Hesterberg's Wilde Brühne ("Wild Stage"). He was born in Bialystock, Russia, the son of an operatic baritone. The family moved to Germany when his mother died in 1905, and Mischa gave his first concert at the age of ten. Like Holländer, Spoliansky was seduced by the cabaret. In fact, it was Victor Holländer who first encouraged him in that direction, bringing him into the Reinhardt organisation. He was commissioned to write (as well as perform in) a musical called *Victoria* based on Somerset Maugham's *Home and Beauty* which toured to Vienna and Salzburg after a successful run in Berlin. In 1922 he met the lyricist Marcellus Schiffer (1892-1932), a leading humorist whose other collaborators included Friedrich Holländer, Rudloph Nelson and the opera composer Paul Hindemith. Their greatest hit was the revue *Es liegt in der Luft* ("It's in the Air") featuring Schiffer's wife Margo Lion and Marlene Dietrich. The setting was a department store, in a spoof on consumerism. One of the songs "Wenn die beste Freundin" ("When the Special Girlfriend") depicted two women shoppers who decide to "exchange" their unsatisfactory husbands for each other. This song became an unofficial anthem for Germany's lesbian community. (Schiffer was gay, and Lion a lesbian.) A "cabaret opera", *Rufen Sie Herrn Plim!* ("Send for Mr. Plim"), produced at the Kabarett der Komiker (Cabaret of Comedians) in 1932 with a book by Kurt Robitschek and starring Harald Paulsen (1895 – 1954) (who had appeared in *Threepenny Opera*) also had a department store setting, with the management devising a unique way of dealing with customer complaints. Mr. Plim's job was to be "fired", thereby acting as a scapegoat for all complaints.

Of course, Germany was dancing toward disaster. "To the Nazis," Liel Leibovitz and Matthew Miller say in their book *Lili Marlene*, "Berlin's freewheeling culture, dominated as it was by leftists, liberals, and Jews, represented an insidious threat to the pure Aryan culture they wished to see reborn in a Germany cleansed of non-Germans. To them, the playful criticism of the ruling classes that the cabaret shows engendered amounted to treason and the black musicians and American jazz that were celebrated in its rollicking halls were a cancerous tumor rotting the German soul."[17] Within a year, Adolph Hitler would become Chancellor, and the curtain would come down – quite literally – on kabarett. However, Marcellus Schiffer would not live to see it – he ended his own life in 1932 with an overdose of sleeping pills.

Like Holländer, Spoliansky fled Germany when Hitler came to power, settling in London and working in films for Alexander Korda, among others. He also wrote propaganda songs for the German language service of the BBC during World War II (although, as an "enemy alien", his work was banned from the domestic service).

Benny Goodman recorded some of his music, and he could count George Gershwin among his admirers. He never worked in English language musical theatre, but not for lack of trying – his musical version of Shaw's *Pygmalion* was never pursued. Back in Germany he did an adaptation of Carl Zuckmayer's 1928 folk play *Katharina Knie,* set in a travelling circus, with book and lyrics by Robert Gilbert (1899-1978). This opened at the Theater am Gärtnerplatz in Munich on 20 January 1957. *Wie lernt man Liebe?* ("How You Learn Love"), described as a "musical party game" also written with Gilbert, based on Sheridan's *School for Scandal*, was produced on stage and television there a decade later. In 1978, he and Margo Lion accepted an invitation to the Berlin Arts Festival in a performance of his music. It was such a triumph that they were invited back again the following year.

Spoliansky did finally make his posthumous English language musical theatre debut in 1999, when *Send for Mr. Plim* was revived in an English adaptation by actor Julian Forsyth at the Battersea Arts Centre in London. *The Guardian*'s Michael Billington wrote, "The piece is pure joy and a total vindication of the form of cabaret opera: it says more in 60 minutes than most musicals galumphingly say over three hours."[18]

The genesis of this version came some years earlier when Spoliansky's daughter Spoli Mills came to see Forsyth in Trevor Nunn's stage production of *The Blue Angel*, which had used some of her father's songs. She then sent him the piano score for *Plim*.

"It's full of pastiche of all sorts of musical styles", Forsyth told me. "It'll switch very quickly from pastiche Richard Strauss or even Wagner or Handelian recitative into a fox-trot or various other jazz rhythms. And it's very fascinating, but I thought, as it stood, for a modern audience, maybe there's a little bit too much of a requirement for audiences to recognise some of the operatic pastiche... Is that going to disengage them from the story if they're going 'oh, there's a little bit of *Rosenkavalier* here', or 'a little bit of recitative that sounds like Handel'? It seemed to me there was more of that than there was of the jazz... It felt to me, at the time, as though we were admiring how clever a composer could be. That worried me slightly."

Then an idea occurred. "As it happened, we made contact with an English vocal group called Cantabile who, amongst other things, do arrangements of German popular songs in the style of the Comedian Harmonists." The latter was a cabaret sextet in Weimar Berlin who patterned themselves after an American group called The Revellers, the original members of which were Harry Frommermann, Erwin Bootz, Roman Cycowski, Aspurach Leschnikoff, Erich Collin and Robert Biberti. They had taken part in another Spoliansky revue, *Zwei Krawatten* ("Two Neckties") which also featured Marlene Dietrich. (Joseph Vilsmaier's 1997 film *The Harmonists* is based on their story.)

Forsyth and his director wife Marguerite decided to bring in Cantabile to play the department store managers. He expanded the roles of the manager and personnel manager in the original version into four, thus forming a vocal quartet. "Cantabile had evolved over a generation or two, and so there was quite an interesting age range", Forsyth explains. "You've got the senior, rather conservative boss, then the next in command is maybe a little bit prickly. He was the one [who], because he could sing counter-tenor as well as tenor, would be the most likely to say something rather dramatic and do it as a kind of Handelian recitative. Then the next one down was the guy who'd worked in Macy's for a year and [is] very astute and always thinking the American way. And then we thought it's interesting to have one guy below him who's got an eye on his job and is younger and will maybe pick holes."

In order to accommodate this, he was able to interpolate other Spoliansky melodies – particularly some originally written for the Comedian Harmonists – into the score. "You would get the feeling that switches in musical style were in some way organically generated by their interaction amongst each other and also whomever else they might encounter." This also resulted in a jazzier, more popular style.

Ultimately, the managers' plan falls apart. "What they don't reckon with is that Mr. Plim turns out to be kind of subversive in the funniest ways. They… give him instructions as to how to behave with these angry customers, and whatever instructions they give to him he takes to its logical extreme. So instead of the customer leaving feeling satisfied that they have actually assisted Wertheim's [Department Store] by getting rid of an unsuitable employee, they end up leaving even more angry. The things they complain about are absolutely ludicrous, but the management kow-tow to them and are terribly obsequious. It just so happens that whatever instruction they give to Plim, whether it's [to] be very apologetic and in fact almost be grateful that your inadequacies have been pointed out to you… He's so grateful for being put on the dole along with millions of other Germans who can barely eat that this lady from the Women's Institute in Leipzig is even more angry when she departs than when she arrives. So they say, 'we obviously got that wrong…you'd better show a little bit of distress'. So of course Plim becomes this wonderful actor. You're never sure whether he just has that mindset – 'Okay, I'll play that to the hilt' and it all just happens to go horribly wrong, or whether there's some subversive element in what he's doing."

Many have taken this to be a critique of capitalism and consumerism, but Forsyth believes it has a more specific target. "The whole idea of the need for a scapegoat – who's to blame for the Wall Street crash that wrecked the German economy – all these loans recalled, the millions of people thrown out of work – who's to blame? Of course, we all know what the Nazi Party's answer to that particular question was."

There were other challenges in adapting *Plim* for an English audience. "A curious thing about cabaret music at that time, which you find in Spoliansky and Schiffer and you certainly find in Brecht and Weill is sometimes the words fit the music in ways you really wouldn't expect. In fact, it's almost deliberately put together in a way that it really doesn't fit. It's anti the normal American way of doing things. Where the music dictates the stress should be is exactly where you wouldn't want it if that person were just saying that sentence."

44

When the New York Shakespeare Festival mounted a revival of *Threepenny Opera* starring Raul Julia in 1976, translators Ralph Manheim (1907-92) and John Willett (1917-2002) attempted to find an English equivalent to this way of phrasing. The earlier Marc Blitzstein (1905-64) translation had aimed to make the lyrics more singable, but in this case producer Joseph Papp felt "it was evident that the intention of its creators had been to violate the musical rhythms so that the force of the language dominated the hearing of its audience. While I admit that the popular and Americanized treatment of Brecht's lyrics are in some instances more beautiful than what appears to be the clumsier and less manageable text in this more authentic translation, on the whole the deliberately crude artistic texture of the original is clearly diminished."[19]

"I'm inclined to agree with Joe Papp that the 'deliberately crude' juxtapositions of text and music in the Brecht/Weill originals is something that translations of those works should try to emulate if one wants to capture the flavour and intentions of the originals", says Forsyth. "But I think Brecht/Weill set a trend... and Marcellus Schiffer was to some extent copying that. But Schiffer and Spoliansky are of course much less edgy and ground-breaking than Brecht and Weill, and I just felt that copying the deliberate idiosyncrasies of the *Plim* prologue for example wouldn't do them any favours with audiences who had never heard any Spoliansky music before... I think to a modern ear it would seem quaint to the extent of almost 'whoever's done that translation hasn't done a very good job', because the words don't go with the music. It would probably seem dated in German too."

"I felt you almost need to forget that people were singing. You need to see them interacting almost as if it were a little intimate play. The interaction between characters needs to be organic and therefore any changes in musical style need to be organic. You need to see somebody thinking, 'Oh, I know how to respond to this, but I will choose to respond to it in a fox-trot.'

The critical success of this version has led to some renewed interest in the piece. There were some initial legal complications, as Spoli didn't own the rights, but now that they have been resolved, Forsyth is translating his adaptation back into German, where it will exist as an alternative to the original.

Although they were working in a very controversial field, there was one thing that Holländer, Spoliansky and Weill had in common – they were all highly classically trained. They all were also clearly enamoured of American jazz and Tin Pan Alley. (While Kurt Weill never actually wrote for the cabarets, Bertolt Brecht did, albeit briefly, and that influence can be heard in *Threepenny Opera* and other works).

The first attempt at cabaret in Vienna was in the cellar of the Theater an der Wien in 1901, when Felix Salten (1869-1945) opened his *Theater zum lieben Augustin* which lasted for only seven performances. Five years later, a more permanent cabaret opened in the same space, called Die Hölle ("Hell"). This was soon followed by Marc

Henry's "Fledermaus" in Kärtnerstrasse, whose contributors included future operetta composer Oscar Straus. One of the most successful and long-lasting was "Simplicissimus", founded in 1912 by Egon Dorn as a restaurant with entertainment. One of its emcees was Fritz Grünbaum, who would later establish himself in operettas as a librettist before dying in a concentration camp. "Simpl" – as it came to be known – survived the war, and still exists.

After Hitler came to power, most of the cabarets in Germany closed. Those that survived were converted into so-called "positive cabaret", which presented a pro-Nazi outlook devoid of any real satire. Lale Anderson was one artist who survived, in spite of her anti-Nazi beliefs and her Swiss Jewish lover. Her story is proof that even a control freak like Joseph Goebbels couldn't stage-manage everything. In 1938, she recorded "The Song of the Young Sentry", a sentimental ballad composed by Norbert Schultze as a setting of a World War I poem by Hans Leip. The story concerned a young soldier who yearns for his girlfriend. Leip combined the names of two girls he had romanced, "Lili" and "Marlene". The recording disappeared without a trace – almost. When Radio Belgrade required some fresh light music to fill their daily broadcast to the German soldiers in Eastern Europe and North Africa, they were given a number of records that had been rejected by the mainstream German broadcasters, including this one. It became a hit with soldiers on both sides of the conflict, and there wasn't anything either Goebbels or Churchill could do to stop it.

Some of the exiled artists took their acts to Austria (until its German annexation), Switzerland, the Netherlands and Britain. After the war, Holländer tried to revive Tingel-Tangel in Munich in the 1950s, and a form of cabaret called Die Distel was tolerated by the East Berlin authorities as a safety valve. It survives to this day in a converted cinema in Friedrichstrasse. Berlin sketch writer Jergen Behrens says, "Cabaret should be a combination of living room and bedroom."[20]

Cabaret of the sort practised in Paris and Berlin was never very big in London, although some indigenous attempts were made. In 1912, Austrian heiress and journalist Frida Strindberg (1872-1943) (nee Uhl), ex-wife of the famous Swedish playwright August Strindberg, established the "Cave of the Golden Calf" in the basement of a merchant's warehouse just off Regent Street. It lasted for just over a year. With the possible exception of Peter Cook's Establishment Club in Soho in the early 1960s, what little cabaret there has been in London has tended toward jazz clubs such as Ronnie Scott's, rather than satire. In recent times, there have been a few nightclubs such as Pizza on the Park and the Pheasantry that feature theatre artists singing a repertoire of Broadway standards.

In the post-war period, the Netherlands developed its own brand of cabaret. Although it owed much to Weimar, it took on a character of its own. Some of the most famous "cabaretiers" included Wim Sonneveld (1917-74) and Toon Hermans (1916-2000) who mixed political and celebrity satire, music and poetry and movement. Their characters were larger than life, but very real as well. Dutch actor and dancer René Driessen remembers artists like De Mounties, and Snip en Snap. "When I was a kid we used to love watching them and especially around New Years Eve and in the Christmas Holidays they would be shown often on TV and the whole country watched them (we only had one or two channels and nobody looked at foreign channels then, which is completely different now). It sometimes saddens me that those people and those times are gone, because it had a real intimate sense of 'home'".

One Dutch cabaret-writing team turned their hands to writing book musicals. Their biggest hit *En Nu Naar Bed* ("And Now to Bed") which opened in Amsterdam on 5 November 1971 with book and lyrics by Annie M. G. Schmidt (1911-95) and music by Harry Bannink (1929-99), was directed by the Canadian-born, London-based choreographer Paddy Stone (1924-86). I will talk more about this and other post-war European musicals in another chapter.

Of course, in recent years, the word "cabaret" has taken on other meanings. When Lisa Appignanesi talks about New York cabaret, she is talking about the stand-up comedy of Lenny Bruce, Mort Sahl and Mike Nichols and Elaine May, and her only musical references are to the jazz of the Beat generation. Yet, that is not the context in which I usually hear the word used today.

In the U.S., there is a monthly magazine called *Cabaret Scenes* with articles on cabaret artists such as Amanda McBroom and John Bucchino. There is no mention of stand-up, and little talk of political satire. Nor is the emphasis on jazz. Many, if not most of the artists listed are in some way connected to musical theatre – either as off-duty actors, or as singers who draw heavily on the Broadway repertoire.

"For a good part of the 20th century, musical theatre songs *were* the majority of the popular songs," says American cabaret singer Karen Oberlin, "so those were the songs being performed in the intimate clubs, even in New York. Everyone performed the theatre songs, including theatrical singers and jazz singers, so I think the infusion of theatre songs was quite natural and continues to be part of the tradition. In an intimate setting, the lyrics have to 'hold up,' and a performer must be living within a song, so theatre songs work well."

"Cabaret has 'evolved' to become 'personal theatre', in other words, the songs are 'acting pieces' that allow the singer to convey something personal to the audience", says singer Anne Kerry Ford. "Some of the best 'acting songs' naturally come from musical theatre. These are usually the songs with the deepest lyrical content (say, over 'pop' songs). Not always... I mean, I have heard all kinds of songs done well in cabaret shows, but the Broadway material almost demands to be sung out of the context of the show they were written for, because they are so lyrically rich. It is fun for the audience to hear them in a different context from the show they were written for, as they can consider the song as a complete work of art in itself, and they usually hear it afresh without the story of the show around it. These songs are gems in themselves, and often they stand up quite well when taken out of context, if they make sense in the context of the cabaret show. It's like deconstructing a dress (read 'Broadway show') to make a quilt (read 'cabaret show'). Both are valid art forms; the same material is just being used in different ways. I personally look for material that has a lot of emotional content, as these are the ones that resonate with me and allow me to use my acting chops. That's why I have made the music of Kurt Weill my metier."

"I believe that the reason Broadway music ended up in cabaret rooms is that performers who are drawn to musical theatre are interested in telling stories through song", says American actor and singer David Cameron Anderson. "These people, if they're at all ambitious, have no intention of waiting for someone to tell them, 'You can sing now,' or 'You may sing now, however your 'type' is (fill in the blank – ingenue, leading man/woman, character man/woman) therefore you may only sing songs that we think 'fit' your type' and continuing, 'The public is not interested in the love lives of the less than beautiful – so you can sing the best friend's song or the fathers song or the janitor's song but, God forbid, you should dare to sing to express how you love or how you are loved' and to the beautiful people, 'you're pretty – you don't get to tell the jokes'… So these disenfranchised performers pick music that matters to them and find a place with a piano and a microphone and a place for the audience to sit and then they sing for all they're worth. And Broadway songs are already story songs so there you have it… Then they find that the Broadway trunk, though substantial, cannot possibly fill hour after hour in cabaret rooms without overexposure so they look at others who write story material – folk writers, country and western writers, literate pop writers."

When a song from a musical is performed in a cabaret, it is stripped naked. Usually with only a piano for accompaniment and no more than two hundred people in the audience, this is a friendly communication between artist and audience that plays to the musical theatre's greatest asset: the lyrics. Whether it is Ann Hampton Calloway singing Frank Loesser or Edith Piaf singing Marguerite Monnot, the effect is the same – they are telling stories to an audience hanging on their every note and word. Jacques Brel understood this, which is why his songs were so easily adapted to the revue format. Size isn't everything. "When Sarah McLaughlin sings 'Angel', accompanying herself on a piano, in the Universal Amphitheatre (seating at least 4,000) it is cabaret to me," says Anderson. On the other hand, "Some brilliant theatre singers are lousy in small venues," says Lorna Dallas. "Imagine Merman reigning in her voice for some place like Jermyn Street? Impossible."

Whether by accident or by design, cabaret and revue have long been a proving ground for new writers who then go on to write full scale musicals. This is true in New York, but it was also true in Paris and Berlin. Vincent Scotto, Albert Willemetz and Henri Christiné wrote for the cabarets in Paris, as did Bertolt Brecht in Berlin.

In London, Mark Bunyan began in the late 1970s "where I managed to skilfully fall between any of the available stools." As an outspoken gay artist, he was deemed too radical for the mainstream (one West End management told him, "We can't put that on the *Val Doonican Show*"), but not radical enough for the "soft-soap socialism of many of the alternative comedians who merely replaced the word 'mother-in-law' with 'the fuzz' and alcohol with cocaine." He ended up playing solo acts in theatres before a largely gay audience until he began to reach a "much wider spectrum who just want to be intelligently entertained."

I got to know Mark through the Writing Block, a group of songwriters who used to meet once a month in Covent Garden to try their songs out on each other – much like the Hydropathes of a century earlier. "I suppose it was an obvious step for me as a narrative-writing cabaret writer... to move into writing narrative musical theatre." His musical *Achilles in Heels* was mounted at the Landor Theatre in South London in 2007.

Cabaret works differently in different places. In Toronto, it has traditionally been allied with revue and dinner theatre, where artists like the late Tom Kneebone and Dinah Christie did revues such as *Oh Coward!* There is a great comedy tradition, beginning with the annual *Spring Thaw* revues that ran from 1948-71. Although *Second City* originally began in Chicago, its Toronto offshoot has largely eclipsed the parent, having spawned the long running *SCTV* television series. In fact, while Toronto cabaret has largely gone in the Broadway-writ-small direction, the sort of political satire that Appignanesi has identified with cabaret has prospered – on and off – on TV and radio. *This Hour Has Seven Days*, which ran on CBC television from 1964-66, combined serious public affairs journalism with biting satirical songs (usually sung by Ms. Christie) and sketches. Former Canadian broadcaster Sandy Stewart describes it as "a lively, provocative and even outrageous program which was required viewing for all intelligent Canadians."[21] (It was taken off the air after network attempts to curtail some of its more controversial subjects.) The spirit of *Spring Thaw* has also survived in the form of *Royal Canadian Air Farce*, first on radio, then on TV.

In Australia, where an annual international cabaret festival has been held in Adelaide since 2001, it has developed an updated form of its own, allied to alternative fringe comedy. "Here, the word 'cabaret' isn't loaded with European and American baggage", says London based performer Barb Jungr. "This is the country that gave the world Robyn Archer, and followed with Caroline Reid's *Pam Ann* and Tim Minchin. There seems to be a fair amount of envelope pushing as far as the genre is concerned."[22] Minchin has more recently enjoyed London success with *Matilda*, his musical adaptation of the Roald Dahl classic. *Keating*, a highly successful cabaret musical with a political theme, will be discussed in the chapter " Larrikins and Sentimental Blokes: Musicals Down Under".

Berlin: Give My Regards to Friedrichstrasse

In a way, perhaps Adolph Hitler was right. It seems that, so far as musical theatre was concerned, there was a master race. Unfortunately for him, they were not the so-called Aryans, but the Jews – the very people he was persecuting. (Evidently he didn't own a mirror, or else he might have noticed that he was not himself blonde haired and blue eyed.) Still, he dedicated himself to ridding Germany of many of the people that had brought it to the forefront of the arts and sciences, resulting in the greatest "own goal" in the history of humanity. He eventually discovered, to his peril, that this included most of the top nuclear physicists who were now devoting their not inconsiderable intellects to making sure that no one atom in his body remained attached to any other. Equally humiliating to him was the fact that most of the greatest musical talents of the Third Reich (save for his beloved Wagner, who was already dead) were either being killed or driven into exile. Musical theatre in central Europe was brought to virtual extinction, and it was all his fault.

Not that Hitler was against the arts. Far from it – after all, he was a failed artist himself. It was just that he didn't like anybody to be better at anything than he was, and so he and his fellow Nazis did not suffer geniuses gladly. When the leading German conductor Wilhelm Furtwängler[1] declared, in the *Deutschen Allgemeinen Zeitung* that the only dividing line in music was not between Aryan and Jewish but between "good and bad art"[2], the Nazi minister for "public enlightenment" Joseph Goebbels replied, "Only an art that draws from the full Ethnicity itself may in the end be good".[3]

It was not always thus. In the late nineteenth and the first quarter of the twentieth century – a period of remarkable racial tolerance – Germany, along with Hungary and Austria, not only had a strong indigenous musical theatre tradition, but it has had an inestimable influence on the rest of the world as well. The dual traditions of operetta and cabaret gave us Weill and Holländer among many, many others.

In fact, Kurt Weill is probably the first name to come to mind when you think of Berlin musical theatre, but he was by no means the first out of the starting gate. In fact, many people probably know the song "Glow-Worm" without realising that it came from a 1902 production of *Lysistrata*, with music by Paul Lincke (1866-1946). Richard Strauss (1864-1949) had suggested Lincke to Kaiser Wilhelm as a court composer, but the Kaiser – who was an admirer of Arthur Sullivan – thought him too vulgar. His early career had been spent writing opera parodies, and he honed his skills in Paris as musical director of the Folies-Bergère. His first great Berlin success was *Frau Luna,* a "burlesque-fantastic-spectacular" with a libretto by Heinrich Bolten-Bäckers (1871-1938), which began in 1899 as a simple one-act operetta. It struck a nerve with its hometown audience.

50

After World War I, the mood and temper of Berlin musical theatre changed. "German language operetta was at the crossroads, not just politically but artistically, as it attempted to reconcile the traditional and the new"[4], says Andrew Lamb. The "traditional" could be typified by the operettas of Strauss and others, while the "new" would include the cabaret-derived works of Brecht and Weill, Benatzky, Holländer and Spoliansky. "Berlin in the years after the First World War was in spirit the most American city in Europe", said Kurt Weill in a 1941 interview. "We read Jack London, Hemmingway, Dreiser, Dos Passos, we admired Hollywood pictures, and American jazz had a great influence on our music. America was a very romantic country for us."[5] Of course, German composers re-interpreted American jazz and Tin Pan Alley and "that re-interpretation created something highly individual and unique," according to Kevin Clarke, director of the Amsterdam-based Operetta Research Centre. "You can sense that in the newspapers of the period... Or you can sense it in [Emmerich] Kàlmàn recycling [Sigmund] Romberg, after Romberg had recycled Kàlmàn (in *Desert Song*). I find this ping-pong game fascinating. At the time, audiences in Germany and Austria [were] obviously much more aware of what was going on on Broadway than now. And instead of just copying it... like now, they used it as a starting point for something new."[6]

Viennese-born Max Reinhardt (1873-1943) was one of the leading directors of the twentieth century. His work straddled barriers between the traditional and new, populism and elitism, and intimacy and spectacle. In Berlin in 1919, he constructed the massive 3,000 seat Grosses Schauspielhaus, a domed arena with a thrust stage and revolve where he staged epic classics such as Aeschylus' *Oresteia*. He became noted for his spectacular productions of *The Miracle* and *A Midsummer Nights' Dream*, both of which were eventually adapted for American audiences. But he also was a pioneer of intimate cabaret with his Sound and Smoke, where he nurtured the early careers of Friederich Holländer and Mischa Spoliansky.

Although he was a great lover of Offenbach, whom he regarded almost as a soul mate – he had staged productions of *La Belle Hélène*, *Tales of Hoffmann* and *Orpheus in the Underworld* – he had, according to his son Gottfried, "a deep aversion to the sham Vienna depicted by coy and sentimental operetta kitsch... He would not give a *Fuchzgerl* for the operetta giants, Franz Lehár, Emmerich Kálmán, Robert Stolz, and the full weight of their carefully calculated schmaltz. He would not even give the negligible time it would have taken to sit through a performance of Oscar Straus's cloying *Waltz Dream* or *Chocolate Soldier*, although he esteemed the musicianship of Straus, a friend ever since they had collaborated on their mutual cabaret debut. And he would not let wild horses drag him into a theatre to sit through the saccharine *Merry Widow* or *Madame Pompadour*, even when their star was Germany's operetta queen Fritzi Massary, whose talent he found irresistible... Even Richard Strauss's *Der Rosenkavalier*, ("The Knight of the Rose") whose first performance he directed, made him uneasy. The elegant sophistication of its first act, the lyrical glamour of its second, followed by the broad buffoonery of its third, was a mixture too smooth for his comfort... While he considered Johann Strauss's music to be of Mozartian quality, the cute slapstick offended him."[7]

Still, he was persuaded to mount a revival of Strauss's *Die Fledermaus*, which opened in Berlin on 8 June 1928 at the Deutsches Theater with the composer's widow Adele in attendance. "As theatre, the Johann Strauss opus has hardly ever been taken seriously", Reinhardt Jr. continues, "With one exception... under Max Reinhardt's direction it took its place under what I would call his flawless productions." (Kurt Gänzl – who is not a Reinhardt fan – disagrees, dismissing it as "gaudy" and "typically big and typically botched".)[8] For this version, the book was revised by Ernst Marishka and the music adapted by Erich Wolfgang Korngold (1897-1957). The violinist Yehudi Menuhin saw this production, "which left me walking on air for three days afterward."[9] He then took his production to Paris, where it received a cool reception. In Vienna, it was pilloried for tampering with such a sacred cow, yet in Milan they loved it. In 1942, an English translation of this version opened on Broadway under the title *Rosalinda* with choreography by George Balanchine (1904-83). The English libretto was credited to John Meehan Jr. (1908-67) and Gottfried Reinhardt (1911-94) and the lyrics by Paul Kerby (1891-1971). *Time* magazine wrote that "Director Reinhardt has whipped *Fledermaus*' drama into a light fluff, flavored it with a medley of Strauss waltzes from other sources, given it a new prologue, a new name (*Rosalinda*) and a decorous, Victorian striptease... that leaves its leading lady more thoroughly clad than many of today's best-dressed bathing beauties."[10] Reinhardt was not officially the director of this production: a former assistant of his, Felix Brentano, had teamed up with Korngold to remount the show using Reinhardt's text and prompt book. When the great director got wind of this (it was Korngold who tipped him off), he stepped in to protect his legacy. It received excellent notices and ran for a total of 521 performances before going on tour.

"Musical quality alone was not sufficient incentive for him to come to terms with absurd stories and characters without character", says his son. "Operetta texts – *Die Fledermaus* not excepted – are synthetic fabrications. Their roles are stereotyped and their actions tend to bog down in structural impasses."[11] In other words, as Oscar Hammerstein demonstrated in *Oklahoma!* the music must serve the book.

Reinhardt was a firm believer in popular theatre. "The so-called 'good' public is in reality the worst," he told his biographer Gusti Adler. "Dull sophisticates. Inattentive, blasé, used to being the centre of attention themselves... Only the gallery is worth anything."[12] German theatre critic Esther Slevogt says, "Reinhardt has never really been forgiven for pointing out that all democratic theatrical arts are dependent on the audience, in other words **the market**. The majority of German theatre makers continue to feel part of an elite with a diffuse task: that of enlightenment, or of truth itself. Max Reinhardt took another path and because of this he is still a provocation to subsidised culture."[13]

The Berlin of Max Reinhardt and of Kurt Weill (1900-50) is the child that was aborted. Reinhardt's Deutsches Theater was nationalised by Hitler in 1933 and eventually became the state theatre of the German Democratic Republic. Reinhardt and Weill, both Jews, became refugees of the Nazis. They had made two failed attempts to collaborate – they had intended to work together on *The Rise and Fall of the City of Mahagonny* and *The Silver Lake*, but were unable to – before finally coming together on the ill-fated *The Eternal Road* in New York in 1937. Although their collaboration never really amounted to much, somehow we are left thinking that it *should* have. These were two of German theatre's brightest talents, but the rise of German nationalism had ironically strangled its sense of national identity. We are left to speculate what, in their hands, might have become of German musical theatre had they not been so rudely interrupted.

The "new" with which the operettas had to come to terms included the influence of the cabarets, which had existed in Germany since the early 1900s. Lincke wrote few new works after 1918 because, according to George Colerick, "he did not have the feel for the new rhythms, especially those from the Americas."[14] It is only too ironic that it was American lyricist Johnny Mercer who adapted "Glow-Worm" into a popular song for the Mills Brothers in the very form that had eluded Lincke himself.

The new generation brought Friedrich Holländer, Mischa Spoliansky and, of course, Kurt Weill. The son of a cantor in Dessau, Weill came to Berlin in 1918 to study under Engelbert Humperdinck (1854-1921), composer of *Hansel and Gretel*, but he returned home, dissatisfied. He worked as music director at a theatre in Lüdenscheid. There he resolved that he would spend his life in the theatre, and returned to Berlin to study under Ferruccio Busoni (1866-1924). His timing was propitious: the end of the First World War had forced Germany to open its borders to foreign cultural influences, including American, French, English and Russian. For Weill and others, this meant exposure to jazz. One of the leading bandleaders touring Europe at that time was Paul Whiteman (1890-1967), a former classical violinist who championed "symphonic jazz" that largely eschewed improvisation. (It was Whiteman's orchestra that commissioned Gershwin to write *Rhapsody in Blue*.) Some might consider the jazz heard in Berlin to be watered down, even corrupted, but this was jazz filtered through German ears. Weill biographer Foster Hirsch writes, "Such jazz-based elements as syncopation, improvisation, a greater use of wind instruments, and a driving percussive beat mixed with native expressionist and atonal idioms... A fusion was born that was to prepare the way for Kurt Weill's music-theatre hybrids."[15]

It was his collaboration with Bertolt Brecht (1898-1956) that was to have the greatest impact on German musical theatre. They both shared a fascination with America – or rather, the America that they saw on the movie screen. To them it was the New World, not yet the world-dominating hegemony that it later became. Weimar Germany was freer than Wilhelmine Germany had been, but it was economically and politically precarious. Of course, Brecht was not one to tread lightly on eggshells. His outlook was radical, both politically and theatrically.

Their first project together was a setting of Brecht's *Mahagonny* poems, a songspiel describing a mythical American city that was later expanded into the three act opera *The Rise and Fall of the City of Mahagonny*. But the major stage work for which they are now remembered came about when a former actor named Ernst Josef Aufricht bought the Theater am Schiffbauerdamm, and was determined to open it on his birthday with a new show. John Gay's 1728 *Beggar's Opera* had recently enjoyed a successful revival at the Lyric Theatre Hammersmith in London, and Brecht's assistant Elisabeth Hauptmann was working on a German adaptation.

Aufricht apparently leapt at the idea, but was reluctant to take Brecht's suggestion that Weill write a new, original score. He had Weill prepare a few songs to "audition", and then gave the go-ahead. *Die Dreigroschenoper*, the "Threepenny Opera", opened on 31 August 1928. The initial reception was not warm, but it gradually caught on, and played for more than 400 performances.

Soon dance bands all over Germany were playing music from the show, including its opening number, "Moritat von Mackie Messer" ("The Ballad of Mack the Knife"), a song written just before the opening to satisfy the ego of actor Harald Paulsen who played Macheath. (He was disappointed then to learn that while the song was about his character, he would not be singing it.)

With all the touring companies, *Threepenny Opera* amassed a staggering 4,200 performances in Germany in the 1928-29 season, and by 1933 had been seen over 10,000 times across Europe. A film was made by director G.W. Pabst in both German and French. The German version cut half of the music, but included several members of the original cast, including Lotte Lenya (1898-1981) as Jenny. Although several attempts were made, it was not a success in the English speaking world until an off-Broadway production opened in 1954 with a translation by Marc Blitzstein and starring Weill's widow Lotte Lenya. "Mack the Knife" became a hit for Louis Armstrong and, later, Bobby Darin.

In stark contrast to conventional operetta – and to later "integrated" Broadway musicals, Brecht believed in keeping the elements separated, in order to "alienate" the audience, maintaining an emotional detachment. "Nothing is more revolting than when the actor pretends not to notice that he has left the level of plain speech and started to sing," he wrote. "The three levels – plain speech, heightened speech and singing, must always remain distinct, and in no way should heightened speech represent an intensification of plain speech, or singing of heightened speech… The actor must not only sing but show a man singing."[16] Richard Kislan, professor of speech, theatre and dance at Glassboro Stage College in New Jersey writes, "Since Brecht theorized much about devices in the theater for breaking illusion and keeping emotion in check through interrupting devices, it was natural for him to insist on wonderful, haunting, and idiosyncratic songs that interrupted the book."[17]

Brecht and Weill followed with *Happy End*, with a book by Elisabeth Hauptmann set in 1920s Chicago among gangsters and Salvation Army recruits. (If it sounds familiar, it's only because Frank Loesser tackled a similar idea with much greater success a couple of decades later – *Guys and Dolls*.) While it contained some enduring songs, including "Surabaya Johnny", it was not a hit.

"The more the newer trends took hold," says historian Andrew Lamb, "the greater the nostalgia for the past, and there were various attempts to satisfy it by overhauling the operetta hits of the nineteenth century."[18] A 1922 revival of *Frau Luna* expanded it by interpolating songs from other Lincke shows, (including the aforementioned "Glow-Worm").

One composer working in Vienna and Berlin who managed to straddle the lines between cabaret, operetta and revue was Ralph Benatzky (1884-1957). Born in what is now the Czech Republic, he studied with Antonin Dvořák (1841-1904) before becoming the musical director of the Kleines Theater in Munich, and later the cabaret venue Bonbonnière. While working within the operetta tradition, he incorporated a jazzy, musical-comedy sound that revealed an American pop influence. In 1931, his greatest success, the "singspiel" *Im weissen Rössl*, for which he wrote the majority of the score, opened at Berlin's Grosses Schauspielhaus, Reinhardt's former home of spectacle. It travelled to London the following year as *The White Horse Inn*. It then opened in New York in 1936 under the same title, but with new lyrics by Irving Caesar. In fact, it was extensively adapted for each country in which it played, including France, Hungary and Australia. Although it was Benatzky's only world-wide hit, he enjoyed other successes in German-speaking countries, including his charming Hollywood satire *Axel an der Himmelstür* ("Axel at the Gates of Heaven") starring Zarah Leander, staged in Vienna in 1936.

Alas, after 1933, musical theatre activity in Germany – and much of Europe – ground to a screeching halt, never to regain its former glory. Not only did Weill, Holländer and Spoliansky leave, but so did Max Reindhardt, deemed by many to be the greatest theatrical director of the century. The rest is a story of "woulda, shoulda, coulda". It did not die a natural death. It was murdered. However, there is a coda to our story. Recently, when riding an S-Bahn train in Berlin and looking at the eclectic mixture of passengers, including some from Turkey and North Africa, I realised just how beautifully Hitler had failed.

Paris: Where Musicals Were Born, and Where They Go to Die

Alain Boublil, the co-creator of *Les Misérables* has said, "France is an empty space as far as musical theatre is concerned. Only old-fashioned operettas, but that's about it."[1] Far be it for me to argue with the most successful French musical writer of the modern era, but he may as well claim that his country has no art, literature or architecture.

Yet, this notion has persisted. Cameron Mackintosh has said, "The French have hardly ever taken to modern musicals, and Paris has proved the early graveyard for most of the worldwide musical successes of the last fifty years; they prefer revivals of operettas, Euro-rock musicals of dubious origin and the occasional short, chic season of American touring musicals – performed in English."[2] Irish music producer Gareth Murphy takes that logic even further, saying "The fact is, with the exception of classical music composers such as Ravel, Debussy or Fauré, France is not really a major player on the world's musical map."[3] What about their film composers – Maurice Jarre, Georges Delerue, Francis Lai? Murphy goes on to say that, "Caught in a split personality between the brooding of Northern Europe and the simplicity of Mediterranean culture, it's almost as if the French still don't know whether music is supposed to be stupid or serious, ironic or first degree… I suspect that theatre is the subliminal reference of what they think music should resemble. Sharing the same stage as thespians, impersonators, comedians and pantomime clowns, French musicians shift gears from mega-seriousness to social satire, even into slapstick muzak. In the French language, both drama and humour are represented by the one word: comédie." I would argue that what Murphy has described here is the essential ingredient of their cabaret tradition, and that may be a strength, rather than a weakness.

The truth is that Paris' relationship with the musical theatre is rather complicated. In the past, it had its own quite vibrant musical theatre scene. The city was also the inspiration for many Broadway and Hollywood musicals. However, these two facts seldom if ever interacted. The odd Parisian number, such as "Mon Homme / My Man" would make it across the Atlantic, and stars such as Maurice Chevalier (1888-1972) and Yvonne Printemps were known and admired by their English language contemporaries. But, for much of the twentieth century – so far as the English speaking world was concerned – a haze of obscurity hung over the musical theatres of Paris.

While the world embraced the music of Edith Piaf, Charles Trenet, Charles Aznavour and Jacques Brel, there was little musical theatre traffic – in either direction – between the stages of Paris and those of New York and London. Few American musicals succeeded in France (with the odd exception, such as *Rose-Marie* or *No No Nanette*), and French musicals didn't travel well to the English speaking world. Why was this?

Even in 1929, when Parisian musical comedy was still at its peak, a reviewer for *Time Magazine* remarked, "French musical comedy is seldom written home about. Tourists are either ashamed about it, or don't understand it, or spend their time in the Louvre".[4] A strange fate to befall the land of Offenbach and Bizet, to be sure. Musical theatre historian Kurt Gänzl says, "If the American writers of musical comedy had studied these gents and their text writers rather more than they did, they might have produced rather better musical comedies. For me, these pieces are the acme of 20th century musical theatre writing."[5]

What is even stranger still is that now the French seem to retain more of an appetite for writing musicals than they do for going to see them – including, of course, Boublil and his partner Claude-Michel Schönberg. Boublil says, "Imagine two people in France creating something for which no tradition exists." Yet France has one of the richest traditions in all of the musical theatre, even if you have to dig a little bit to find it. Not only that, but Boublil and Schönberg are very much a part of it. Of course, *Miss Saigon* doesn't have the sauciness that has run through much of the Parisian musical comedy, from *Orpheus in the Underworld* to *Irma La Douce*. But still, Schönberg grew up listening to *Carmen* (Bizet) and *Tales of Hoffman* (Offenbach), while Boublil was steeped in Aznavour and Brel. And it shows. Their ballads have the highly wrought intensity of a Piaf chanson. "Empty Chairs at Empty Tables" could easily have come from the pen of Jacques Brel. (And Brel himself was a champion of musicals, having played in *Man of La Mancha* for 180 performances in 1968.)

History is written by the victors. Just as Thomas Edison – and not the Lumière Brothers – is credited with the invention of cinema, the Americans get all the credit for inventing musical comedy. Yet, even American musicals like *Gigi* and *Can-Can* seem to tacitly acknowledge that, from the Chat Noir to the Moulin Rouge and the Folies-Bergère, Paris has all of the ingredients.

Théâtre des Bouffes-Parisiens

In front of the Théâtre des Bouffes-Parisiens in Rue Monsigny in the second arrondissment there is a historical plaque indicating that the theatre, once run by Jacques Offenbach, was where the world premieres of *Orpheus in the Underworld*, *Veronique* and *Phi-Phi* took place. The first theatre on the site, the Théâtre Comte was opened in 1826 by Louis Comte (1783-1859) a ventriloquist who ran it as a children's theatre until his retirement in 1854. Two years later his son Charles sold a part interest in the theatre to Offenbach, who used it to present his own works until

1862. However, Offenbach may have been a great showman, but he was a poor businessman. Management passed to a man named Varney – who proved to be even worse, for he reduced the number of Offenbach shows presented, nearly bankrupting the theatre. All the same, he rebuilt it as an eleven hundred seat house, causing Offenbach to temporarily sever his ties with it in 1864 because the re-opening had been delayed. In spite of this, for over one hundred fifty years the theatre has been associated with the name Offenbach, and continues to be the premier venue for French musical comedy.

It was not the only musical house of importance in the French capital, however. Nearby in Boulevard Montmartre, the Théâtre des Variétés had been in business since 1807, and would house a number of Offenbach premieres, including *La belle Hélène*, *La Grande-Duchesse de Gérolstein*, *La Périchole* and *Les Brigandes*, and many years later, Reynaldo Hahn's *Ciboulette*. Also in the Opéra Quarter is the Théâtre Edouard VII, opened in 1916, which presented many of the Sacha Guitry shows, including *L'Amour Masque* with music by André Messager and *Mozart* with music by Reynaldo Hahn. The Théâtre Mogador, built in the manner of an English music hall, hosted Messager's *La Petite Functionnaire* in 1921 as well as two of the few Broadway musicals to take Paris by storm – *No No Nanette* in 1926 and *Rose-Marie* in 1927 – and continues as a commercial musical house to this day, recently housing *The Lion King* (in French). The 200 seat Théâtre des Capicines built in 1889 which presented André Barde and Charles Cuvillier's *Son p'tit frère* in 1907 and Maurice Yvain's *Yes* in 1928 still exists, but not as a theatre. In 1993 it became a museum for the perfume maker Fragonard. The tiny Théâtre Marigny in the Champs-Elysées was originally established in 1835, but gained its greatest prominence as Offenbach's first Bouffes-Parisiens before his move to the Théâtre Comte. The present building, dating from 1880, received Messager's *Coups de Roulis* in 1928. The 450-seat art deco Théâtre Daunou, which housed one of Maurice Yvain's greatest hits, *Ta Bouche* was built in 1921. The Théâtre Nouveautés, also built in 1921 in Boulevard Poissonnière – the fourth of that name – would present its follow-up, the equally successful *Pas sur la Bouche*. The Théâtre de la Michodière, where Messager's *Passionnément* opened in 1926, was built in the previous year for the impresario Gustave Quinson. Even the Folies-Bergère presented operettas in its early days, before gaining renown for more exotic popular entertainment.

Since Offenbach, there have been many composers who achieved great success within France – and sometimes in central Europe, but little if any of their work is known in English speaking countries. The reasons for this are complicated, and do not necessarily always reflect on the quality of their work. In some cases, the libretto lost too much in translation. In others, the frankness of the subject matter was deemed unsuitable for either British or American tastes.

Many French musical comedies were farces on the Feydeau model, a form that has seldom adapted well in English musicals. Lehman Engel writes, "The farces of Feydeau and Labiche cannot accommodate music because they are extremely complex without the additional and probably more confusing burden of another element. Also they are swift and the inclusion of songs would only slow them down. Without speed, they would fail to make their incessant – almost unrelenting – comic points."[6] *A Funny Thing Happened on the Way to the Forum* is a rare exception, because the songs offer a relief from this breakneck pace. "Farces are express trains, musicals are locals", explains Stephen Sondheim. "Savoring moments can be effective while a farce is gathering steam, but deadly once the train gets going. That's why the songs in *Forum* are bunched together in the first half of the first act, where there is more exposition than action, and then become scarcer and scarcer, until eventually in the last twenty minutes before the Finale there are no songs at all."[7] It could be argued, however, that in the case of a show like *Pas sur la bouche* the music gives a pretence of elegance and sophistication to what is otherwise a vulgar form.

Opéra-Comique, Paris

André Messager (1853-1929), a pupil of the composer Camille Saint-Saëns (1835-1921), did double duty as a serious composer during the day while his nights were spent as a conductor at the Folies-Bergère. (Like many French composers of that period, he had one foot in so-called "serious" music, the other in popular culture.) His first break came when the composer Firmin Bernicat (1843-83) died prematurely while writing the score for *François-les-Bas-Bleus*, which Messager was commissioned to complete. He then combined light operettas with ballets and more substantial comic operas such as *La Basoche*, produced at the Opéra Comique in Paris in 1890. (An English version was produced in London in 1891 by Richard D'Oyly Carte.) His commercial breakthrough came seven years later when *Les P'tites Michu* was staged at the Bouffes-Parisiens, and was solidified the following year by *Véronique* with a libretto by Albert Vanloo (1846-1920) and Georges Duval (1847-1919). The plot concerned the pending arranged marriage between an aristocratic woman and a libertine. The two have never met, but when the young woman hears of the libertine's seduction of a shop worker, she sets out to teach him a lesson. Being an operetta, they fall in love.

Messager also enjoyed a career as a conductor at the Opéra-Comique (where he conducted the world premiere of Debussy's *Pelléas et Mélisande*) and at London's Royal Opera House and the Paris Opéra. For a time, this took him away from composition, and by the time he returned, the fashions had changed, and he adapted. In 1919, he worked with the English librettist of *Maid in the Mountains* Freddie Lonsdale (1881-1954) on an adaptation of Booth Tarkington's *Monsieur Beaucaire* which played 221 performances in London, and opened in Paris in 1925.

During World War I, a profound change began to take place. People sought an escape from the carnage going on around them, and with the US entry into the war, American soldiers brought with them American popular culture. "They wanted singing, dancing, light comedy or even crude farce," says French historian and lecturer Jules Bertaut "and the stimulant of a perpetual rhythm to beat down consciousness."[8] It was the beginning of the jazz age. Historian Jeffrey Jackson writes that "Jazz, the music that 'makes men crazy', was already starting to shape the era that some in France would come to call *les années folles* — the crazy years. Jazz was not just music, it seemed. Rather, it marked the onset of a new and challenging age."[9] The American musical had not yet become the world-beating juggernaut that it was in later decades. American (and other foreign) popular music forms were, to the French, exotic. Even a traditionalist like Messager was an admirer of jazz, as was Debussy.

Henri Christiné

The Parisian musical comedy emerged into the post-war, modern era of the "années folles" in a quite literal sense, for it was on the day after the armistice was signed that *Phi-Phi* premiered. Originally conceived for the two hundred seat Théâtre de l'Abri, it was moved at the last minute to the much larger Bouffes-Parisiens, which had unexpectedly gone dark. The scene painters and costumiers were offered percentages in lieu of their fees – as it turns out, a lucrative option.

Phi-Phi tells the story of the Parthenon sculptor Phideas in Ancient Greece and his quest to find a model for his statue of Virtue. Having found her, he aims to relieve her of said virtue, but of course complications ensue.

The music was by Henri Christiné (1867-1941) a former schoolteacher who was born in Geneva to a French watchmaker and his wife. He rebelled against his strict upbringing by pursuing unconventional interests, marrying a travelling cabaret singer and writing songs for her. He had already written a handful of forgotten stage works before *Phi-Phi*, the show that would make his reputation. His popular songs were performed by Mistinguett, Yvonne Printemps and many others. The book and lyrics for *Phi-Phi* were by former lawyer Albert Willemetz (1887-1964) in collaboration with Fabien Sollar.

Willemetz is credited with more than 3,000 songs, including "Mon Homme", a success for Mistinguett (nee Jeanne Bourgeois, 1875-1956) in 1916 that, in its English form as "My Man" was later a hit for American comedienne Fanny Brice. (This was a case of a song moving from the Folies-Bergère to its American off-shoot, the *Ziegfeld Follies*.) His other collaborators included Arthur Honneger, Maurice Yvain, Vincent Scotto, Moisés Simons and Georges Van Parys. He eventually was made a director of the Bouffes-Parisiens, and was president of the royalty collection agencies SACEM[10] (1945) and CISAC[11] (1956), the only person to serve in that capacity in either organisation who could not read music.

Phi-Phi ran for more than a thousand performances. In May 1919, London producer C.B. Cochran announced that he had acquired the British rights, and that he intended to present it later that season at the London Pavilion.[12] The following year, E. Ray Goetz made a similar announcement for the American rights in New York.[13] Three years later, Londoners were still waiting. *The Daily Mirror*'s gossip columnist "The Rambler" remarked, "In spite of the critics, Mr. Cochran, I hear, is determined to produce another revue, or musical extravaganza, or something of that sort."[14] Evidently, "The Rambler" was taken to task by Mr. Cochran, for only three days later he wrote, "Mr. Charles B. Cochran writes to me to say that I have diagnosed his new production *Phi-Phi* wrongly. I said it was either a revue or a musical extravaganza or something of that sort. Mr. Cochran tells me it is to be an 'operette', with music by Christiné. I must admit that I find it hard to make a definite distinction between Mr. Cochran's revues, musical extravaganzas and operettes."[15]

Alas, when it finally opened on 16 August 1922, it did so in such mutilated form that it surely was not worth the wait. A new English libretto by Fred Thompson and Clifford Grey removed the sauciness of the original, and the score was augmented by Herman Darewski, Nat D. Ayer and even Cole Porter (who contributed a number called "The Ragtime Pipes of Pan"). It starred Clifton Webb, Evelyn Lay and Arthur Treacher, and expired after 133 performances.

The American production fared even worse. A tryout by the Shuberts, with an entirely different book by Glen Macdonoughy and Harry Wagstaffe Gribble with lyrics by E. Ray Goetz and additional music by Arthur H. Guttman opened and closed at the Globe Theatre in Atlantic City in the same year. It was never seen again in the U.S.

Only the Hungarians seemed to "get" *Phi-Phi*. An adaptation by Jenő Helta played for more than 200 performances after it opened in Budapest on 7 October 1921 (as *Fi-Fi*).

Phi-Phi may not have changed the world, but it did change the face of Parisian musical theatre. In the 1920s, Paris was presenting forty musicals per year. While French musicals of the twentieth century tend to be lumbered with the label "operetta", it is a misnomer, if you accept Andrew Lamb's definition of a show with "swirling melodies, lush orchestrations, and the romantic doings of palaces and princes". A show like *Phi-Phi* is no more an "operetta" than is *No No Nanette*. The quasi-classical operettas were – in the main – overtaken by the more overtly sexual comedies with modern dances and popular music.

Willemetz and Christiné followed this up on 10 November 1921 with *Dédé*, whose cast included a music hall singer named Maurice Chevalier making his book-musical debut as a profligate dandy named Robert. It ran for nearly three years, although Chevalier biographer Edward Behr dismisses it as "an unbelievably old-fashioned piece of part-spoken, part-sung theater, with a creaking, contrived plot and a host of contrived characters."[16] Kurt Gänzl, on the other hand, praises a score that "rippled with melody and dancing rhythms".[17] Willemetz and Christiné, whom Chevalier would cite as his favourite songwriters, later gave him one of his most popular hits, "Valentine", in 1925, which he also sang in the 1935 Hollywood film *Folies-Bergère de Paris* which was made in both French and English-language versions.

Willemetz worked likewise with André Messager on *Passionnément!* (1926) about an American woman who leaves her jealous, possessive husband for a younger man, and *Coups de roulis* ("Roll of the Waves") (1928), a shipboard romance and Messager's final score.

Reynaldo Hahn

Reynaldo Hahn (1875-1947), born in Caràcas, Venezuela to a Venezuelan mother and a German father, was also, like Messager, a conductor at the Paris Opéra. A child prodigy, he had already established himself as a serious composer and critic before turning to operettas in the 1920s. Although he was one of many Parisian musicians to show an interest in jazz, his operettas remained doggedly traditional. His first great success was *Ciboulette* in 1923, in which a flower girl seeks to become an actress. Then he teamed with actor playwright Sacha Guitry (1885-1957) for a series of "comédie-musicales" in which the music played a supporting role to the text. Guitry himself would star in a non-singing role, opposite his second wife, Yvonne

Printemps (1894-1977). The first of these was *L'Amour Masqué* (1923) in which a young woman falls in love with the photograph of a young man, not realising that he is the elegant older gentleman who has paid her a visit.

In 1925, Hahn took on another musical for Guitry — a story that Messager had turned down — about *Mozart*, starring Printemps in a cross-dressing role as the teenage composer. In 1933, he and Guitry (now divorced from Printemps) turned to a more cynical approach with *Ô mon bel inconnu* ("O My Handsome Stranger") about a married man who joins a lonely hearts club, unaware that the three women he is corresponding with are in fact his wife, his daughter and his maid. American opera historian Richard Traubner says it was "too refined and slight for a public that was slowly nurturing a taste for thumping spectaculars."[18]

Vincent Scotto

Vincent Scotto (1876-1952) was a cabaret songwriter of the belle epoque who eschewed so-called "high culture". An untrained musician who played the guitar by ear, he nevertheless managed to turn out some 4,000 songs and 60 musicals, many of which are still performed in France. Born in Marseilles to Neapolitan parents, his songwriting career began while he was still in his teens. His songs were performed by Maurice Chevalier, Josephine Baker ("J'ai deux amours") and Edith Piaf ("Les mômes de la clouche"). Henri Christiné told him, "Vincent, your songs will be sung in every street and home in France."[19] In 1931, his musical *Au Pays du Soleil* was a big hit. The book was co-written (with René Sarvil) by Henri Alibert (1889-1951), Scotto's son-in-law, who also starred as a man falsely accused of murder. As in *Rose Marie*, all ends happily and he is reunited with his true love. Inspired by Marcel Pagnol's Marsellais plays, this was the first in a series of "Opérettes Marseillaises" that would play Paris's Moulin de la Chanson. Throughout the 1940s, his work became more serious, such as *Violettes impériales* at the Théâtre Mogador in 1948, and he scored some 200 films, including Pagnol's *La Femme du Boulanger* (which formed the basis for Stephen Schwartz and Joseph Stein's 1976 musical *The Baker's Wife*). He was made a Chevalier of the Légion d'Honneur. Kurt Gänzl calls him "one of the most memorable French songwriters of his age."[20] Although his works are sometimes referred to as operettas, like Maurice Yvain, Scotto wrote in the popular music form of the time.

It was Maurice Chevalier who first introduced Albert Willemetz to a composer whom he had known in the infantry a decade earlier, Maurice Yvain (1891-1965). The son of a trumpet player from the Opéra-Comique, Yvain was already a successful cabaret songwriter when he turned to writing musical comedies. It was with Willemetz that he wrote the massively successful *Ta Bouche* in 1922, with a book by Yves Mirande at the Théâtre Daunou for impresario Gustave Quinson (1867-1943). *Ta Bouche* opened on Broadway on 27 November 1923 at the Fulton Theatre as *One Kiss*, for a brief run, with a largely interpolated score. Quinson also controlled the Théâtre des Nouveautés, for which he put Yvain together with librettist André Barde (or Bourdonneaux) (1874-1945) whose *Son p'tit frère* had been a big pre-war hit a generation earlier. The result was the similarly titled *Pas sur la Bouche*, directed by Leon Benoit-Deutsch who, according to Yvain, "seemed not a man of the theatre at first glance"[21], but who nevertheless delivered a hit. Yvain was particularly pleased to be given an orchestra of seventeen musicians – unusually large for that theatre, and for which the front row of seats had to be removed.

The story of *Pas sur la Bouche* is a farce about a woman who discovers that her husband's new business partner is a man to whom she was once secretly married. Yvain describes the show's headliner Régine Flory, as "the pet peeve" of wives, having "superb eyes" and "a body you can't take your mind off of"[22]. She was already a star in both Paris and London, but it would all soon come to an end in 1926 when she committed suicide over a failed love affair in the office of the manager of Theatre Royal Drury Lane during the run of *Rose Marie*.

Pas sur la Bouche was "adapted" into English as *Just a Kiss*. Following a tryout at the Princes Theatre in Manchester, it opened at the original Shaftesbury Theatre (destroyed in the blitz on 17 April 1941) on 8 September 1926, produced by Harry Grattan. The setting was changed to Windsor and Mayfair with a new libretto by Frederick Jackson, and Yvain's score augmented by new songs by Vivian Ellis and Phil Craig. *The Times* said that "with a little attention, *Just a Kiss* should be quite a success."[23] Evidently that attention was not paid: it lasted for 93 performances. It played more successfully in Budapest, and toured North America – in its original French.

Unusually, *Pas sur la Bouche* was remade as a feature film in 2003 – almost eighty years after its stage debut (and seventy years after it was filmed for the first time) – by director Alain Resnais, starring Audrey Tautou and Lambert Wilson. Several of Resnais' other films show a strong musical theatre connection: His 1997 film *On connaît la chanson* ("Same Old Song") interpolated popular French songs into the story, and he made a documentary about George Gershwin in 1992. His 1974 film *Stavisky* featured an incidental score by Stephen Sondheim.

In 1923, Yvain and Willemetz collaborated on *Là-Haut* ("On High") which was intended as a vehicle for Chevalier at the Bouffes-Parisiens. However, although it was a hit, Chevalier was upstaged by his co-star Dranem (1869 - 1935), and left the musical theatre behind for good after suffering a nervous breakdown.

"Les Six" member Arthur Honneger, the Swiss opera and ballet composer best known for *Pacific 231* was commissioned by Willemetz to write the score for his 1930 adaptation of Pierre Louÿ's 1901 novel *Les Aventures du Roi Pausole* about a king with

365 wives whose chaste daughter Aline runs away with a visiting dance troupe. Its frank sexuality insured a long run at the Bouffes-Parisiens. Towards the end of his life, he taught at the École Nationale where his students included future *Baker Street* composer Raymond Jessel.

American popular music was not the only foreign influence on Parisian musicals. During the prohibition era in the U.S., wealthy Americans travelled to Havana to the night-clubs, where they were entertained by Latin rhythms. One of the hits to emerge from Cuba in the 1920s was "El Manisero" ("The Peanut Vendor") by composer Moisés Simons (1888-1945). This song was sung in Spanish by Rita Montaner and in English by Antonio Machin. It was also performed by Louis Armstrong and Duke Ellington, and decades later an excerpt was sung by Judy Garland in *A Star is Born*. Aside from writing dance hits, Simons was a composer of Zarzuelas, the Spanish equivalent to opéra-bouffe. He had already had works performed in Barcelona before the popularity of such South American dances as the rumba, the samba and the conga brought him to Paris with Rico's Creole Band. His musical *Toi c'est moi* was presented at the Bouffes-Parisiens on 19 September 1934, with a book by Henri Duvernois (1875–1937) and lyrics by Albert Willemetz, Marcel Bertal, André Mouezy-Eon, Louis Maubon and Robert Chamfleury and was filmed in 1936. The story tells of a Parisian malefactor who is sent to the Caribbean to keep him out of trouble.

Although – with a few exceptions – French musicals of the twentieth century have had a very limited impact outside of their native land, a few French theatrical song writers have enjoyed some international success – even if we may not be aware the provenance of the works in question. I have already mentioned Maurice Yvain's "Mon Homme" which became Fanny Brice's hit "My Man". Fans of Baz Luhrman's *Moulin Rouge* may have noticed Canadian singer Rufus Wainwright's rendition of what sounds like an old Parisian street song. It was in fact "Complainte de la Butte", written for Jean Renoir's 1954 film musical *French Cancan*. The lyrics were by Renoir, and the music by Georges Van Parys (1902-71), a man with a solid background in cabaret and musical comedy.

Van Parys began as a pianist at the cabaret Chez Fyscher in 1924, and in 1927 he enjoyed his first success with *Lulu* at the Théâtre Danou. This show then travelled to Budapest, and was the first in a series of musicals with lyricist Phillipe Parès and book writer Serge Veber. His wartime musical *Une Femme par Jour* ("A Woman per Day"), with a book by Veber and lyrics by future film director Jean Boyer opened at the Théâtre des Capucines in 1943, and was filmed in 1948. His later works included the spectacular *Les Chasseurs d'images* at the Théâtre du Châtelet in 1947, and *Minnie Moustache*, a parody "western" with a libretto by Jean Broussolle and André Hornez which opened at the Théâtre de la Gaîté-Lyrique in December 1956. In total, he would compose more than sixty scores for the theatre, in addition to some 350 films, beginning in 1930 with the first French screen musical, René Clair's *Les Million*. In recent years, Sudden Théâtre has toured an anthology revue of Van Parys songs called *Comme de Bien Entendu*.

Moulin Rouge

French Cancan offers us a unique contrast to *An American in Paris*, released three years earlier, showing the different American and French approaches to musicals. "Renoir... doesn't do anything as obvious as having a painting come to life", says American director and film scholar Peter Bogdanovich. "It's not studied. It feels like it's in his bones. It's in his blood, and it's just there in every image."[24] Unlike the American musical – according to Bogdanovich – Renoir doesn't sentimentalise his characters. "Danglard [the fictional founder of the Moulin Rouge played by Jean Gabin] is very casual about his affairs. When he's pinned down at the end and [Nini] says 'I want you to myself', he says, 'What, do you want to put me in a cage like a canary?'... It's totally different from the way the American would do it. It is, in fact, totally realistic in terms of that kind of person." Although the film has not been widely seen by English speaking audiences, it was a hit on its home turf.

The real Moulin Rouge opened in 1889 on Boulevard de Clichy in Montmartre. It was built as a cabaret by Joseph Oller (1839-1922), who also owned the Paris Olympia music hall. It gained notoriety as the place where the can-can was reborn. Originally a working-class dance, the Moulin Rouge introduced courtesans to perform seductively for male patrons. As the night-club became more fashionable and respectable, the courtesans were replaced by professional dancers, and in its heyday the club was headlined by the likes of Josephine Baker (1906-75), Edith Piaf and Mistinguett. Henri de Toulouse-Lautrec designed a famous series of posters for the club.

There is one aspect of Parisian musical theatre that has had an unmistakable influence on Broadway. That is the Folies-Bergère at 32 Rue Richter in the 9th arrondissement, which in turn was patterned after London's Alhambra music hall in Leicester Square. An announcement in the *Album des Théâtres* in 1867 proclaimed that "the performances to be shown in the new hall will be a combination of various genres:

Operetta, lyrical fantasy, pantomime, song and acrobatic display."[25] When it opened on 2 May 1869 as the Folies Trévise, the Duc de Trévise, who did not want his name to be linked to such lewd entertainment, pressured the management into changing the name. On 13 September 1872, the name was changed to Folies-Bergère after a nearby street. (The word "folies" is derived from the Latin "foliae", meaning "leaves", although in this context it means "field", suggesting a place of open-air entertainment, or a place where clandestine lovers may meet.)

It took time for the new venue to catch on. The Franco-German war, the siege of Paris and the Commune had to be endured, but after a decade or so Paris began to experience a renaissance, and the Folies-Bergère was the beneficiary. The first "glamour revue", *Place aux Jeunes* opened on 30 November 1886. This was the template for what was to follow, the world that the novelist Colette knew very well. The stars of the Folies-Bergère later included Josephine Baker and her pre-Carmen Miranda "banana dance", and Maurice Chevalier.

In 1895, Florenz Ziegfeld (1867-1932) was travelling in Europe, looking for a new star. He found one in Anna Held, who was under contract to the Folies-Bergère. After paying $1500 to buy her out of her contract, he took her to New York to star in his production of *A Parlor Match*. It was at Held's suggestion that Ziegfeld presented an American version of the Folies-Bergère. The first edition, which opened on 8 July 1907 at the roof-top Jardin de Paris in New York was called *Follies of the Day.* The title was drawn from librettist Harry B. Smith's newspaper column, thus giving the word "follies" a double meaning, referring to human foibles. These "revues" (Ziegfeld also imported the French spelling of that word) ran in annual editions until 1931. Stars of the *Ziegfeld Follies* included Fanny Brice, who made an American hit out of Maurice Yvain and Albert Willemetz's "Mon Homme" (My Man).

The first French composer since Offenbach to enjoy world-wide success with a book musical was Marguerite Monnot (1903-61) who is perhaps best known as Piaf's favourite songwriter. She trained with Nadia Boulanger (1887-1979), who also trained the Broadway composers Charles Strouse and Marc Blitztein, as well as orchestrator Robert Russell Bennett. Poor health had forced young Marguerite to give up a career as a concert pianist and she turned instead to popular music. After many hits (including "Hymne à l'Amour", "Milord" and "La Goualante du Pauvre Jean"), she first turned to writing for the theatre with *La P'tite Lili*, an operetta with book and lyrics by Marcel Achard starring Piaf, Robert Lamoureux and Eddie Constantine which lasted for seven months in 1951 at the ABC Music Hall in Paris.

Then on November 12, 1956 came her biggest success, when *Irma La Douce* opened at the Théâtre Gramont. The book and lyrics were by Alexandre Breffort (1901-71). He expanded a short story he had written for the satirical magazine *Le Canard enchaîné* (of which he had been editor since 1934) which he had already turned into a twenty-minute cabaret sketch in 1949 at the Cabaret Chez Gilles for the Compagnie Grenier-Hussenot, *Les Harengs Terribles.* ("Harengs" is an argot slang term for a man who lives off the avails of prostitution.) When he and Monnot expanded it into a full-length entertainment, he was emphatic that it should be a "comedie-musicale" and not an operetta.

Bob-le-Hotu introduces the action: "The story we are about to tell you is the story of a ménage à deux – something you don't see everyday!" The story concerns a naïve member of the Paris underworld (a law student in the English version) named Nestor-le-Fripé ("Rumpled Nestor") who falls in love with a prostitute and becomes her protector. Wanting her to himself, he disguises himself as a wealthy patron named Oscar who buys her exclusive services. When the strain of maintaining this double life becomes too much for him, he "kills" Oscar – and is convicted of murder. (Only through bribery is he able to convince the authorities that he didn't actually "murder" himself.)

The original production was directed by René Dupuy who also played the narrator, Bob-le-Hotu, proprietor of the Bar-des-Inquiets ("Bar for Worried People"). For the leading role of the prostitute Irma, Juliette Greco and Colette Deréal were considered, but the part finally went to Colette Renard (1924- 2010), who was married to the show's musical director Raymond Legrand. Another Piaf collaborator, Legrand's son Michel was the un-credited co-arranger (for a four piece on-stage band). Nestor was played by Michel Roux, who had also appeared in the original sketch. *Le Figaro* said, "Alexandre Breffort achieved a slight of hand in dealing with a difficult subject without for one second falling into the trap of vulgarity." It transferred to the larger Théâtre de l'Athénée and ultimately played for a total of 962 performances, including a 1967 return engagement.

Translating a musical from one language into another is always a tricky business. Michael Kunze, who in addition to being a successful lyricist and book writer in his own right has also created German-language translations of *Evita*, *Chicago* and many others, maintains that it is more adaptation than translation. "I try to become the original librettist and lyricist," he told me, "writing the whole show again in German. It is more important to keep the original intentions and atmosphere than to stick to the words. All my partners saw it the same way, Tim Rice, Fred Ebb, Stephen Schwartz, even Stephen Sondheim. Likewise, I never demand a word-by-word translation from my authors."

Irma La Douce managed to achieve what few of even the best French musicals could manage: it was successfully adapted into English. Bandleader Henry Hall had seen the show in Paris and obtained the rights, which he then sublet to Donald Albery (Donmar Productions) and Binky Beaumont (H.M. Tennent Ltd.). Monty Norman (1928-), David Heneker (1906-2001) and Julian More (1928-2010) had already collaborated on the music business satire *Expresso Bongo*. On the strength of this, they were approached by the producers to provide an English libretto for this French hit.

It is fair to say that the English version of *Irma la Douce* is an adaptation rather than a translation. The challenge was enormous, for all the elements that had defeated shows like *Phi-Phi* were there in spades: a risqué subject, a distinctly French flavour, and liberal use of slang terms such as "grisbi" (money), "poule" (prostitute), "mec" (pimp) and "millieu" (Paris underworld), and expressions like "dis-donc" (you don't say), not to mention Breffort's penchant for puns. Imagine trying to translate the Damon Runyon dialects of *Guys and Dolls* and you'll get the idea. Even in Paris, a glossary was provided in the programme.

"After several versions had been thrown in the wastepaper basket", wrote Julian More, the principal author of the book, "we eventually hit on the right way to present *Irma* to English audiences: to avoid use of Bronx or cockney slang equivalents[26], so beloved of sub-titlers and so killing to Gallic atmosphere; to use instead a few French argot terms and to adapt the lyrics freely, taking Breffort's thought line but creating our own shapes, and in some cases writing completely new lyrics to Monnot's music."[27] For example, they cut the original opening number "Because" and created a new number, "Valse Millieu", (using the same melody as the title song) in which Bob-le-Hotu introduces the slang terms we are about to hear. In some instances, melodies and the characters who sang them were entirely re-assigned, and the musical structure adjusted. What had originally been "Il a Raison" ("He's Right") sung by Irma became "That's a Crime", sung by Bob-le-Hotu. "Avec les anges" (literally, "with the angels"), with a very slight melodic alteration became "Our Language of Love." (In the English version, what had been a recurring verse is used only as a recitive at the beginning, and the two syllable "an-ges" becomes the one sylable "love".) Because Elizabeth Seal was a dancer, choreography by John Heawood was added, which was largely absent in the original.

The collaboraters resisted advice to sanitize the story and dialogue, and to add more female characters – Irma being the only woman among fourteen men. Director Sir

Peter Brook (1925-) maintained, "The English version was a faithful translation of the original French production – give or take a few score terms in Montmartre argot. We did take liberties there… The story, characters and author's attitude are unalterably French. Our friends advised us to change the locale to London or New York. But we felt the local flavour of the 'millieu' – that is, the community of prostitutes, procuerers and thieves of the back streets around Pigalle, must be maintained."[28]

Of course, in those days, all scripts had to be submitted to the Lord Chamberlain's office (the censor). "He to everyone's surprise passes our script intact", writes Brook in his published journal. "He only cuts, without explanation, one word, 'Kiki' – and I haven't the heart to tell him that this in Paris slang simply means 'the neck'."[29]

"In Paris it was, and is, of its own strange kind, a masterpiece," wrote Harold Hobson in the *Sunday Times*. "One did not notice there the absence of offence. One was conscious instead of the actual presence of virtue, of a love that is, of all quiet things, of generosity and response to kindness… In London, the cast bar their minds against all thoughts of evil, whilst in Paris, the company, with glowing innocence, seem unaware that evil could possibly exist."[30] *Punch* made a similar comparison: "In Paris, one saw the ugliness of Pigalle through a haze of fantasy, and Colette Renard played Irma with such a shining simplicity that one could have almost taken any of one's aunts to see her… This was a trick, I think, that only the French know how to manage… English is a poor language for wrapping squalor."[31]

Following tryouts in at the Pavillion Theatre, Bournemouth (where it opened 24 June) and Brighton, *Irma la Douce* opened at London's Lyric Theatre on 17July, 1958, where it ran for a record-breaking 1,512 performances starring Elizabeth Seal and Australian actor Keith Michel (later replaced by Shani Wallace and John Neville). The music was re-orchestrated by another French composer, André Popp, who had arranged many of Jacques Brel's early recordings and would later write the hit "Love is Blue".

The Times wrote, "Treated clumsily, the frivolous anecdote which *Irma la Douce* expands into a musical comedy could only hope to raise sniggers. Happily, the book of M. Alexandre Breffort is adroitly written, and though it goes somewhat heavily into English a special sort of innocence has been retained, and the audience at the Lyric, at any rate in the first half, is kept in a perpetual ripple of open and more or less sunny laughter."[32] The *Manchester Guardian* called it "thin stuff and… it seems paradoxically thinner in this export version because Peter Brook's vigour in production swells the volume of what is more acceptable when left sleazy and frail."[33] Although most critics had nothing but praise for Elizabeth Seal, the *Observer* claimed she was the show's weak link: "vocally too weak and coy to suggest a convincing whore."[34] On the other hand, the *Daily Herald*'s Harry Weaver complained that "Not even Liz Seal's vitality and urchin charm or the hard work of Keith Michell make this an evening to remember. Maybe *Irma* should have stayed in the original French."[35] However, *Tatler*'s Anthony Cookman wrote, "The delightful thing about the adaptation of *Irma la Douce* at the Lyric is that it somehow contrives to extract the innocent absurdity of the original French musical and make it easy for us to swallow the absurdity neat."[36]

The "prompt book" of the London production reveals that two songs were re-written during the run – "Valse Millieu" replaced the lines "Millieu's the name of the underworld mob / Poule is the girl who goes out on the job / Mec is the fellow who pockets the cash / Grisbi's the cash which is lovely to stash" with "This is the Paris that hides from the day / Waiting 'til night for the stranger to stray / This is the world to forget or forgive / Sinner or saint, we have all got to live". The lyrics for "Wreck of a Mec" were also entirely replaced. Before opening in New York under the aegis of David Merrick, the show went through yet another transformation. "Très Très Snob" (which in the original version had been "C'est Polyte le Mou", or "It's Spineless Polyte") was rewritten as "Sons of France". A very Broadway sounding overture was added, as were two major dances.

Irma la Douce opened at the Plymouth Theater (following a two-week tryout in Washington, D.C.) on September 29, 1960 with the same director (and the same three stars) but with new choreography by Canadian-born Onna White and dance arrangements by future composer John Kander and additional orchestrations by Robert Ginzler (who did the same chores on *Gypsy* and *Bye Bye Birdie*), and ran for 524 performances. Howard Taubman in the *New York Times* wrote, "Trust the French to make vice as innocent as a fable."[37] *Time* magazine explained that "by putting its bad apples at the top of the barrel and its milk of human kindness inside Pernod bottles, *Irma la Douce* endows its harmless story with a nice tingle of iniquity, even a certain mixture of sweetness and bite… Marguerite Monnot's score has a gay street-music tinniness that can have resonance too, as in the rousing wail of 'From a Prison Cell' or the ring and bounce of 'There is Only One Paris for That'".[38] John Chapman in the *Daily News* declared, "There won't be a more captivating new musical on Broadway all this season than *Irma la Douce*".[39] John McClain in the *Journal American* said, "Here is authentic French atmosphere which will entrance anyone who loves the byways of Paris and harkens to the lilting music of Montmartre."[40] The *New York Post*'s Richard Watts Jr. decided that "its chief virtue as a musical play is that it has taken the materials of cynicism, sentimentality, mockery and what might be termed sexual preoccupation and woven them into an integrated whole that posesses strikingly imaginative style and originality. In this achievement it is greatly aided by Marguerite Monnot's charming score".[41] Only the *Herald-Tribune*'s Walter Kerr seemed not to have been swept away. "It's a pity that someone couldn't have decided that the evening had an impish point to make and then stuck to it, instead of letting it gradually transform itself into a sort of poor man's *Beggars' Opera*, or even, at times, into a beggar's *Beggar.'s Opera*. There is imagination, and to spare. But there is no staying-power, no hearty filling inside the showy meringue."[42]

A German production opened on 24 January 1961 at the Theater der Stadt in Baden-Baden, and an Australian company opened at Theatre Royal, Sydney on 25 February of the same year. A Spanish-language version opened in Buenos Aires at Teatro Smart on 23 October 1963, and a Hungarian version opened in Budapest on 4 November 1964.

Following *Irma*'s world-wide success, Monnot was invited to write songs for Walt Disney (interesting, in light of *Irma*'s low-life subject matter), but she didn't want to leave France. In 1960, she and Breffort wrote one more musical together, *L'Impasse de la Fidélité* which starred the music-hall chanteuse Patachou at the Théâtre des Ambassadeurs. The following year she died of a ruptured appendix at the age of 58.

The film rights to *Irma* were sold to the Mirisch Corp. two months before the Broadway production had even opened, but they had to wait until the stage show had run its course before they could begin shooting. Director Billy Wilder then hired Shirley Maclaine, who had recently starred in the film of Cole Porter's *Can-Can* to play the title role, and Herschel Bernardi, who would later star in *Fiddler on the Roof* was cast as Inspector LeFevre. The supporting cast included Bruce Yarnell who had starred in a Lincoln Center revival of *Annie Get Your Gun* opposite Ethel Merman, and Canadian character actor Lou Jacobi, who had appeared in the London productions of *Guys and Dolls* and *Pal Joey*, as Moustache (Bob-le-Hotu in the stage version). Even Jack Lemon as Nestor has been known to put across a song, and the presence of André Previn as musical arranger certainly pointed toward this being a musical. Yet, as Wilder and his co-screenwriter I.A.L. Diamond progressed with their adaptation, they gradually reached the conclusion that the songs had to go. "I have nothing against music", he says, "but the more I went into that story, the better I thought it was. And for me, the numbers got in the way. So, first, one of them went. Then another one went. And, one day, I made the decision, and we threw the whole score out and made it a straight picture."[43]

Thus Marguerite Monnot's music was relegated to the background (although "Dis-Donc" is virtually staged as a musical number, even although no lyrics are sung except for a brief exclamation of the title). Monnot and Breffort were both credited as the original authors of the play, without any specific reference to music. André Previn won an Academy Award for his adaptation of her themes, including "Language of Love / Avec les Anges" and "Dis-Donc". Interestingly, in her later one-woman-show, Maclaine performed some of the songs that she would have sung in the role had she been given the chance. While the film was, at the time, the most commercially successful of all of Wilder's, it is not one of his best remembered. Many feel that by cutting out the songs, he cut out the heart. As Wilder's biographer Ed Sikov writes, "The wonderful … thing about Hollywood musicals is that characters can tap immediately into their emotional lives by opening their mouths and singing... Love, joy, regret, despair, bliss, triumph — these are the mainstays of musical comedy, but for Billy they're too quick, easy and pretty."[44] For *The Guardian*'s Richard Roud, the film reminded him of the story of Lichtenberg's knife. "As every schoolboy knows, George Lichtenberg was an eighteenth-century German satirical writer who invented the knife without a blade whose handle was then removed. Following what we might call Lichtenberg's law, then, this plotless musical has now had its songs and dances removed. Surely this is madness and the result is pretty disastrous."[45] Interestingly, cutting the songs did not speed the plot along: it still runs well over two hours.

Irma la Douce was adapted for French television in 1972, starring Marie-Claude Mestral as Irma and Jean-Pierre Moulin as Nestor. It was directed by Paul Paviot, and first broadcast on 17 February 1972. The original French stage version has been revived in Paris several times, including a major production at the Opéra-Comique in 2000, directed by Jérôme Savary (1942-). *L'Express* called it "a delight in pictures and song." The *New York Times* said this production "has everything going for it: good singers, good dancers, good costumes, good sets that spin and open up like gigantic dollhouses. It also has Savary's characteristic frenetic pace, busy staging and visual gags, leaving never a dull moment. Here's a chance to spend two hours with some bad guys you can't help but love."[46]

It's hard to know how Breffort and Monnot felt about the English version. After Breffort's death in 1971, Colette Renard said, "You never knew if he was happy or unhappy. He loved to make people laugh, but personally, I never saw him laugh."[47] Breffort himself never understood *Irma*'s international appeal. "There are feelings that do not make it across borders", he said. "My heroine is so typically Parisian that you couldn't even transplant her from Belleville to Ménilmontant!"[48]

However, what distinguishes *Irma la Douce* from *Phi-Phi* and other French musicals that failed in translation is that Messers Brook, Norman, More and Heneker respected their source material. Of course, as soon as you move anything outside of its native language you separate it from its culture, but the fact that they attempted to preserve as much French atmosphere as the English language could accommodate surely counts for something.

Irma was not the only French musical on Broadway at the time. *La Plume de ma Tante* ("The plume of my aunt"), a revue devised by Robert Dhéry (1921-2004) with music by film composer Gerard Calvi (1922-) and lyrics by Francis Blanche and Ross Parker which had already run for three years at London's Garrick Theatre, opened on Broadway at the Royal Theater on November 11, 1958 and closed on December 17, 1960 after a total of 835 performances. *Time Magazine* called it "as engagingly French as it is abundantly funny."[49] The ensemble was awarded a special Tony Award in 1959. Calvi and Dhéry also created the 1965 production *La Grosse Valise* with lyrics by Harold Rome and conducted by Lehman Engel which played for twelve previews and seven performances at New York's Fifty-forth Street Theatre.

In the period following World War II, at precisely the same time that the American musical was reaching its apex and was beginning to be taken seriously as an art form, the precise opposite happened to the French musical. "A kind of concensus between artists, politicians and intellectuals chucked light entertainment out", says actor and singer François Raffenaud. "Artists had to be 'serious' and 'philosophically' if not 'politically' committed. A generation of amazing lyricists and performers emerged, but operetta became a symbol of superficiality."[50] It had failed to keep pace with the new developments that were happening on Broadway, and – in my opinion – to fully develop the dramatic potential of their own chanson tradition. This was further complicated by the fact that some artists, including Albert Willemetz and Sacha Guitry were accused of collaborating, (and I don't mean in the words and music sense).

A few, such as Vincent Scotto and Francis Lopez (1916-95) continued to write. Lopez, who trained as a dentist, had a major hit with his first show *La Belle de Cadix* with a libretto by Raymond Vincy that opened at the Casiono-Montparnasse in 1945 and ran for two years. He balanced large scale musicals with intimate shows, including *Quatre Jours à Paris* and *La Route Fleurie*. Kurt Gänzl says, "Unsophisticated though it may often be, the rythmic, sentimental and immsensely singable music of his earliest opérettes is in the happiest tradition of popular light musical theatre."[51] His later works, written without Vincy, were less accomplished, and his final work, *Les Belles et le gitan*, was staged in 1993. But somehow the French writers had failed to move with the times. "With their old-fashioned style rooted in European dance rhythms and their old-fashioned lyricism, Lopez's shows did not stand a chance in New York or London", says Andrew Lamb.[52]

While the musical stages of Paris appeared to the outside world to be moribund, there came an international success in a most unlikely medium – the cinema. *Irma La Douce*'s uncredited arranger Michel Legrand (1932-), another pupil of Nadia Boulanger, had become a world-class jazz musician and film composer. Teamed with French "New Wave" auteur Jacques Demy (1931-90), he created the first in a series of Gallic-flavoured musical films. *Les Parapluies de Cherbourg* ("The Umbrellas of Cherbourg") was a through-sung musical about young love and teenage pregnancy set against a backdrop of the Franco-Algerian war in the 1950s. Although it had an industrial port setting and gritty subject matter, Demy bathed his film in such glowing Technicolor that it was literally seen through rose coloured glasses. The result was a soaring melo-drama which included the Oscar nominated hit song "I Will Wait for You". Writer and actor Tom Shea calls it "as cinematic a musical as there's ever been; it's a superb application of French New Wave film techniques to the movie musical genre."[53]

Demy explains, "I try to fight the belief that musicals can't make it in France. There've been counter-examples like *West Side Story*. Plenty of Stanley Donan [the director of *Singin' in the Rain*] musicals have done well in France and were superb. We haven't made many in France, but when we've tried… they were charming, done with a sense of lightness and charm that created a dreamy atmosphere." [54]

"It's just love that you send out in a certain manner, a way of communicating that I find more interesting if it's sung", Demy continues. "It can be more tender, more generous, more violent, more aggressive, whatever... That's what interests me. It's a language, my language." Demy and Legrand set out to give their recitative "language" the same rhythm as speech. Although professional singers were pre-recorded, and the songs were later lip-synched by the actors, the two sets of performers worked in close collaboration. The actors were present during the recording sessions, working with their singing counterparts on phrasing and intonation. (This also happened when Marni Nixon dubbed Deborah Kerr's voice in *The King and I*.)

I first saw the film when it was re-released in a restored print in the 1990s. My initial reaction was, "I wonder how many times Boublil and Schönberg saw this before they wrote *Miss Saigon*?" I got my answer in 2008, when *Marguerite*, which they wrote in collaboration with Legrand, opened in London. Michel Legrand says, "[Demy] wanted an opera, he got one. It was entirely sung. He wanted it to be clear, self-evident, he wanted it as a kind of song throughout the film, a single through line, from start to finish... Audiences wept, it was so sad. We'd planned it... Jacques and I wrote on the score: 'First hanky, page 38... Second hanky...' So we had... a scoreful of hankies."[55]

The *Umbrellas of Cherbourg* was adapted for the English-speaking stage in 1979 by Sheldon Harnick and Charles Burr (in collaboration with Demy and Legrand) and directed by Andrei Serban. It enjoyed a brief run of 79 performances in New York at the Public Theatre, and received its Paris stage premiere in the same year at the Théâtre Montparnesse using a small orchestra. The English version opened in London at the Phoenix Theatre on 10 April 1980. It lasted only twelve performances. This version was revived at the Gielguid Theatre in London in March 2011 by Kneehigh Theatre's director Emma Rice. The *Guardian*'s Michael Billington decreed: "Watching the stage version is like seeing a Technicolor film rendered in black and white: Lez Brotherston's set, with its partitioned steel structures, seems determined to evoke the reality of Cherbourg, whereas the point of the story is that it is a romantic fairytale... What is lost are the very things that made the film so original. One is the way in which the fluid camera movement matched the seamless recitative of the Legrand score: take that away, and you are left with a show that, with the exception of 'I Will Wait for You', seems strangely lacking in musical or dramatic highlights. The other missing ingredient is the candy-coloured artifice of the film, in which even the wallpaper matched the characters' costumes."[56] *Variety* largely concurred: "Oddly, Rice doesn't appear to have adjusted the lyrics first heard in Sheldon Harnick's translation in a production at Gotham's Public Theater in 1979. Hearing a cast using English accents to sing such American phrases as 'I guess' and 'trimming the tree' is jarring."[57]

Demy and Legrand followed up the original film in 1967 with *Les Demoiselles de Rochefort*, also starring Deneuve as well as her sister Françoise Dorléac. It also included guest-stars Gene Kelly and George Chakiris, and was choreographed by Irish-born Norman Maen. "It's... a musical that periodically defamiliarizes – 'makes strange' – the form of the musical", says American film critic Jonathan Rosenbaum. "Some American viewers may find it difficult to feel their way into such an aesthetic overload… Received wisdom on musicals is that the genre's greatest achievements – such as the entertaining Astaire-Rogers steamrollers and *Singin' in the Rain* – are triumphs of engineering, co-ordination and expertise… Unless you conclude that the only reason for 'technique' is to express what you want to say, the technical shortcomings of *Les Demoiselles de Rochefort* are bound to be disappointing."[58]

Since then, Legrand has established a major career in both France and Hollywood as a composer. His films include *Summer of '42* and *The Thomas Crown Affair*, for which he wrote the song "The Windmills of Your Mind" with lyrics by Alan and Marilyn Bergman, with whom he would work again on his only English-language film musical, the Oscar-winning *Yentl*.

More recently, Legrand wrote a musical for the stage that was deliberately evocative of Offenbach's "opéra-bouffe" style. "I have always loved Offenbach, so inventive, so droll, with splendid harmonies."[59] The result was *Le Passe-Muraille*, with a libretto by novelist Didier Van Cauwelaert (1960-) based on a short story by Marcel Aymé about a man who can walk through walls. It ran for a year at the Théâtre des Bouffes-Parisiens in Paris in 1997 (where it won the Prix-Moliere for Best Musical), and, with an English adaptation by Jeremy Sams, transferred to the Music Box theatre on Broadway – for a brief run – as *Amour* in 2002. The *New York Times* declared, in a mixed review, "even charming is too weighty a word to describe the appeal of *Amour*", a "twinkling trinket of a musical".[60] The critical consensus seemed to be that Van Cauwelaert's libretto – with its intricate wordplay – didn't translate well, and that perhaps it was too small a show for a Broadway theatre. Sams told me that it "mystified Broadway audiences and critics. They said it wasn't like an American musical and they were right!"

Soon after, Alain Boublil (1941-) wrote a stage adaptation of *Les Demoiselles de Rochefort*. More recently, Boublil and Schönberg collaborated with Legrand on another project, *Marguerite*, a Second World War updating of Alexandre Dumas' *Our Lady of the Camelias*. Thus Legrand, who has also worked as an arranger with Maurice Chevalier,

Jacques Brel and other stalwarts of the French music hall and "chanson" traditions, embodies at least one link between the musical theatre of the Belle Epoch and that of *Les Misérables*.

Of course, the latter would go on to eclipse all that had gone before it. However, unlike *Irma la Douce* or *The Umbrellas of Cherbourg*, it was not really a French show that had been adapted into English. Beginning as a concept album and then staged in a Paris arena, *Les Misérables* was entirely reconceived by producer Cameron Mackintosh and directors Trevor Nunn and John Caird.

Alain Boublil and Claude-Michel Schönberg (1944-) were French pop songwriters who had ventured into the world of theatrical spectacle in 1973 at the Palais des Sports in Paris with *La Revolution Française*. They were enamoured of *Jesus Christ Superstar*, *West Side Story* and *Oliver!* In fact, it was the latter show that would give them their greatest inspiration, for the Artful Dodger's rendition of "Consider Yourself" reminded Boublil of the character of Gavroche in Victor Hugo's novel. "As soon as the Artful Dodger came onstage, Gavroche came to mind. It was like a blow to the solar plexus. I started seeing all the characters of Victor Hugo's *Les Misérables*—Valjean, Javert, Gavroche, Cosette, Marius, and Éponine—in my mind's eye, laughing, crying, and singing onstage."[61] He and Schönberg recorded *Les Misérables* as a concept album in 1980, which was staged by director Robert Hossein at the Palais de Sports in 1982. A tape of this production found its way, via Hungarian director Peter Farago, to Mackintosh. "It was an instant combustible decision", he told Sheridan Morley and Ruth Leon. "By the fourth track I had already decided that I had to do it."[62]

Rather than simply assigning the rights, Boublil and Schönberg became part of the creative team, which eventually included South African-born lyricist Herbert Kretzmer. "The project was probably too patrimonially French for anyone else to have done it in a way that would be what the show is today"[63], says Boublil. The show would ultimately be expanded from one hour to three, and only about a third of Kretzmer's lyrics were translations of Boublil's originals. Although the original Royal Shakespeare Company production at the Barbican Theatre received tepid notices, Mackintosh proceeded with a transfer to the West End, and he hasn't looked back since. (Ironically, one of the cuts made during the transfer was "Little People", Gavroche's answer to *Oliver*'s "Consider Yourself".)

Although I have argued that the modern musical began in Paris with Offenbach, there is little evidence that the next generation of French musical writers have any consciousness of their heritage. *Nôtre Dame de Paris*, with original lyrics by Canadian-born Luc Plamondon (1942-) and pre-recorded music by Richard Cocciante (1946-) enjoyed some success in Paris and in Plamondon's native Montreal, but it flopped dismally in London. According to Kurt Gänzl, "It was equipped with embarrassingly lowest-common-denominator lyrics and a ramming, repetitive score".[64] Another show with lyrics by Plamondon and music by Michel Berger (1947-92) called *Starmania* has had an equally tough time outside of the French speaking market, in spite of English lyrics by Sir Tim Rice.

Jeremy Sams (1957-), who wrote the English adaptation of *Passe-Muraille/Amour*, argues that "The idea of dramaturgy [in the Anglo-American sense] in a musical is totally absent in Offenbach and all French works, including, fascinatingly, the French (pre Cameron [Mackintosh]) version of *Les Miz*." He argues that this is also true of French drama. "Structure, in the post 1940s sense, has no interest to the French. French shows have nothing in common with, and no influence on the structured American musical." He adds, "I'm personally glad of this, since the 'song shows' of France lead to wonderful things like [Charles Trenet and [Jacques] Brel, to [Francis] Poulenc and [Arthur] Honegger's operettas, to Michel Legrand's movie musicals – all things I love." But, he adds, "What they don't lead to is Broadway."

I believe that Paris may have had an impact on international musical theatre in a very indirect way. It was the haunt of Porter and Gershwin, and although there is scant evidence that French musicals inspired them per se, one must assume that something in Parisian culture attracted them. When Gershwin was in Paris working on *An American in Paris*, he consulted with Maurice Ravel, Francis Poulenc and others. Ravel was something of a mentor, and Gershwin returned to New York with eight bound volumes of Debussy scores in his luggage. Similarly, Porter studied in Paris at the Schola Cantorum with Vincent d'Indy. The Schola opened in 1896 as an alternative to the more operatic Paris Conservatoire. Porter would be hired to interpolate songs into the English adaptations of *Phi-Phi* and other continental shows. Satie and Ravel were major influences on the work of Stephen Sondheim[65] – just listen to Satie's *Trois Gymnopédies* then listen to "Goodbye for Now" (the theme from the film *Reds*), or to "Someone is Waiting" from *Company*.

While few French musicals have been international successes – not for lack of trying – Paris was the undisputed birthplace of operetta, the Folies-Bergère and the cabaret – three of the most basic building blocks of the modern musical. Yet somehow the notion that the city of lights is a musical dead spot has been allowed to take hold, and nothing that has emerged in recent years seems likely to change that perception. However, the fact that it took other hands – German, British and American – to integrate these elements does not in any way detract from the credit due to their originators.

In my mind – and this is, of course, the view of an outsider – there is one song that sums up the musical voice of Paris. I first heard it sung by Maria Friedman in an English version by her then-husband Jeremy Sams called "Paris in the Rain". Although it comes from a film, "Complainte de la Butte"'s pedigree covers all bases: its composer Georges van Parys has written for cabaret, café-concert and musical comedy, and the lyrics by Jean Renoir sum up the melancholy spirit of Montmartre and the Moulin-Rouge. Little wonder that Baz Luhrman chose it to set the scene for his opus.

Declaration of Independence: The American Musical

That the American musical developed from European operetta and musical comedy is well documented. While the primary thrust of this book is the work that exists away from the centres of New York and London, I feel that, as an example for others to follow, it is useful to look at how American (and British) musicals developed their own distinctiveness.

British North America is, in a sense, a partitioned country, much as Ireland is. It is divided between those whose loyalty remained with the British Crown (or at least with a European way of life) and those who set out to create a new nation. The former, of course, became Canada, and the latter became the United States of America. In Canada, for much of the first century of its existence as a nation-state, its mother culture was that of Britain (for the Anglos) and France (for the Francophones). Their evolution (not "revolution") toward democracy mirrored that of Britain, which had begun with the Magna Carta and continued through the English Civil War. In the United States, on the other hand, deliberate and concerted efforts were made to differentiate themselves from their former colonial masters. They consciously set out to change their language, dropping the "u" from words like "colour", and changing "zed" to "zee". This was not just natural evolution, but a deliberate effort at nation building. In *The White Jacket*, Herman Melville proclaimed, "We Americans are the peculiar, chosen people… We are the pioneers of the world; the advance guard, sent on through the wilderness of untried things, to break a path in the New World that is ours."[1] They had decided to re-invent themselves, and the year 1776 had become, in their minds, the year "one".

The American musical is not – in my view – a separate art form from its European parent, any more than American English is a separate language from British English. That said, the development of a distinctively American form of the musical, like the changes in the language, was deliberate. For much of the first century of its existence, American music struggled for acceptance against the much more ubiquitous European forms.

Musicologist Wilfred Mellers defines American culture as "an extreme evolution from the European consciousness".[2] When America began to import musical comedies from Britain and Europe in the nineteenth century, they were filtered through their own very American sensibilities. *HMS Pinafore* was wildly popular when first produced there, but not for entirely the same reasons as at home. "The Savoy operas were… a somewhat different thing for the Americans than they were for the English," says Raymond Knapp, a professor in the Department of Musicology at UCLA. "The political basis for Gilbert's humor created not only a sense of recognition in America, but also an awareness of difference, for political structures and issues, too, had diverged dramatically. And the music itself was distinctly more European than American, with little or none of the diverse African-American inflections, already then present to some extent in American music (in minstrelsy and spirituals), that would eventually develop into idioms of jazz and blues. These subtle shades of difference helped Americans to recognize and appreciate the ways in which their own development had diverged from that of their English counterparts; in conjunction with Gilbert's often pointed critique of English mores, these easily perceived differences encouraged Americans to see themselves in a more favorable light."[3]

It is inevitable, given the radically different milieu that the European immigrants found themselves in, that American music would begin to develop a voice of its own. Mellers says of early American composer Charles Ives (1874-1954), "If he was to be an honest creator, he had to take his materials from the world around him: which was the provincial community of the hard-bitten farmer, the small business-man and tradesman. Here was a certain measure of pioneering vitality, mixed with a somewhat blighted religious ethic; of refinement or 'culture' there was no trace. In musical terms, this life meant the town band (which Ives's father directed), ragtime, the corny theatre tune, the chapel hymn. All these were crude but full of conviction, since they were aspects of a way of life."[4]

The Broadway sound was established by the generation of Jewish and Irish immigrants who came to New York in the latter half of the nineteenth century. These people were outsiders with something to prove. Much is written about the Klezmer sounds from Eastern Europe (whose improvisational nature made it an easy soul mate for jazz). But the Celtic strains of Irish music made their impression as well, eventually emerging as modern bluegrass. Although his music doesn't sound particularly Celtic, George M. Cohan, a second generation Irish American who grew up on the vaudeville stage, gave his work an aggressively patriotic zeal. There was a reason for that aggression: the Irish, like the Jews, had not yet been accepted as true Americans. "The Irish were culturally displaced", says Ethan Mordden, "a clan in a strange land. Cohan assimilated the Irish. His musicals were not pure Yankee: they were symbolic of a time in which the Yankee melting pot yielded a richer stock from its infusion of races. One of the reasons he got such bad press in his early years is the sociological impact of his shows. They celebrated racial integration: this was a controversial topic in the early 1900s."[5]

More than anybody, it was Jerome Kern (1885-1945) who, starting with his Princess Theatre revues, brought maturity to the nascent American form. Kern was, in fact, strongly influenced by the central European operetta, for some of his earliest successes had been with songs interpolated into American productions of European musicals. Sometimes this involved travel to London, where he met and collaborated with future *Jeeves* author P.G. Wodehouse. It was in another show imported from London, a 1914 musical called *The Girl from Utah*, that he introduced "They Didn't Believe Me". This song, says music historian Andrew Lamb, "symbolised the emergence of American theatrical song, in which swirling melodies, lush orchestrations, and the romantic doings of palaces and princes were replaced by simple, gently tripping melodic lines and lyrics that expressed the workaday sentiments of ordinary people."[6]

"The four year cataclysm helped to crystallize America's confidence in her own culture", says Lehman Engel of the period following World War I. "Whether in a practical or in a deeper, spiritual sense, the war brought a crucial period of independence to the American theater."[7] Jaded by a war they had fought in only reluctantly, by the 1930s Americans had become more culturally isolationist. Although this may have been, at its heart, a reactionary tendency, it also brought out a spirit of radicalism in the arts. In her biography of Leonard Bernstein, Meryle Secrest writes, "The role of American composers in building a brave new world was to create a uniquely American contribution, based on the New England heritage of hymns, dances and folk songs and on the rich and exploitable vein of Negro rhythmic patterns and tone colors."[8] New Hampshire based composer and educator John Warthen Struble writes, "The imagination of America was turned inward during the Depression, toward things American, and foreign musical influences held less power than at any previous time in our history"[9].

One tangible result of this was the Works Progress Administration's Federal Music and Federal Theatre programs. In 1935, composers like Aaron Copland (1900-90) and Marc Blitzstein (1905-64) were given grants to write music in an American style and on American subjects. Blitzstein wrote the left-wing agit-prop musical *The Cradle Will Rock*, which was directed by Orson Welles for the Federal Theatre (although, due to its political content, WPA support was withdrawn), with musical direction by Lehman Engel. In 1942, conductor André Kostelanetz commissioned Copland and Kern (among others) to write orchestral pieces based on American historical figures. Kern chose Mark Twain, while Copland ultimately settled on Abraham Lincoln.

Broadway has always prided itself in being a "melting pot", made up largely of immigrants from Eastern Europe or of first-generation Americans. Irving Berlin was born in Russia, but arrived in New York when he was a small child. But what of the composers who had already received their training and begun their careers in their home countries?

Victor Herbert (1859-1924) was born in Dublin and at the age of twenty-four became the principal cellist in the court orchestra at Stuttgart before emigrating to the U.S., where he played with the orchestra of the Metropolitan Opera. His first operetta, *Prince Ananius* was a success in 1894. "There were always hints of his Irish heritage in his music", says Alan Jay Lerner, "which frequently gave his melodies a wistful tenderness."[10] Broadway conductor Lehman Engel says, "Although his avowed purpose was to further Viennese operetta, he unconsciously succeeded in creating a style that represented the first significant step away from the European models. His melodies were simpler, more easily remembered, and easier to perform. His harmonic sense was less sophisticated, and although he was a highly skilled musician, he chose to shed musical complexities, which had been the hallmark of the Europeans."[11]

Vernon Duke (1903-69) was born Vladimir Dukelsky, in Parfianovka, Russia where he went to school with George Balanchine. After arriving in New York, he worked on *Garrick Gaieties* for the Theatre Guild. He also wrote serious works under his birth name, although according to Alan Jay Lerner, "Duke proved to be more successful than Dukelsky".[12] He wrote revues with Yip Harburg including *Walk a Little Faster* starring Beatrice Lillie in 1932 that featured the song "April in Paris".

Rudolph Friml (1879-1972) studied under Antonin Dvořák at the Conservatory in Prague. He visited the U.S. in 1902 as accompanist to Jan Kubelik before moving there in 1906. In 1912 he met music publisher Max Dreyfuss who encouraged him to write his first operetta, *Firefly*. He had a major hit in 1926 with *Rose-Marie*. "Friml's musical composition and improvisation never departed from the tradition that was his European musical heritage", writes Richard Kislan. "He detested the new music of syncopated rhythms and dismissed the songs of the modern composers as 'freakish, unmusical and exaggerated'. For him, melody blossomed under his fingers and rhythm would never be allowed to get out of control."[13]

Frederick (originally Friedrich) Loewe (1901-88) was born in Berlin to Austrian parents. His father Edmund Loewe played Prince Danilo in the first Berlin production of *The Merry Widow* and also starred in Oscar Straus's *The Chocolate Soldier*. "Fritz" is said to have studied piano in Berlin with Ferrucio Busoni – who also taught Kurt Weill – and Eugene d'Albert, although biographer Gene Lees disputes this. He came to the U.S. with his parents to do a show for David Belasco, but Edmund Loewe died during rehearsals. He played piano in a 1931 revival of *Die Fledermaus* on Broadway. After meeting Alan Jay Lerner in 1942, together they would write several of the most enduring Broadway musicals of all time, including *Brigadoon*, *My Fair Lady* and *Camelot*. "Fritz Loewe's musical sensibilities – unlike those of [George] Gershwin, [Jerome] Kern, [Harold] Arlen, [Frank] Loesser, [Arthur] Schwartz or [Vincent] Youmanns – were untouched by black music", says Lees. "They were entirely European. He did not emigrate to the United States until he was twenty-three, by which time his musical character was formed."[14] He died in 1988.

Sigmund Romberg (1887-1951) was born in Nagykanizsa, Hungary and studied in Vienna. He was sent to the U.S. by his parents in 1909 to discourage him from writing music. (Clearly Europeans didn't acknowledge New York as any kind of cultural Mecca then.) He worked in a pencil factory for $7 a week and played in an orchestra and wrote dance tunes. In 1914, was hired by the Shubert Brothers as a staff composer, where he worked on fourteen musicals in just over two years. According to Alan Jay Lerner, "He had assembled over the years a library of all the great operas, operettas, *lieder* and orchestral works that had ever been written. He read them all carefully and made notes next to the hundreds and hundreds of orchestral and vocal parts. Perhaps it would only be four bars, but next to it he would write 'good baritone solo' or 'soprano'. He then kept a catalogue of all his notes. When the time came to sit down to write a score, if he were about to write a baritone solo, he would check his files for a 'good baritone solo', etcetera. Perhaps he would not use it verbatim, but it would give him a start. The wheeze around Broadway during the war was that Romberg's music was suffering because there were no German scores being shipped in."[15] Richard Kislan says that Romberg "understood the stage… [He] saw in operetta a stage medium whose potential for the evocation of deep feeling increased in proportion to the skilful addition of great music… [he] became the most celebrated American operetta composer to speak out on the importance of the book… Romberg knew that great music in the theater without acceptable dramatic context wastes away or overwhelms the drama altogether. Consequently, he believed it to be his duty to create a complete score with mutually agreed-upon allegiance to the story well before the casting and rehearsal period."[16]

Kurt Weill is one of the clearest examples of an immigrant coming to Broadway with a pre-existing reputation in the musical theatre. Some critics are divided over Weill's work after he went to New York. Former literature director of the Arts Council of Great Britain Charles Osbourne says that in New York "Weill became more relaxed politically. In Berlin he would never have considered writing for the established bourgeois theatre. In New York, however, he began to understand the lure of Broadway, and for a time he succumbed to it."[17] (By "for a time", we should read "for the rest of his life".) Osbourne calls *Knickerbocker Holiday* "a Broadway musical… a superior Broadway musical, certainly… but a Broadway show nevertheless." With *Lady in the Dark*, "his capitulation was complete." That is certainly a fashionable view, but not entirely an accurate one. In Berlin, Weill contacted his publisher frequently to ensure that his music was being played in all the top dance halls. Brecht may have been a Marxist, but Weill's politics were far less dogmatic. His biographer Foster Hirsch says, "Weill's American work, judged as compositions for the theatre, is of a quality that is comparable to his European catalogue, and is arguably more diverse."[18]

Other American-born songwriters acknowledge European influences. As a teenager, Jerome Kern studied at the Heidelberg Conservatory in Germany. "Kern had his musical roots in the fertile Middle European and English school of operetta-writing", says Richard Rodgers, "and amalgamated it with everything that was fresh in the American scene to give us something wonderfully new and clear in music-writing."[19] Ira Gershwin acknowledges a debt to W.S. Gilbert. "Gilbert was the greatest, no question of that. If he were alive today, he'd be doing good musical-comedy songs."[20] In London, Ira and his brother George contributed to a 1924 revue called *Primrose*, co-produced by George Grossmith, whose father had starred in many of Gilbert and Sullivan's productions, including the original *HMS Pinafore* and *The Mikado* (as Ko-ko). *Primrose* included a song in four-part harmony called "Four Little Sirens We" that parodied Gilbert's "Three Little Maids from School".

The final triumph of Broadway as the primary centre for musical theatre following the Second World War happened for a number of reasons. Since many of the leading composers of European musicals were Jewish (and most of those who weren't staunchly opposed Fascism), there was an exodus of talent, and much of it went to either New York (Kurt Weill) or Hollywood (Friederich Holländer). In England, Vivian Ellis and Ivor Novello continued to ply their trade, but began to look increasingly tired and old-fashioned next to the more brash work that was coming out of New York. And, of course, in 1943 the operetta world of Oscar Hammerstein II met the musical comedy world of Richard Rodgers, and we've never looked back since.

Thus began what is often referred to as the golden age of Broadway – beginning with *Oklahoma!* in 1943 and running until the late 1960s. While the social and technological changes of the post-war period brought about a widening gap between musical theatre and popular music, Broadway continued in the evolutionary path that it had begun with *Show Boat* in 1927. However, the seeds of its decline (in influence, if not in quality) had already set in. Whereas popular music had, with the invention of magnetic tape, become something that could happen any time and in any place, the American musical was still firmly centred on Broadway. Only by touring, or being produced by regional stock companies (or adapted into films) could its impact spread beyond New York. And, as mid-westerners like to say, New York is *not* America.

Entr'acte: A New World Order

The New World(s)

What I have laid out thus far is a fairly traditional account of the development of the musical, albeit filtered and re-interpreted from an international perspective and with more emphasis on cabaret than most histories give. In the first "Act" I have explained how musical theatre developed out of opera in Europe, was influenced by cabaret and music hall, then migrated to New York. It suffered a calamity at the hands of Hitler, and was usurped by the new kid on the block.

It is in Act II that we are entering hitherto largely unexplored territory. In the post-war period, there was a seismic shift in the popular music industry with the birth of rock. One of the other after-effects of Word War II was the final dissolution of all of the European empires, especially that of Great Britain. With that came a cultural awakening in the former colonies, and a new sense of national identity. There was a sense that smaller countries, long hidden in the shadows of the great powers, were entitled to speak to themselves and to the world in their own voices.

I experienced this "renaissance" myself in my native Canada. After the war, we Canadians gained our own citizenship (1947) and our own flag (1965). The centennial of confederation in 1967, which culminated in Expo '67 in Montreal, awakened a new interest in Canadian culture that is continuing to unfold.

The other countries I have explored tell, to varying extents, similar stories. Just as the Americans declared their independence from European operettas, so are Australians, Canadians and others attempting to break free from the Broadway and West End hegemonies. Some, like South Africa, have overcome oppressive regimes and are just beginning to flower. Other countries such as Japan and Argentina reveal their own traditions. Even the European "motherlands" are slowly returning to musical life. As the economic centre of gravity inexorably shifts towards Asia, countries like Korea, Singapore and China are entering the field.

At this point, my analysis becomes largely speculative. It is unfinished. In some cases, even "un-begun". I am looking for the seeds that can be planted and watered; the foundations upon which an indigenous musical theatre form might be built. As indicated in the "overture", this is a search for signs of live. Nobody can say with certainty which "seeds" will grow. What we can do is look at the "soil conditions". My belief is that a unique culture exists in every country, but not all have learned how to articulate it. Some countries, such as Japan, Canada, Australia and Argentina, have at least some history with the musical theatre form. Others, like Korea and Singapore, are entirely new to the game. The challenges and obstacles they face are vast. This is not a survey of past accomplishments, but an anticipation of future potential. In most cases, there is not yet a canon of work to be examined. What there is, I believe, is a common principle: each is trying to play to the world by firstly playing to its own audience.

86

Before we jump into Act II and the new developments by the old world's "offspring", I want to talk about some of the changes that have helped to bring about this new world order: the rock revolution and globalisation.

The Rock 'n' Roll Syndrome

The arrival of rock music affected musical theatre – and the rest of popular culture – in much the same way that the arrival of a meteor affected the dinosaurs. Everything that came before was swept aside. For popular music, the date was 9 July 1955, when Bill Haley's "Rock Around the Clock" hit number one on the *Billboard* charts. Some music critics actually cite this as the date when popular music began – apparently dismissing Irving Berlin and Cole Porter entirely.

Of course, it's all nonsense. The Beach Boys' Brian Wilson says, "I've always loved George Gershwin. The earliest music I remember hearing is 'Rhapsody in Blue'"[1], while Paul McCartney grew up with ambitions to be the next Cole Porter, and his company owns the publishing rights to works by Frank Loesser, Jerry Herman, Meredith Willson (the Beatles once recorded Willson's "'Til There Was You") and Charles Strouse. In fact, both have recently released albums that are love letters to the classic American songbook: McCartney's 2012 CD *Kisses on the Bottom* and Wilson's 2010 release *Brian Wilson Reimagines Gershwin*. These pre-baby-boomers grew up in the era of Tin Pan Alley. John Lennon could talk about Buddy Holly, but Hoagy Carmichael was part of the mix too, as was a whole raft of British folk-music and music hall tradition. Not so for the generation that followed them.

Nowadays, the pop music world's approach to Tin Pan Alley and Broadway resembles the way Christian Creationists rationalise the existence of dinosaurs: they belonged to a mythical earlier world, if indeed they existed at all. For folk music to be heard, it had to be called folk-rock. For jazz, it had to be fusion. So fundamental was the post-war demographic shift for the record buying public that everything without a rock beat was marginalised, if not entirely obliterated.

A number of forces came together to create this meteor: some were economic, some technological. The invention of magnetic tape meant that music could be recorded anywhere, not just in the major studios. In the U.S., the establishment of Broadcast Music Inc. (BMI) in the 1940s broke the monopoly of ASCAP on the licensing of music on the airwaves. (The first was controlled by the songwriters and publishers who were concentrated in New York; the second by broadcasters across the U.S.) These two developments brought about a change in whose songs were being sung. Songs about "hillbillies" were now being written by hillbillies, not New York songsmiths. Nashville was on the rise. Impresario Billy Rose said in 1956, "Not only are most of the BMI songs junk, but in many cases they are obscene junk pretty much on a level with dirty comic magazines… Today it is a set of untalented twitchers and twisters whose appeal is largely to the zootsuiter and the juvenile delinquent."[2]

Even before this, there was a kind of class distinction between Tin Pan Alley and Broadway. The former, with songs like "Three Little Fishies (Boop Boop Diddum)" and "Mersey Dotes" aimed for a less sophisticated audience than the works of, say, Cole Porter. Although Tin Pan Alley briefly morphed into the "Brill building" set with writers like Jeff Barry, Carole King / Gerry Goffin and Burt Bacharach / Hal David, in the post-Beatles era, most singers were expected to write their own songs. This meant that song writing – and especially lyric writing – became a less specialised art. Since the music tended to be written by guitar players who didn't read music, it seldom existed in a precise enough form to be concerned with marrying individual words to individual notes. When the songwriter is also the performer, it becomes easy to simply shoehorn the words into the melody, rather than carefully crafting the metre to the rhythm or the open vowel to the whole note. Lyrics became, at best, sung poetry (fraught with meaning, but lacking in musicality) and at worst, doggerel. This has affected the music as well. "At least 150 years ago", says composer Howard Goodall, "the very slowness of making a notated score of a piece of music meant that the creator had to live with it and think about it for a period of time before it was released to the world."[3]

The old guard certainly had their backs up. Tom Lehrer famously lumped rock and roll in with "other children's records"[4]. As English pop music historian Ian Whitcomb (himself a one-time rock star) says, "It was a cry from the heart, not the pocket-book. Long-held deep beliefs of a civilized way of life were being assaulted by hillbilly songs of fightin', boozin', cheatin'; by rhythm and blues songs about getting' loaded, wantin' a bow-legged woman and rockin' all night long. But worst of all was assault by rock 'n' roll noise, which when coherent seemed to be solely concerned with sex, violence and our own people. All those years of gradual growing away from crude ragtime and jazz towards a disciplined fine art of reticence (with maybe hints of suggestion) all wiped out by our wives and children leaping about to Chuck Berry on the phonograph!"[5]

"Rock had its own sophistication, rhythmic and street-wise," argues singer-songwriter Paul Simon, "but its shallower harmonic well has never provided even its best songwriters with the abundance of great melodies that Gershwin poured forth in less than two decades of work... Rock critics have consistently derided orchestral or symphonic fusions as pretentious and bourgeois, while exalting the nihilism of punk and alternative bands as the best way to purify and revitalize rock and roll. Perhaps the deeply ingrained oral tradition in rock has left an indelible mark on the psyche of its musicians: beware the written form, the manuscript paper with notes, clefs and musical direction in Italian. It's a credo of rock that raw is true, yet in the adjacent world of jazz no such constraints hinder its composers."[6]

Somewhere along the line we lost Mozart's (and Leonard Bernstein's and Kurt Weill's) notion of elevating the public's taste. (Not that this approach was always successful – following a performance of *Othello* at London's Old Vic in the early nineteenth century, the great actor Edmund Keane snarled at the audience: "I have played in every civilised country where English is the language of the people, but in all my life I never acted to such a set of ignorant, unmitigated brutes as I now see before me."[7]) Pop music became – in theory – more democratic. Kids got together in their parents' basements and garages and formed rock bands. They made demo tapes on portable tape recorders. The new music acts came from the working class areas of Detroit and Liverpool. On the other hand, the new generation of Broadway writers came from privileged backgrounds. Stephen Sondheim's family owned a major garment manufacturer, while Andrew Lloyd Webber's father was the head of the London College of Music. The musical – which was born alongside democracy – had lost its common touch. Still, it took a few years for Broadway to lose its edge.

In Britain, at around the same time, a similar shift occurred in the legitimate theatre. When John Osbourne's *Look Back in Anger* opened, it spelled the end for the "well-made plays" of Noël Coward, J.B. Priestly and Terrence Rattigan. However, since it tended to appeal to an older and wealthier audience, the "well-made" musical continued to dominate on Broadway for at least another decade. Alan Jay Lerner said, "as a theatre-goer and theatre lover I somehow cannot find it in my heart to rebel against a well-made play. The great plays of history have usually been splendidly constructed, most often with whopping good parts, and both author and audience have gone home quite contented."[8]

Until the mid-1960s, Broadway cast recordings were a major force in the record industry. Then, when rock and roll came on the scene, a new youth market was discovered, and the "singles" charts were geared toward transistor radios, meaning that the limitations of guitar-based music were confounded by poor sound reproduction. (The arrival of hi-fi only partly mitigated this; the damage had been done. Rather than allowing for subtlety, it simply made the floor vibrate.) Instead of appealing to a smaller group of people with a lot of money to spend, they began to target an enormous group with pocket money. It wasn't so much that the same people changed their tastes as that they were supplanted by a new, younger market and the record companies turned to them, largely to the exclusion of all others. Record stores now had youthful employees with an extensive knowledge of the rock world and little or no knowledge of anything else. The latest music was played in-store at high volumes, and the other clientele gradually fell (or were driven) away.

I've never entirely bought into the whole 1960s myth. (I was there, and I *do* remember it.) The generation that preached peace and love hurled their music as an offensive weapon. For me, the era of great music and radical politics was the 1930s, when you had Gershwin, Ellington and Porter. Rather than being forced against their will to fight Communism in Korea and Viet Nam, young men were being *prevented* from fighting against Fascism in Spain. I know of no more effective protest song than Yip Harburg and Jay Gorney's "Brother, Can You Spare a Dime?", written for the 1932 Broadway revue *Americana*. The '60s were a time of rebellion; of drugs, sex, peace and social justice. Later on, that generation would say, "Weren't we silly", and then dump the peace and justice and keep the drugs and sex. Small wonder that they grew up to

90

become the neo-conservatives of the nineties, favouring free markets and general hedonism with the odd military intervention but eschewing social spending. The irony is that John Osbourne became a right-winger, whereas J.B. Priestly remained a socialist. *Easy Rider* actor Dennis Hopper was a Republican. Rodgers and Hammerstein were outspoken liberals. Andrew Lloyd Webber and Tim Rice are not. Who's a rebel now?

I'm not saying that the rock revolution was entirely bogus. But when I saw the recent British film *The Boat that Rocked*, I was nauseated by what a self-absorbed lot they all were. I can say this, because it is my own generation that I'm talking about. The film dealt with the explosion of pirate radio stations in Britain in the 1960s, when the BBC confined rock and pop music to one weekly programme. In the end, the film triumphantly claims victory when the British airwaves become overwhelmed by this revolution. What it doesn't say is that the poles were reversed, and the other non-rock forms were ghettoised. If you didn't buy into this totalitarian regime, you were written off as "square". (People with an intimate knowledge of only their own generation's music were now "broad-minded", whereas those with a wider spectrum, who knew very well that 90% of what they were hearing would inevitably be consigned to some future rubbish bin, were "narrow-minded".)

That said, I should, for the purposes of full disclosure, state what my own relationship with 1960s pop and rock has been. I feel I expressed it best in the following item which appeared originally in *Musical Stages* magazine under the title "An Epiphany":

I am undone.

For twenty years, I have dedicated myself heart and soul to writing musical theatre. Not campy gags either, but sophisticated, dramatic stuff. I've studied the greats - Sondheim, Gershwin, Hammerstein - and have entered into erudite discussions of the under-appreciated works of Schmidt and Jones. My record collection includes the works of Brecht and Weill sung in the original German by Lotte Lenya. So why did I risk chucking it all by exposing my dark secret?

It happened by accident. As I felt myself being sucked inexorably into the vortex of cyberspace, I stumbled on a website that would draw me back into my deep and distant past, and force me to confront the truth. My formative influence was not *Anyone Can Whistle*. Nor was it *Candide*. Nor *Porgy and Bess*. It was "Sugar, Sugar" by The Archies.

Yes, I'm out of the closet now. As an eleven-year-old, I gave hours of pleasure to my family as I played that song over and over again, at least twenty times a day. Stigmatised by some as "bubble gum" pop, it was, for me, an act of open rebellion. Not "Born To Be Wild" so much as

Born to be Reviled. My idolatry of a pop group whose only public face was as a semi-animated cartoon show in the ghetto of Saturday morning TV certainly set me apart.

Eventually, I put all this behind me, moving on to the concerns of underscoring the nuances of subtext. Within ten years, the only musical impression the name "Sugar" would conjure up was in the first Broadway incarnation of *Some Like It Hot*. The truth was safely buried - until I stumbled upon www.rondante.com. Suddenly I found myself holding information that, thirty years earlier, I would have climbed over the bodies of old ladies to obtain – such as, who they really were. I could now rejoice in the knowledge that among those clapping their hands and exclaiming "Honey, honey" were Ray "Everything is Beautiful" Stevens and Ellie "Leader of the Pack" Greenwich. And guitarist Hugh McCracken would later grace albums by both John and Paul (of the Beatles - you've heard of them?) Or that the female voice claiming "I'm gonna make your life so sweet" was Toni Wine, who wrote "Groovy Kind of Love". I comforted myself in the knowledge that lead singer Ron Dante would later produce *Ain't Misbehavin'* on Broadway.

Now as I listen to the mp3 files downloaded from the website, I find myself thinking – "Ah, that's how you write a hook song!" Jeff Barry may not have been Larry Hart, but he knew how to get his tunes lodged in your brain.

Now a slightly worrying thought occurs to me. As I struggle to champion a return to melody on the musical stage, is it possible that the bubblegum pop of my youth had a lasting impact?

There go my chances of ever being invited to join the Mercury Workshop.[9]

At least, on the last point, I was happily proven wrong: I have been a member of what is now Mercury Musical Developments since 2003. Ron Dante himself may have thought this vignette "the funniest I have ever received about my recording of 'Sugar, Sugar'", but I was being serious.

So how does rock (and all the other forms that followed after it) fit in to the musical theatre scheme of things? Philip Hedley, former artistic director of London's Theatre Royal Stratford East argues ruefully that *Hair*, the first successful rock musical on Broadway, didn't appear until fourteen years after "Rock Around the Clock" hit the airwaves. Of course, *Hair* wasn't the first musical to employ rock idioms – *Bye Bye Birdie* had done that eight years previously, and London's *Expresso-Bongo* was even earlier than that. In fact, even in the so-called "golden age" of Broadway, few successful musicals drew on just one style, form or fashion. If there were any "ragtime musicals", "jazz musicals" or "big band musicals", they have long been forgotten. Lehman Engel says, "Ragtime is a style or vocabulary, not an all-inclusive language."[10] Even Scott Joplin's *Treemonisha* cannot be considered a "ragtime opera". Engel says the same for jazz and rock – they can be employed as styles, but are not complete forms in themselves.

Shows like *A Chorus Line* and *Company* have incorporated rock music without truly being "rock musicals". "I only use rock where I think it's emotionally justified", Stephen Sondheim said in 1970. "Too many people use it because it's the contemporary sound. There's a mystique about rock that it's an arcane language. One of its salient features is the freedom of form, which I think is terrific."[11] Lehman Engel said, "I am not against rock as such but only against the fact that it is born of 'freedom' more rigid and limiting than anything that ever before existed in music."[12] Mark N. Grant, in *The Rise and Fall of the Broadway Musical*, claims that "the theatre loses richness and power as a narrative and literary medium when it panders to the audience before it serves the play. Such a theatre may well generate a carnal excitement, but it cannot function as an evoker of Aristotelian pity and terror. Paradoxically, heightened engagement of sensation and rhythm alienates the theatregoer from a true emotional engagement."[13]

"Rock 'n' Roll", says American cultural observer John Lahr, "put a premium on energy, not expertise".[14] Traditional musical theatre writing thrives on expertise. Jim Betts, the artistic director of Toronto's Script Lab once said to me, "With what I've heard recently of the generation of Canadian musical theatre writers that came after the Lehman Engel era, the traditional 'craft' is not something that seems very important any more. I think that's a shame."

Can the craft of the classic Broadway musical be applied to contemporary musical forms – i.e., rock, hip-hop? Of course it can, if people demand it. When Cole Porter was writing, people demanded smart rhymes. I once heard Leonard Cohen talk about how perfect rhymes "delight the ear". But he confessed that he sometimes used false rhymes, because the audience that he writes for don't mind. "They are really false rhymes but they are close enough that the ear is not violated", he maintains. "In English, we love to hear these coincidences we call rhymes. It does delight us for some odd reason, we are delighted by inventive uses of sonic coincidences."[15] Nowadays, pop writers not only aren't fussy about perfect rhymes, they sometimes even actively avoid them, thinking that they sound pretentious. I don't agree.

I was lucky in that, not only did I have musical theatre heroes as role models, but I sometimes even got to meet them. Shortly after moving to London, I had lunch with the late Dick Vosburgh, the lyricist behind *A Day in Hollywood / A Night in the Ukraine*. Although he was born in the US, he had lived most of his life in London (which didn't put one dent in his accent) and had written comedy material for everybody from John

Cleese to Bob Hope. He had even appeared in an episode of *Monty Python's Flying Circus*.

Over a meal in Leicester Square, he gave me a lecture on why Alan Jay Lerner's lyrics to "On the Street Where You Live" were sloppy. Ignoring the obvious fact that it should have read "*In* the Street Where You Live", he went straight to the line "People stop and stare / they don't bother me / There is no place else on earth where I would rather be." It was the pairing of the phrases "bother me" and "rather be" that irked him. I suggested that it depended on the accent of the singer, but he told me I had missed the point. "Bother me" and "rather me" would be fine. That is what is called a "triple rhyme". But although, as written, the syllables rhyme individually, they do not rhyme as a unit because of the changed consonant on the last syllable.

Why does this matter? Well, to most people who have been raised on the so-called "slant rhymes" of late twentieth century pop lyrics (in which "time" pretends to rhyme with "mine"), it doesn't. But in the theatre, the audience is lost if they can't understand the lyric the first time they hear it. They can't study the words on the back of a record sleeve. Accurate rhyming helps the listener to anticipate the word, thus aiding clarity. I tend to compare it to a well-made piece of woodwork, in which the nails are invisible.

In the late seventies – early eighties, a shift occurred in musical theatre, similar to the one that had already overtaken pop music (although not as all-consuming). As a new generation began to grasp musical theatre, the values changed. *Jesus Christ Superstar* begot *Les Misérables*, and *Hair* begot *Rent, Spring Awakening* and *Next to Normal*, and the theatrical world hasn't been the same since. London's stage schools began turning out Michael Ball and Frances Rufelle clones. The pop power ballad became, in the theatre, an overwrought catharsis in which sheer volume was equated with emotional intensity. André Previn complains that musicals have "degenerated into the screeching and wailing of the adolescent pop stars of the week, leering with teenage concupiscence and flashing their pimples."[16] Shows like *The Producers* and *The Drowsy Chaperone* seemed to be a nostalgic counter-attack. The students of Lehman Engel adopted a "if you can't join 'em, beat 'em" tactic, becoming more esoteric, with mixed success. Others struggled to create a "contemporary" musical – *Rent, Spring Awakening* – evidently equating "contemporary" with "under thirty", as if youth culture were somehow underrepresented. Musical theatre became polarised between the Sondheim and Lloyd Webber camps – or, perhaps more accurately, between traditional Broadway and something that had not quite defined itself.

But let's be honest. Musical theatre writers are a snobbish lot. The accuracy of our rhyming has become a demarcation point that places us on a higher plain than those untutored, boorish pop writers. That and the fact that most pop musicians wouldn't know a music score from hieroglyphics allows us to believe we can bar the great unwashed from our hallowed halls. (One further bit of disclosure is necessary at this point: I *can* read music. What I *can't* do is play any instrument proficiently.)

Therefore, part Sondheim, part "Sugar, Sugar", I am caught between two poles. I share the anguish of those who long to preserve the craft of the "traditional" musical theatre. I also understand how staid those old musicals seemed to me as a youth. I can remember the excitement when my sister's high school did *Bye Bye Birdie* in the late 1960s. (It didn't hurt that none other than Chita Riveira came out to coach the cast.) This was a show with a contemporary feel – and with rock 'n' roll. The following year, my sister groaned when she learned that they would be doing a really corny, old-fashioned 1940s style show – *Guys and Dolls*. Looking back on it, which show seems dated now?

Universality Part 1: "Do They Understand This Show in America? It's So Japanese!"

Before I begin to talk about the musicals that have been springing up in diverse places, from Sydney to Seoul, from Toronto to Tokyo, and from Buenos Aires to Johannesburg, I need to pose the question, "What is meant by universality?" What does it mean when we say that the best musicals have "universal appeal"? Does it mean that they will be perceived the same way, whether they are playing in New York, London or Madagascar?

"Certain musicals play better within their own country than outside", says London producer Sir Cameron Mackintosh. "*Guys and Dolls* has always proved to be the longest running musical in New York when it is revived, whereas in England it would be *Joseph* [*and the Amazing Technicolor Dreamcoat*], *Oliver!* and *My Fair Lady*. *A Chorus Line* and *Hello, Dolly!* are two of the longest running musicals of all time in New York, yet only managed to run a couple of years in London, whereas *Fiddler on the Roof*, *Phantom* [*of the Opera*], *Les Misérables* and *Cats* have proved to be universal long runners. Inevitably, some shows play better in major cities rather than out of town, and occasionally vice versa."[1]

While this book is primarily about indigenous musical theatre outside of New York and London, I believe it's also important to look at how Broadway and West End shows are perceived outside of their natural habitat. What makes a musical universal? Why is it that some musicals play successfully all over the world, when others don't? Obviously, in purely commercial terms, it is desirable for a musical to be a success in all the key markets. But we've already seen that many fine French and German musicals failed to make the transition into English. Also, an Australian political satire such as *Keating* tackles a subject that would be virtually unknown outside of its native country. Does that make it less valid? Just because a show doesn't work globally, does that mean it isn't good?

When *Fiddler on the Roof* opened in Japan for the first time, one of the producers asked the show's book writer Joseph Stein, "Tell me, do they understand this show in America?" Perplexed, Stein replied "What do you mean?" "It's so Japanese!"[2] Yet this statement can be read two ways. Many will interpret it to mean that *Fiddler* is so "universal" that it works in even the most remote cultures. On the other hand, it deals with arranged marriages, a concept that exists in Japan's recent history, but not in America's. Japanese director Amon Miyamoto agrees. "We have a 'so traditional' way. We have to be careful always. Our parents say, 'Tradition! Tradition!'"

Even the most "universal" shows will be perceived differently in each country where they play. Broadway conductor Lehman Engel wrote, "When one thinks of *My Fair Lady* in Turkish, *Man of La Mancha* in French, and *Fiddler* in Japanese, a number of important questions arise: How do a cockney flower girl and her snobbish speech-teacher friend find empathy in a poor country like Turkey? How does a musically very American version of a Spanish classic find favour with super-critical French audiences? How does a show about Polish [sic] Jews at the turn of the century relate to Japan?"[3]

When a Broadway musical succeeds abroad, the circumstances of its success are as unique and individual as they were in its original production. For example, in Paris – a city that is notoriously reluctant to embrace American musicals – *Man of La Mancha* was helped by the presence of the legendary Belgian troubadour Jacques Brel (1929-78) in the title role. (Brel also provided the French translation.) Engel concludes, "The answers to these questions are to be found in two considerations: the universality of the original material… and the excellence of the transformation based on a profound knowledge and understanding of local people and customs." Please note that in each example Engel cites, it is an American show set in a foreign (i.e., non-American) locale.

Engel had his own experience with cultural exports.[4] He took *Porgy and Bess* to Ankara, Turkey in 1968, where the "Buzzard Song" gave them particular problems – there are no buzzards in Turkey. "So many things were different", says Ira Gershwin. "Idiomatic things like crap game. They had to hunt for its equivalent in Turkish. Very, very difficult."[5] He later told Engel, "I do sense though you feel that all the discomfort, the sweat and the rage you went through were worth it for the respect and acclaim you finally received."[6]

A show's universality can be hampered by ignorance and/or insensitivity. If, in seeking to create a show with "universal" appeal, you also want a show that will withstand the test of time, one should bear in mind that future audiences may be more enlightened about the places and situations in your story than past or present ones have been.

It is very seldom that either Broadway or Hollywood pays any attention to my home country Canada, but it does happen. Most infamous (to Canadians) is *Rose Marie*, the 1924 operetta with musical chores shared by Rudoph Friml (1879-1972) and Herbert Sothart (1885-1949) and a libretto by Oscar Hammerstein II and Otto Harbach with locations spanning from the Rocky Mountains across the Saskatchewan prairie to the ballroom of Quebec City's Chateau Frontenac. It played for 557 performances on Broadway, two years at London's Theatre Royal Drury Lane, and an amazing 1,250 nights at Paris' Théâtre Mogador. A North American tour included a stop at Toronto's Royal Alexandra Theatre in January 1925.

The hero was a Mountie of the Dudley-Do-Right ilk. Now, we laugh at the "Indian Love Call" ("when I'm calling yo-o-o-o-o-u") for all the wrong reasons. But it is the even more distorted 1936 film version starring Nelson Eddy and Jeanette MacDonald that has become a buzzword for American misperceptions of Canada (even though it was produced by the Canadian-reared Louis B. Mayer.) "Everybody loved *Rose Marie* when it was first issued because everybody loved Jeanette MacDonald and Nelson Eddy", says Canadian author Pierre Berton. "The idea of a scarlet-coated Mountie carolling his way through the forests in the company of a girl whose brother he is seeking for murder was perfectly acceptable to a nation of moviegoers numbed and dazzled by celluloid make-believe. The joke was only understood years after the event."[7] The film even included one interpolated song – "Some of these Days" – by a Canadian-born songwriter, Shelton Brooks (1886-1975).

The Royal Canadian Mounted Police, who – despite Mayer's concerted efforts – declined to be involved with the film, regarded it as an embarrassment. In the late 1960s, when Prime Minister Pierre Trudeau said Canada was about to shed its "*Rose Marie* image", Friml's secretary replied, "Shame on you! … The beautiful legend of *Rose Marie* is as much a part of Canadian history and tradition as is the French language in Quebec."[8] Alas, "history" is largely what *Rose Marie* has been consigned to, although it has enjoyed the odd Canadian revival over the years, including some in French. You didn't have to be Canadian to know that the plot was ludicrous: the Germans saw right through it from the beginning, and so it flopped in Berlin. Now, finally, through Canadian-created shows like *Due South*, Canadians have been able to share in the joke.

In spite of its long run at the Charlottetown Festival, where it plays largely in front of American tourists, Don Harron (1924-), author of the book for *Anne of Green Gables - The Musical*, has never believed that his show should even be attempted on Broadway. "We learned long ago it's not that kind of show. *Anne of Green Gables* is not *Annie*."[9] He adds, "I have been at many Broadway opening nights and seen the brittle sophistication of the first niters [sic] who were much more interested in being seen than seeing anything on that stage. Londoners were different, in their ratty fur stoles they wanted to see a show and enjoy it."[10]

Harron's conviction has, alas, grown a new wrinkle. Although his version, written in collaboration with Norman Campbell (1924-2004), Elaine Campbell (1925-2007) and Mavor Moore (1919-2006) is authorised by the original *Anne* publishers (to which they continue to pay royalties), the Americans now consider the story to be in the public domain[11]. (Under US copyright law, anything published before 1923 is automatically up for grabs, whereas in most other countries, the copyright would last until 70 years after the author's death.) While the name and likeness of Anne is a trademark owned in Canada by the Anne of Green Gables Licensing Authority, American writers are not obliged to seek permission or pay royalties before writing their own versions. So off-shoots such as *Anne with an E* have proliferated. Most recently, a new version was presented off-Broadway at the Lucille Lortel Theatre by Theatreworks USA. The libretto was by the noted lyricist Gretchen Cryer (1935-) and the score by composer Nancy Ford, creators of *I'm Getting My Act Together and Taking it on the Road*. Believing it to be a story that transcends national boundaries, their script makes little reference to its setting. In fact, actress Piper Goodeve, who played the title role, was unaware that it was set in Canada. She conceded, in reference to the Charlottetown Festival version, "I can see how it's upsetting that it's not their version in New York."[12] Canadian independent producer Michael Rubinoff put it more succinctly. "We should protect one of the few musicals that have become a Canadian institution at home and abroad," he told the *Ottawa Citizen*'s Kate Goodloe. "The original has been around for over 40 years. I can only imagine the outrage if I decided to announce a new version of *Les Misérables*."

While the original novel may be regarded as in the public domain in the U.S. and Canada, it remains in copyright in Europe. While others may adapt the novel, they may not produce souvenir merchandise without permission of the Anne Authority, which is jointly controlled by the L. M. Montgomery estate and the Province of Prince Edward Island. David MacKenzie, then-Chief Executive of the Confederation Centre, producers of the Charlottetown version, said "I think there's a little bit of jealousy come forward because I'd love for that show on Broadway or off Broadway to be *Anne of Green Gables - The Musical*, the Charlottetown Festival version, and hopefully some day it will be"[13] Montgomery herself fumed when an early silent movie of the story showed the Stars and Stripes flying over Avonlea schoolhouse. I doubt that any American could conceive of how it would feel if the rest of the world were unaware that *Huckleberry Finn* actually took place, not on the Yorkshire Humber, but on the Mississippi.

One other Canadian-based story made it to Broadway, but since the success of *The Happy Time* was modest, it is virtually unknown in the land of its setting. When producer David Merrick originally approached playwright N. Richard Nash (*The Rainmaker*) to write the book, Nash preferred instead to do an entirely original story. However, Merrick held the rights to a 1950 Broadway play by Samuel A. Taylor that in turn was based on stories by Robert Fontaine, concerning a Francophone family in the Ottawa Valley in the 1920s. Ultimately, Nash rewrote his story to incorporate some of Fontaine's characters, and moved his setting to Canada. Composer John Kander (1927-) and lyricist Fred Ebb (1928-2004), fresh from their success with *Cabaret*, were brought in to write the score (after Cy Coleman and Dorothy Fields had declined). The only Canadian involvement was star Robert Goulet (1933-2007) (who won a Tony award) and Oscar winning filmmaker Christopher Chapman (*A Place To Stand*), who designed the film projections. It has been revived in a number of American regional theatre productions, including Goodspeed Opera House and Signature Theatre.

What happens when a successful British musical is remounted on Broadway, and "tweaked" for American audiences? There is a British tendency to balk at the very gloss that Broadway prides itself in. Don Black (1938-) was already an Academy Award winning lyricist when he began writing for the West End stage. Beforehand, he had been asked to write lyrics for *Bar Mitzvah Boy*, a 1978 musical based on Jack Rosenthal's 1976 TV comedy. The music was by Broadway legend Jule Styne (1905-94). Although

Styne had been born in London's East End, he grew up in the U.S. and was a New Yorker through and through. Whereas the original BBC teleplay had been low key and subtle, Styne and his fellow American director Martin Charnin insisted the musical had to be big and brash. "They brought to it this New York veneer," says Black, "this show-stopping polish, that was wrong for it."[14] Its production at London's Her Majesty's Theatre closed after seventy-seven performances, but it would lead to Black's next assignment, and to a difficult Broadway transfer.

Song and Dance had begun life as a song cycle with music by Andrew Lloyd Webber called *Tell Me on a Sunday*, written as a vehicle for actress Marti Webb. It told of the romantic misadventures of an English girl set adrift in America. After a successful stage adaptation (combined with Lloyd Webber's Paganini *Variations*), plans were made to bring the show to Broadway, but Lloyd Webber and producer Cameron Mackintosh both felt it needed to be seen through American eyes. Director and lyricist Richard Maltby Jr. (1937-) was brought on board, and Bernadette Peters signed to star. "I knew something was wrong at the beginning," says Black, "when Bernadette... asked me to show her Muswell Hill... 'because I want to see where this girl comes from'... We spent the day there, and she kept asking things like, 'What does the character's Dad do?' And I'd say, 'Well, we don't talk about her Dad'. She needed to know. 'Could he have owned one of those sweet shops?'... she'd persist. And I'd say, 'Er, yeah'. And she'd reply, 'Great. That helps me.' That's when I realised: she was having to consciously motivate herself to get the character. Call it method acting. Whatever. Marti never asked any of that. She *was* the girl, and that was it, and that was why there was a truth to it with her."[15] "The attempt to Americanise, supposedly authenticate, *Tell Me on a Sunday* for a New York audience, was a dismal failure", says London theatre critic Michael Coveney, "insensitive to the fact that Black's heroine's absorption of American detail was filtered through her predominantly Muswell Hill persona."[16]

Even with Sandy Wilson (1924-)'s *The Boy Friend* (1953), which was a hit on Broadway, there were tensions. While the original Players Theatre production was performed with just two pianos and drums, producer and director Cy Feur decided that the Broadway production needed to be flashier and broader. He also felt it required an orchestra, with jazzier arrangements and faster tempos. An outraged Wilson became persona non grata at rehearsals. Original London director Vida Hope wrote, "The whole show is performed with all the high gloss and efficiency of the modern American musical... But inevitably, some of the tenderness has vanished."[17] (It's interesting to note that, fifty years later, when the similarly pastiche Canadian musical *The Drowsy Chaperone* was adapted for Broadway, its original creators openly embraced the more polished Broadway approach.)

It is difficult, if not impossible, for a writer from the most powerful nation on earth to fully understand what life is like for those who live under its domination. In dealing with this question of "universality" and cultural sensitivity, there is one Broadway show that gives me a great deal of trouble. Not that I dislike it – on the contrary, *The King and I* has, since my childhood, been one of my favourite musicals. Lehman Engel regarded it as one of the fifteen all-time best, and it has been staged successfully in countries as far afield as Japan and Israel – but never in Thailand, the land of its setting. In fact, it has been banned there. "The Thai people find *The King and I* in its movie and Broadway play forms offensive because it caricatures His Majesty King Mongkut in such a denigrating and condescending manner", wrote the Honourable Nitya Pibulsonggram, then-Thai ambassador to the United States in a 1997 letter addressed to Christopher Cox of the *Boston Herald*[18].

When Rodgers and Hammerstein adapted Hungarian playwright Ferenc Molnár's 1909 drama *Liliom* to become *Carousel*, they avoided the problem of a foreign culture by changing the setting from Budapest to New England, thereby Americanising it. Hammerstein was uncertain that his audience would accept a foreign locale. "There was no way of knowing how the public would be thinking", he said.[19] Clearly, a change of setting would not be possible for *The King and I*.

It was leading actress Gertrude Lawrence (1898-1952) who initiated the project. She had optioned Margaret Landon's 1943 novel *Anna and the King of Siam*, and initially approached Cole Porter, then Noël Coward to write the score.   Rodgers and Hammerstein declined at first, deeming Landon's story too episodic in nature, but they were persuaded when they saw Rex Harrison in the non-musical 1946 film of the book.

The novel was in turned based on the highly fanciful memoirs of the Welsh school teacher Anna Owens, who travelled to Bangkok in 1862 to be a teacher for the children of King Mongkut. Here is where the trouble begins. Owens, (who added her husband's middle name to his surname to become Leonowens in her writings) felt the need to spice up her stories by adding harrowing tales of harem girls and torture. She didn't limit her fantasy to descriptions of the Siamese court – she also re-invented much of her own back story. She was born in India, and while she considered herself to be Welsh, she evidently never did make it to the British Isles. (She wasn't the only colourful member of her family: her great nephew William Pratt became the actor Boris Karloff.) Crucially, she also portrayed herself as the king's most trusted adviser, whereas the historical record reveals otherwise: King Mongkut kept extensive journals during this time, in which Mrs. Anna's name occurs only once, and in a very trifling reference. It is likely that their contact was minimal, if in fact they ever even met.

However, American audiences and theatre professionals in the 1950s were unconcerned by any of this. This is Lehman Engel's assessment of *The King and I*: "The arrogant King of Siam has sent for a Welsh schoolmistress, Anna, to educate his numerous children and wives. It is the King himself, however, who needs Anna's help – although he doesn't admit it and seldom accepts it without protest. Anna, a widow with a young son, has needs of her own. The audience's strongest wish is to see both of them helped, and each of them in this situation is the only one who has the power to help the other."[20] Of course, Engel's concerns are for the needs of the Broadway musical, not for the accurate portrayal of Thai culture.

"In this age of 'political correctness'", counters the Thai ambassador, "it is stunning to sit through a performance of *The King and I* and to see not only the King, but all the Thai people portrayed via an extreme example of ethno-centricity as childlike, simple, and hopelessly unable to cope with the arrival of westerners. The British, however, are portrayed as superior beings, gently trying to uplift their naïve hosts. The wonderful music and the visual treats of the production camouflage the real insult that lies at the core of the play. Imagine if there were a similar caricature of Benjamin Franklin or Abraham Lincoln. Would you find it amusing to laugh at them, particularly if it requires a foreigner to teach them the necessary veneer of civilized behaviour? I doubt Americans would find it funny." Bearing in mind that, under this king's rule, Thailand was the only southeast Asian country that was able to withstand the assault of Western imperialism in the nineteenth century, he may have a point. If somebody were to make a film or play about the American Revolution in which the redcoats were the heroes and George Washington a terrorist, it might not be banned[21], but it certainly would not be popular stateside.

Still, in the "Occidental" world, *The King and I* is a beloved musical, written by two men with impeccable liberal credentials: both were active supporters of Roosevelt's New Deal who campaigned vigorously against racism in all its guises. I'm sure they would be appalled to find that they had caused offence. Perhaps, though, they should not have been surprised. After all, this was written for American consumption, and at that time you were thought to be very progressive if you portrayed non-whites as sentient beings. They had already fought a brave battle to retain the interracial romances in *South Pacific*. Clearly, showing the king of Siam as a cultured, progressive man who was fluent in Sanskrit and Latin (and who impressed westerners with his expertise in astronomy) would not fit that era's idea of an exotic "noble savage". Rodgers own approach to authenticity is revealing: "It seems more than likely that if one were to attempt to reproduce with accuracy the court of the King of Siam in the year 1860, he might have to show the king as an individual quite unattractive (physically at least) to the Western eye. The palace itself might show a certain weird charm, but there would probably be a strange odour about the palace coming from the kitchen where strange and not entirely palatable foods were being prepared. Continue this technique and let it include the philosophies, the physical discomforts and the appearance of the Siamese women and it seems probable that you would end up repelling completely the Western eye, ear, nose and sense of touch."[22] Clearly Thailand's tourism industry was still in its infancy, and Americans had not yet developed their taste for Thai cuisine. In any case, one has to wonder if the only Thai women Rodgers had seen were the Ladyboys of Bangkok.

Viewed as a work of fiction, *The King and I* is a landmark of musical theatre. Viewed as a representation of history, it is a travesty. Sadly, it is all that many Westerners know of King Mongkut.[23]

The film musical *Hans Christian Andersen* also raised similar hackles in Denmark, even though screenwriter Moss Hart, composer-lyricist Frank Loesser and producer Samuel Goldwyn made no pretentions that this was a biography. Its star Danny Kaye told a Copenhagen press conference that the film was "just another fairy tale, an entertaining film built on an incident which might have taken place in Hans Christian Andersen's life."[24] However, the Danish critics complained that the film reflected a German, rather than a Danish setting: the names "Hans" and "Copenhagen" were given German pronunciations, and the actors dressed in Bavarian costumes. Nevertheless, fifty years later this would not stop the city of Copenhagen from an adopting the song "Wonderful, Wonderful Copenhagen" as the theme song for its tourism promotion.

As we've seen with the examples of *Hans Christian Andersen*, *The King and I* and *Rose-Marie*, it is very seldom that any Broadway musical set in a foreign "exotic" country ever truly works when exported back to that country. Even *Les Misérables* failed in Paris when re-imported from London. One of the few exceptions to this is Lerner and Loewe's *My Fair Lady*. Perhaps this is because it was based on an Anglo-Irish source (Shaw's *Pygmalion*) and because Alan Jay Lerner (1918-1986) was educated in England. (Still, it didn't stop him from writing "*On* the Street Where You Live" instead of "*In* the Street...") Even its initial director Moss Hart was of English parentage. Actor and writer Steve Nallon has a more elaborate theory. "It is difficult to think of a show that is more 'British'", he says. "The 'Britishness' of *My Fair Lady* is really found in its 'Englishness', or more specifically 'the cold-blooded murder of the English tongue'. But Shaw's obsession with the way the English speak, perfectly captured in 'Why Can't the English?', is only a means to an end. Higgins properly hits the nail right on the head when he sings, 'The verbal *class distinction* by now should be antique'... It seems to me that *class distinction* is at the heart of *My Fair Lady*, and indeed the lifeblood of every British musical."[25]

On the other hand, Lerner and Lowe's *Brigadoon* presents a highly romanticised view of Scotland. "Much of this comes from the invented traditions of Scotland, such as kilts and clan tartans", says Jennifer Oates, Associate Professor at Queens College, City University of New York. "The Scots played a role in creating these as a way to recover or assert a national identity after merging with England in the Union of 1707."[26] This is what Colin McArthur refers to as "Scottish Discursive Unconscious" in his book *Braveheart, Brigadoon and the Scots: Distortions of Scotland in Hollywood Cinema*[27]. This image, according to Oates, is not an American view of Scotland so much as an idealised view put forward by the Scots themselves in the literature of Sir Walter Scott, the comedy of Sir Harry Lauder and promotions of Scottish tourism.

Something similar happened more recently with the enormously popular *Riverdance* phenomenon. Laura Farrell-Wortman, who holds a BA in Irish literature from New York University, asserts that its greatest success was in "the creation of a recognizable brand... Coming as it did during the rise of the Celtic Tiger economy, the show was the product of a nation in transition, seeking a new global identity to match their new global economic prowess. *Riverdance* was able to take a traditional, rural cultural form – Irish step dance – and bring it up to date, modernizing it and reimagining the possibility inherent within it."[28]

Andrew Lloyd Webber (1948-) and Tim Rice (1944-)'s musical *Evita*, based on the life of Argentine first lady Eva Perón, has never been professionally staged in Buenos Aires. However, contrary to some claims, it is not banned. It seems more likely that the people of Argentina prefer their own versions of their history. A number of plays and films have dealt with the subject, both critically and favourably, including at least two musicals: *Eva, el gran musical argentino* (1986) and *Evita - Volveré y seré millones* (1989) are both dealt with elsewhere in this book. The Argentine critical consensus of the Lloyd Webber/Rice version seems to be that it is a miscomprehension of Argentina's complex political dynamics. One essayist criticises "*Evita's* oversimplified dismissal of Perónism as simply 'common or garden fascism' (Rice's phrase), with no understanding of or appreciation for the complexities of Perón's Justicialist Party, a political movement that included factions from the Right, the Center, and the Left." [29]

How important is this type of cultural authenticity in a musical? In 1976, Stephen Sondheim (1930-) and John Weidman (1946-) made a concerted effort to make a culturally sensitive portrayal of the Japanese in *Pacific Overtures*, but some critics questioned the decision to try to tell it from the Japanese point of view when surely the Japanese could tell their own story much better. Director Harold Prince told the *New York Times'* David Oyama, "It would be arrogant and stupid for me to suggest that what we did was Kabuki, but what fascinated me most – and what I did try to infuse into *Pacific Overtures* – was the peculiar energy of Japanese theater and their unabashed enthusiasm for theater itself."[30] Then this version was seen on television by a young would-be director named Amon Miyamoto (1958-). At the time, he found it rather "weird" seeing a Japanese theatrical form – Kabuki – combined with Western music, but a couple of decades later, in 2000, he was given the opportunity to stage this show at Tokyo's National Theatre when the rights to another play by famed novelist Yukio Mishima (1925-70) fell through. Until then, the National Theatre had never considered doing a musical. "The musical was seen as a kind of cheap entertainment in Japan", says Miyamoto. But the artistic director read the script without the music, and decided it was "good enough". While Harold Prince had staged the original in a pastiche of Kabuki style, Miyamoto felt that it was better suited to the simpler and less flashy Noh style. "Like minimalist, not like a spectacle. Not Kabuki way."

Japanese audiences were sensitive to the perceived historical inaccuracies of John Weidman's script, particularly regarding two of the principal characters. "For example, Kayama [a samurai] and Manjiro [an imprisoned fisherman] never met each other [in real life]", says Miyamoto. "But I don't care, because how the two men go in different directions is more important for me." (In the show, Manjuro becomes fiercely anti-Western, whereas Kayama embraces the new world.) Miyamoto's version made it to New York in two incarnations. First, his National Theatre production was presented in Japanese at Lincoln Center in 2002, where the *New York Times* said it "has been directed with verve and imagination... In reinterpreting an American musical about their own country, Mr. Miyamoto and company have bestowed a great gift upon New York: a chance to see muscle-flexing Americans as aliens at a moment when it is especially crucial for the United States to understand how it is perceived internationally."[31] Michael Feingold in the *Village Voice* said, "Rumi Matsui's starker sets and Emi Wada's less ornately patterned costumes seemed built out of a whole culture's visual sense, not designed with a distancing specialness born of research."[32]

Two years later, he returned to restage it, this time in English, at the Roundabout Theatre. He found working with American actors required some adjustment. "It was a big shock when I first worked on Broadway in 2004. Japanese casts don't oppose you. They just listen to what you tell them as to a teacher and say 'yes'," he told *CNN Asia's* William Andrews. "But that's horrible! I want to do work together. We have to communicate and share ideas. I tried to work in the usual Japanese way in America but on the third day of rehearsal the cast told me I had to change."[33] Of this production, Feingold remarked that "Miyamoto's cast demonstrates its success, ironically, by seeming far less rooted in an Asian sensibility than the original. But then, this, too, suggests Miyamoto's approach, which often seems to make Broadwayish what the original strove to make more 'Japanese'."[34] Of course, this is not surprising, given that the original production was by an American "Japanophile", whereas this was by a Japanese-born "Broadway Baby".

There is a song in *The Drowsy Chaperone* that contains the intentionally very Politically Incorrect lines "What is it about the Asians / That fascinates Caucasians? / What is it about the Asians / That's so nice? / Is it the won-tons? The egg-roles? The rice?"[35] This sort of exoticism – and the potential for cultural misunderstanding – has long fascinated writers. "Whenever one culture looks at another, especially from so remote a distance," says Raymond Knapp, Professor of Musicology at UCLA, "it cannot help essentializing differences, so that often what will barely register for an insider stands out in high relief for an outsider, forming the basis for stylistic imitation... Part of the problem is, to be sure, that the point of exoticism is largely *not* to fully understand the Other, but to keep it usefully at a distance so that its foreign flavour might be savoured."[36]

In an article in *Studies in Musical Theatre*, Doctoral candidate Jessica Hillman writes, "Musical theatre, as a popular and populist art form, reflects and absorbs America's highly sensitised identity politics, making issues of ownership and authenticity central."[37] When in 2004 a new revival of *Fiddler on the Roof* opened on Broadway directed by Englishman David Leveux, some dubbed it "Fiddler with no Jews" or "Goyim on the Roof" because Leveaux cast his non-Jewish compatriot Alfred Molina as Tevye, the milkman. Thane Rosenbaum of the *Los Angeles Times* said it lacked a "Jewish soul"[38]. In an attempt to further "universalise" an already internationally successful show, some complained that its ethnic identity was watered down. There were also complaints when another non-Jew, ironically named Norman Jewison, directed the 1971 film version, in which the ethnic identity was heightened. However, what Jewison did was to return the story to its Eastern European roots – to the world of the Sholem Aleichem stories and the Marc Chagal paintings that had inspired the show in the first place. Some felt that it lost some of the humour that it had on stage. If that's true, it certainly didn't hurt the film's international appeal. Perhaps more significant than his being a protestant, Jewison was a Canadian. *Fiddler on the Roof* – as a movie – was no longer being seen from a New York perspective.

In February 2005, I received an intriguing email from a Dubai-based company called Capacity World. It said, "We are now preparing for a great fantasy musical production" and that they were looking for a lyricist and book-writer. Hisham Abdel Khalek, their artistic director, "reaming with all our best regards", asked me to send samples of my work.

Alas, as it turned out, this was to be somebody else's adventure. New York based book writer and lyricist Stephen Cole, whose credits include *After the Fair* and *Night of the Hunter*, also received a similar email, only in his case, it asked point-blank: "We want you write musical. How much?" This show would be performed only once for the opening of Aspire Sports Academy, the world's largest glass-enclosed soccer arena, in the presence of Sheikh Hamad bin Khalifa Al Thani, the Emir of Qatar, and a thousand foreign diplomats. For the music, they ultimately settled on composer David Krane, an established Broadway dance arranger and protégé of Leonard Bernstein whose credits included the film versions of *Chicago* and *Nine*.

Krane and Cole had never met before, but they bonded instantly, and soon they were on a flight to Dubai, where they were given their remit: the spoilt son of a Sultan has been locked away in a palace and wants to possess a star from the sky. The settings were to include a desert and a sea, and it must travel in time to Egypt of the Pharaohs, ancient Greece and the Stone Age. The show was to include pearl diving, falconry, a score of camels, ten Arabian stallions and a major sporting star. Cole had to turn these requirements into a coherent plot. He decided, first of all, that the reason why the son was locked in the palace was that his father wanted to protect him from the world. The star that he craved was turned into a magical character who came down from the sky and took him on adventures to ancient Greece, Egypt and pearl diving in Qatar. (They were able to persuade the producers to omit the Stone Age.) Each journey would teach the boy lessons about brain, heart and strength, the qualities of a good sportsman. They had six weeks in which to write it. The show would, like its venue, be called *Aspire*.

Back in New York, they turned out a song a day. "We wrote as if we were writing Broadway's next Tony Award-winning musical", Cole wrote in the *Dramatists Guild Quarterly*. "I did some of my best lyrics and the music was filled with the mystery and beauty of Arabian nights, with a little Broadway and pop thrown in for good measure."[39] They managed to turn it in a week early. "It had everything: camels, soaring stars, singing Sultans, dancing sports celebrities, flying carpets, King Tut, and a small chunk of Homer's *Odyssey*."

There were learning curves: after they auditioned the score for the producers in London, they were met with a stony silence. They were told that they could not use the name of "Allah" in a song lyric – even if it did refer to apple pie with ice cream (i.e., "à la mode"). Krane had, for local colour, quoted one Arab folk tune that he was told could only be played during Ramadan.

These problems fixed, Krane went with orchestrator Larry Blank to Bratislava to pre-record the score with a seventy-piece orchestra. They also tried to pre-record the chorus using Slovakian singers, but the phonetically rendered results were unacceptable, so the chorus was re-recorded in London.

Then they found out, to their stupefaction, that they were not to be included in the casting, nor would they be invited to attend any rehearsals. The director had a background in Italian opera, and had never seen a musical.

They arrived for the final rehearsals to find the show, according to Cole, "in a shambles. The cast was tanned but under-rehearsed. No run-through ever got past the third song. The lights were rented from a local disco, the Russian dancers were choreographed by a kindergarten dance teacher from Boca Raton, the sets were so huge that some of them didn't fit on the stage, the effects (including a wall-to-wall LED screen rivalling Times Square) didn't work, there were flying accidents, backstage fights among the hundreds of Arabs required to push the huge sets around and no one spoke the same language." And it played in English in front of an audience who, without the full Arabic translation in their programs, wouldn't have a clue as to what was going on.

Yet, somehow it all came together, and the Emir gave it a standing ovation. They asked for a Broadway-style musical, and they got one. The only thing that didn't happen was their third and final payment, due upon performance. In Cole's words, "Our producers had folded their tents and tiptoed into the desert, never to be heard from again." He later told me, "It was certainly an adventure and I am glad I didn't miss it."

Since they had always felt like they had been living in a Bob Hope / Bing Crosby "road" movie, they decided that "maybe art imitates Arabs" and conceived a new show about the experience, called *The Road to Qatar*. "We treat the Arabs with affection", Krane told Kathryn Boughton of the *Litchfield County Times*. "You can't make fun of them. I feel we have done a small bit for peace in the world."[40] It opened at the Lyric

Stage in Dallas, Texas on 9 October 2009. "It's the company's giddiest yet, with a production as nifty as a terrific band of New York pros can make it,"[41] wrote Lawson Taitte in the *Dallas Morning News*. The *Dallas Voice*'s Arnold Wayne Jones said, "Because it's autobiographical, *The Road to Qatar...* has the immediacy of insane guerrilla theater."[42]

If a show doesn't have "universal appeal", does that mean it's not as good? Norman Campbell, the composer of *Anne of Green Gables - The Musical* once told me, "It is very important that we are able to write musicals that are about we Canadians, and about our own scene. To be inhibited by making it universal just by taking away place names and issues is a mistake."[43] Imagine if the Broadway producers of *1776* had worried about whether it would play well in London? (It didn't.) A show can be well written, well crafted and still be of its time and place. Surely there's nothing wrong with that.

Universality Part 2: A Sense of Time and Place

The ironic thing about universality in a musical is that it usually requires a very specific setting in order to work. It's when that setting, that time and place is so clearly articulated that even a person who has never been there can appreciate its sense of detail that you have a show that transcends borders.

In the mid 1970s Canada's Charlottetown Festival produced a musical based on the film *The Rowdyman*, which told a story set in a Newfoundland out port. Jamie Portman of the *Southam News Service* complained that "there is no real sense of time and place – despite [actor and co-author Gordon] Pinsent's careful Newfoundland dialect... The idiom is certainly not Newfoundland, only Broadway derivative."

This is one of the problems that I constantly ran up against in my native country. Because the musical is regarded as an American art form, it has not been taken seriously by the Canadian cultural establishment. A part of the problem is that there has been no musical-theatrical form that clearly evokes Canada. This was my initial reason for researching the roots of the Canadian musical in my previous book, *Broadway North*. In it, I asserted that one reason that it is so difficult to define Canada in terms of music is that we have been so pre-occupied with appealing to foreign markets that we have failed to develop our own identity. It is there, I believe, beneath the surface. For me, God is in the details.

I once saw a low-budget Canadian film called *My American Cousin* that depicted a place I was familiar with so vividly that I felt that it was my life up on screen. The funny thing is, Steven Spielberg evidently agreed with me (and hired its ingénue for a part in one of his films). And I'm pretty sure he didn't grow up anywhere near Penticton, British Columbia. But because writer and director Sandy Wilson was writing about what she knew (and managed to impart that knowledge coherently), it worked. More recently, the internationally successful television series *Being Erica* has clearly delineated its Toronto setting.

There is no formulaic approach to this. John Gray (1946-), the author of *Billy Bishop Goes to War*, told me "a lot of people start thinking of other musicals when they write, and not that space, that theatre, that stage, those actors. The more you have that in mind, the more you are in touch with the form."[1]

I am not arguing that every Canadian musical has to be set in Canada or be a Canadian story. (Or Australian, or South African.) If Australians write a show – especially if it is aimed at an Australian audience – it will have an Australian point of view. That's not the tricky part. People writing musicals in those places should know how to evoke their own milieu.

That said, musical "authenticity" can be ambiguous. Often the music that we associate with a particular place is not actually from there. The American popular music of the Tin Pan Alley era is largely European and African in origin, but achieved its popular success in New York, and is indelibly linked to that place. The folk music of the British Isles evolved into the folk music of the Appalachians and gave birth to bluegrass. Music does not have to originate in a place in order to reflect it.

In Broadway's golden age, writers thought nothing of "evoking" Thailand in *The King and I*, Scotland in *Brigadoon* and France in *Can-Can*, safe in the knowledge that few in the New York audience would have ever been to any of those places. In fact, few would have seen any foreign films, and their knowledge of foreign shores would be limited to books that were probably written by American writers. Broadway conductor and teacher Lehman Engel wrote, "Richard Rodgers… set shows in the Oklahoma Territory, the New England coast about 1873, the South Pacific of World War II, Siam, San Francisco, Salzburg, and many other places, but the basic melodic, harmonic and rhythmic style are all quite recognizably Rodgers. Here and there, there are colorations. The melodic style of *Oklahoma!* is unrelated to that of *Carousel*. *South Pacific* has its "Orientalisms" ('Bali Hai,' for example), Salzburg is here and there slightly more 'musical' musically than *Oklahoma!*, but throughout all of it, it is obviously American and Rodgers."[2]

On the other hand, Engel criticised *Cabaret* for trying too hard to sound like Weimar-era Berlin. "I cannot understand why so much of *Cabaret* sounded like Kurt Weill… In the end, this sort of thing must fail since at best it is only an imitation." Yet Vincent Patterson, the American director who mounted a revival of *Cabaret* in Berlin in 2006 says, "I am really blown away that [John] Kander and [Fred] Ebb and Joe Masteroff, who wrote the book, had not come to Berlin before they wrote this piece. They did this while sitting in New York… Somehow the muses got inside of them and informed them of not only the story that was so powerful, but the sentiment and the sounds of the music and the dialogue and the way people spoke and the feeling of this time."[3] Composer John Kander had immersed himself in the music of not only Kurt Weill, but of Friedrich Holländer, Mischa Spoliansky and others of that period. Of course, it *is* an imitation – albeit a particularly skilful (and appropriate) one. (Engel later conceded that "*Cabaret* is a far better show than I had at first thought".[4])

Times have changed. Not only are people better travelled now, but the chances are that Broadway shows are not playing strictly to New York (or even American) audiences anymore. Broadway and the West End are now more reliant than ever on tourists, and the centre of gravity is shifting.

110

Another factor is that people in other parts of the world are getting tired of being portrayed as stereotypes. Brazil is not populated by exotic women who wear fruit bowls on their heads. Canadians do not live in igloos (nor do their policemen ride on horses wearing bright red tunics), and Australians are not all crocodile-hunting bushrangers.

However, that only covers what they are *not*. Discovering what they *are* is a whole lot more difficult a process. How do you write a show that is set in Australia and make it instantly recognisable without resorting to stereotypes?

"When you hear Australians sing in their accent, you know exactly where you are because it's such a remarkably different accent", says Aaron Joyner, artistic director of Melbourne's Magnormos Theatre. "Admittedly, musical theatre style is actually easier to sing in the American accent. The vowel sounds are a lot easier. There are some words that when we're working on a specific song the Australian way to say the words just doesn't really resonate very well, so quite often the temptation is to quickly go back into the American. It can be difficult for our musical directors to hone that in and my ear has become very attuned to it." This means that composers need to be sensitive to the difference in language, and think about how a word is going to scan when they set it to music. It may also be a clue that could lead composers and lyricists to a more comfortable Australian style of scansion.

Søren Møller, the artistic director of a Danish musical theatre workshop called Uterus says, "I think that [a distinctly Danish point of view] will shine through what we do. I'm not a missionary about that, but I'm hoping that it will shine through that this is a Uterus developed project, that it's developed in Denmark and that it has a certain kind of feel to it that comes from the culture, and defining your own culture is first and foremost. Being part of that organic development of the Danish culture in musical theatre, that's a given that we're part of that. There [are] a lot of Danish composers, and its deep within our soul, and at the same time we've also been under the influence of the same thing by the Americans that everybody else has in the world. I think it's just a big melting pot, but I do think that a Danish composer, being brought up in Denmark, will bring some of Carl Nielsen [composer, 1865-1931] and the lullabies that we carried as children into the work that we do, and I think that will shine through."

Of course, audiences for musicals like to be transported to some place exotic and unfamiliar – hence the popularity, in the West, of *South Pacific* and *The King and I*. In Japan, on the other hand, the Takarazuka Revue's productions, such as *Rose of Versailles*, are often set in Europe, and of course *Anne of Green Gables*, which is wildly popular there, is set in Canada. I had an illustration of this in Singapore when I met some members of their musical theatre community for dinner in an international buffet called "The Line" at the Shangri-la Hotel. I was only interested in food from Singapore and Malaysia, whereas one of my hosts, Stella Kon, ordered roast beef with Yorkshire pudding. "This, for me, is exotic", she explained.

I even find in London that there is a fascination with all things American. It is, to the British, "exotic" in much the same way as *My Fair Lady* is to Americans. For Kurt Weill and Bertolt Brecht, American culture was seen through the rose-tinted filter of Hollywood. As a result, shows like *Happy End* are America as seen through a Teutonic distortion lens.

There are two American musicals from the so-called "golden age" that have deliberately set out to evoke a peculiar kind of rural Americana. Although they are musically contrasting pieces, the points in common between *The Music Man* (1957) and *110 in the Shade* (1963) are quite striking. For one thing, they each tell the same basic story – that of an outsider, a conman, who comes to a small town, stirs up the population, captures the heart of the local spinster, then finds or brings about some kind of redemption. Of greater significance to me, Meredith Willson (1902-84), the author of *Music Man* was a native of Iowa, where the show was set. Similarly, composer Harvey Schmidt (1929-), lyricist Tom Jones (1928-) and book writer N. Richard Nash (1913-2000) were all native Texans.

Musicology professor Raymond Knapp calls *The Music Man* "the most perfect of American musicals"[5]. Willson had already established himself as a proud native of Mason City, Iowa in his popular radio appearances as a musician and humorist. It was his friend and fellow composer Frank Loesser who encouraged him to write a musical about his home state.

"Iowans like myself recognize the characters," says Roberta Freund Schwartz, associate professor of historical musicology at the University of Kansas. "Meredith Willson always thought of the musical as a valentine to his native state, albeit one that did not idealize its inhabitants... Iowans have a reputation for being stubborn, pragmatic, direct and sometimes contrary."[6]

Part of the musical personality of *The Music Man* was a product of Willson's having been a flute player in John Philip Sousa's band, but much of it came from his years as a band-leader on various radio shows. Like Paul Shaffer on David Letterman's late night talk show, his talent for comedic banter soon became evident, and he was given the part as the resident Iowa 'hick'. It was then that he developed a technique for writing comedic "speak songs" to be performed by the programme's vocal quartet. These became the prototypes for the stunning "Rock Island" number that opens *The Music Man*, which Stephen Sondheim describes as "surely one of the most startling and galvanic openings ever devised"[7], as well as for the half-sung, half-spoken "Ya Got Trouble". "Willson's stubborn efforts to emphasize rhythm over rhyme and to create songs with the quality of dialogue were driven by a desire to make the 'River-citezians' [sic] in *The Music Man* sound like Iowans", Schwartz says. "As Iowans do not have a distinct regional accent, Willson used other means to characterize his fellow Hawkeyes." In discussing the song "Iowa Stubborn, she says "The music itself is stubborn: the incessant repetition of a small number of rhythmic motives creates a piece that seems as intractable as the folks who sing it."[8] Professor Knapp points out that "every problem is solved specifically through music". The townspeople are literally seduced by the power of music, and so is the audience.

It has a surprisingly unsentimental effect. Not that Broadway guru Lehman Engel was impressed: "The makers of *The Music Man* must have felt that they were in trouble when they resorted to an exercise in terpsichore involving a number of fat ladies in Grecian costumes, and the music reached for adrenalin in the form of an old-fashioned American-type march, '76 Trombones'."[9] He used this as an illustration of why that show would not be revivable. Sadly, Engel died before he could be proven wrong.

110 in the Shade, with book by N. Richard Nash (based on his play *The Rainmaker*) and music by Harvey Schmidt and lyrics by Tom Jones is not as well known by the general public as *The Music Man*, but it is held by many to be one of Broadway's hidden gems. The music is closer to the ballets of Aaron Copland than to the bluster of Sousa. "[*The Rainmaker*] had a story line about an old maid and a magician that had mythic proportions and cut right through to the heart", says Jones.[10] Schmidt and Jones had both grown up in Texas in the thirties and forties, and knew the setting well. "We searched our own youths and memories of Texas in the summer"[11], Jones says. Like the plays of Horton Foote, there is a soulfulness, an epic quality to it.

Sometimes a show's distinct sense of time and place is a product of its creators' imagination. Frank Loesser had already mastered the idiosyncratic speech patterns of Damon Runyon in *Guys and Dolls*. When he attempted to adapt B.J. Chute's fantasy novel *Greenwillow*, which is set in an un-specified place and time, he once again gave the characters eccentric phrases such as "Any flimsy-dimsy looking for true love better smile me no good-deary-good-day".[12] The show was not a success; it ran for just 97 performances at the Alvin Theatre in 1960, although Brooks Atkinson of the *New York Times* wrote that "Mr. Loesser has provided a warm and varied score that captures the simple moods of the story... The makers of *Greenwillow* have never faltered. Mr. Loesser has taken care of that by writing music out of personal musical convictions."[13] On the other hand, *Time Magazine* reported, "Whatever the charm of *Greenwillow* the novel, the play is as vague in its storytelling as in its geography. It offers lovers but no proper love story, devils but no improper temptations, and the sort of artificially flavored language that tries to be folk poetry but turns out as horrible prose. Doubtless some people will think it delightful, but anyone with memories of a J. M. Synge must find its whimsies bogus, while people with memories of a J. M. Barrie should find its cuteness grim."[14]

While *The Sound of Music* is at its heart an American musical, there is still a very definite sense of place. Of course the film version was able to make stunning use of its Alpine setting, but Sarah T. Ellis, a Ph.D. student in Theatre and Performance Studies at the University of California at Los Angeles argues that Richard Rodgers' (1902-79) music constitutes a place in and of itself. "In *The Sound of Music*, the reiteration of music via orchestral and sung reprises continually reinscribes a sense of place for the von Trapp family, regardless of their physical location. The very sound of music encompasses both a nuclear family and value system for the von Trapps – a transportable, or transposable, sense of place... the von Trapp family nests in their nuclear family and ideals of freedom by way of the very sound of music."[15] In other words, it is when they sing together – in harmony – that they are at home.

Of course, *The Sound of Music* is based on a true story, albeit with a very fanciful reworking. About the only things that were true were the fact that Maria was studying to be a nun, she did marry Baron von Trapp, the family did sing and they left Austria. However, she was never governess to all seven children – only to one – and she and the Baron had been married for twenty years by the time they "escaped". He was a loving and attentive father who certainly never forbade his family to sing. He was never drafted into the German navy – as an Italian citizen, he could not be – and their rather routine "escape" was by train. In fact, they rented out their home during their absence, and returned to it at least once during Hitler's occupation.

Even *Grease*, in its original Chicago incarnation, had a definite local feel to it, although much of this was lost when it transferred to Broadway. Its creators, Jim Jacobs (1942-) and Warren Casey (1935-88) met in 1963 as part of the Hull House Theatre, whose prime director Bob Sickinger was later my collaborator on two projects. The original version of *Grease* opened at a converted streetcar barn, the Kingston Mines Theatre in 1971, where it reflected Jacobs' own memories of Taft High School. The script was riddled with local references to places like Palmer House, Melrose Park and Lakeshore Drive. Local critics championed the show, and New Yorkers began to take notice. Producers Ken Waissman and Maxine Fox suggested they would produce it in New York if certain changes were made. "We were told it was necessary to make the characters loveable, instead of scaring everybody", Jacobs told the *Chicago Tribune*'s Chris Jones. "The show went from about three-quarters book and one-quarter music to one-quarter book and three-quarters music."[16] Where the original had been an ensemble piece, the Broadway version shifted its emphasis to the characters of Sandy and Danny.

In 2011, something resembling the original version was presented by director P.J. Paparelli, using a combination of the original rehearsal script and some restored cut material, stripping it of most of the songs added for Broadway, including "Summer Nights". "Everyone involved here has made sure that the kids of Rydell High – or, if you peel back the thinnest of disguises, Taft High School circa 1959 – are finally allowed to be kids again," writes Chris Jones, "mocking one another as Polacks and spaghetti benders, obsessing over tattoos, cup sizes and prophylactics floating down the Chicago River, and generally doing what working-class kids did and what parents teachers and ratings-obsessed filmmakers fear."[17]

And so, as shows move from one place to another, they either adapt to the foreign environment, or else their audiences do. (Or they die trying.) The rules are, I believe, changing. During the period of the so-called "golden age" of Broadway – the 1940s and 1950s – only the very wealthy could afford to travel abroad. Now nearly everybody can do it. Therefore it stands to reason that this change will affect how foreign locales are depicted in musicals. Any sense of "otherness" that is concomitant with the "exotic" will change with it. Before any other cultures can take their place in the new musical theatre world order, they will have to do some soul searching to discover what that place might be; to find their own voice.

ACT II: The Offspring

"Who Will Buy?" – Lionel Bart and the Post-war British Musical

For much of the twentieth century, the impact of European popular music on the rest of the world – the United States in particular – had been pretty laughable. "Since the heyday of Gilbert and Sullivan and the demise of the Viennese operetta, the leadership in musical theatre has belonged to the Americans," said *Time*'s Michael Walsh in 1988. "British musicals, when they were considered at all, conjured up images of ageing vaudevillians with straw boaters and canes barking strophic ballads at nodding pensioners."[1] The days of Vivian Ellis and Ivor Novello had passed, leaving little impact on the world scene. Then two things happened. One was in the sphere of pop music, the other in the theatre.

I don't think I need to tell you much about John, Paul, George and Ringo. The Beatles and the British invasion that they led are common knowledge. However, it had implications for musical theatre that cannot be understated. It wasn't just the beat. It may not have even been the music at all. It was the fact that four working class lads from Liverpool had captured the world's imagination.

The real change, of course, goes back a little further. In 1945, despite the fact that Winston Churchill had led Britain through the war, the British people decided they wanted a change – a new social contract, really. They elected Clement Attlee and the Labour party. This was a part of a massive social upheaval that accompanied post-war austerity. There was, of course, the sexual revolution and the rock revolution. But more fundamentally, the class system finally began to break down, and it became fashionable to speak in a working-class accent. In the so-called straight theatre, the "angry young man" John Osborne supplanted the "well-made plays" of Noël Coward and Terrence Rattigan.

In London, all social classes attend the theatre (including pantomimes) at some point in their lives. In New York, it is largely the domain of the middle classes. According to a survey commissioned by the Society of London Theatre in 2008, the average London theatregoer earned £31,500 per year, while the average Broadway audience member earned a whopping $195,700.[2]

In many ways, Lionel Bart (1930-99) exemplifies the post-war British musical. Unlike any of his American counterparts, he actually moved into musical theatre from the rock 'n' roll world. He continued to straddle both spheres: his circle of friends included Coward and Rattigan as well as The Beatles. Although he began his career writing revue material for the left-wing agit-prop Unity Theatre, it was as a songwriter for Tommy Steele ("Rockin' with the Cave Men") and Cliff Richard ("Living Doll") that he achieved his first success.

117

While Bart is credited as the sole author of the book, music and lyrics for *Oliver!*, actor Ron Moody (who originated the role of Fagin) writes in his memoirs that he substituted many of Bart's lines with the original Dickens, changing for example "How d'ya do?" to "I hope I shall have the honour of your intimate acquaintance?" "Bart's script seemed rather too evenly spaced, even sparse, with short bursts of dialogue alternating with a page or two of lyric. We soon discovered, however, that this simple balance played incredibly well."[3] At the time, Moody wrote in his diary, "[Bart] is no marvel and all his tunes are derivative, some incredibly so, but he is workmanlike and clear cut in his decisions", although he more recently commented, "How strange to read that opinion fifty years later, when the entire score has been enshrined in the archives of musical comedy greats."[4]

"It's hard now to realise how thoroughly he transformed the British musical", wrote Michael Coveney in London's *The Independent*. "He mined an entire semi-submerged territory of music hall, parlour songs and cockney anthems and filtered them through an idiosyncratic gift for rhythm, phrase-making and song construction."[5] Within a very short time, Bart would achieve a kind of prosperity that would rival Andrew Lloyd Webber's. In 1959, he had two shows – *Fings Ain't Wot They Used T'Be* opened at Theatre Royal Stratford East on 17 February, while just over three months later, on 28 May, *Lock Up Your Daughters* (for which Bart contributed only lyrics to Laurie Johnson's music) opened at the Mermaid Theatre. Over the following year, both shows would successfully transfer to London's West End, and on 30 June 1960, he would make it a hat trick with the show that would seal his reputation – *Oliver!*

Bart learned from the American musicals and applied their principles to British culture. It is in this way that he serves as an example to people in other parts of the world who want to create indigenous musicals. Like the Broadway writers of the golden age, he learned to use street vernacular in his lyrics. While he was writing *Blitz* he said, "I've gone back to English folk groups and based things on English street cries and English nursery rhymes. And I'm a Jew, so there are Jewish things in it, too. I use jazz where it comes in… I'm not a musical scholar but I have a good ear and I've gone into musical origins. Jazz, real African jazz, isn't far from Jewish music, which is quite close to Gregorian, and leads on to Celtic music and then to English folk songs and Cockney street chants."[6]

Oliver! inspired a rash of imitators – *Pickwick*, *Scrooge*, even Andrew Lloyd Webber's early work – but Bart was determined not to repeat himself. His theme song for *From Russia With Love*, for instance, sounds nothing like anything in *Oliver!* Although *Oliver!* is perhaps the only Bart musical to withstand the test of time, *Blitz!* (1962) and *Maggie May* (1964) were modest successes, and only the catastrophic failure of *Twang!!* (1965) and the still-born *La Strada* have blighted his reputation as Britain's greatest post-war musical writer.

Bart was not alone in his desire to drag the post-war British musical into the modern era. Nor was he the only person trying to create a distinctive British form of musical. Author and playwright Wolf Mankowitz (1924-98) declared in 1965: "Those of us who have been working for the musical theatre for some years would like to make it categorically clear we are not concerned to create pastiche American musicals. We are driving towards a specifically British musical theatre."[7] His efforts included the pop music satire *Expresso Bongo* (1958) and *Make Me an Offer* (1959) and his co-conspirators – Monty Norman (1928 -), Julian More (1928-2010) and David Heneker (1906-2001) would dominate the British musical from the late 1950s through the early 1960s. (Heneker would achieve his own international success in 1963 with *Half a Sixpence*.)

They and others pioneered what theatre historian Adrian Wright calls the "verismo" musical, which should "offer an accurate reflection of real life... Verismo holds up the glass to life, the unflattering light of day, sordidity, pans across the drawing room with its chintzy cheeriness to the kitchen sink."[8] (This is similar to the principal of "putting the audience on stage" put forward by Gratien Gélinas and Mavor Moore in the chapter "Canada – Still Deciding What it Will Be".) *The Crooked Mile* (1959) with book and lyrics by Peter Wildeblood and music by sometime Noël Coward accompanist Peter Greenwell depicted Soho's gangs and prostitutes, albeit sweetened with sentimentality. Its score included the ballad "If I Ever Fall in Love Again", sung by the American expatriate Elisabeth Welch. However, after *Oliver!*, the trend turned toward chirpy, nostalgic literary adaptations (*Pickwick, Half a Sixpence*) and, according to Wright, "The British musical was almost done with holding a mirror up to life".[9] (For a detailed account of the more obscure post-war British musicals, see Wright's book *A Tanner's Worth of Tune*.)

Andrew Lloyd Webber (1948-) may ultimately have turned to Puccini-esque quasi-operatic romantic schmaltz with *Phantom of the Opera*, but his first un-produced collaboration with Tim Rice (1944-), *The Likes of Us* sounds like he'd slipped into a coma with the *Oliver!* cast album on auto-repeat. Still, by the time *Jesus Christ Superstar* rolled around – actually their fourth collaboration – he had found a way to combine the form of a Broadway musical with the kind of quasi-symphonic rock heard in the final tracks of The Beatles' *Abbey Road*. "The urgent and forceful nature of the rock idiom was there," says Kurt Gänzl, "but the bones that lay under the surface of the score were of a more thoroughly classical shape. Just as the jazz and ragtime idioms had been adapted for song and, eventually, for show music, here was the rock idiom being modified into a theatrically acceptable and dramatically effective style of music by being cross-bred with the solid tenets of a more regular style of theater music."[10] "Influences abound," writes Alan Jay Lerner, "but they are filtered through a very distinctive musical personality, which gives his music a sound of its own... [He] speaks in the popular musical language of the day, more literate but, nevertheless, contemporary through and through."[11]

The musical theatre establishment has been reluctant to embrace Lloyd Webber. They complain that his music is bombastic, that his scores are all interchangeable, and that he is more interested in being theatrical than in being dramatic. It may also be that he is a victim of his own success, and that, as with Rodgers and Hammerstein before him, over-familiarity breeds contempt.

Aside from Andrew Lloyd Webber, successful British musicals have been thin on the ground. The landmark critical successes have been even fewer. Therefore, the two shows I'm going to examine here were not commercial successes, but were nevertheless highly regarded. (Although Adrian Wright doesn't mention them, I wonder if they might not fall into the verismo category?)

Musically, *The Hired Man* (1984) would appear to be as far away from *Oliver!* as you can get, although I believe that composer Howard Goodall (1958-) had taken some of the same lessons on board. Telling a love story set among a Cumbrian coal-mining community in the years leading up to World War I, Goodall combined English folk music with the sort of choral sounds he learned as a chorister at Oxford. Although it ran for only 164 performances at London's Astoria Theatre, it raised great hopes in some people's minds.

He set out to be a serious composer – and he has several choral works to his name, but it is his work with Rowan Atkinson and the *Not the Nine o'Clock News* team that defined Goodall's early career. Even now, he is probably best known for the theme from the TV sitcom *Red Dwarf* (Jenna Russell singing "I'd like to lie shipwrecked and comatose, drinking fresh mango juice…") and his work on *Blackadder* and *Mr. Bean*. In fact, what sets him apart is his ability to write richly textured music that is also highly melodic. "Goodall caught the English choral tone magnificently", says Kurt Gänzl[12]. Although he has continued to write musicals, including *Girlfriends* (1987), *Days of Hope* (1991) and *Love Story* (2010), he has never fully embraced the values of Broadway.

Instead, he has been in demand as a presenter of television programmes *about* music. In this way, like Mozart Weill and Bernstein, I count him as a composer who aims to elevate popular tastes.

When I first heard that somebody had written a musical about Viv Nicholson, a woman who won the pools in the early 1960s and then lost everything, I thought, "Who cares?" However, a number of people whose opinions I trusted were raving about it, so I finally went to see *Spend, Spend, Spend* by composer Steve Brown and author Justin Greene, which opened at the Picadilly Theatre on October 12, 1999 following an initial production in 1998 at West Yorkshire Playhouse.

Ian Shuttleworth in the *Financial Times* had declared it "the most glorious new musical I can ever recall seeing". Ian Bradley, in his book *You've Got to Have a Dream*, called it "a classic example of a musical based on a subject which would previously have been treated via a kiss-and-tell biography or a television documentary. At the end I was left asking the question what was added to the story by making it a musical?"[13] While I was still not entirely won over by its principal character, the score was, alongside *The Hired Man*, probably the best in any British musical of the last quarter century.

It won the *Evening Standard* award for Best Musical, and star Barbara Dickson managed to capture an Olivier Award. She told journalist Piers Ford, "It really speaks to me, which is important for an artist. I always feel that if you're not moved when you read something, there isn't much point in doing it. She is a fascinating character, and I think it's because of the subject matter. She was a poor woman who won money that they spent like water, and then her husband died. [Greene and Brown] just went headlong at it."[14] It managed to hold on for the better part of a year before going on tour, and was revived at the Watermill Theatre in Newbury, Berkshire in the summer of 2009.

Brown, whose TV work includes *Spitting Image*, *The Ant & Dec Show* and *I'm Alan Partridge*, had previously attempted a musical version of *Elmer Gantry* but was spurned by the rights holders. More recently, he tried to do *It's a Wonderful Life*.

For a couple of decades now, in many people's minds, the great hope of British musical theatre has rested on the shoulders of lyricist Anthony Drewe (1961-) and composer George Stiles (1961-). They differ from Brown and Greene or from Goodall in that, unusually for European writers, their forté is musical comedy.

They met at Exeter University in the early 1980s, and won the first ever Vivian Ellis Prize in 1985 with *Just So*, a musical based on stories by Rudyard Kipling. Under the auspices of Cameron Mackintosh, it was produced first at the Watermill Theatre in Newbury, then at London's Tricycle Theatre. The rights were optioned by Steven Spielberg, but the proposed animated film never materialised, and neither did a West End production. *Honk!*, their update of the ugly duckling tale, also began at the Watermill, where I saw it in December 1993. Back then it was called *The Ugly Duckling (or, The Aesthetically Challenged Farmyard Fowl*. It was later produced at the National Theatre, and has since been seen more than a thousand times at regional theatres around the world.

When Cameron Mackintosh acquired the stage rights to *Mary Poppins*, one of the conditions dictated by the late author P.L. (Penelope) Travers was that the writers must be British. Mackintosh knew that audiences would expect to hear the songs by

Richard M. and Robert B. Sherman from the Walt Disney movie – which Travers loathed – so he asked Drewe and Stiles to rework them. Following a tryout at the Bristol Hippodrome, *Mary Poppins* opened at the Prince Edward Theatre in 2004, directed by Sir Richard Eyre.

In spite of that show's success – both in London and New York – Stiles and Drewe have yet to emerge as the bankable household names that many people believe they have the potential to be. Yet they are two of only a small handful of people in Britain who make a full-time living from writing musicals. Their latest project, *Betty Blue Eyes*, with a book by American writers Ron Cowan and Daniel Lipman based on Alan Bennett and Malcolm Mowbray's 1984 satirical screenplay on postwar rationing *A Private Function*, opened at London's Novello Theatre on 14 April 2011. The *Evening Standard*'s Henry Hitchings called it "a production with heart and an unusual mixture of gentleness and naughtiness. Though not an instant classic, it's satisfyingly meaty."[15] The *Guardian*'s Michael Billington said, "This is a rare show in several ways. It is a genuine 'musical comedy' rather than a through-composed pseudo-opera… The success of this show relies on the fact that the songs grow out of, and are always proportionate to, the situation."[16] It closed after seven months, but this has not curbed Stiles' optimism. "I don't want to come over as a Pollyanna", he told *The Stage*, "but I have good reason to think we might be entering a pretty rich vein of British musical theatre. It's a staggeringly broad church… and I would rather celebrate that than harp on about great work not having longer runs."[17]

More recently (and successfully), Roald Dahl's *Matilda* was adapted by English playwright Dennis Kelly and Australian comedian and songwriter Tim Minchin at the Royal Shakespeare Company, which transferred to the Cambridge Theatre in London's West End in 2011. "Dennis Kelly's adaptation grips from the start", said *The Times* . "Jokes and numbers come thick and fast…Tim Minchin's lyrics, to his own music, are so good that the temptation to write them down could, at any point, make you miss some extraordinary sight."[18] "The Royal Shakespeare Company has struck gold with this wildly entertaining musical", wrote *The Independent* "Dennis Kelly's clever adaptation and the witty, intricate songs by Aussie comic Tim Minchin create a new, improved version of Dahl's story."[19] The *Evening Standard* said, "In this lovingly created show, *Matilda*'s magic positively sparkles. There's a cleverness in the writing which ensures that, while it appeals to children, there is plenty for adults to savour…it's blissfully funny…There's a playfulness throughout that proves intoxicating."[20] The RSC produced the transfer itself, and it is estimated that it recovered its £2.6 million investment in early 2012.[21] It won seven Olivier awards, including Best Musical.

At the far end of the spectrum from *Betty Blue Eyes* and *Matilda* is *London Road*, a music-theatre piece by documentary playwright Alecky Blythe and composer Adam Cork, developed with director Rufus Norris at the National Theatre Studio. It opened at the Cottesloe Theatre on 7 April 2011. Blythe recorded testimonies from those who had been affected by a series of murders of prostitutes in the London Road area of Ipswich. The verbatim accounts were then set to music by Cork, retaining the rhythm of the original speech. "The presence of music alters how we hear these words, forcing us to pay attention to the exact intonation used in the act of reproduction", says Sarah Whitfield of University College Falmouth. "*London Road* does something remarkable, in occupying this troubled space between song and spoken dialogue. It opens a different road for music theatre, not at the expense of the musical, but by demonstrating the possibilities for collaborations between unlikely practitioners, and the benefits of the kind of institutional support and protection the National Theatre is able to give new work."[22] Critic Mark Shenton found the result to be "totally absorbingly different… bursting into arresting, affecting life… an innovative and challenging show".[23] Perhaps this is a return to verismo?

Europopera

While British musicals survived and sometimes even prospered, the Second World War decimated continental European musical theatre. French musical comedy breathed its last gasp with the operettas of Vincent Scotto and Francis Lopez and the international success of *Irma La Douce*. In Spain, the Zarzuela tradition began to fade out after the Spanish civil war. In Germany (and all the countries it had occupied) Hitler had either killed or driven away the talent pool, and the city of Vienna saw fit to demolish many of its celebrated musical houses. It seemed that not only had the skills and the talent pool been lost, but the whole art form – especially in France and Austria – had been tainted.

Still, there were pockets of activity, usually inspired more by the then-current American and British fashion than by any indigenous tradition.

In 1992, Vienna's Theater an der Wien housed the most successful post-war German language musical, *Elisabeth*, with book and lyrics by Dr. Michael Kunze (1943-) and music by Sylvester Levay (1945-). The story concerns the life of Austro-Hungarian Empress Elisabeth, wife of Emperor Franz Josef. In this show, her "leading man" wasn't the emperor, but a young man who is the embodiment of Death. Kurt Gänzl calls it "a landmark in the history of the European stage."[1] The original production ran for six years. *Variety*'s review by Larry Lash said, "*Elisabeth* is never less than entertaining as it tells its tale of a tragic life, but when it takes on history, it truly soars."

Michael Kunze was born in Prague in 1943 to Austrian parents and grew up in Munich. He studied law, history and philosophy, and in the late sixties turned to writing pop lyrics, becoming the first German ever to win a Grammy award. In the early seventies he met Sylvester Levay, a Hungarian composer who had worked in Hollywood, providing the theme music for television series such as *Airwolf*. His hits included "Fly, Robin, Fly" and "Get Up and Boogie".

Initially, Kunze was not a fan of musicals – "my idea of a Broadway show was people dancing with a straw hat"[2] – until some New York colleagues took him to see *The Wiz*. "I was excited because it was contemporary, and it told a story with my kind of music."

"I don't feel at all linked to the tradition of the Viennese, German or French operetta", he explained to me. "But I did like the *Threepenny Opera* of Brecht and Weill and most of their other works, and I may have been influenced by them."

He was asked by Andrew Lloyd Webber to translate *Evita* into German. This led to further adaptations of *Follies*, *Aspects of Love*, *Cats*, *A Chorus Line*, *Phantom of the Opera*, *Company*, *Little Shop Of Horrors*, *Into The Woods*, *Kiss Of The Spider Woman*, *Sunset Boulevard*, *The Hunchback Of Notre Dame*, *The Lion King*, *Aida*, *Mamma Mia!!* and *Wicked*.

Then he began writing his own original shows with Levay. *Elisabeth* was their first hit, but they have also written *Mozart* (1999), *Rebecca* (from the Daphne DuMaurier novel, 2006) and *Marie Antoinette* (2006). An English version of *Rebecca*, adapted by Christopher Hampton is in the works. However, his first venture into English-language musicals was not such a happy occasion.

Dance of the Vampires, with music by American pop songwriter Jim Steinman (1947-), who wrote Meat Loaf's *Bat Out of Hell* album, was based on a Roman Polanski film that was released in 1967 under the more farcical title *The Fearless Vampire Killers (or, "Pardon Me But Your Teeth are in my Neck")*. Although he wrote it in English, it was first produced in German in Vienna in 1997 where it ran for two years in a production directed by Polanski himself. Five years later, it opened at the Minskoff Theatre on Broadway, starring Michael Crawford.

The New York producers brought in playwright David Ives (1950-) to Americanise the dialogue. At the time, Kunze told Ellis Nassour, "I'm completely happy with it... I'm not able to write in the 'Broadway' style... There're people here who can do this type of thing so much better."[3] However, seven years later, he would tell me "The *Dance of the Vampires* Broadway version was not an authorised adaptation of my musical. It was rather a mutilation." Needless to say, the Broadway run was short and the reviews scathing. He explained to me, "I gave that interview at a time when I knew that David Ives and Jim Steinman had mutilated my book and lyrics. I wouldn't have been professional nor practical to complain about it to the press. I had to keep smiling, but I was not 'completely happy', quite the opposite. If you know Broadway and the Rialto gossip[4], you don't want to feed bad rumours before an opening. I've learned from that experience to make sure I have contracts that cannot be circumvented."

In Amsterdam, two writers with a background in cabaret created a book musical called *En Nu Naar Bed* ("And Now to Bed") which opened at the Carré Theatre on 5

November 1971. The book and lyrics were the work of children's author Annie M. G. (Maria Geertruida) Schmidt (1911-1995), and the music was by Harry Bannink (1929-99). The director was the Canadian-born, London-based Paddy Stone (1924-86), who had worked with Japan's all-female Takarazuka Revue and who later choreographed the film *Victor/Victoria*. It told the story of Frans, who since birth has been presided over by a good fairy played by Mary Dresselhuys and a bad fairy by Conny Stuart, who guide the course of his life, taking on different human forms: as a teacher, as a checkout lady, as a customer in a shop, as a psychiatrist. The show ran for 345 performances, and produced the hit song "Vluchten kan niet meer" ("There is no more escaping it").

Bannink and Schmidt began their collaboration in 1965 with *Heerlijk duurt het Langst* ("Delicious lasts the longest") which, like *En Nu Naar Bed*, starred Stuart and was directed by Stone. Schmidt had been a popular columnist with the newspaper *Het Parool* and had written cabaret songs for cabaret artist Wim Sonneveld and a radio series called *De familie Doorsnee* ("The Average Family"). Sonneveld, known to English-speaking audiences for his role of Boroff in the film of Cole Porter's *Silk Stockings*, had starred in a very successful Dutch-language version of *My Fair Lady*. After this, Schmidt was much in demand as a translator of lyrics, but finally she told producer John de Crane, "As long as I still have as many new ideas, I won't translate anything." At this point, de Crane replied: "If you still have so many ideas..."

She teamed with former dance band pianist Bannink, who had been Sonneveld's tutor on *My Fair Lady*. "The first one is most precious to me, says Bannink. "We both made beginners mistakes, but we were convinced it would be good. That wasn't overconfidence, but a sacred naiveté. We've become addicted to this genre, but that huge feeling became a lot less strong later on. More professional and thought through. With each next show we knew exactly when the intermission had to come and that's a pity, because you have to retain your child-like innocence."[5]

Coming from a Dutch cabaret tradition, and working with one of the Netherlands' most famous authors, the lyricist was queen. "Holland is the country of the church, so of the word", says the composer. "When I hear that seven applicants for the Cabaret Academy [in Amsterdam] sang Bannink songs at the audition, then I'm very satisfied." Bannink and Schmidt worked together for the next twenty years. Their other

126

shows included *Foxtrot, Wat een planeet* ("What a planet", 1973) and *De dader heeft het gedaan* ("The culprit did it", 1984).

Schmidt disliked the slickness of American musicals. Neither did she moralise like her Dutch cabaret contemporaries. "I don't answer the question: What is good, what is bad? I say in every song: Look at the lunacy of this. What do you think about that?"[6] Bannink, who is said to have written some three thousand songs, also eschewed the standard reprise form structure of a Broadway score, leaving it to director Stone to provide a unifying visual concept. Bannink later became the chief composer for the Dutch version of *Sesame Street*, and has a theatre named in his honour in his home town of Enschede. Schmidt was awarded the Hans Christian Anderson award for her children's literature. She ended her own life in 1995, and Bannink passed away four years later.

Jos Brink (1942-2007) was an actor, lyricist and comedian who came into musical theatre via cabaret. In 1972 he teamed up both professionally and personally with Frank Sanders to form the cabaret group Pierement. Their musicals together included *Masquerade* (1979), *Madame Arthur* (1985) and *Max Havelaar* (1987). Later in his life he became a Protestant minister and campaigner for gay rights.

The first Dutch musical ever to open on Broadway was *Cyrano*, based on the play by Edmond Rostand. The original Dutch book and lyrics were by Koen van Dijk and the music composed by Ad van Dijk. The English adaptation was by Peter Reeves and Sheldon Harnick. Producer Joop Van den Ende (1942-) told Marlise Simons of the *New York Times*, "I try to be in step with or ahead of a trend. But an American audience can be quite different from ours. The United States is sometimes far behind us and sometimes far head."[7] It opened at the Neil Simon Theatre on 21 November 1993 and, although it was nominated for Tony awards for Best Musical, Best Book, Best Score and Best Costume Design, it closed after only 137 performances. Ben Brantley in the *New York Times* wrote that the music "recalls the mechanically propulsive score of *Les Misérables*"[8]. *Variety*'s Jeremy Gerard dismissed it as "a thundering mishmash of unspectacular spectacle, non-musical music and anti-romantic romance."[9] The director Eddy Habbema and leading actor Bill van Dijk were both responsible for the extremely successful Dutch language production in Amsterdam the previous year. The composer and lyricist later collaborated on *Joe*, a musical based on the 1944 film *A Guy Named Joe*, (which had already been remade by Steven Spielberg in 1989 as *Always*), about a pilot who comes back from the grave to mentor a young protégé.

Ciske de Rat
©Joris-Jan Bos Photography

While none of these shows have had a successful life beyond their native country, I believe that a more recent Dutch musical may have international potential. *Ciske de Rat* ("Ciske the Rascal") is a trilogy of children's books begun in 1941 by Piet Bakker. It has been adapted for film twice, in 1955 and 1984. The star of the latter version, Danny de Munk later became a musical theatre star, playing Marius in *Les Misérables* in Amsterdam in 1991. He returned to the story that made him famous, playing the older Ciske in a massively successful musical version, which opened in Amsterdam on 5 October 2007.

The book and lyrics of the musical were written by André Breedland and Maurice Wijnen and the music was by Henny Vrienten (1948-), one time member of the 1980s Dutch ska/reggae band Doe Maar and a protégé of Harry Bannink. Vrienten had also scored a number of Dutch films, including *The Vanishing* and *Left Luggage*, and contributed one song to the Bannink and Schmidt revue *Foxtrot*.

The story of *Ciske*, set in Amsterdam in 1934, concerns eleven year old lonely street urchin Franciskus "Ciske" Vrijmoeth, a sort of "arse-kicking" Oliver Twist, who has no friends. After pouring ink over his teacher's head, he is forced to change schools, but he is befriended by his new teacher Bruis. He would rather live with his father Cor, a fisherman who is absent much of the time, but instead he is stuck with his alchoholic mother Marie and her abusive new boyfriend. During a heated altercation, he stabs her and is sent to prison. The story is told from the perspective of the older Ciske, who has been drafted into the army of occupation in 1940.

The show was directed by Paul Eenens and presented by Dutch theatrical giant Stage Entertainment, owned by billionaire media mogul Joop Van den Ende, who is also a major player on Broadway and in the West End and produced both the Dutch and English incarnations of *Cyrano*. *Musical Stages'* Sebastiaan Smits says, "It's been a long time since I've been enthusiastic about a Stage Entertainment musical, but after such disasters as *Three Musketeers* and *The Wiz* they finally got it right."[10]

I asked director Paul Eenens if they have considered adapting it for export. "*Ciske* is so very typically Dutch in every way", he explained. "The story is Dutch heritage, the music is composed with typical Dutch influences, the political and social context of the story is very Dutch, the characters are very Dutch etc. As you mentioned, *if* the show would be brought to another country that would ask for intelligent adaptation and an answer to the question *how* this story can/should be told in a specific country. We are not saying that adaptation is not possible or that the show will not be adapted for another country in the future. The story is strong enough and has universal elements in it. But until now the focus was/is completely on the Dutch run and success of the show that is now in its second year with more than 500 shows… And we are proud of the fact that an original brand new Dutch musical creation and story is so incredibly successful amidst and next to lots of originally foreign musicals with foreign topics."

I would argue that its unique Dutch character is what might make it interesting to a foreign audience, provided that it is adapted intelligently and that they retain its Dutch millieu. The score is tuneful and well-shaped, the story is heart rending without being mawkish, and if any Dutch musical has a chance in the English speaking world, this may well be it.

Sweden's Benny Andersson (1946-) and Björn Ulvaeus (1945-) have been extremely successful with *Mamma Mia!!*, derived from the back catalogue of their former band "Abba", and to a lesser extent with *Chess*, the pop opera written with Tim Rice that ran for three years in London and about that many weeks in New York. However, these shows were all originally written in English, and were first mounted in London. *Kristina* is another matter. Based on Vilhelm Moberg's 1949 novel *The Emigrants* which was filmed in 1971 starring Max von Sydow and Liv Ullmann, the story follows a Swedish family as they emigrate to the new world. A hit when first mounted in Sweden in 1995, an English version with lyrics by Herbert Kretzmer (1925-) received a concert performance in New York at Carnegie Hall starring Louise Pitre in 2009. "Major asset is Andersson's [and Ulvaeus'] music," says *Variety*'s Steven Suskin, "which on first hearing is more impressive than *Chess*. Trouble is, there's way too much of it – song after song after endless song."[11] As of this book going to press, it has yet to receive a full staging in English.

One country that has, so far, failed to develop any strong musical theatre tradition is Ireland, and I'm not really sure why it hasn't. This is, after all, the birthplace of Victor Herbert, and the ancestral home of George M. Cohan. It is the land of Oscar Wilde and George Bernard Shaw. Celtic music and dance permeates the Irish soul – and yet, they have never managed to put all these elements together into an integrated whole. The nearest Ireland has come to a successful piece of musical theatre has been *Riverdance*, with an original score by Bill Whelan (1950-) and choreography by Michael Flatley. However, *Riverdance* was a dance spectacular with a loosely defined theme, but no book or characters as such.

There have, however, been some recent attempts. Alastair McGuckian (1936-)'s *Ha'penny Bridge* is what is euphemistically referred to in the business as a "vanity project". McGuckian, a farming systems designer who financed the show himself, had the initial idea while stranded in Saudi Arabia during the first Gulf war. He also wrote the book, music and lyrics. The story concerns love and divided loyalties during Ireland's 1922 civil war. It was initially produced at the Cork Opera House in 2000, then remounted in an expanded version at The Point, Dublin, in June 2005. "It's the first time that West End production values are really being brought to bear on a musical premiered here; the kind of production values that audiences expect after *Riverdance*," McGuickan told *The Sunday Times'* Michael Ross. "We went to London to get the people we needed. It's very expensive to stage. It's certainly running into big money now. There are about seventy people working on this, it would be impossible to recoup the investment in Ireland."[12]

"This could have been Ireland's answer to *Les Misérables*", wrote Patricia O' Callaghan of Radio Telefis Eirreann. "Their revolution, our civil war. It could have been great. But, judging by the finished production, our civil war was the lesser exciting of the two."[13] The *Village*'s Colin Murphy wrote, "As drama, this musical is awful, though probably marketable. Each scene looks like a set piece from some kind of theme park, cabaret numbers perhaps for a Las Vegas 'Irish Experience'."[14]

Still, McGuickan didn't give up. A CD was produced, and he hired noted Broadway orchestrator Larry Blank to rework the score for a proposed North American premiere at the Princess of Wales Theatre in Toronto in May 2008 before travelling to San Francisco's Golden Gate Theatre on a pre-Broadway tour. The director was to be Stratford Festival veteran Donna Feore, and American actress Anika Larsen (*Rent*, *Xanadu*) was announced to star. Then, five weeks before rehearsals were due to start, producer Garrett McGuickan – the composer's son – announced, "Despite the outstanding job our creative staff has done reshaping the book, music and lyrics of the show, we, as producers, feel the production is not yet commercially ready."[15] It seems that not enough American cities signed up to make a tour viable, and no Broadway theatre was able or willing to take the show in. "I've given two years of my life to the project", Feore told Richard Ouzounian. "I'm angry for myself, but I'm disappointed for my creative team and my cast, who have given so much to the show."[16]

Improbable Frequency, a musical satire with book and lyrics by Arthur Riordan and music by Conor Kelly and Sam Park, (calling themselves "Bell Helicopter") received a warmer critical reception when it opened at the Dublin Theatre Festival in 2004. It was remounted at Dublin's Abbey Theatre in March 2005. The story concerns some suspicious calls to a Dublin radio request show in 1941 that catch the attention of Britain's MI5, resulting in a meeting between the English poet John Betjeman and the physicist Erwin Schrödinger, calling into question Ireland's claimed neutrality. The *Irish Independent* described it as "slick and seamless throughout, with touches of brilliance...a landmark achievement". *The Village* called it "the first great Irish musical." When it opened in December 2008 at New York's Off-Broadway 59E59 Theatre, the *New York Times*' Charles Isherwood found it to be "a bit like early Stoppard crossed with a Gilbert and Sullivan operetta. Most unexpected is how consistently this strange concoction entertains..."[17]

In 2006, an Irish musical film called *Once*, made on a budget of €130,000 was enthusiastically received by both the critics and public. The score was written and performed by its two leading actors, Glen Hansard ('1970-) and Markéta Irglová (1988-). The story concerns the burgeoning relationship between a Dublin busker and a young Czech woman. The song "Falling Slowly" won an Academy Award for best original song. A stage adaptation directed by John Tiffany with a new book by Irish playwright Enda Walsh (1967-) opened at the New York Theatre Workshop on December 6, 2011, and transferred to Broadway's Bernard P. Jacobs Theatre on March 18, 2012. It won the 2012 Tony Award for Best New Musical.

While there have been a number of European shows in the post-*Les Miz* "Europopera" mode, few of them have succeeded beyond that continent. Perhaps the prospects are better for shows like *Improbable Frequency* and *Ciske de Rat*, which make a virtue of their specific milieux.

Canada – "Still Deciding What It Will Be"

To some people, my home country Canada is boring – the very incarnation of ennui, and Toronto, its economic and cultural epicentre, doubly so. Yet others claim the latter as the third largest centre for English speaking theatre, behind New York and London.

Once upon a time, Toronto was a very puritanical, Presbyterian city – hence the epithet "Toronto the Good". There used to be a joke that a competition offered a first prize of a week in Toronto. Second prize was two weeks. On the other hand, "Born to be Wild" was written by a Canadian named Dennis Edmonton, under the pseudonym Mars Bonfire, and first recorded in 1968 by a Toronto band called Steppenwolf.

Now, it is an exciting, vibrant city of over five and a half million people, one of the most cosmopolitan in the world. But still, it struggles with its past reputation. There are some who seem to feel that it should not get ideas above its (colonial outpost, branch plant) station. For others, it's the dour wallflower that longs to soar and sing. The Toronto Transit Commission recently unveiled its remodelled Museum subway station, giving it a theme and décor related to the neighbouring Royal Ontario Museum, and hoping to purge its reputation for resembling the world's longest public lavatory. There were the inevitable reactionaries who objected to this desecration of its heritage, claiming it would spoil the system's uniformity. Fortunately, the TTC didn't listen. (No doubt these people objected to Toronto native architect Frank Gehry's reinvention of the Art Gallery of Ontario, too.)

The journalist Robert Fulford has said, "Canada remains a place without final definition, a place whose inhabitants have not all made a total commitment to its existence, a country that is forever reshaping itself… We have no 'foundation myth,' as the anthropologists say. Canadians did not emerge slowly from the mists of time, far back in unwritten history; nor did we, like the Americans, found our state on Enlightenment principles inscribed in a sacred constitution; nor can we, like the Israelis, look for national legitimation through either ethnic history or a covenant with God. We lack ethnic, religious, and ideological identity. We came slowly together, gathering in sparse settlements on the Atlantic coast and later the Pacific coast, and along the way slowly filling the arable land between. Even today… it is not 'settled' in the way many countries are."[1]

Then again, Rudyard Griffiths, co-founder of the Dominion Institute, asserts that "History shows that ours is a political community built on shared democratic values and institutions rather than on ethnicity, region or language." Griffiths maintains that, for Canada's founders, "loyalty to Canada meant a lifelong commitment to the idea of a free and equal citizenry engaged in a great democratic experiment… to advance a single goal: the establishment of a new nation, Canada, as an egalitarian, democratic, economically ambitious and less sectarian society – a wholly Canadian vision that was consciously distinct from Britain's and America's."[2] Neither of these views factor in the ethnically based nationalism of Quebec, nor the regional loyalties that exist in both the western and Atlantic provinces.

There is a bridge across Vancouver's First Narrows that could stand as a metaphor for Canadian culture. The Lions Gate Bridge was, when it opened in 1939, the highest suspension bridge in the British Empire. However, it is not internationally famous in the way that the Sydney Harbour Bridge and San Francisco's Golden Gate are. I had always wondered why this was, until a recent visit to Vancouver. As my plane flew over the city, I looked down on Stanley Park and the North Shore mountains, yet I could not see the bridge. Painted a deep green, it was invisible against the water. Standing at the entrance to one of the most spectacularly beautiful harbours in the world, it accentuates its environment, but does not dominate it. Instead, it is a quietly graceful structure. (However, it hasn't gone entirely un-noticed: a major film studio, Lionsgate Entertainment, is named after it.)

Canadians have tended to eschew mythology altogether, preferring their heroes to be merely life-sized (Paul Bunyan being the notable exception). Putting aside visions of Mounties and beavers, it's hard to find a Canadian stereotype. In order to have one, we would have to at least be known for *something*. Sadly, the Canadian cultural identity has been largely either stifled or absorbed into the larger (and louder) American one. In 1971, Toronto-born rock musician Robbie Robertson said, "There's no Canadian music... There is no music that you can say, 'Oh, that's Canadian' – know what I mean? It's North American music – different countries, but you hear the exact same music, from blues to cowboy."[3] Singer k. d. lang would appear to disagree. "The landscape, sparse population, long winters and proximity to nature all contribute to a very introspective, melancholic (and I use that word not in a negative sense) kind of spiritualism – they contribute to an openness and humility."[4]

Take away the mythology from art and you are left with journalism. It's a recipe for blandness. But then, I would argue that the notion that Canada has no mythology is in itself a myth.

Until the late 1960s, what we saw on stage, TV and the cinema and what we heard on the radio were almost entirely under foreign control. There was no indigenous Canadian music industry, and professional theatre was just developing. A few isolated songs emerged, such as Ruth Lowe's "I'll Never Smile Again", first performed by the Percy Faith Orchestra on CBC Radio in 1939, and Elizabeth Clarke's "There's a Bluebird on Your Windowsill", originally written in 1947 for the patients of a Vancouver children's hospital. However, artists like Hank Snow and Wilf Carter were lured to Nashville, and their Cape Breton Celtic roots became indistinguishable from country and western. Similarly, light music composer Robert Farnon (1917-2005), an early member of radio's *The Happy Gang*, left for Britain. (Tony Bennett once said, "The people of Canada should build a statue to Robert Farnon for his unparalleled and magnificent contribution to music this century".[5])

Even now, the home-grown media exists in the shadow of Hollywood and Broadway. TV shows like *Flashpoint*, ostensibly set in Toronto, are like "no name" brands – they don't really represent any place at all. (When it was shown on British television, it was introduced as a new "stateside" drama.) Occasionally, shows like *Due South* and *Being Erica* defy this trend, proving the folly of looking over your shoulder for the answers. As somebody who has lived and worked in Toronto and Vancouver, I know that there is a distinct identity, but it gets buried when even our public broadcaster encourages its artists to speak with an American accent. It seems that the producers feel that the market demands American clones, even though common sense tells us this is a recipe for mediocrity.

Traditionally, the phrase "Canadian musical" has always been treated as an oxymoron. Back in 1948, the future Canadian novelist Margaret Laurence (then a newspaper columnist at the *Winnipeg Citizen*) wrote: "It seems to be very difficult to capture the much more rugged atmosphere of Canada in a musical comedy... They must deal in subtle wit, and the wit of this country is not generally found in the super-civilized repartee. They must be gay, and while this country has great potentialities for humorous writing, it is not basically gay... I feel that the Canadian scene simply does not lend itself to good musical comedy. Just as great tragic drama flourished in Elizabethan England, the time and the tone of a country almost always sets the pattern of its artistic creation. Until musical comedy actually fits in with the life of our people, and until it can be written with more spontaneity than at present, I think we would be better to forget about it for a while."[6]

Ironically, this was written in the same year that *Spring Thaw*, the world's longest-running annual professional satirical revue first appeared. This was the show that would begin the long process of proving that Margaret Laurence was wrong. In fact, "fitting in with the life of our people" was what *Spring Thaw* was all about. Founder Mavor Moore took his inspiration from *Les Fridolinades*, the Montreal revues conceived in 1937 by Gratien Gélinas who, according to Moore, "deserves the credit for insisting that Canadian theatre had to start putting its audience on stage."[7] Among the shows that it influenced are *Rowan and Martin's Laugh-in*.

Moore later adapted this approach to include book musicals. When he founded the Charlottetown Festival, he set out to commission new Canadian musicals, and *Anne of Green Gables - The Musical*, with book by Don Harron, music by Norman Campbell and lyrics by Campbell, Harron, Moore and Campbell's wife Elaine, was their first great success. It began life when Campbell, a television producer with the Canadian Broadcasting Corporation, had a ninety-minute slot to fill. Actor Don Harron was reading *Anne of Green Gables* to his daughters Martha and Mary (the latter grew up to direct the films *American Psycho* and *The Notorious Betty Page*). "I suggested to the

Campbells that it would make a good TV musical", says Harron, "because the heroine has such an imagination that the only way to render her expressive outbursts in a dramatic form would be to set them to music."[8] Of Lucy Maude Montgomery's original book, Robert Fulford says: "Everyone has an imagination, and everyone is encouraged to deny it – or at least fence it in. The world teaches us early that our imaginations are dangerous or frivolous. The world tells us to stop dreaming and be serious… Anne's unique ability to invest her surroundings with world-shaking, heaven-storming possibilities – this is what gives her story the power of enduring myth. That's also what makes her such a peculiarly Canadian heroine – like the best Canadian artists, she turns an unpromising landscape into a proper home for the imagination."[9]

Anne of Green Gables, Theatre Under the Stars, Vancouver, 2004
(Photo courtesy Roger Smith)

Anne has been playing in Charlottetown every summer since 1965, and has played well over three thousand performances. Until the recent Broadway success of *The Drowsy Chaperone* it was Canada's best-known musical, and the first Canadian book musical to receive world attention.

Anne essentially went through three major stages of development. Firstly, it was adapted as a ninety-minute live television special in 1956 starring Toby Tarnow as Anne and John Drainie as Matthew. This version was repeated in 1958 with Kathy Willard as Anne. Then, in 1965, came the stage version at Charlottetown. However, between 1965 and 1969, it remained a work in progress. For the first season, the orchestra consisted of two pianos, percussion and trumpet. A number of new songs were added – including "Open the Window", "Did You Hear?" and "The Words", which had lyrics by the Festival's founder Mavor Moore, because Don Harron was tied up with filming commitments. After the success of the first season, musical director John Fenwick re-orchestrated the score, and since that time Campbell and Harron secured a contractual commitment for a minimum of nineteen players in the pit. In subsequent seasons, more numbers were added, including "General Store".

In 1969, Canadian-born London impresario Bill Freedman brought the show to London's New (now Noël Coward) Theatre, where it opened on 16 April. For the first time, a Canadian book musical was on foreign turf. "Bill Freedman didn't want the critics to know that it was a Canadian show in any way"[10], says Norman Campbell. *Mame* was about to open in London starring Ginger Rogers. It had songs called "Bosom

135

Buddies" and "Open a New Window". *Anne* had "Bosom Friends" and "Open the Window". The latter was easily solved by changing the title to "Learn Everything", a hook in the original lyric. "Bosom Friends" was another matter – this required an entirely new song. However, Don remembered that a recurring line in the book was "Kindred Spirits". And so, with the help of a piano loaned by none other than Liberace, "Kindred Spirits" was added to the London score, and eventually to the Charlottetown version as well. However, Freedman also wanted a more up-tempo number for Hiram Sherman, as Matthew, to sing in the first act. "(I Can't Find) The Words" was replaced by "When I Say My Say", while a reprise of "The Words", sung by Marilla in the second act after Matthew's death, was retained as a stand-alone number. (This change was never incorporated into the Canadian version of the show, although it remains as an appendix to the published script.)

While it was generally warmly received by the London critics, *Anne* closed after a respectable but loss-making 319 performances. "I was very unsophisticated in 1969", says Freedman. "I should have toured it. I would not have done it today without two stars."[11]

Anne has been presented several times in Tokyo in a Japanese language production by the Shiki Theatre Company. Aside from the translation into Japanese, according to Harron, the script is the same as the Canadian version. "There was no strangeness", says Norman Campbell. "Everyone thought we should react to a Japanese girl wearing red pigtails, but it was perfectly natural... The cast was excellent, all of them being good musicians and having great schooling in theatrical arts."[12]

Since then, Canada has developed a handful of musicals that have earned international reputations. John Gray (1946-) and Eric Peterson (1946-)'s *Billy Bishop Goes to War* played briefly on Broadway and in the West End in the 1980s, but it would take another two decades before Canada would have an unqualified Broadway hit.

Still, Canadian musicals have struggled to find acceptance within their own theatre community. "To this day, musicals are excluded from most literary and playwriting competitions and prizes," says S.G. (Sharolyn) Lee, Executive Director of the Imperial Theatre in St. John, New Brunswick. "There has been little serious academic study of musical theatre, and within many of our 'legitimate' actor training institutions there is still considerable prejudice against musical theatre."[13]

In 2006 *The Drowsy Chaperone*, with book by Bob Martin and Don McKellar, and music and lyrics by Greg Morrison and Lisa Lambert, opened at the Marquis Theatre on Broadway, where it broke box office records after winning five Tony Awards (including best book and best score.) The musical, in which a lonely divorcee sits in his apartment listening to the cast recording of his favourite "1920s" musical, had begun on the fringe in Toronto in 1998, and graduated through many incarnations before making its move south.

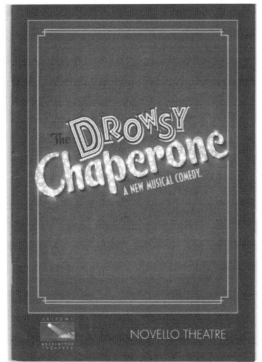

Bob Martin attended Lawrence Park Collegiate (folk singer Neil Young's alma mater) with two of his future collaborators, Lisa Lambert and Don McKellar. Even then they dreamed up mock musicals. The late Marian Grudeff (1927-2006), a veteran of *Spring Thaw* who co-wrote the score for the Broadway musical *Baker Street* with Ray Jessell (1929-), remembered Don as an English student at Victoria College. "He looked like a rabbinical student", she told me in 2004. "He played Hysterium in *A Funny Thing Happened on the Way to the Forum*. He had a lot of charisma on stage. He's a very musical man. He'd come over and sit beside me on the piano and we'd go over a whole book of different songs."

McKellar and Lambert recalled their friendship with Grudeff to Sandy Thorburn, musical director of a production of *The Drowsy Chaperone* at Thousand Islands Playhouse in Gananoque, Ontario. "I'd never sung in public before and I felt hopelessly nervous and out of place, until the accompanist [Grudeff] beckoned me over to her piano and privately, gently, probed the limits of my voice. 'Not much there', she confided, 'but what voice you have is musical and has character'... With humour and inexplicable generosity she taught me Hysterium's song 'I'm Calm'. I performed it for the director and I got the part. I still have no idea why she took the time to draw me out of my shell, but the next year, when I was asked to helm the annual Vic musical *Salad Days*, I accepted on the condition that Marian was the musical director."[14]

Lambert and Martin were also in that production. "At that time I was obsessed with musicals," says Lambert, "and when I learned of Marian's history I was beside myself. Don and I started spending time at her house – a little Broadway haven in the middle of polite North Toronto... It wasn't long before she was mentoring me; I would bring her rough lyrics and confused melodies and she would show me how to turn them into real songs. And when Bob Martin and I started creating musical revues at the Fringe of Toronto Festival, Marian was an integral member of the troupe. Together we wrote such bizarre routines as 'We're the Only Tulips on the Track Team', 'Le Chef Grotesque' and 'That Haircut Doesn't Suit You, Mr. Green'. (And not only was Marian an inspired collaborator, she had a way of directing and accompanying singers and non-singers so that they sounded better than they had a right to.) "

McKellar says, "We never would have written a musical if we hadn't met Marian. It's inconceivable. She simultaneously glamorised and demystified Broadway. Her affectionate and irreverent anecdotes made it irresistible and somehow within reach. Heaven for 'Man in Chair' would have been an evening with Marian Grudeff: trading tidbits of musical comedy arcana, laughing himself silly and singing into the night."[15]

It was their work with Grudeff that led to the creation of *The Drowsy Chaperone*. "Her influence is all over it", says Lambert. "She and I often discussed creating a strange, archaic show with, as she put it, 'first-rate second-rate songs'. One of my big regrets is not thanking Marian in my Tony acceptance speech. She's why my dreams came true."

When Bob asked Lisa to be the "best man" at his wedding to Janet Van de Graaff, the wheels of *The Drowsy Chaperone* were set in motion. Lisa and Don, together with Greg Morrison, a composer whom Bob had introduced them to, began to write a forty-minute pastiche 1920s musical about the marriage of two people (who happened to be named Robert Martin and Janet Van de Graaff) as a stag night entertainment. This very first incarnation was performed on 9 August 1998 at the Rivoli on Toronto's Queen Street. It was open to the public, and was advertised in the newspaper. The show, at that point, contained a half-dozen songs, of which two, "Aldolpho" and "An Accident Waiting to Happen" survived into the Broadway production. "It was broader at first", composer Greg Morrison told an American Theater Wing symposium *Working in the Theatre*. "The original score spanned greater periods – a forties song, a thirties song, a twenties song – and as the show developed, that was one of the things that the score honed more into – developing specifically as a twenties show."[16] Among the titles that didn't survive was one called "Hey, Sourpuss". That first book, which contained the basic plot of the musical within the show, was written by McKellar in collaboration with Matt Watts and the actors.

They decided it shouldn't end there. Bob Martin joined the team as a co-writer, and the character of the Man in Chair was born – a would-be raconteur, an obsessive show-queen who can – and does – recount every detail about his favourite 1928 musical, *The Drowsy Chaperone*. "I would say one of the greatest evolutions was the character of the Man in Chair", Don McKellar told the *Working in the Theatre* symposium. "We realised early on that he was really the lead character and in a way his story is the real story arc of the script." Lisa Lambert told me, "It's all about the private place – the bedrooms where musical-theatre-fan teenagers record their YouTube renditions, etc." Lambert herself played the title role, and McKellar played the Latin lover, Aldolpho, while Janet Van de Graaff played her own namesake. Also in the cast was Jonathan Crombie, who would later replace Martin as the Man in Chair on Broadway and on tour. A new song, "It's an Over-rated World (With Seven Underwhelming Wonders)" was created for the title character to sing. This version, now an hour long, opened on 2 July 1999 at the 181 seat George Ignatief Theatre as a part of the Fringe of Toronto Festival, directed and choreographed by Steven Morel. Robert Crew of the *Star* pronounced it "so much fun it's barely legal." John Karastamatis, director of communications for Mirvish Productions, waited in line for one of the half dozen sold out performances.

On 24 November 1999, with backing from Mirvish Productions and a $120,000 budget, Karastamatis presented the show for a three week run at Theatre Passe Muraille, directed by Sandra Balcovske, a director from Second City. Two more songs were added for this version: "Cold Feet" and "I Do I Do in the Sky". It won the "Pretty Funny Comedic Play" and "Pretty Funny Director of a Comedic Play" awards at the Canadian Comedy Awards. By this time, Matt Watts' name was no longer included among the collaborators. "It hurt", Mr. Watts told Susan Dominus of *The New York Times*, "but I'm still very close to them all."[17] He was not left out entirely. While in its transition from fringe comedy to Broadway musical the improv performers were necessarily replaced by singing and dancing triple threats, the creators made sure their friends received a share of the royalties. "If anything, they've been overly concerned and caring about it." There is still something of Watts' contribution left in the final script: "All that monkey imagery that's still in the play, that came from my obsession."

On 7 June 2001, Mirvish Productions presented a full-scale production directed by Daniel Brooks – artistic director of Necessary Angel Theatre Company – at the Winter Garden Theatre. "Show Off", "Bride's Lament", "Message from a Nightingale" and "I Remember Love" were added for this version. The set consisted of a bare stage with six doors and a chair. "I think the design was supposed to support a big farce section that got pared down later in the rehearsal process", explained Lambert. Martin told the *Working in the Theatre* symposium, "We had to make a choice as to whether we allow the show to be an evocation of the musical – in other words, do we have a neutral place where both worlds co-exist like a metaphor for the theatre of a blank space where anything can happen? Basically that decision was made for us by our very small budget at the Winter Garden to be perfectly frank, but we knew that there was something unsatisfying about that, so we wrestled with the idea of fully realising the real world."

Xtra!'s Gordon Bowness called it "a delightful combination of high camp and low shtick that often leaves you breathless with laughter."[18] But Richard Ouzounian, theatre critic for the *Star*, was apparently underwhelmed. "This is probably a musical for people who hate musicals, and secretly think there'll all silly and trivial. I don't, and so I was less than amused by most of the proceedings. There are people who will enjoy this, and I wish them well. I just don't agree with them. But most of all, let us hope this is where the expansion of *The Drowsy Chaperone* ends. I really don't want to see it further 'improved' a year from now at the Hummingbird [now Sony] Centre, or – heaven forbid – Skydome [now Rogers Centre]." His comments seem strange in light of two things – firstly, it has since been described as a "valentine" to the musical. Secondly, in his former guise as host of CBC Radio's *Say It With Music*, Ouzounian himself bore an uncanny resemblance to the Man in Chair. Lisa Lambert swears the character wasn't based on any real person, although Bob Martin told *NOW Magazine* that he "is based on someone with [Ouzounian's] enthusiasm, someone who's maybe a little bit too much into the show, someone who bores people by talking about their original-cast albums. Basically it's what Richard Ouzounian would have become if he weren't successful."[19] And, of course, *The Drowsy Chaperone* certainly didn't end there. (And Bowness added, "Richard Ouzounian hated *Drowsy*, so it's got to be good.")

American producer Roy Miller saw the show at the Winter Garden, and with Paul Mack, presented a showcase of it at the National Alliance for Musical Theatre's Festival of New Musicals in New York in 2004. (Among the cast was Broadway veteran Christine Ebersole.) Co-producers Kevin McCollum and Bob Boyett came on board at this point.

The show's title was a cause for some concern. McKellar and Lambert had originally seen it as a plausible title for a forgotten twenties musical. In fact, they deliberately wanted a bad title. At one point they considered changing it to *The 'Oops' Girl* (a reference to the Janet Van de Graaff character), but ultimately the title remained unchanged.

A new director was brought on board. Casey Nicholaw, who had been nominated for a Tony award as best choreography for *Spamalot*, would make his Broadway debut as both director and choreographer. "We knew that in order for the show to be truly effective, the musical within the show had to be fully realised, with great voices, great dancers, great costumes," Martin told the *Working in the Theatre* symposium. One of the first decisions made was to ditch the six doors. Instead, a realistic setting of the Man in Chair's apartment was created, which could be magically transformed into the settings for the musical within the show. "We were excited when we thought about the idea of a director-choreographer, because the show is not just about dancing, it's about movement, and the set itself is almost like another character in the show. It's constantly transforming, and it's absolutely crucial that we had somebody at the helm who knew how to move the action around with the characters in and out of these two worlds that we're presenting."

So many shows from other countries have gone to New York and lost their souls to producers who had no understanding of their original concepts. "It was certainly something we were really scared of", McKellar told Phil Hahn of CTV News, "but it never entered into that territory where we sold out or betrayed our initial impulse... At first, when we had our American partners involved we were sure that was going to be an issue, and it would lose its irony... but fortunately we had, in our producers and our director and our creative team, collaborators who were able to understand the importance of the tone, and the irony that we came with – and encouraged us to stick with that."[20] Of course, this is a show that benefited from Broadway gloss, as opposed to one smothered by it (as others have been). In its transition from Toronto to New York, the show did lose one joke – expressing his hopes for a good evening's entertainment, the Man in Chair originally prayed, "If it must be a Canadian play, please don't let it be a *Canadian* play." However, having seen it play so successfully in its original pared-down incarnation, the American producers knew that they mustn't throw the baby out with the bath water.

A tryout production was arranged at the Ahmanson Theatre in Los Angles. Three new songs, "Fancy Dress" (the opening number), "As We Stumble Along" (replacing "Over-rated World") and "Toledo Surprise" were written.

For the Broadway opening, "I Remember Love" was replaced by "Love is Always Lovely in the End". "'I Remember Love' seemed to come out of nowhere", Larry Blank, the orchestrator, remembers. "It didn't land very well in L.A. and it was decided that a new number would help. The new number seems to work much better in the general scheme of the show... but I always thought 'I Remember Love' was the better, more fun song. And I had more fun with the orchestration as well." There were other changes – a ballet in the second half, following the "Bride's Lament" was also lost. "*Drowsy* was a very good show in L.A.," says Blank, "and it became much more polished and focused in N.Y. Once in previews in N.Y., the most attention was paid to cleaning up 'Accident Waiting To Happen' and smoothing all of the 'best man' transitions. Like most successful shows, this one was positive from the go, and the fixes were mostly cosmetic. A lot more credit should go to Casey Nicholaw who really pulled it together."

Associated Press' Michael Kuchwara called it a "disarming, delightful soufflé".[21] Howard Kissel of the *New York Daily News* found "cause for rejoicing. It's full of wit and high spirits".[22] The all-important *New York Times* critic Ben Brantley said "The gods of timing, who are just as crucial to success in show business as mere talent is, have smiled brightly upon "The Drowsy Chaperone," the small and ingratiating musical that opened last night at the big and intimidating Marquis Theater." But he added that, "Though this revved-up spoof of a 1920's song-and-dance frolic, as imagined by an obsessive 21st-century show queen, seems poised to become the sleeper of the Broadway season, it is not any kind of a masterpiece."[23] Still, on the night I attended – two days after the opening – the audience was warm and healthy. The show won seven Drama Desk awards, including Best Musical, best book and best score. It also won the Best Musical award from the Drama Critics Circle, and was nominated for thirteen Tony awards, including every category for which it was eligible.

The first Canadian show since *The Dumbells* (a First World War comedy troupe that played on Broadway in 1920) to be an unqualified Broadway hit, it repaid its $8 million cost within thirty weeks before finally closing at the end of December 2007 after 674 performances. The London production didn't fare quite so well; starring Elaine Paige in the non-starring title role, it finished after only eight weeks at the Novello Theatre, although it managed to be nominated for five Olivier awards (alas, losing to *Hairspray*). It has since enjoyed a successful pared-down revival in one of London's fringe theatres.

I was amazed to find that some people in the musical-loving community took serious offence to *The Drowsy Chaperone*. What is even more amazing is that these were some of the real life Men in Chairs – the people I would have expected to be the show's biggest fans. On an on-line discussion group, I heard some object – with no apparent sense of irony – to the portrayal of a stereotypical "show queen" as a lonely, neurotic obsessive-compulsive with no apparent social life – then proceeded to lambaste the show for its "inaccuracies" – the belting voices, the brassy orchestration, and the obvious fact that there were no cast-recordings in 1928. This actually turned into a heated argument about the "willing suspension of disbelief". I wondered if the show had simply cut too close to the bone.

There were great hopes for a triumphant homecoming, but an opportunity was missed when it was decided that it would not have a sit-down Toronto production. Mirvish Productions decided to pass, thinking that it was too soon after its original production. (Also, they had lost heavily on *The Producers*, *Hairspray* and *Lord of the Rings*.) Instead, a new company, Dancap Productions decided merely to open its North American tour in Toronto (with an all-American cast, save for its star Bob Martin).

It received a rapturous reception at the Elgin Theatre (which is downstairs from the Winter Garden, where Mirvish presented the first full-scale version). Even Richard Ouzounian re-evaluated the show. "It's interesting to see how the show has changed over the years. When it first started out, everyone was thrilled that four local authors (Martin, Don McKellar, Lisa Lambert and Greg Morrison) had succeeded in conveying their unique sense of musical comedy hijinks to a theatrical audience. But as the work got closer to Broadway, the glitter got a little blinding and the sizzle sometimes threatened to overwhelm the steak. Well, a year on Broadway, a largely new touring cast and a return to this city where it all started has done wonders. In many ways this is probably the best, most balanced and most ultimately satisfying of the show I have ever seen. What makes it special? I call tell you that in two words. Bob Martin. He's always been *The Drowsy Chaperone*'s secret ingredient."[24]

Still, I believe that an open ended Canadian production would have been a greater triumph. It has, however, found a home among Canada's regional theatres, having been staged at the now-defunct Vancouver Playhouse in Christmas 2008, and at Edmonton's Citadel Theatre and the National Arts Centre in Ottawa in 2009. Playhouse artistic director Max Reimer told *Equity Quarterly*'s Matthew Hays, "Even though it has less name recognition than something like *The Sound of Music*, I wanted to put it on here. We had amazing success with it. It was great to put on a Canadian show that the audiences took to so strongly. I really hope that there are more musicals like it."[25]

An Australian production opened in 2010 in Melbourne – where it broke box office records – starring Geoffrey Rush. It has even been presented in Tokyo, directed by Japan's top musical man, Amon Miyamoto, who had brought his Japanese production of *Pacific Overtures* to New York in 2000. "I love this Canadian focus", he told me. "This

142

is how they loved musicals long distance. That's good for me. It's all in his imagination, his own creation. This is a Canadian viewpoint. That's what made me very excited when I saw it on Broadway. It touched my heart. I cry a lot. Japanese people looking at Broadway and Canadian people looking at Broadway, the distance is similar."

Anne of Green Gables - The Musical and *The Drowsy Chaperone* actually have one very important thing in common. Both were originally created by a group of people who had been drilling together for a long time. In the case of *Anne of Green Gables*, Don Harron, Mavor Moore, Director/choreographer Alan Lund, Barbara Hamilton and much of the ensemble came from *Spring Thaw*, whereas *The Drowsy Chaperone* came out of Toronto's Second City and other improv comedy traditions.

How "Canadian" is *Drowsy Chaperone*? It has often been described as a love-letter to the American musical – but, as the Japanese director observed, that letter was definitely post-marked Toronto. "We've always felt that there is a Canadian angle," says Don McKellar, "which is sort of the Man in Chair, that he has this perspective outside of Broadway. In a way, he's watching as we watched from across the border and imaging what it's like and being titillated by it, and also critical."[26]

Co-author Bob Martin is a former artistic director of *Second City*, and co-creator of the superb TV mini-series *Slings and Arrows*, and Don McKellar is an actor, writer and film maker of some note in Canada. Through the character of the "Man In Chair", it possesses that detached irony that has long been a trademark of Canadian humour. Although few foreign observers pick up on this, it is clear to me that the Man In Chair's apartment is in Toronto. The souvenir programme that was sold at the theatre makes it clear that he visits New York *as a tourist*. He views Broadway from a distance. In fact, crucially, he has never actually seen his favourite 1920s musical of the title; he simply knows it by its cast album – the same way I first became acquainted with the great Broadway shows. (I didn't see a musical in New York until 1996, after I'd been writing them for almost twenty years.)

Lisa Lambert told me, "For me, the apartment is my bedroom in the North Toronto house I lived in growing up in Toronto – my crappy record player and Broadway cast recordings I stole from my mother's collection."

Since *Drowsy*, Nicholaw and Martin have collaborated on *Minsky's*, with music by Charles Strouse and lyrics by Susan Birkenhead based on the 1968 film *The Night They Raided Minsky's*, which tried out at the Ahmanson Theatre, opening 6 February 2009. He also collaborated with Thomas Meehan on the book for the 2010 Christmas show *Elf*, also directed by Nicholaw, with music by Matthew Sklar and lyrics by Chad Beguelin. .

The Drowsy Chaperone was not the only Canadian success in New York that year. Three graduates from Queens University brought their camp fringe show *Evil Dead – the*

Musical from Toronto's Tranzac Club to New York's off-Broadway New World Stage, where it opened on November 1, 2006. The idea was first conceived in a bar in 2002 when comedy writer George Reinblatt was enjoying a drink with fellow Queens alumni Christopher Bond, who was appearing in a production of *The Rocky Horror Show* at the time. They decided that they too could create a cult horror musical, based on Sam Raimi's *Evil Dead* series. With Raimi's blessing, they brought in composer Frank Cipolla and put it together on the fly. They thought they were doomed when it opened on the night of the great Toronto blackout, when even the streetcars were left – quite literally – dead in their tracks. But then a strange thing happened. Line-ups began forming for tickets. People were willing to wait ten hours just to get in. Word spread, and *Evil Dead* fans from all over North America began to congregate. This attracted the attention of producer Jeffrey Latimer, who had presented the Toronto production of *Forever Plaid*. He booked it in to the Montreal *Just for Laughs* festival, which then attracted American interest. Multiple Tony award-winning choreographer Hinton Battle signed on as a co-director for the New York production. It played for 126 performances and 34 previews before shuttering on 17 February 2007. A cast recording was issued by Time Life Music. It then moved back to Toronto where it enjoyed another run of four months at the Diesel Playhouse. A Korean production opened in Seoul in 2008.

When *The Drowsy Chaperone* opened on Broadway, Bob Martin said "In terms of creating shows for Broadway, I would hope that *Drowsy Chaperone* shows that it is possible."[27] I had hoped that Toronto would respond to all of this activity by getting a bee in its collective bonnet. Yet Toronto's commercial theatres seem to have been in sleep mode. (Many believe the city has yet to fully recover from the 2002 outbreak of SARS.) The 2007 edition of the *Time Out Toronto* guide says, "For the past 20 years, Toronto has been passing itself off as the third largest theatre centre in the English speaking world, after London and New York. This holds true in terms of the number of venues and independent theatre companies in the city, but is debatable in terms of quality or government support."[28] It is often claimed that the market is too small to support a viable commercial theatre, but Garth Drabinsky claimed that his production of *Phantom of the Opera* drew on a market of twenty million people from a 250-mile radius of the city.

Is Toronto really "Broadway North"? I've argued that Toronto's theatre district needs a brand. Like Broadway and the West End, the area on King and Yonge Streets where the Royal Alexandra, Princess of Wales, Elgin/Winter Garden, Panasonic and Ed Mirvish theatres are located needs an identity. The potential is there: these theatres, in addition to the Sony and St. Lawrence Centres and the Four Seasons Opera House, as well as Roy Thomson and Massey Halls are all in easy walking distance of each other, and are close to the top hotels and restaurants. Perversely, the area that advertises itself as the "Entertainment District" does not include the theatres of Yonge Street, nor the St. Lawrence Centre. This is the equivalent to Broadway not including the theatres on Forty-Second Street, or the West End ignoring Shaftesbury Avenue. I received the following "explanation" from the office of the Toronto Entertainment District Business

Improvement Area: "Our mandate is to support and promote the businesses located within our boundaries only...I believe it would be the responsibility of the City of Toronto and Tourism Toronto to promote Toronto theatres as a whole."[29] I know that we Canadians like to shoot ourselves in the foot, but do we have to actually shove our big toes up the barrel of the gun?

Sadly, we Canadians have an unfortunate habit of stepping back from the brink of greatness. In the same week that my book *Broadway North: The Dream of a Canadian Musical Theatre* came out, Canadian Stage presented a new Canadian musical called *The Story of My Life* with songs by Neil Bartram and book by Brian Hill, starring Brent Carver and Jeffrey Kuhn. Bartram, from Burlington, Ontario, and Hill, from Kitchener, met in Toronto while performing in the revue *Forever Plaid* in the early 1990s. Their previous musical *Somewhere in the World* ran for five seasons in Charlottetown.

The Story of My Life tells of a lifelong friendship between a writer (Carver) and his childhood friend and muse, told in flashbacks after the latter's death. I considered this lovely little show to be a shining example of all that was right with Canadian musical theatre, but alas the Toronto critics had other ideas. The *National Post*'s Robert Cushman said it was "close to unbearable", and even made reference to the title of my book in saying, "This isn't the dream of a Canadian musical, and it's too mild even to be the nightmare of an American one."[30]

However, that was not the end of the line for *The Story of My Life*. On February 19, 2009, it opened at the Booth Theatre on Broadway in a production directed by Richard Maltby Jr., starring Will Chase and Malcolm Gets. Ben Brantley in the *New York Times* wrote: "In addition to jettisoning the usual excesses of tourist-trapping extravaganzas, they have tossed away such niceties as originality, credibility, tension

145

and excitement."[31] *Variety*'s David Rooney said, "This flavorless new musical is not exactly terrible, but it's not terribly interesting, either."[32] But Michael Kuchwara of Associated Press disagreed. He called it "a heartfelt little musical that has the courage of its sweet-tempered, low-key convictions."[33] Peter Filichia, in his *Theatremania* blog, concluded that "it deserved far more respect than it got."[34] In a personal email to me, he cited author Ethan Mordden's assessment of the decline of the Broadway musical, saying that "stupid people like stupid things"[35]. Perhaps "sweet-tempered" and "low-key" is just too Canadian for New York. It closed after only five performances. It has been successfully mounted in Korea, and appears to have a future in regional theatre productions. Sadly, Canadian Stage's financial position has since deteriorated to the point that in the following season they produced no Canadian works – musical or non-musical – on their main stage.

In 2007, the Shaw Festival in Niagara-on-the-Lake, Ontario, presented the world premiere of *Tristan*, a musical by Jay Turvey, an actor with the company, and Paul Sportelli, the festival's musical director.   Based on a story by Thomas Mann, the show opened at the Courthouse Theatre on 28 July 2007, directed by Eda Holmes. Turvey and Sportelli had previously collaborated with librettist Morwyn Brebner on the Dora Mavor Moore award-winning *Little Mercy's First Murder* at Toronto's Tarragon Theatre in 2003, so hopes were high. The *Hamilton Spectator* called it a "brave and beautiful evening of theatre"[36], and the *Niagara Falls Review* proclaimed, "Instead of just staging excellent musicals, [the Shaw Festival]'s now creating them."[37] Alas, the Toronto papers were less generous. Richard Ouzounian of the *Toronto Star* found it to be "a well-intentioned disappointment"[38], while *Now*'s Jonathan Kaplan wrote, "The composers' songs are often elegant and moving, alternately simple and richly textured, their lyrics clever. The narrative, however, with its talk of art and love, is too stretched-out to hold our interest."[39]

In 2011, they followed it up with *Maria Severa*, starring Julie Martell as Maria, which opened at the Courthouse Theatre on August 5, 2011, directed by Jackie Maxwell. "The score is a considerable achievement", said *Variety*'s Richard Ouzounian. "Unfortunately, the book Turvey and Sportelli have concocted doesn't have the weight or the originality of their songs. It's a pretty predictable affair about an aristocratic bullfighter, Armando (Mark Uhre), who falls in love with the lowly Maria (Julie Martell) but loves her for her art as well as her physical charms."[40] In a similar review in *The Star*, he elaborated that "their story of the poor Portuguese prostitute who invented the art song form known as *fado* demands a score of passionate depth and they provide it. Haunting melodies, unexpected harmonies and ever-changing rhythms are just a few of the things they do to make their music soar. And the lyrics fit smoothly and often powerfully to fill in the feelings underneath."[41] "The songs they've written for Maria herself," says the *National Post*'s Robert Cushman, "are melodically moody and

146

rhythmically complex; a number that she shares with a street-walker friend, titled 'Bread and Butter', comes over like Portugal's answer to Brecht and Weill. Sometimes the score strays further afield, or maybe that should be closer to home; the ensemble number "At the Bullfight", is high-end contemporary Broadway, and so, even more, is the beautiful love-duet 'I Can't Touch You with Words'. The lyrics can be pungent, though they can also, too often, sound earnestly explanatory." [42] Like Ouzounian, he found the weakness to lie with the book, which he felt was strong on atmosphere but weak on structure.

In 2009, Tarragon produced *Mimi, or A Poisoner's Comedy*, a musical about French serial killers with book and lyrics by comic actors Nick Roberts and Melody Johnson and music and additional lyrics by Allen Cole, whose previous scores have included *Pélagie* and *The Wrong Son*. Richard Ouzounian of the *Star* wrote, "When this show is good, it's very, very good, but when it's bad, it's better."[43] Robert Cushman of the *National Post* wrote, "The delight of *Mimi*… is that it's written by people who know how. That makes it a phenomenon among new musicals, Canadian or other."[44] Only Christopher Hoile of *Eye* didn't quite agree: "A musical so ineptly written and directed it is a waste of the considerable talents of all those involved."[45]

Of course, Ontario is not the only part of Canada where musicals are being developed. In Winnipeg, there is a group calling itself White Rabbit Productions (formerly the Canadian Musical Theatre Development Group) that aims to develop new work through workshops and showcases. Although it is a small city, it has always been a place of cultural importance. In the 1950s, the Manitoba Theatre Centre became Canada's first regional theatre, and the Royal Winnipeg Ballet is world-renowned.

Winnipeg writer and composer Danny Schur has taken an independent road to success, and managed against the odds. Already known as the composer of the theme song for the 1999 Pan Am Games, his musical *Strike!* managed to achieve a certain degree of national attention, largely due to its historic subject matter. Based on a 1919 general strike in which a Ukrainian immigrant was killed by the Mounties, *Strike!* was workshopped privately in 2003, and mounted independently at an outdoor theatre in Kildonan Park two years later with backing from the labour movement and the Ukrainian community (of which Schur is a member). CBC Radio's said, "it's a story that fills your heart with goodness and hope and expectation for the future. Whether or not the specific aspects of this particular moment in history… will travel – I don't know."[46] The *Winnipeg Free Press* said, "*Strike!* is not so impressive that it takes the art of musical theatre anywhere it hasn't been before. But it is intelligent and curiously touching."[47] A revised version played at Saskatoon's Persephone Theatre, and a concert version was broadcast nationally on CBC Radio in 2007.

Canada has long had excellent training facilities for performers, beginning with the musical theatre program at the Banff Centre, to the more recent one at Toronto's Sheridan College, where Jim Betts teaches a course on Canadian musicals. Vancouver's Capilano University also offers a musical theatre course.

Canadian performers have long been a staple of Broadway and the West End, from Robert Goulet to Victor Garber. In 2012 the Stratford Festival's hit production of *Jesus Christ Superstar*, directed by Des McAnuff (1952-) opened on Broadway at the Neil Simon Theatre on 1 March 2012. Composer Andrew Lloyd Webber has described this production as "definitive", saying "I've never really been happy with it before... now it's right."[48] Alas, although it was nominated for a Tony award for best musical revival as well as for best featured performer Josh Young (as Judas), it closed on 1 July 2012 after only 116 performances. During the awards broadcast, presenter Ben Vereen evidently didn't know the name of North America's premier classical theatre company, calling it the "Stamford Festival". "That was really the last straw, wasn't it?"[49] says *Toronto Star* critic Richard Ouzounian.

With all of this activity, you would think that Canada's cultural leaders would take notice. You would be wrong. The Canadian Broadcasting Corporation, in particular, has yet to wake up and smell the latté. These mandarins act as a sort-of control valve to turn off the flow of oxygen whenever something looks like it might be in danger of getting too interesting. Over the past decade, a number of Canadian shows have enjoyed some measure of international success, including *Two Pianos, Four Hands* and *Da Kink in My Hair*. And yet, since cancelling Richard Ouzounian's Sunday afternoon series *Say It With Music* (from which the creators of *The Drowsy Chaperone* are said to have gained some of their inspiration), CBC Radio has virtually expunged show music from its national airwaves, claiming that the world's most popular theatrical form does not appeal to a wide enough audience. To be fair, they did broadcast live versions of Vincent de Tourdonette and Allen Cole's *Pelégie* and Danny Schur's *Strike*, (but only after these works had achieved a fair measure of success on stage) and a regional program called *North by Northwest* featured *Broadway North* five years after its publication. But the one organisation with the resources to nurture musical theatre writers is just plain not interested.

It seems unlikely that this situation will change any time soon: in September 2008, they appointed Denise Donlon, a former president of Sony Music Canada and one-time producer for rock-video channel MuchMusic as Executive Director of CBC Radio. Although she protests that "as a public broadcaster, we have to do our best to reflect the diversity of the country",[50] she has devoted her entire career almost exclusively to youth pop culture. Under her reign, Radio 2 has switched away from a classical format towards one that favours contemporary popular music. In April 2012, as a result of a $3 million cut in funding, all drama was eliminated from CBC Radio One.[51]

Although founded by Mavor Moore with the intention to develop new Canadian musicals, inadequate funding has led the Charlottetown Festival to the decision to largely abandon the development of new Canadian musicals on their main stage, and to mount imported shows like *Buddy*, *Hairspray* and *Ring of Fire*. "All of our cast, crew and everything we perform, produce and construct is done by Canadians", says the Confederation Centre's Chief Executive Jessie Inman. "Also, I believe that sometimes when a show meets the multicultural spirit in the evolution of Canada's multicultural society that from time to time we do pick a script that may not have originated in Canada, but it does meet our identity as a nation as a diverse national mosaic."[52] (In her vocabulary, "from time to time" evidently means "for the past half decade".)

The Centre was established in 1964 with a mandate to "inspire Canadians to celebrate the creative vision of Confederation and Canada's evolving nationhood by showcasing the nation's visual and performing arts and artists." Inman maintains, " I don't think that it's outside of our mandate to pick something that's written by someone else and we might refer to Johnny Cash [*Ring of Fire*] this year {2012} as an example."

Shows like *Ring of Fire* may keep the box office ticking over merrily, but they do nothing for the development of the indigenous form. Then again, perhaps Prince Edward Island and its largely American tourist audience is not the best development ground for Canadian theatre – musical or otherwise. "As you will realise," says Artistic Director Anne Allan, "we are now so conditioned to 'creating to sell' which can be most frustrating and yet necessary for the ongoing and future of Canadian musicals in a time which is very delicate in the arts. Each year I have tried to bring to the fore new works but risk because of untried material, is a difficult word for managements! The work continues with many workshops each year and we are working towards a brand new Canadian Musical for 2015. I will conduct two workshops this year [2012] in the hope that they will be presented for the 2014 50th [anniversary] celebration. I am a strong advocate for Canadian Theatre and new works. The 'We are Canadian Series' I created for the Young Company. *Canada Rocks – A Celebration*, was received with much success."[53]

But still Canadians with talent and ambition leave. Not just to earn more money, but to earn more respect. Film director Norman Jewison has said, "Artists need to feel that their work is appreciated. They need approval. When the encouragement to produce their best work doesn't exist in their own country, they go somewhere else..."[54] This problem is not unique to Canada. In Australia, they call it the "cringe factor". If it's home grown, it can't be good. And if it becomes too successful, the "tall poppy syndrome" will soon cut it down to size.

While Toronto has yet to emerge as the major theatre capital I believe it could potentially be, it is not dead. *We Will Rock You* and *Dirty Dancing* may not have been Canadian shows, but they did give Toronto one advantage: American tourists could come to Toronto to see a show that was not (yet) playing in New York. And their nationally televised search for a new Maria for Andrew Lloyd Webber's production of *The Sound of Music* did raise the profile of Toronto as a centre for musical theatre.

This trend began when Mirvish Productions hosted the North American premiere of *Buddy – the Buddy Holly Story* which had been selling out in London. They then transferred this production for a short-lived Broadway run. They had greater success with *Mamma Mia!*, which originally settled in for a 26 week Toronto run in 2000. When that show transferred to Broadway (with its Canadian star Louise Pitre in tow), they recast the Canadian production, and it continued for another four years.

With *Dirty Dancing*, a new precedent was established that I think could have interesting implications. This production, a stage adaptation of the film, originated in Australia, then transferred to London. Producer Amber Jacobsen told the *Globe and Mail*'s Kamal Al-Solaylee, "We Australians feel that we're quite like Canadians. We did think about that. We're part of the Commonwealth."[55] Since then, the Mirvishes have also hosted the North American premiere of *Priscilla, Queen of the Desert* prior to its Broadway engagement. It might be interesting if shows were to start moving directly between Melbourne or Sydney and Toronto, before trying their luck in London or New York.

One area in which Australia is ahead of Canada is in the encouragement of aboriginal musicals, although there have been some recent developments in this regard. Thomson Highway (1951-), Canada's pre-eminent native playwright collaborated with composer Melissa Hui on *Pimootewin (The Journey)*, an opera written entirely in Cree and based on First Nations legends. The story tells of how the Trickster and the Eagle, who miss their friends who have died, visit them in the land of the dead, and attempt to bring them back to life. It received its world premiere on 15 February 2008 at the St. Lawrence Centre in Toronto then mounted a regional tour. "When culture is alive, it's dynamic and relevant," director Michael Greyeyes told CBC News. "Our culture, Cree culture, is exactly that – it's always being redefined, reinvented, reinvigorated and so for us to in effect hijack the form of opera to tell our stories, Cree stories, I think is a really crucial lesson that we share with these communities."[56] Highway, himself a classically trained pianist, is the author of the hit plays *The Rez Sisters* and *Drylips Ought to Move to Kapuskasing*.

Beyond Eden is a show written by two white men that tells the true story of an attempt to save the totem poles of the ancient Haida village of Ninstints, a United Nations World Heritage site in Northwestern British Columbia. Bruce Ruddell, a composer of choral and chamber music and Bill Henderson (1944-), a former member of the rock band Chilliwack worked together on the show that premiered during Vancouver's Cultural Olympiad in 2010. It was the culmination of thirty years' work for Ruddell, who was inspired by his friendship with Bill Reid, the late Haida carver who was involved in the original rescue attempt. After first trying it as a choral composition, it was Broadway director Harold Prince who suggested he turn it into a musical. *The Vancouver Sun*'s Peter Birnie wrote, "While this story of a real-life expedition in 1957 by Victoria anthropologists to recover (steal?) totem poles on Haida Gwaii is gorgeous to look at and lovely to listen to, it's also a genuinely compelling and largely successful attempt to blend 'white' and 'Indian' sensibilities."[57]

Cathy Elliot is a status member of the Mi'kmaq First Nation who is also a well-established composer, lyricist and book writer based near Toronto. Her previous works include *Fireweeds: Women of the Yukon*. She is the principal writer behind *The Talking Stick*, a presentation by the Confederation Centre's Young Company for the Summer 2011 Charlottetown Festival. A free forty-five minute lunchtime outdoor presentation, it includes First Nations stories and legends from across Canada, using music, dance and spoken word.

Perhaps the most promising developments are the announcement of a new company in Toronto called Theatre Twenty, and the creation of Sheridan College's Canadian Music Theatre Project. Launched at the Panasonic Theatre on 20 January 2011, Theatre Twenty will be an artist-run company dedicated exclusively to musical theatre. Among its members are Louise Pitre, Colm Wilkinson and Brent Carver, all of whom have trod the boards in both London and New York and even won Tony Awards. They also boast a commitment to new Canadian musicals, beginning with a workshop of an English version of a Quebec musical based on Michel Tremblay's play *Les Belles Soeurs*. Its initial season, beginning in 2013, will include a production of Stephen Sondheim and George Furth's 1970 Broadway musical *Company*, and *Bloodless*, by Winnipeg composer Joseph Aragon, based on the notorious Edinburgh body-snatchers Burke and Hare. It will be directed by Wilkinson.

Vancouver also has a new company dedicated to treating musical theatre as an art form. Patrick Street Productions presented Adam Guettel and Craig Lucas' *The Light in the Piazza* in September 2011, winning the Jessie Richardson award for outstanding production. "We have a huge creative community in the theatre, and they all go 'I want to do it my way'", Artistic Producer Peter Jorgensen told *The Georgia Straight*'s Janet Smith. "That's the way [wife] Katey and I started too. I had a certain idea of how musicals should be done, and I wanted to see if I could make that happen."[58] In the same year, Touchstone Theatre, together with the Arts Club Theatre presented *In Tune Conference –Creating the Great Canadian Musical*. Among the guest speakers were composer-lyricist Jim Betts, who was a student of Lehman Engel. Their purpose, according to their press release was to "engage in a community-wide consideration and celebration of how we currently develop new musicals in Canada, and what kind of scenarios might encourage more work and greater success and profile for work created." A second conference is planned for 2013.

The Canadian Music Theatre Project, like Denmark's Uterus workshop, is attached to an established musical theatre school, in this case Sheridan College in

Oakville, Ontario. Their first two projects, *Come from Away* by David Hein and Irene Sankoff, and *Central Park Tango* by Robert Gontier and Nicky Phillips were showcased at Toronto's Panasonic Theatre on 10 April 2012. "Establishing a permanent headquarters for the development of new musicals is a culturally significant event in Canada"[59], says Michael Rubinoff, Associate Dean of Sheridan's performing arts school.

As a centre for commercial theatre, Toronto remains a city on its way up. Its history hasn't happened yet. Novelist Nino Ricci has said, "Toronto is still deciding what it will be. We're still finding out what it means to be Torontonian. Our mythology has yet to be written."[60] Or, to quote one of the first hit Canadian show-tunes, it's still "waiting for the sunrise". The artists are ready. They just need to bring the public onside.

Larrikins and Sentimental Blokes: Musicals Down Under

When Mark Twain visited Sydney in 1895 he described the Australians as "English friendliness with the English shyness and self-consciousness left out."[61] Until my own recent visit, all of my perceptions of Australia came from the films of Peter Weir, Bruce Beresford and Gillian Armstrong. *Picnic at Hanging Rock*, *Breaker Morant* and *My Brilliant Career* were my touchstones. For many other people – especially in Britain – Australia is the land of Kylie Minogue and of the TV soap opera in which she once starred, *Neighbours*. (Two of my colleagues who assisted me with this book, Peter Pinne and Ray Kolle, were writers for that show.) My introduction to Australian musical theatre came through *Once in a Blue Moon*, a CD made in 1994 by the Australian Broadcasting Corporation featuring the Melbourne Symphony Orchestra with guest soloists in a television concert of songs from Australian shows.

I had always suspected that if my homeland were to be twinned with any other country, it would be our antipodean cousins. Both are former British colonies, with relatively small populations spread over a vast territory, much of which is barely fit for human habitation. Both are also under foreign cultural domination, from which they have sought liberation and validation. Australia has one advantage over Canada – its isolation from the rest of the world. That is also its disadvantage. (Similarly, Canada's proximity to the United States is both its advantage and its disadvantage.)

When I travelled from London to Sydney in November 2008, I flew across Russia and India, taking a gruelling twenty-one hours (not including my nine hour stop in Singapore). I had flown to the other end of the world to be in a country that was culturally so similar to my own. I was there to see a production by Kookaburra, Australia's National Musical Theatre Company, and to witness OzMade Musicals, a showcase of new Australian musical theatre. Wanting to gain a feel of the countryside, I travelled by train from Sydney to Melbourne. The 962 km journey took just over eleven hours, calling at stations with names like Wagga Wagga, Cootamundra and The Rock. Although we grazed the Southern Highlands of New South Wales, most of the journey was relatively flat and extremely dry. My fellow passengers informed me that it hadn't rained in seven years. Less than three months later, Victoria and parts of New South Wales would be devastated by bush fires, destroying 1,800 homes and killing 173 people.

In Melbourne I was a guest on a radio show called *Broadway at Bedtime*, presented by Will Conyers and P.J. Buchanan. Part of my initial impression had been that Australians projected a more confidant image than Canadians did, but I soon learned that they also suffered from something called the "cringe factor", similar to Canada's "national inferiority complex". Our two countries certainly had much in common – especially in our pursuit of a cultural identity. Will told me about the Australian actress Jill Perryman, M.B.E. (1933-), who worked in the business for some forty years, playing leading roles in shows like *Hello, Dolly!* before finally having a chance to sing in her own accent in *The Boy from Oz*.

Dr. Peter Wyllie Johnston, a theatrical historian at the University of Melbourne, and author of a number of articles on the history of Australian musicals, was one of those struck by the similarities between our countries. "You've got the physical commonality with a huge country spread over big distances… The creative people aren't all concentrated in one place… We have Melbourne and Sydney forever as rivals and neither of them really co-operating."

Comedy and Her Majesty's Theatres, Exhibition Street, Melbourne

Of those two cities, it is Melbourne, with a population of about three and a half million – slightly smaller than its rival – that comes the closest to having a Broadway-like, clearly defined theatre district. Actor John O'May told Will Conyers, "When you are performing at Her Majesty's and something's on at the Comedy and something's at the Princess and the Regent is going all of a sudden the city … is lit up … and it is one of the most exciting things… it becomes a part of what a city's life is." [62] You can stand in front of the Athenaeum Theatre in Collins Street and look over the road to the Regent. Both of these theatres have long histories: the Athenaeum dates from the 1830s, while the Regent – which has a ballroom attached beneath the 3,500 seat main auditorium – was built in 1929 as a cinema with live entertainment. Similarly, the Comedy and Her Majesty's Theatres are directly opposite each other in Exhibition Street, while the Princess is nearby in Spring Street, near the Victoria Parliament House. All were built on the sites of earlier nineteenth century theatres from the Victorian gold-rush era.

Sydney, on the other hand, has a less coherent infrastructure, having lost most of its historic theatres. There is no entertainment precinct per se. While there are several major venues, including both commercial and non-profit, they are spread out. The Seymour Centre, for example, where Kookaburra performed most of their shows, is part of the University of Sydney campus near Central Station, and lacks a street frontage and the nearby restaurants and coffee bars that support audience development.

In the past, Canadian and Australian actors worked freely in Britain in the days when a Commonwealth passport meant open borders. Cyril Ritchard, Keith Michell, Michael Blakemore and Sir Robert Helpmann were among a large Australian Diaspora in London, just as Christopher Plummer, Cec Linder and Bernard Braden were from Canada.

In the beginning, the Diaspora was long on talent and short on national identity. The Australian-born actor and playwright Oscar Asche (1871-1936) created the musical *Chu Chin Chow* as a reworking of the story of *Ali Baba and the Forty Thieves* in 1916, with music by Frederic Norton, an Englishman. In 1920, the Tivoli circuit brought it to Australia. The London production ran until 1921, making it one of the most popular musicals of that period.

John Stange Heiss Oscar Asche was born in Geelong, Victoria in 1871. His Norwegian father had practised law in Oslo, but had become an innkeeper after moving to Australia. Young Oscar was educated at Laurel Lodge, Dandenong, and travelled to China as a teenager. Upon his return, he articled for a short time with an architect, then lived in the bush and worked as a jackaroo (agricultural trainee) on a sheep station before announcing to his parents that he wanted to become an actor. His father sent him to study in Norway, where the playwright Henrik Ibsen told him he should return to his own country and work in his own language. Instead, he went to London and worked to lose all trace of his Australian accent. As a result, "Oscar Asche... was regarded as British," says Dr. Wyllie Johnston, "and if you look up a lot of English books on the musical, it's claimed as a British musical of course, and there's no reference to the fact that he was Australian."[63]

Such was the fate of any Australian who wanted to write musicals (or act in them, for that matter). Not only did they have to leave Australia, but they had to stop being Australian. There was no infrastructure at home to support them, and the commercial producers of the day took precious little interest in developing local talent. Again, something any Canadian could relate to.

The process of developing an indigenous Australian musical theatre has been a slow and laborious one. Among the first entirely Australian shows to be professionally staged was the mysteriously titled *FFF*, an "Australian Mystery Musical Comedy" by Clement John "Jack" De Garis (1884-1926) and Reginald Stoneham (1879-1942) that opened at the Prince of Wales Theatre in Adelaide on 28 August 1920. De Garis was a dried-fruit magnate with considerable charm as well as artistic ambitions. According to impresario Claude Kingston, in "one of those blinding mental flashes which he mistook for inspiration"[64], he conceived a musical comedy with a title whose significance was known only to himself (if even that). He managed to sell it to the Tivoli circuit's Hugh D. McIntosh, partly by flattering him by naming one of his characters "Hugh D. Collins".

(This was a man who was reputed to be so persuasive that he managed to sell a piece of real estate to a police officer who had just arrested him for writing bad cheques.)

Although the Adelaide production lost money, De Garis posted a guarantee against losses, allowing it to open in Perth on 29 September, where according to Claude Kingston, "takings hardly met the cost of lighting the theatre". Still, it moved on to Melbourne, where De Garis claimed "a record box office success"[65] when it opened at the King's Theatre on 9 October. The *Melbourne Herald* said, "There seems to be no adequate reason why Australian song-writers should not find as much inspiration in Croajingalong as the Americans have found in Dixie."[66]

Australia's southern neighbour, New Zealand, was also trying to establish its identity on the world stage. Established as a British colony in 1840, "English-speaking theatre became an integral part of its culture almost immediately", says Julie Jackson-Tretchikoff, a Ph.D. student at Auckland University, "although the predominantly English/Scottish European population in Auckland numbered only 2,000 compared with approximately 20,000 indigenous Maori."[67] The first musical theatre production, an evening of songs, was performed in a men's pub in 1841. Amateur operatic societies were formed, in part, because "the new migrants needed a sense of identity, of belonging to a community where the music was familiar in the harsh, frontier society so far from Great Britain".[68]

Although most of this activity involved amateur productions of British, European and, later, American musicals, some New Zealanders longed for the big-time, and to express their own voices. Poet and journalist Arthur Adams (1872-1936) teamed with Australian-born, Leipzig-trained composer Alfred Hill (1869-1960) to write an operetta called *Tapu, or a Tale of a Maori Pah*. When Adams showed this to Australian impresario J.C. Williamson in 1898, he bought it immediately, and hired Adams as his literary secretary.

The original Australian constitution had left a provision for New Zealand to join the Federation as a state, and at the time that *Tapu* was written, this was seriously under consideration. The plot is set in a Maori village, where an Australian delegate is awaited to discuss New Zealand's entry. At the same time, an acting troupe arrives on the scene, and their actor-manager is mistaken for the Australian diplomat. The title refers to a Polynesian concept of spiritual restrictions, and is the origin of the English word "taboo". *Tapu* received its world premiere in Wellington's Opera House on 16 February 1903.

J.C. Williamson saw the show in Wellington. This renewed his interest, and he mounted a tryout production in Auckland before moving it to Melbourne, Brisbane and Sydney. The *New Zealand Times* announced that, "For the first time on any stage there was produced an opera which essentially belongs to New Zealand".[69] However, the critics reserved all of their praise for Hill, and Adams had evidently abandoned the book to other hands long before the opening. The late New Zealand broadcaster Peter Harcourt wrote, "Adams had simply failed to get the mixture right. His theatre people, with their posturings and protestations, were figures of fun who amused him and gave him an opportunity to mock their blurring of fantasy and reality. The Maori characters were another thing altogether, and the use of more or less authentic Maori poi dances and the haka never failed to bring an ecstatic audience response. In short, the component parts of Adams' libretto were like oil and water and no amount of shaking and stirring would ever have caused them to blend."[70] His play *Mrs. Pretty and the Premier* was presented by Melbourne Repertory Theatre in 1914 and at His Majesty's in London in 1916.

After *Tapu*, Hill teamed up with another journalist, the American-born John Youlin Birch (1872-1951) to write *A Moorish Maid* (1905). While its initial productions in Auckland and Wellington were well received, an attempt to bring it to London ultimately collapsed. Hill would go on to become on of Australia's leading composers, and was appointed to the Order of the British Empire and a Companion of the order of St. Michael and St. George. Both Adams and Hill would make their careers in Australia.

For much of its history, commercial theatre in Australia and New Zealand – and especially musical theatre – was dominated by one company: J.C. Williamson Ltd., known to people in the business as "The Firm". At one point it even claimed to be the largest theatrical firm in the world. James Cassius Williamson (1845-1913) was actually an American who had come to Australia on tour as a dialect comedian under contract to George Coppin. Four years later, he acquired the Australasian rights to *H.M.S. Pinafore* for £300. To Williamson, "A good play should appeal to the eye, to the heart and to the mind, in that order."[71] For the next thirty years, he built up an empire that included the Princess and Her Majesty's theatres in Melbourne and Her Majesty's in Sydney (among others), for which he imported stars such as Sarah Bernhardt. He fought – successfully, for a time – against the formation of an Australian actors' union. The company was often accused of behaving like a monopoly, and of taking little or no interest in the development of indigenous Australian theatre, claiming that Australian audiences did not want to see themselves on stage. "The commercial theatre has, at times, resembled the last bastion of colonialism", wrote lecturer, actor and director Malcolm Robertson in 1977, "as it has sought desperately to preserve its dependence on the English theatre and, to a lesser extent, the American theatre, for its continuous existence, seemingly oblivious to what was happening around it."[72]

When Williamson died in 1913, the control of "The Firm" passed to four brothers, John, Nevin, E. J. and Frank Tait, who in conjunction with other partners (Williamson's former associate Sir George Tallis, Ernest C. Rolls) guided the company for the next half century. Some of their successes included the D'Oyly Carte Opera Company, the Borovansky Ballet and, in 1947, a tour of *Annie Get Your Gun* that heralded a stream of imported Broadway musicals.

At first it was the Australian performers, rather than writers, who managed to break through and light up the stages, both at home and abroad. "We became known as a sort-of glorified summer stock out here", says actor Tony Sheldon (1955-), whose grandmother was a leading lady in the Tivoli variety circuit. At the beginning of the twentieth century, companies such as J.C. Williamson would import the entire original casts of shows from England and America, including silent film star Harry Langdon in *Anything Goes*. Gradually, they began sending out the second string casts – the understudies who would still invariably be billed as 'Direct from Broadway', with Australians playing supporting roles.

Then the Second World War began, and the ships carrying the imported stars stopped coming. "Rather than not do anything, we started a series of revivals of shows like *No No, Nanette*," Sheldon explains. "We became very, very good at reproducing Broadway musicals using Australian performers. Rather than creating original works, we cultivated the performers. We became known for our energy, for our commitment, for being triple threats: we have very good dancer-singer-actors in Australia – a lot more than in England. All the way through to the sixties and seventies, we compared very, very favourably against English performers who were known as being wishy-washy in comparison to the very robust Australian style of performing, which came from our culture. We're a beach culture; we're an outdoor culture. The dance teachers were tougher... We suddenly realised, 'yes, we are capable of performing leads'."

Then in 1957, *The Pajama Game* was presented with an all-Australian cast. This happened because a proposed tour by Margot Fonteyn had been postponed, leaving theatres in Melbourne, Sydney and Adelaide dark. The star was Sheldon's mother, Toni Lamond (1932-), half-sister of singer Helen Reddy. "J.C. Williamson took a bit of a risk with that", says Sheldon. "It went through the roof. It ran two and a half years." The cast also included Bill and John Newman and Tiki Taylor (John Newman's wife), who sang "Steam Heat". Although J.C. Williamson returned to their old practice of importing leads for *My Fair Lady*, the precedent had been set. Jill Perryman got the lead in *Funny Girl*, and Nancye Hayes (1943-) played *Sweet Charity*.

Today, Australia still produces top-drawer musical theatre performers, including Caroline O'Connor (1962-), Philip Quast (1957-) and Hugh Jackman (1968-). Unusually, the leading school for musical theatre, the Western Australian Academy of Performing Arts – of which Jackman is an alumnus – is located in Perth, at the opposite end of the country from the two leading theatre centres of Sydney and Melbourne. Sheldon is on the faculty there. Over seven hundred people a year audition for eighteen places (nine men and nine women). Other major programs include the National Institute of Dramatic Art in Sydney and the University of Ballarat in Victoria.

Of course, for Australia to really have a vibrant musical theatre scene, they would have to create their own shows. *Collits' Inn* with book by Sydney journalist Thomas Stuart Gurr (1884-1967) and music and lyrics by Isobel Varney Monk (1892-

1967) was the result of a 1932 Light Opera and Revue Competition sponsored by Sydney singing teacher Nathalie Rosenwax. The setting for the story was the historic inn built in 1823 by Pierce Collits, an Irish convict who had been transported to New South Wales twenty-two years previously. The story was a highly romanticised account of Collits' daughter's marriage.

Although it failed to win first prize, Rosenwax decided to mount a production of *Collits' Inn* with her students in Sydney in December 1932. The opening was attended by the New South Wales governor. There was a repeat performance at Mosman Town Hall in March 1933, and in June an abridged version was broadcast nationally on the Australian Broadcasting Commission's radio network. They then submitted it to J.C. Williamson Ltd., but were told that it was no good. Then, when they were ready to give up, Melbourne-based film producer Francis William Thring (1882-1936) came forward, saying that "a country which could produce a [Nellie] Melba, a Florence Austral and many other world-famous names, should surely possess individuals capable of providing the material for musical productions equal to those from abroad."[73] He had equally ambitious plans for the Australian film industry, having in 1931, written, produced and directed *Diggers*, the first successful Australian sound feature.

Hoping that it would be the first in a series of Australian musicals, Thring opened *Collits' Inn* at the Princess Theatre in Melbourne on 23 December 1933 starring Gladys Moncrieff (1892-1976), Australia's most popular star of light opera who had made her name in the English operetta *The Maid of the Mountains* in Melbourne in 1921. This expanded version of *Collits' Inn*, which employed Australia's first revolving stage, contained the "corroboree ballet", said to be a transcription of an authentic aboriginal chant that Monk heard in Kiama which she hoped would rival the "totem" dance in *Rose-Marie*. According to Wyllie Johnston, Monk's transcription of the chant was pretty accurate in its original version. "Unfortunately, the musical director of the Thring production took it upon himself to change the [time] signature. It's in 9/8 in the original, but [he changed it] to 3/4. It suddenly becomes rather conventional."

The Age said that "the most uproarious enthusiasm with which the play was received from start to finish, and the gasps of amazement and admiration that resounded through the theatre as that ingenious novelty a revolving stage revealed several scenes of spectacular colour and beauty left no doubt at all as to the success of the show." *Smith's Weekly* said "its Australian—and its good". The Sydney *Daily Telegraph* said "It was with a distinct shock that the audience realised that this play was Australian; that some one had had the audacity to use gum trees (magnificently reproduced gum trees) as a setting; that someone had realised the potentialities of a corroboree for ballet. Something for even New York to become excited about." The Melbourne *Argus* proclaimed "It satisfies as no *Rose-Marie* or *Lilac Time* can satisfy." It ran for sixteen weeks in Melbourne before moving to the New Tivoli Theatre in Sydney for eight weeks.

Thring had ambitious plans to make a film of the show, but they were never realised. Only a sound recording (on nitrate film) was ever made, and this is now preserved in Australia's National Film and Sound Archive. Thring produced a second Varney Monk musical, *The Cedar Tree*, which opened 22 December 1934 at the Princess Theatre in Melbourne, also starring Gladys Moncrieff. According to Dr. Wyllie Johnston, "J.C. Williamson, the huge theatre chain in Australia… were very upset that Thring was being so successful, and so when *The Cedar Tree* moved from a successful season in Melbourne to another season in Sydney, they gave it the worst theatre in town, and it closed after three or four weeks in the middle of a summer heat wave." Thring died in 1936.

Collits' Inn sparked a brief flurry of activity that would include *Blue Mountain Melody* for J.C. Williamson with music and lyrics by Charles Zwar (1911-89), (whom Thring had hired to augment the *Collits' Inn* score, adding the song "They're in Love") and a book by cartoonist J.C. Bancks (creator of the *Ginger Meggs* comic strip) and starring Cyril Ritchard which opened on 22 September 1934 at Sydney's Theatre Royal. "A lot of Australian stuff was terrible," Sheldon says, referring to some of the other nameless product that ensued. "We deserved to have the cringe factor."

As in Canada, many of those who had talent left for greener pastures. Zwar moved to London, where he played piano for revues at the Gate Theatre near Charing Cross. He contributed songs to *Sweet And Low*, *Sweeter And Lower* and *Sweetest And Lowest* with Hermione Gingold and had a modest hit in 1952 with *Bet Your Life* starring Arthur Askey, Julie Wilson and Sally Ann Howes. In New York, where Gingold had already used some of his songs in *Murray Anderson's Almanac*, a revue of his songs – *From A to Z* – ran briefly at the Plymouth Theatre, and back in London, his musical *Marigold* (with lyrics by Alan Melville) was staged in the West End at the Savoy for seventy-seven performances in 1959.

Edmond Samuels (1895-1973) was a Sydney pharmacist (and proprietor of the "world-famous headache bar") who also "dabbled" in writing popular songs. Many of his customers were theatre people – he touted himself as a "hangover expert" – and as a result he managed to have one of his songs performed at the Tivoli variety theatre. As a regular first-night theatre-goer, he became particularly enamoured of musicals such as *Showboat* and *Rose Marie*. "I studied the production methods, becoming deeply immersed in this type of show", he later wrote. "Being so very Australia-minded, I felt it was time someone created a musical with an Australian flavour, using our natural scenery for its setting."[74] Encouraged initially by F. W. Thring, he wrote *The Highwayman*, but found no takers in his native country. With English book writers Guy Bolton and Clifford Grey[75], he rewrote it as *At the Silver Swan*, the "first attempt by a young, super-patriotic and ambitious Australian to present a musical play with an Australian background on the London stage."[76] It opened at the Palace Theatre, London starring Alice Delysia on 19 February 1936 (after a tryout in Glasgow) and closed after fifty-three[77] tortuous performances.

160

Fourteen years later, Samuels would try again, this time in his own country. He even managed to interest the theatrical giant J.C. Williamson in backing his venture under its original title, *The Highwayman*. This was no mean feat; Williamson's were notoriously disinterested in local talent, on or off stage. However, what they actually did was to encourage him to death (almost). Samuels had seen it all before in London, where it appears that some "angels" hadn't quite earned their wings: his backer's auditions for *Silver Swan* exposed him to the quasi-criminal machinations of some theatrical financiers. In Australia, Williamson's kept stalling on signing a contract, and shortening the length of booking they could promise him.

Finally, he joined with expatriate American director Carl Randall and managed to snatch the "resting" cast of the recently closed *Annie Get Your Gun* from under the Williamson's noses. He booked the King's Theatre in Melbourne, controlled by the Fullers' group, JCW's competitors, where it received a warm reception. Perhaps too warm: Melbourne was in the throes of the worst heat wave in half a century, and the King's Theatre had no air conditioning. Still, it ran for three months and was seen by 100,000 people.

They decided to transfer the show to Sydney, where Samuels secured another Fullers' theatre, the Palace. Only a five-week slot was available, and the theatre was small, but Samuels preferred to stay out of the Williamson's stable. The Australian Broadcasting Commission aired a condensed version of the show on radio, and EMI eventually made a recording of excerpts from the score.

"There [were] key people spread around the place at different times who created musicals seemingly, sometimes, out of nothing", says Dr. Wyllie Johnston. As was the case in Canada, "when you do the research you find there's actually a big background there. In many cases [we find] people with a lot of depth of knowledge and understanding who've done a lot of work about how to write shows and eventually have at least one success." Although, unlike Canada, Australia never had any equivalent to either the Lehman Engel workshops or the Charlottetown Festival, "we did have a few people who went to the West End and came back determined to try to create something of a good standard." However, distance was always a problem – not just the distance between centres, but from the rest of the world and the creative communities. "If they had a success, it came, it went, people forgot about it. There was nothing that really kept the whole tradition alive."

The Phillip Street Theatre, established in Sydney by the Scottish-born impresario William Orr in 1954, was one of the first regular outlets for writers. John McKelllar created the *Phillip Street Revues* (1954-71), which, like Canada's *Spring Thaw*, "for the first time held a mirror up to Australian culture, particularly suburban culture," according to Tony Sheldon. Even the expatriates were persuaded to return: Charles Zwar contributed to 1964's *Is Australia Really Necessary?* Other productions included *A*

Cup of Tea, A Bex and a Good Lie Down (1965). Among the acts to emerge from these revues was "Dame Edna Everage", the brainchild of actor Barry Humphries' (1934-). This led to other offshoots: *Revue '60* was a television show whose English-born head writer Chris Bearde (1936-) later went to Toronto and wrote for *Nightcap*, the *Spring Thaw*-influenced CBC local satirical show that would inspire *Rowan and Martin's Laugh-In*. When the latter show began in 1968, Bearde teamed with Canadian writer Alan Blye to join that show's writing staff in "beautiful downtown Burbank".

Lola Montez: Frank Wilson and the Ladies of the Town
Photo by Fred Carew from Elizabethan Theatres Trust production courtesy Peter Pinne

Lola Montez (1958), with music by Peter Stannard (1931-), lyrics by Peter Benjamin (1930-2008) and book by Alan Burke (1923-2007), told the story of the Irish-born Spanish dancer's time in the mining village of Ballarat, Victoria. It was originally tried out by the Union Theatre Repertory Company in Melbourne where it opened on February 19, 1958. The Australian Elizabethan Theatre Trust, established in 1954 as a nurturing body for the performing arts, then chose it for a full production. "Things happened thereafter beyond the authors' control",[78] Stannard told me. George Carden (1913-1981), an Australian expatriate who had choreographed the variety shows at the London Palladium for many years, was engaged as director-choreographer. He brought over one of his English dancers, Mary Preston, to play the lead role. Preston was then in her early twenties, while the real-life Lola had been thirty-seven when she came to Australia. "And Mary didn't have much of a voice", says Stannard. What the composer calls the "blown-up" version opened under their auspices on October 1 at Her Majesty's Theatre in Brisbane, where it ran for five weeks. While the critical reception was warm, the audiences were small, and things did not improve when it opened in Sydney on October 22. Still, EMI produced a cast album – the first stereo recording to be made in Australia, and so the show's reputation grew. One song, "Saturday Girl", was touted as Australia's first hit show tune. It was later produced on both radio (1959) and television (1962). A revised version opened December 3, 1988 at the Playhouse Theatre, Canberra. "The show still bobs up somewhere in the country every now and again," Stannard says. "Even Japan plays some of the music on radio and the trickle of royalties is welcome!"

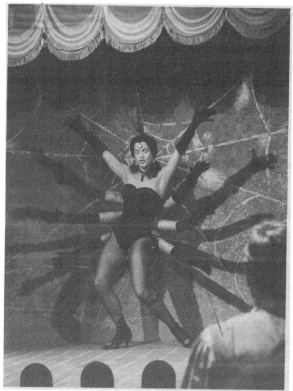

Brigid Lewisham (Lola) performs her Spider Dance in ABC-TV's production of *Lola Montez*, telecast nationally on May 7, 1962.
Photo courtesy Peter Stannard

The same writing team were later commissioned by the ATN7 network to write a musical for television called *Pardon Miss Westcott*, which was broadcast nationally on Christmas Eve, 1959. Since then, Stannard has largely returned to his day job as an advertising executive, with occasional forays into music and theatre.

"The trap we fell into was trying to emulate the Broadway musical, and we just weren't good at it", says actor Tony Sheldon. "It was strange to do a show about Lola Montez coming to the gold fields in about 1850, which is about miners. Everybody goes, 'let's make it like *Paint Your Wagon*', but Australians don't want to see a bunch of gold miners getting up and doing dance numbers because it's not in the Australian character."

While *Lola Montez* seemed to be following the American model, *The Sentimental Bloke* by Albert Arlen (1905-1993), Nancy Brown (1909-2003) and Lloyd Thomson, revealed an English influence. Peter Wyllie Johnston calls it "our most successful original score of the twentieth century". Arlen had worked as a musician and composer in London, where his *Alamein Concerto* (1944) had been recorded by Mantovani. He began working on *The Sentimental Bloke* in 1950, based on C.J. Dennis's poems *Songs of a Sentimental Bloke*, (which had also been made into a silent movie in 1919) but it took more than ten years for it to reach the stage. This show managed to tap into Australia's "larrikin" humour of defiance of authority and irreverent self-deprecation. He tried to interest managements in both Australia and London, but with no success. Finally he and his wife Nancy Brown mounted it themselves with an amateur cast at Albert Hall in Canberra on 7 March 1961.[79] This came to the attention of theatrical giant J.C. Williamson, who presented it in what was meant to be a limited six week season at Melbourne's Comedy Theatre on 4 November 1961.[80] Edwin Ride played the title role, as he did in the original amateur production. This was extended to five months, then a tour was mounted to Adelaide, Brisbane, Sydney and New Zealand. Nancy Brown later complained, "Not one management asked us if we had anything else we could show them. Our work went as if for nothing."[81]

At this time, there were a handful of Australians who were having some success abroad. Queensland-born Ron Grainer (1922-1981), now best remembered as the composer of the *Dr. Who* theme, collaborated with English librettist Ronald Millar (1919-98) for *Robert and Elizabeth*, based on *The Barratts of Wimpole Street*, which enjoyed a healthy run of 948 performances at the Lyric Theatre in London's West End in 1964, which producer Garnet H. Carroll later brought home to Australia.

In parallel to the Canadian experience, Australia also began to develop a more nationalistic "alternate" theatre. Both countries were influenced in this by London's Unity Theatre and by Joan Littlewood's Theatre Workshop. "By the 1950s", explains Dr. Wyllie Johnston, "you had a grass-roots movement that grew up that was strongly connected to the trade union movement, which was very concerned to depict other parts of Australian life." *Reedy River*, which premiered at Melbourne's left-wing New Theatre on 11 March 1953, had a book by Dick Diamond (1906-89) about a shearers' strike in the 1890s that made use of traditional folk songs. "This was considered very radical and not terribly okay by the establishment and by the prevailing political forces of the 1950s when the conservative government was in power under [Robert] Menzies. Yet it had tremendous popular support and went right around Australia and travelled to London where it was also successful."

Robyn Archer (1948-), Australia's leading interpreter of the songs of Brecht and Weill and of the Weimar cabaret says, "One can stage a biting anti-government satire which will be guaranteed to appeal to at least half the population, simply because no matter how the gerrymander works in favour of a Liberal Party [i.e. conservative] victory at elections, at least half the population always votes Labor."[82] "This was the beginning of a separate tradition of musical theatre which really took off a lot more in the late seventies and into the eighties when Nick Enright and Dennis Watkins came into their own and began to write musical theatre", says Dr. Wyllie Johnston.

The Ballad Of Angel's Alley was a 'pocket opera' concerning thieves and prostitutes by television writer Jeff Underhill (1927-78) and composer Bruce George. It was first tried out at Melbourne's New Theatre on Boxing Day in 1958 as a co-operative venture, because no commercial producer would take it on. "Most managements in this country can't even read a score", said Underhill at the time. "They have to go to New York or London to find a musical that they can put on here." [83] In 1962, it was successfully remounted by the Melbourne Theatre Company. Frank Murphy in *The Advocate* (Melbourne) called it "a delicious extravaganza, written in a mock serious style that capitally captures and sustains the old ballad melodramas".

Beginning on 14 May 1966, Melbourne's Emerald Hill Theatre presented Australia's first rock musical, *A Bunch of Ratbags*, with music by Peter Pinne (1937-) and lyrics by Pinne and Don Battye (1938-). The book by Battye was based on a novel by William Dick about gang warfare in Melbourne in the 1950s. Pinne says, "When Don Battye and I first started writing we deliberately eschewed going the 'gumnuts and wattle' route (period works about the bush and searching for gold etc.), which up until that time had been the subjects of the only Australian musicals we had seen. We wanted to write something about contemporary Australia." Leonard Radic in *The Age* wrote, "This is an all too rare venture in Melbourne's theatrical life – a locally written and commissioned musical which holds up the mirror to aspects of Australian life. On these grounds alone it is worth applauding... It has its deficiencies and its weaknesses, granted; it also has vitality, colour and a measure of authenticity."[84] Jean Battersby in the *Canberra Times* added, "The potential of this musical for large scale professional production is impossible to ignore."[85] Pinne and Battye would collaborate on several more musicals, including *Caroline*, *Red, White and Boogie* and *Prisoner Cell Block H*, which played in London's West End in 1995, starring Lilly Savage.

Another milestone in the progress toward a distinctly Australian musical style was *Flash Jim Vaux*, a ballad opera presented by Nimrod Theatre, where it opened 28 April 1972 with book and lyrics by former radio producer Ron Blair (1942-) and music by Terry Clarke and Charles Colman based largely on traditional tunes. Based on the true story of a prisoner who had been wrongly transported to Australia three times, "It worked because it was intrinsically Australian", says Tony Sheldon. "It suited the material. It wasn't imposing a sort of Broadway sensibility."

Reg Livermore (1938-), a veteran of the Phillip Street Revues who had appeared in the Australian cast of *Hair*, wrote a rock musical – with a score by Patrick Flynn – about *Ned Kelly*, which opened at the Adelaide Festival Theatre on 30 December 1977.

Grahame Bond (1943-) and Jim Burnett (1947-)'s *Boy's Own McBeth*, about a forty-two year old man who contrives to stay in school in order to secure free room and board, opened on 11 July 1979 at Kirk's Gallery in Sydney, and has, according to Peter Pinne, "been one of the most performed original Australian musicals playing over 600 performances around the country. It also played a gig in Los Angeles."

One of Australia's best known writers – both of musicals and straight plays – was the late Nick Enright (1950-2003), who may be best known internationally as the screenwriter of the film *Lorenzo's Oil*. "Nick in particular began to steer the musical in a more self-consciously Australian direction", says Dr. Wyllie Johnston, "but also one that had a bit more political substance in it." Some of Enright's shows as book writer and lyricist included *The Venetian Twins*, a two-act musical comedy based on Carlo Goldoni's 1747 play *I due gemelli veneziani* ("The two Venetian twins"), in turn based on the Menaechmi of Plautus; *Orlando Rourke* (1985) with music by Alan John (1958-), produced at the Adelaide Festival Centre by the State Theatre of South Australia; *Summer Rain* – about a travelling tent show in the outback in post-war New South Wales – with music by Terrence Clarke (1935-), first produced by the National Institute for Dramatic Arts at the Parade Theatre in Sydney on 19 October 1983 and later by the Sydney Theatre Company; and *Mary Bryant*, with a score by David King, which opened at the Ensemble Theatre, Sydney, on 5 September 1988 after a production at the Western Australia Academy of Performing Arts (Hugh Jackman's alma mater) in Perth.

Then, Australian musical theatre suffered one of its greatest box office setbacks. *Manning Clark's History of Australia – the Musical*, based on the six-volume history by Professor Manning Clark (1915-91), opened at Melbourne's Princess Theatre on 16 January 1988. The book was by Tim Robertson, John Romeril (1945-), and Don Watson (1949-), with music by Martin Armiger (1949-) and George Dreyfus (1928-), and it was produced by John Timlin.

It was mounted to commemorate the bicentennial of the establishment of the first permanent British settlement in Australia (which was, of course, a penal colony). "This was a musical which attempted to put a particular point of view about the history of Australia which accorded with Manning Clark's view, and which had tremendous support from the government at the time under Bob Hawke and a lot of other people but sadly, the public didn't buy it", says Dr. Wyllie Johnston. The *Sun News–Pictorial* declared it "A tawdry and tacky affair, enough to give the Bicentennial a bad name".[86] It ran for five weeks and then closed. "It's only been produced a couple of times since in amateur productions, and once in America by a Jewish guy from Melbourne who was a drama teacher who took it there to show the people in Texas and Arkansas and places like that the history of Australia from a rather left-wing point of view," says Wyllie Johnston. "One can't imagine how it went down."

David Reeves wrote the music for *Seven Little Australians* with lyrics by John Palmer (1940-) and book by Palmer and Peter Yeldham (1927-). It opened on 22 June 1988 at the Comedy Theatre, Melbourne. "That would be the closest thing we have to *Anne of Green Gables*," says Dr. Wyllie Johnston. The story, based on a novel by Ethel Turner, is about a widower with seven children. "It's a perennial part of Australian culture." It was presented as a large-scale production, "clearly influenced by Rodgers and Hammerstein, especially *The Sound of Music*." *Variety*'s review possibly reveals more about Australia's notorious cringe factor – not to mention civic rivalry – than it does about the show, complaining that it "trivializes the subject and sets Aussie legit back 90 years… Chances are this musical will best succeed in Melbourne, appealing as it does to a conservative, undemanding audience. First-nighters were in raptures. Families in search of old-fashioned idealism and innocuous entertainment will be pleased. More discerning folk in Sydney, however, might be less likely to pay top prices for something the likes of which they could see free of charge at their local shopping center any lunchtime."[87] It ran for about seven months in Melbourne, grossing around three million dollars.

The show that has probably achieved the highest international profile would be *The Boy from Oz*, with a book by Nick Enright telling the story of Australian singer and songwriter Peter Allen (1944-92), using Allen's own songs. Directed by Gale Edwards (1954-), it opened on 5 March 1998 at Her Majesty's Theatre, Sydney. Jill Perryman told me, "It took me fifty years of singing and acting in musicals from the U.S. before *The Boy from Oz* came along in which I was overjoyed to play the mother of Peter Allen who was such an icon in our musical history, and it *was* a strange feeling singing in a broad Australian accent."

"The authors went to great pains to work out what was Peter Allen's demon", says Tony Sheldon. "This man whose stage persona was this camp, devil-may-care, let's have a good time, 'I Go to Rio' thing, yet all his songs were about loss and loneliness. The author, Nick Enright, spent nine drafts trying to pin down what was the demon that drove this man. He pinned it down to his father's suicide. Peter Allen's father shot himself in front of Peter... when he was a child, and Peter and his mother were left to clean the blood off the walls. This was something that scars a person terribly. What they chose to do, through many drafts, was to not mention this – you just knew there was something dogging him until the end of the show. They kept the suicide off-stage, then it all built to the song 'Tenterfield Saddler', which he wrote about his father, which is Peter Allen's most personal song. It's what *The Boy from Oz* hangs on."

Sheldon draws a big breath. "The first thing that happens when they take the show to America is they cut the song. They cut the entire suicide as a plot point, and they finish with 'I Go to Rio' instead. And the producer gave an interview and said, 'Peter Allen never had a dark side.' So you've immediately emasculated the entire project in one fell swoop." The original Australian production sold around a million tickets and grossed about sixty million Australian dollars. The Broadway production, starring Hugh Jackman, had a new book by Charles Busch and a new American director. It ran for a year – the duration of Jackman's contract.

167

Director Gale Edwards followed *The Boy from Oz* in 2004 with *Eureka* (a musical about the 1854 Eureka stockade miners' rebellion) with book and lyrics by Maggie May Gordon, Gale Edwards and John Senczuk and music by Michael Maurice Harvey, a show which "celebrates our national story and I think that, as Australians, the audiences will want to stand up and cheer."[88] When critics failed to do that, she told Will Conyers, "*Eureka* is an interesting example of a show that drew on a tremendous wide range of Australian resources, and was very close to being fantastic, but was completely destroyed by the critics. I think Germaine Greer … gave it 'zero'. You can't give it 'zero'. Not acceptable. You can say that you didn't like this and this and this about it, but you can't actually give a show which cost five million dollars and drew on that kind of power and had that sort of expertise and was such a valiant and noble effort – you can't give it zero because that is actually contempt."[89] One of the cast members was Nancye Hayes, who told broadcaster Peter Thompson, "It's been a hard road to hoe with the Australian musical, but we will not give up, we are determined to get one up there."[90]

In recent years, the creation of new Australian musicals has been supported by a biannual prize established by Jeanne and Richard Pratt ($50,000 to the winners, plus $30,000 towards a workshop by Pratt's own The Production Company). "The purpose of this award is to stimulate the creation of music theatre," said Jeanne Pratt in a press release dated November 28, 2002. "When we began advertising for entries late last year, we expected we would get perhaps a dozen or two. With six weeks to go before entries closed – June 30 – we had 10 or 12. But in the following final weeks, another 132 entries came flooding in! Clearly, this award has been a powerful creative catalyst."

The first Pratt Prize was awarded to *Sideshow Alley* by Paul Keelan and Gary Young. The story tackled themes of acceptance and prejudice in a touring sideshow in 1950s Australia. Following a workshop directed by Gale Edwards, the show was picked up by Melbourne based producer Jim McPherson, whose massively successful tour of *Menopause – The Musical* had been directed by Young. A full stage production of *Sideshow*, under Young's direction, opened at the Playhouse in Brisbane in 2007. The authors aimed for a distinctly Australian feel to both the music and words. "I think it's time musicals became more Australian," said Gary Young. "Plays have become much more localised but musicals are late off the mark dealing with Australian stories. And this is an original story, script and score, set in Australia with Australian slang, about Australians."[91] He elaborates, "Where else in the world but here is any one going to say to you, 'Sorry mate, I was flat out like a lizard drinkin!' or 'I was off like a bride's nightie!' or 'Crikey love, you're all dolled up like a Mungandai squatter!'"[92]

Many people's hopes were riding on this show – not just those of the creative team. It opened on February 3, 2007 following ten days of previews. "At last the arrival of a new musical that isn't strung together from a back catalogue of popular tunes", said the *Herald-Sun*. "*Sideshow Alley…* is that rarest of things in today's conveyor-belt culture – an unashamedly Australian tale replete with larrikins, show people, dry humour, slang and sentimentality."[93] Rosemary Duffy of *State of the Arts* wrote, "The show's good-natured, unrestrained larrikinism reminds us just how distinctive preglobalized Australia was."[94] Yet, in spite of some very vocal support, audiences simply didn't turn up in sufficient numbers, and in fact some performances were aborted due to poor ticket sales. Planned engagements in Melbourne and Sydney were cancelled.

Melbourne-based Magnormos Productions have produced an annual festival since 2002 called OzMade Musicals. Artistic director Aaron Joyner explains, "The idea was to have a production company that could produce Australian work, as well as key international work… There wasn't really anything happening for Australian writers." Beginning with a concert on Australia Day (January 26), he presented a concert of songs from Australian-written musicals. Finding that it was hard to attract an audience on a public holiday when many people were away, he has since moved the show to November, but the idea has remained the same, "to create pathways for writers to get their work demonstrated, developed and presented in front of an audience of people that includes media and producers and practitioners and the general industry, and actually get the work showcased in a classy presentation."

He has the same funding problem that people with similar plans have in the U.K. and Canada. "Unfortunately, musical theatre is problematic to the Australia Council because it's a multi-discipline art form. Therefore, when you go to apply, you have to choose between applying for music, dance or theatre or even literature, depending on what stream it is. So, it's very confusing when you speak to one board and they say, 'well, you really should speak to *this* board'. To date, we've never had a member of the theatre board attend OzMade, despite multiple invitations. And we've never been successful in grant applications, despite attempts every year. However, last night[95] we did have our first Australia Council representative from the music board." As in other countries, the cultural bureaucrats tend to view musical theatre as being commercial, and therefore not worthy of government support. OzMade has received corporate sponsorship from companies like Yamaha Music, who provide musical instruments, and the BMD group, a Brisbane-based construction company who have set up a cultural fund. The performers and musicians work for nothing, but as Joyner explains, it's a chance for them to "work in their own accent, which is something that rarely happens in Australia for musical theatre performers."

So far, they have sent one show, *Joe Starts Again* (2004, book by Martin Croft and Mark Fletcher, music by Dean Lotherington and lyrics by Martin Croft) to the New York Musical Theatre Festival, whose then Artistic Director Kris Stewart is an Australian. They would have sent *All Het Up* the following year but, although it had been accepted, they were unable to raise the financing.   Other shows developed by Magnormos have gone on to be short-listed for the Pratt Prize.

The Hatpin, with music by Peter Rutherford and book and lyrics by James Millar received its world premiere on 27 February 2008 at the Seymour Centre in Sydney. It told the horrifyingly true story of a home for orphans in which the charges were murdered by their supposed guardians. Neil Litchfield in *Stage Whispers* wrote, "It's premature to say step aside *Les Miz*, but Australia's 19th century downtrodden get their turn at musicalisation in this show. *The Hatpin* was quite riveting, despite some musical and dramatic unevenness, not unexpected in a brand new work. Occasionally, the score was only solid, but it also reached genuine heights."[96]

"I went to one of the first workshops of it when it was in its purest form, and it was the Australian *Sweeney Todd*," says Tony Sheldon. "I mean, you just sat there going, 'This is a knockout!' I went to a meeting at a leading Australian theatre company the next day, [talking to] somebody that had been there. I said 'Wasn't that the most thrilling experience?' and they said, 'Yeah, pity it's never going to get on'. My heart dropped to my boots because I knew that these people were just looking at the economic viability of putting on a dark show like this. Anyway, the show was then workshopped considerably over the next two years and I watched it get worse and worse with every successive reading. It was like, 'You've got to have a big number to close act one' or 'We need an up tune here'. Suddenly the show became this little bastardised piece. I don't like the current version of *The Hatpin*, and the one that opened commercially starring Caroline O'Connor – all my friends whom I trust said, 'Oh, God, it was a hard night to get through. It was really boring'. Well, that's not the show I saw two years [earlier] in its purest form when it should have been allowed to just go on then without anybody tampering with it. It came from the writer's heart, and they knew of what they wrote at the time, and then they listened to far too many people."

Peter Cousens (1955-), who appeared in the original production, says "Originally it was much more of a whodunnit, and you never really knew who, out of that family [committed the murders] but the way it was redone, it became reasonably obvious early on who were the culprits. It became a kind of a thriller, really, about how they were finally entrapped. You knew where you were heading as an audience." It was presented for six performances at the New York Musical Theatre Festival, but received a cool critical reception. David Finkle of Theatremania.com complained of "agitated melodic lines and... quasi-poetic lyrics"[97].

In 2006, Cousens launched a new company, Kookaburra, with the bold ambition to be "Australia's National Musical Theatre". Their offices were in Australian Hall, the former home of the Phillips Street Revues. "The company is committed to the art form, and developing the art form", Cousens told me in November 2008. "What that means is not only developing new work, but it's developing audiences to be educated to what other sorts of musicals there are, and also giving opportunities to people who work in the industry in this country who usually get locked out of musicals because they're directed, produced, choreographed and designed overseas. Even the actors are basically told what to do, in terms of what an actor did in London and in America." This is a business that Cousens knows very well, having acted in franchised shows such as *Les Misérables*. "We're about doing musicals that wouldn't necessarily be produced by commercial producers... We have to balance a way of doing work that is reasonably artistically motivated but also has an opportunity to support us in terms of being able to sell it... As a company, it's never been about 'Australian musicals', whatever that is. The company is committed to the art form, and therefore the programming needs to come from anywhere that's good."

One of their initiatives was to be called The Nest, a development programme for new works, managed by Clive Paget, former Associate Director of the Bridewell Theatre in London. There were also school tours of Stephen Schwartz's *Emperor's New Clothes* and Jason Robert Brown's *Songs for a New World*. When I met them in November 2008, they were developing a new educational show with Craig Christie, co-author of *Eurobeat* , an Australian show that enjoyed a summer run at London's Novello Theatre in 2008. Although it wasn't a Kookaburra production, they did provide some peripheral support to *The Hatpin*, and Cousens informed me that they had workshopped six works in 2008, with a view to taking one forward to production in 2009 – "as long as we can get it funded".

Kookaburra's initial offerings met with mixed results. *Pippin* was neither a commercial nor a critical success. "Audiences couldn't cope with *Pippin* because it was so out of left field", says Cousens. "It had a backpacker who blew himself up at the end. It had resonances with terrorism and all sorts of things."

Their second show, *Company*, was helmed by Australia's most internationally celebrated director of musicals, Gale Edwards. The opening at Sydney's Theatre Royal was attended by the show's composer Stephen Sondheim, and both reviews and box office were promising. But then, something happened that would haunt the company for the rest of its short existence. A couple of weeks into the run, actress Christie Whelan, who played the supporting role of April, came down with pneumonia. On this particular evening, one of the company's sponsors was in, and there was no room in the budget for understudies.

When contacted by telephone, Cousens decision was, rather than to cancel the performance, to simply cut the scenes and songs that Whelan was involved in. (This included the songs "Barcelona" and "You Could Drive a Person Crazy".) "I was trying to put a very positive spin on the fact that all was well [and] that nothing had gone on at

171

the theatre that was a problem for the public to be made aware of,"[98] he told the *Sydney Morning Herald*. Unhappy with this decision, one member of the cast got in touch with the composer, who demanded an immediate public apology, or else face the withdrawal of the rights for subsequent performances. The following evening's performance was cancelled while a replacement was found for Whelan. The company issued a statement saying, "Kookaburra celebrates the work of Stephen Sondheim and [book writer] George Furth and apologises for interfering with the integrity of their work".[99] Cousens told me, "With a five week run, the last thing you want is an understudy running around and paying for. Yes, we had an incident on *Company*, but it didn't affect the show."

Aaron Joyner says, "That was a sad day for the company and a sad day for Australia's theatre industry really, to have pissed off one of the art form's legends. It was not a great thing to happen, for a company that had made a big splash about being the saviour of the art form." The story soon travelled around the world. In London, *The Stage*'s Mark Shenton described it as a decision "so dumb that it beggars belief"[100], although the alternatives may not have seemed palatable at the time. It is not uncommon, outside of Broadway and the West End, for a show not to have understudies. Should they have cancelled the show and risked losing the support of the sponsor who was in that night? As a part of their settlement with Sondheim and Furth, they added a charity performance in aid of Oz Showbiz Cares and the Actors' Benevolent Fund.

Alas, the problems didn't end there. The company's next scheduled production, Adam Guettell's *Floyd Collins*, was cancelled due to poor ticket sales – "a disastrous piece of programming on my part", says Cousens. "It probably needed to be in a theatre that held a hundred people." A proposed Sydney transfer of the new Australian musical *Sideshow Alley*, which had opened in Brisbane, was also cancelled. "*Sideshow Alley* is a wonderful Australian musical," Cousens told *The Australian*, "but we want to protect it from the crowded 2008 season."[101] A co-production with the Really Useful Group of Andrew Lloyd Webber and Don Black's *Tell Me on a Sunday* received tepid reviews, and while their production of the American musical *Little Women* (which I saw) was well received, it lost money. Sadly, Australia's recession-ridden economy could not sustain them, and several major sponsors pulled out. While they did receive some emergency funding from the New South Wales government, they subsisted largely – in Cousens own words – on "a wing and a prayer and an overdraft." In late December 2008 – one month after I met Cousens – Kookaburra's staff was laid off, and Artistic Producer Peter Ross accepted a job with another company.

As before, the media and the blogosphere were full of rude comments. One particularly virulent post from a former theatre critic dismissed Kookaburra as "a time whose idea never came."[102]

David Spicer in *Stage Whispers* feels that Kookaburra lacked adequate financial oversight. Their administrative overhead and promotional budgets were, say industry sources, disproportionate to their potential revenue. "Who was monitoring Kookaburra and giving Peter Cousens guidance? ... Is there any surprise that if you have a board of directors of a music theatre company filled with people who appear to have limited experience in music theatre that they are not going to be able to provide much assistance? Does Macquarie Bank [one of their sponsors] have a Board made up of people in the main with no merchant banking experience?"[103]

"I think it's very sad for a company that is announcing themselves as the country's national music theatre that in the first two years of programming they haven't staged an original Australian work", says Aaron Joyner. "And they did make the announcement to do so – *Sideshow Alley* – and unfortunately made another media announcement to say they were not going to do it, which I don't think gave much confidence to the form or to their programming choices." But, to give Peter Cousens his due, it's very difficult to make bold choices without sound financial backing. As he discovered, when it comes to getting sponsorship and government support, you first need both the chicken and the egg.

Joyner believes, "Since Kookaburra really didn't do anything new for the art form, or advance local writing in any significant way, I doubt it will be a noticeable loss to the community or the public over the medium term." Dr. Peter Wyllie Johnston adds, "With important financial support from the Macquarie Bank... along with at least one substantial bequest given to it [from another now-defunct theatre company with sympathetic aims], Kookaburra had a rare opportunity to advance Australian musicals. It conspicuously failed to do so, preferring to dabble in well-traversed American musicals and a couple of failed experiments that did nothing to advance the Australian musical."

The last production of their season, the off-Broadway hit *I Love You, You're Perfect, Now Change* was cancelled. The company collapsed, having amassed debts of A$1.6 million.

"Starting a musical theatre arts company in Sydney meant sailing uncharted waters", Cousens wrote in the *Sydney Morning Herald*. "Brisbane, even Melbourne, may have been easier. Sydney is a tough, parochial city determined to prove itself and terrified of failure. If you really walk on the world stage, the potential for failure is just part of the action."[104] However, one unnamed sponsor told the *Herald*, "It was great to see opportunities open up for performers, but no one seemed to make informed or inspired choices."[105] Certainly, important lessons are to be learned from Kookaburra's experience, but one hopes that Cousen's original vision of a company "committed to developing the art form" will survive. Perhaps if the company had begun more modestly, worked in co-productions with established companies, and allowed itself to grow organically, it may have survived.

A recent development in Australia is the aboriginal musical. When Jimmy Chi's (1948-) semi-autobiographical *Bran Nue Dae* opened at the Festival of Perth in the Octagon Theatre on February 22 1990 following a tryout in his hometown of Broome, a dam broke. "Australia has always had a big issue with its native heritage", says Dr. Wyllie Johnston. While shows like *Collits' Inn* and *The Highwayman* featured Aboriginal "corroborees" as an exotic feature, *Bran Nue Dae* was the first musical to be written from the native perspective. This led to the foundation of Black Swan Theatre Company, under the patronage of Janet Holmes à Court, the then-owner of London's Stoll Moss Theatres chain.

"*Bran Nue Dae* is a musical in the Western European popular stage tradition", says Paul Makeham, drama professor at Queensland University of Technology. "It is clearly influenced by the Hollywood musical film genre as well. Yet the play amalgamates the generic conventions of the popular musical with those of Aboriginal oral culture, including those formalised in the tradition of the song cycle. Thus the structural motif of the journey in *Bran Nue Dae* is overlaid onto the specifically Aboriginal form of the song cycle, a type of ritual journey of re-enactment which, like Chi's play, is also 'a musical journey' and a renewal of origins. For the landscapes encountered by the play's travellers are to a large extent sung; through a combination of words, music and images, these landscapes embody aspects of Aboriginal philosophy and consciousness."[106] The musical styles, which incorporate reggae, gospel and country-and-western as well as Broadway, stem from the imported music and films Chi was exposed to in Broome as a young man.

However, to non-Australian ears, *Bran Nue Dae* did not *sound* Australian, and this was a problem for former Theatre Royal Stratford East director Philip Hedley who remarked, "It's a wonderful show, an important show, but it was a mystery to me as to how it arrived at its shape, particularly why it had so many Western borrowings in it."[107] Another Melbourne critic, Catherine Lambert, complained that "although the music explores a range of styles from country to rap, many of the songs are overly simplistic and trite".[108] Wyllie Johnston counters, "The interesting thing about the community in Broome is that it's been a very multi-cultural society for a long, long time. We've had a tremendous number of influences coming and going... via radio, TV, stereo, but also with people visiting there. Jimmy Chi said that he grew up with all these eclectic influences around him musically, and this is why his own music has that kind of feeling... He didn't go for the cliché things, which you can easily do." "Aboriginal Australia's triumph in survival has been its easy ability to appropriate any cultural tool it needs to make strong statements", says Robyn Archer, who was artistic director of the 1998 Adelaide Festival. "Jimmy Chi and his collaborators appropriated a further form, the popular musical, to make a new kind of statement in the widely travelled and televised *Bran Nue Dae* and, subsequently, *Corrugation Road*."[109]

This raises an interesting problem for those wishing to export their shows. They don't always live up to our stereotyped expectations. A friend of mine's father was a well-known Scottish-born jazz trumpeter who had emigrated to Canada. When somebody sent him a recording of bagpipes he said, "I left Scotland to get away from that stuff!" We non-Australians may have a mental picture of what an Aboriginal musical ought to be that won't necessarily tally with contemporary reality. I believe that the same principal will also apply to other countries. In Argentina, they do tango shows for the tourists, but the domestic audiences have other ideas.

Bran Nue Dae was made into a film in 2009 starring Ernie Dingo and Geoffrey Rush, directed by Rachel Perkins. It has led to other shows written, at least partly, by Aboriginal writers and composers. Wesley Enoch (1969-), with composer John Rodgers (1962-) wrote *The Sunshine Club*, about a native serviceman returning from World War II and encountering racism in the dance halls. *The Australian*'s Veronica Kelly hailed it as "a brilliant new landmark in Australian musicals".[110]

The birth of the Adelaide Cabaret Festival in 2001 has encouraged the birth of a new, distinctly Australian form of cabaret musical. *Shane Warne – The Musical* opened at Melbourne's Athenaeum Theatre late in 2008, about the Australian cricket star, written by and starring cabaret artist Eddie Perfect. The director, Neil Armfield (1955-), was responsible for another hit cabaret musical, Casey Bennetto's *Keating*, about the former Labor Prime Minister.

"The joy of Eddie Perfect's *Shane Warne* musical is that it absolutely acknowledges that sport is the obsession in Australia", says Tony Sheldon. "There is no interest in culture, really, from a very high level. We've had Prime Ministers who have never set foot in a theatre in their entire term. And so the opening number of *Shane Warne* is three families at a back yard barbecue in the sixties, and they're all out there in their thongs with their stubbies, their beers, and they're saying, 'How's young Kevin going?' 'Oh, he's great. He won footie this week.' And then, 'How's young Kaylene?' 'She's a champion swimmer'. Then they go, 'How's young Fred?' and his parents say, 'Oh, he's wonderful. He's just got a scholarship to medical school where he's developed a theory on brain surgery.' And they all just stare. 'Oh yeah, that sounds nice.' And they all go back to talking sport. It sets the tone for what the show is going to be about, which is hero worship of a man whose great skill is he can throw a ball... It sums up the Australian character so well."

At first, Warne was angry about this unauthorised musical, but once he saw it, he was evidently won over. So was the Australian cricket establishment: Eddie Perfect was invited to sing the national anthem on the opening day of the test match against South Africa on Boxing Day at the Melbourne Cricket Ground. The show was a hit in Melbourne, but sadly closed after a mediocre three week run in Sydney.

Tony Sheldon was the star of another show that I saw in Sydney. *Priscilla, Queen of the Desert* is, to date, the most commercially successful stage production in Australian history. Based on Stephan Elliot (1964-)'s 1994 film about a trio of Sydney drag queens who become stranded in the desert when their bus ('Priscilla') breaks down, with a score made up of 1980s disco hits, it has grossed more than A$90 million and been seen by a million people on its home turf.

There was a point in the show's early workshops when the question was raised – should it be a 'jukebox' musical, or should it have an original score? "I must confess I was one of the people who said, 'I think you're in very, very dangerous territory there," Sheldon told me. "I mean, I look at *Thoroughly Modern Millie*, that score, and you think, what is it? It falls between two stools. I am concerned about that mixture. I don't know how that works. Still, after two years with *Priscilla*, the reviewers say, 'We wish the songs were more specific.' But I don't think we would have run two years without the songs that we have. It's what people relate to. The minute that overture starts, and the first notes of 'I Love the Night Life', people scream in the audience. So I understand why people rush to the jukebox as an alternative form now. It will die out I'm sure, but it seems to be what people want to hear now. The pre-sold title seems to be all now. Base your show on a famous film or a famous book and half your work is done."

Once more, a lot of hopes were riding on this show. "That, as a musical, I think could be the un-locking of a door for a new generation for Australia, even though it's a jukebox", said Aaron Joyner in 2008. "It's still created by Australians... If they do good box office success like they are, then it allows producers to have a bit more confidence in what the next product could be."

On 24 March 2009 it opened at the Palace Theatre in London with Sheldon in the role of Bernadette (created in the original film by Terrence Stamp), starring alongside former soap star Jason Donovan. Sheldon told the *Australian Times*, "To play an Australian character in an Australian musical on Broadway or the West End has always been my dream. And now, after 45 years as an actor, my dream has come true."[111]

London News said, "It's difficult not to be swept away by this riotously enjoyable show."[112] *London Lite* called it "a real dazzler".[113] Simon Edge in the *Daily Express* said, "All wrapped up as a shiny, pink bowed package, this sumptuously dressed show works gloriously, with its parade of ever more jaw-dropping costumes an utter feast for the eye."[114] Nicholas de Jongh of the *Evening Standard* said, "At a time when escapist musicals are all the rage, here's a rare one that takes you happily out of yourself and into daring places your wildest fantasies might never have dreamed of visiting."[115] But for the *Guardian*'s Michael Billington, "Given the unexplored riches of Australian theatre, it's a pity that artistically buoyant country should now be represented in the West End by this garish throwback in which camp is determinedly overpitched,"[116] while Michael Coveney in the *Independent* declared, "Donovan, it has to be said, seems to have lost what little stage personality he had developed as Joseph in the dreamcoat, and turned, well, rancid – while the long-standing Australian drag queen Tony Sheldon, who starts off promisingly as a dead-ringer for Kim Cattrall and descends into big-mouthed anonymity, and Oliver Thornton as the wicked Felicia – look like Friday night acts at the long-ago Vauxhall Tavern."[117] Rebecca Jones of the BBC decided, "You could pick this show apart if you wanted to – it isn't subtle and the content is a bit thin, but if you want a fun night out with toe-tapping tunes, you'll love it."

Co-writer Allan Scott (1940-) said, "It is curious the way in which a show, no matter its history, doesn't seem to exist or be considered 'real' unless and until it plays in London. The fact that *Priscilla Queen of the Desert – The Musical* has been seen by over a million Australians is, as it were, no more than a bagatelle of Commonwealth trivia. Apparently it is only when we open in London to be seen and judged by British audiences and British critics that we really exist."[118]

Its next stop was Toronto, where it opened at the Princess of Wales Theatre on 26 October 2010, prior to a Broadway transfer. Richard Ouzounian in *Variety* said it was "light years superior to the London production in terms of production standards, pacing (it's 30 minutes shorter) and the emotional honesty of the leading players."[119]

One of the producers of the North American incarnation was actress Bette Midler, and she conceded that some changes have been made to appeal to middle-American sensibilities. "You still get the flavor that has always been part of *Priscilla*, but it's not quite as down and dirty, not as in your face so much so that you might pull back," she told the *New York Times'* Patrick Healy. "It manages to have all the fun of camp without too much of the dark side of camp and drag. Which for Broadway, I think, is a good thing."[120]

The story has also been restructured to shift emphasis onto Tick, the drag queen looking to reunite with his estranged son Benji. "The thinking was that in America having a child say he needs his father would convey the stakes of the road trip immediately to an audience,"[121] said Simon Phillips, the director.

Priscilla opened at Broadway's Palace Theatre on 20 March 2011. *The New York Times'* Charles Isherwood wrote, "While it is performed with gleaming verve and infusions of bawdy humor – Tony Sheldon, who has been with the show from its Australian debut, is particularly winning as the gracious-lady transsexual Bernadette – Priscilla feels monotonous and mechanical... Like Priscilla the bus, Priscilla the musical moves in fits and starts under Simon Phillips s direction, trundling along as a series of interchangeable, aggressively rambunctious dance routines interspersed with catfights and scenes of moist sentiment in which bonds are forged and secrets revealed. (The choreography by Ross Coleman is mostly uninspired music video-style callisthenics.) It doesn't help that the songs are often awkward fits for the dramatic situation."[122]

"I do know we're capable of producing work that can stand up in an international landscape", director Gale Edwards told Will Conyers. "I lament the fact that we have to be told that something's been a big hit on Broadway or the West End before we quite trust it. I think money is a big problem in getting shows produced. For a country the size that we are, and cities as big as Melbourne and Sydney, there are fewer commercial producers than there should be, and therefore fewer opportunities because fewer shows get done. I think we have some of the best musical talent – musical performers, particularly – in the world... but they're largely unemployed... I long for a time when musical theatre really comes to the fore... because I think musical theatre's terribly important and often looked down upon for all the wrong reasons."[123]

In 1958, drama critic Bruce Grant said, "The important fact is not the success in London or the failure in New York but the first success in Australia... the important thing now is to get plays on and to get Australian people to see them."[124] Like their Canadian cousins, the Australian creative community are ready. They just need to bring the Australian public with them.

South Africa: Freedom is Coming

Alan Jay Lerner once said, "It is highly unlikely that any spectator from the days of stone seats to the present has ever learned anything from the theatre. He may experience the entire lexicon of emotions; be tickled to laughter or moved to tears; be stimulated, mystified or exalted by the grandeur of language. But leave the theatre genuinely intellectually changed? Never."[1] But what if theatre was the only avenue of communication open to you? One of the questions often asked in creating a new musical is, "What are the stakes?" Who is Laurie going to go to the box social with – the nice guy or the sociopath? What if the stakes were higher? In South Africa, music and theatre are credited with helping to bring down the Apartheid regime.

While it has been argued that the development of musical theatre coincided with the development of democracy, in some places the relationship was even closer. For South African writers like Mbongeni Ngema, the struggle for freedom actually involved singing and dancing. With no access to a free press, theatre became one of the few practical modes of expression open to them through which they could communicate with a mass audience. Lerner is correct in that theatre is not an efficient means for conveying facts. However, when it comes to emotions, it's another story. And I believe that something that can touch your heart can indeed change your attitudes. (Films like *Gandhi* and *To Kill a Mockingbird* affected many people that way.)

In 1994, when the first democratic elections were held in South Africa, a friend of mine, Dr. Theo Shippey, at the time the vice-chancellor of a polytechnic school in Capetown, told me that the country's first priority – ahead of housing and poverty – should be to promote education. *Sarafina!*, Mbongeni Ngema's 1987 musical, also says that education is the key to liberation. It tells the story of an inspiring teacher in a Soweto (SOuth WEstern TOwnships) high school and her relationship with her brightest pupil, Sarafina. At the time, the pro-apartheid government insisted that black pupils be educated in Afrikaans rather than in English. This provoked riots in which a number of students were killed by the security police. Through the course of the show, this teenage girl becomes radicalised through exposure to violence. To Ngema, liberation was now in the hands of children.

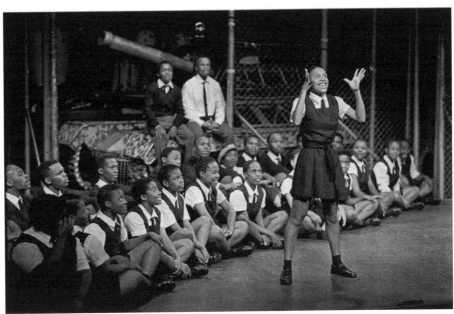

Sarafina
©Ruphin Coudyzer FPPSA

The music for *Sarafina* was written by Ngema in collaboration with exiled South African trumpeter Hugh Masakela, who saw this as an opportunity to return to his roots. "All the years I've been living [in the U.S.], I've never been able to get down with the real musical vernacular of the township", he told the *New York Times*' Robert Palmer in 1987. "This show has been a real opportunity for me to do the real thing, not the hybrid."[2]

For Ngema, it was important that his show be accessible to an international audience. "The important thing about life is that when someone says something in their language, you can understand it because the feeling comes before the word", he told Rina Minervini of Johannesburg's *Sunday Star*. "If someone says 'I love you', you will understand it in any language. Sometimes we get stuck in words and lose the feeling, because you want every word right, everything to be grammatically correct and in real life, people are not always correct."[3]

Sarafina! originally opened 12 June 1987 at the Market Theatre of Johannesburg in what South African impresario Percy Tucker called, "an electrifying and unforgettable evening."[4] The Johannesburg *Sunday Times* reported that "at rehearsals, one could not help feeling the raw texture, colour and beat of the townships. *Sarafina!* vibrates with joy and energy."[5] It played for ten weeks before a pre-arranged transfer to the Lincoln Center's Mitzi E. Newhouse Theatre in New York, where it opened in October. In his review of the show for the *New York Times*, Frank Rich wrote: "So potent are the songs, the performers and Ndaba Mhlongo's hard driving band that one can usually tolerate Mr. Ngema's considerable sloppiness in other areas. As drama, *Sarafina!* is an attenuated, if well-meaning, grab-bag."[6] The *Christian Science Monitor*'s John Beaufort wrote: "*Sarafina...* throbs with an energy that reinforces the urgency of its message. The message, of course, is freedom."[7]

Then in February 1988, it moved to Broadway's Cort Theatre, where it settled in for the next two years and was nominated for five Tony Awards. It then toured North America, and came to London's Hackney Empire in 1991. In 1992, white South African director Daryl James Roodt turned it into a film starring Whoopi Goldberg, and produced by Anant Singh. Towards the end of the shoot, Singh called the entire cast and crew together to meet Nelson Mandela. The late Miriam Makeba, who was starring in the film, was called on to sing. She introduced the song as "My Beautiful Mother", but it was actually an adaptation of the old Sophie Tucker hit, "My Yiddishe Momma". The film was a massive hit on its home turf, but passed largely unnoticed elsewhere.

"The show contravenes every rule of the dramaturg's craft," wrote Wilborn Hampton in the *New York Times*. "For example, what is perhaps the most emotional scene in the show — the funeral of several classmates killed by riot police during a demonstration — comes toward the end of the first act. Ninety-nine directors out of 100 would put that moving scene at the end of the show. But in *Sarafina!*, the show, like life, goes on... It has been suggested that the rousing and evocative Mbaqanga music — the street music of South Africa's black townships — is what keeps people lining up for tickets... But that is only part of the reason the Cort Theater is sold out nearly every night. Perhaps the main reason the show strikes such a chord of unity with its audiences is the young men and women in the cast... When the cast scatters across the stage and up the aisles in the face of police submachine-gun fire and tear-gas canisters, the audience knows it is seeing young men and women who have actually faced bullets and groped through a fog of tear gas on a school playground."[8]

South African journalist Mark Gevisser wrote, "One way or another, *Sarafina!* became the benchmark musical of the time... The play defines the way most Americans think about South Africa, and it defines the way most young black South Africans think about theatre... The pastiche of political anger and comic burlesque, fused into a form of struggle-minstrelsy, has become the almost inescapable formula for how to make black South African theatre: liberating in the possibilities of success it presents, oppressive in the limitations of style it imposes."[9]

Sarafina is now sometimes criticised for its sentimentality. "One thing the play was, was entertaining", says actor and director Jerry Mofokeng. "One thing it wasn't, was illuminating of the South African situation."[10] However, seen in the context of its time, it had a very specific job to do. When his company arrived in New York in 1988 for the Lincoln Centre production, Ngema told his cast that they were ambassadors for the black people of South Africa, to tell a story that the newspapers either couldn't or wouldn't tell. It may appear to be sentimental because of their tendency to smile and laugh through adversity – simply because they know no better way of dealing with it.

When asked how he wanted Americans to respond to the show, Ngema replied, "Racism is the problem of the whole world."[11]

When engaged in a struggle, never underestimate the importance of a cheerleader. "By singing a song… you bring a lot of confidence to the soldiers"[12], says freedom fighter Peter Dimba. Fellow activist Lindewe Zulu adds, "Even when we're dying, the feeling was that when people have died, if you mourn them for too long, it demoralises your spirit. So as a result, even when we used to go bury some of our comrades who had been ambushed along the way, we never used to cry. We used to sing."[13] When activist and musician Vuyusile Mini was hanged in 1964, he went to the gallows singing.

In fact, South African musicals provide a unique challenge to Western audiences. In African culture, people really do break into song in real life situations. The challenge in playing to international audiences is that the Africans do not feel the need to justify singing psychologically in the way that, say, American or British creators do. To some, this creates a feeling of awkwardness or naiveté. On the other hand, perhaps Western writers could learn lessons from this apparent ease in musicalising their emotions.

Ngema's background couldn't be further from that of a conventional musical theatre writer. He was born in Verulam, near Durban in 1955. According to his biographer, "While the conventions of European drama and spectacle existed completely outside of Ngema's orbit, he was exposed from the earliest possible age to a form of theater directly related to the dramatic enactments presented at the courts of the great Zulu kings before the undoing of the sovereignty – a pageantry both solemn and joyous, in which he took part every weekend until he was ten years old."[14]

While English director Peter Brook (1925-) and Polish director Jerzy Grotowski (1933-99) were important influences, the musicals of Mbongeni Ngema exist almost entirely without reference to the American/European conventions of musical theatre. "In an American musical like *Fiddler on the Roof*" writes former Lincoln Center Director of Special Projects Laura Jones, "each musical number advances the story or defines some aspect of the character singing the lead vocal. But the structure that supports *Sarafina!* is based on rules of musical composition, orchestration and harmony, and not on Aristotle's *Poetics* or any concept of the 'well-made play'. Each song is an abstract, spiritual expression, arising organically, as songs do in South African life, out of group experience and feeling. The audience becomes intimately involved with the characters moving about before them, living onstage for nearly three hours, displaying every shade of pathos and humor."[15] (This approach is not unheard of in American musicals: see *Godspell*.) To say that *Sarafina!* is primitive is not in any way derogatory. Singing and dancing as an act of defiance is musical theatre in its purest and most heightened form.

Ngema ran into a problem when in 2004 he mounted a revival to celebrate ten years of South African democracy. "The first time I did *Sarafina*, I didn't have to explain anything," he told the *Boston Globe*'s John Donnelly. "The kids experienced it first-hand. But these kids in this new production didn't have a clue about what it was like. I ask them, 'Do you know what a state of emergency is?' They say no. I tell them what it means, and you see their faces change and their eyes open."[16]

A 1996 sequel, *Sarafina 2*, attempted to deal with the AIDS crisis, but was aborted with the loss of its entire 14 million Rand budget (over $3 million US), which had been supplied by the South African health ministry. Health commissioner Dr. Nkosazana Zuma allegedly used funding from the European Union that had been earmarked to combat aids to commission the new show from Ngema, bypassing the State Tender Board. Money also allegedly changed hands even before the contracts were signed. On top of this, the actual depiction of AIDS was highly inaccurate. "It was a genuine scandal", says theatre historian Professor Michael Simpson. "Funds were misused, and for a show with low-paid inexperienced performers, it was unbelievably expensive, and with little to show for all the expenditure."

In 2008, Ngema was in the spotlight again when he was commissioned by the Mpumalanga provincial government to create *Lion of the East*, a musical which celebrated the life of African National Congress activist Gert Sibande, who led a successful boycott of potato farmers. Defending its enormous 22 million Rand budget, Ngema told the *Mail & Guardian*, "Like all great musicals, like *The Lion King*, I'm taking you to a world standard... There will be a large cast, a big set, costumes, sophisticated lighting, everything will be done on that large scale."[17] However, the artistic director of Grahamstown's National Arts Festival, Ismail Mahomed maintains that the same amount of money "would keep a number of festivals running for a number of years and create work for thousands of people... this level of miscalculation and mismanagement is standard operating procedure there."[18] This kind of carelessness seems to have been rife; in 2008 a play commissioned by the Department of Human Settlements from TV personality Mpho Tsedu also cost R22 million before being cancelled after only sixty performances.

Sarafina! had its progenitor in the township musicals of Gibson Kente (1932-2004), who began his writing career with *Manana, the Jazz Prophet* in 1963. Percy Tucker calls him "a substantial force in building a theatre audience in the townships."[19] His next show, *Sikalo* came two years later and even became popular with white audiences. Most of his works centred around the shebeen, a sort-of speakeasy, and the characters who frequented them. Although Kente eventually fell out of favour because his later works were deemed to be "counter-revolutionary", he trained a great number of black actors and writers, including Ngema. However, Kente's work had little direct impact on audiences outside of the South African townships.

In 1958, lawyer-turned-novelist Harry Bloom (1913-81), step-father of actor Orlando Bloom, went with his friend Ian Bernhardt of the Union of Southern African Artists to hear some black singing groups in the Eastern townships. Wanting to develop a vehicle to display these talents, he set out to find a story to turn into a "jazz opera". In February 1959, *King Kong* opened in Witwatersrand University Great Hall on February 2, 1959 – one of the few venues where a "mixed" creative team would be permitted. The music was by a black jazz musician and journalist named Todd Matshikiza (1921-68) who became immersed in the jazz scene of Sophiatown, a suburb of Johannesburg where, from the 1930s until the 1950s, a multiracial and multicultural music scene was allowed to flourish. From this vibrant scene, artists such as Hugh Masakela (1939-) and Miriam Makeba (1932-2008) emerged, and the highly rhythmic Mbaqanga (Zulu for "cornmeal porridge") music was born of a fusion between American jazz and traditional African harmonies. (Both of these artists would figure in *King Kong*; Masakela as a musician and Makeba as an actress, and that show's eventual international success brought both of them to a new audience.)

Nathan Mdledle (King Kong) with Miriam Makeba and Joe Mogotsi
Photo courtesy Percy Tuicker

I should explain that *King Kong* was not the story of a giant gorilla. Rather, it told the tragic tale of South African heavyweight champion boxer Ezekiel "King Kong" Dhlamini who was convicted of murder, but who became a folk hero for his defiance of white rule. (He is reputed to have taken his name from a movie poster.) The script was by Bloom, and the lyrics were by journalist Pat Williams. The director Leon Gluckman had worked in England as resident producer at the Nottingham Rep, and as an actor at the Old Vic, having trained in the U.S. at Yale University and Pasadena Playhouse. According to impresario Percy Tucker, Gluckman "felt strongly that black and white would have a great deal to give each other if only they were free to do so".[20] All except Matshikiza were white (although the show was popular with black audiences). This would create a problem for Matshikiza: "Every night I dreamed I was surrounded by pale-skinned, blue veined people who changed at random from humans to gargoyles. I dreamed I lay at the bottom of a bottomless pit. They stood above me, all around, with long, sharpened steel straws that they put to your head and the brain matter seeped up the straws like lemonade up a playful child's thirsty picnic straw. I screamed, yelled myself out of the nightmare, and fell off my bed each night I saw the brain straws. I dreamed Black names were entered from the bottom of the register and White names from the top. And when a black man told a white man to go to hell, there was no hell. And when a white man told a black man to go to hell, the black man did go to hell."[21] He said to set designer Arthur Golderich, "Tell them to stop… having meetings without me although it's about my music." They agreed, but the meetings always took place in hotels that were barred to blacks, and required evasion of house detectives.

With a three-month rehearsal period – not a long time for a cast of sixty-three performers with little or no professional experience – Gluckman set about his near impossible task. Many of the actors were cooks, nannies, gardeners and delivery boys by day, while working as equals with their white creative team by night. Percy Tucker was one of those charged with arranging safe transport for them, delivering them back to their servant quarters. "I was much affected by this anomaly and could only guess at how the people concerned coped with their schizophrenic existence."[22]

The Johannesburg press responded enthusiastically. *The Star*'s Oliver Walker wrote that *King Kong* was his "greatest thrill in twenty years of South African theatregoing", while the *Sunday Express* said, "There is such boundless vitality in all the acting, the dancing and the mime that you will want to leap from your seats."

Percy Tucker's company Show Service handled the box office. "An unwelcome view of human nature was revealed by those customers who came to the box office and said, 'Of course, I'm not a racist, and I've got nothing against them, but I really don't want to sit next to a black person.' In those cases, I made sure whenever possible that they would be sitting next to a black person."[23]

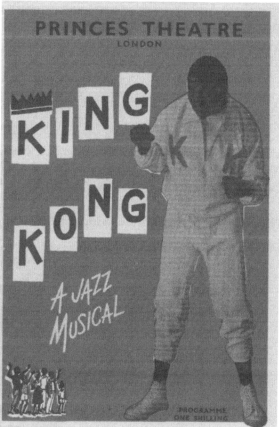

Following a five-week run, *King Kong* then embarked on a South African tour, although the Pretoria city council refused permission for the show to play in the administrative capital, in spite of a press campaign. Across the country, the show was seen by over 200,000 people, over two-thirds of whom were white.

In April, London bandleader and impresario Jack Hylton sent his right-hand man Hugh Charles (composer of "We'll Meet Again" and "There'll Always Be an England") to Johannesburg to see the show. In February of 1960, Gluckman travelled to London to finalise arrangements for a West End transfer. Uncertain at to whether the South African government would issue passports to the cast, he auditioned British-based black artists. He also announced that the show would be re-worked for Anglo audiences, with some rewrites, new songs and traditional costumes. The actors were also sent for elocution lessons. As the cast gathered at the airport for their departure on 7 February 1961, they burst into a chorus of "Nkosi Sikelel' iAfrika" (God Bless Africa), a hymn composed in 1897 by a teacher named Enoch Sontonga which became the anthem of the freedom struggle and eventually the national anthem of a democratic South Africa.

Matshikiza's music was re-orchestrated by other hands. In his autobiography, he says: "I have been watching my music go from black to white to purple"[24], but the British critic Angus Wilson wrote, "The European applause was not patronage, the African applause was not partisanship, both were responding to the genuine laughs and thrills of a first-rate performance".[25] Compared to *Sarafina!*, *King Kong* sounds much more like the American jazz of Duke Ellington, although its African roots come out in some splendid a capella singing.

King Kong was presented at the Princes (now Shaftesbury) Theatre in London, opening on February 23, 1961 for a run of more than eight months. Author Kurt Gänzl told me that "they couldn't sell the front rows of the stalls because of flying bodily fluids". The *Times* wrote: "We come to realize in the course of the evening that this is a show to which strict standards of professional slickness cannot be applied. Stemming from an amateurish impulse and retaining most of its original character, *King Kong* must be taken on its own terms; and it is then very enjoyable. On any other terms there is much fault to be found... Against all these faults which American professionalism would be swift to remedy can be set virtues rare in the musical light theatre. The authors are so steeped in the special ways of life in the gang-ruled shantytowns of South Africa that the material may be said to infuse the style in which it is treated... They seem to be conditioned by the particular locality to which the characters belong; and it is perfectly easy to take what appear to us as stage clumsiness in our stride and to yield ourselves up to the rhythm and the vitality. Mostly the dances are frankly erotic..."[26] Bernth Lindfors, Professor of English and African Literatures at the University of Texas at Austin, says the critics "yielded to the temptation to fasten on what seemed to be the crudest aspects of an animated performance."[27]

Future rock star Cat Stevens, at that time a thirteen year old musicals aficionado and *West Side Story* fan whose parents owned a restaurant nearby, became one of the show's "groupies", seen frequently hanging around stage door.

The programme carried a curious note saying, "In staging the production of *King Kong* in London, Jack Hylton has received every courtesy and co-operation from the Union Government and wishes to record his appreciation." This "courtesy and co-operation" was evidently lacking when book writer Harry Bloom was charged in Capetown with making a false statement while applying for a passport, although Bloom maintained, "I am here quite legally"[28]. In fact, many of the cast members and creative team would seek political asylum in Britain. (Makeba, who had already moved to the U.S., did not join the cast in London.)

A proposed Broadway production fell through, and the company headed back to South Africa on 7 December. Percy Tucker believes that its adaptation to English tastes "watered down the magic".[29]

"It is impossible to overstate either the impact or the significance of *King Kong* in apartheid South Africa of the period", says Tucker. "It gave dignity to the black population of the country and brought recognition of black talent. For white theatregoers it was an eye-opener, and for the theatre itself, a triumphant vindication of the efforts to promote its development and widen its horizons."[30]

It was revived unsuccessfully in Johannesburg in 1979 by American director Joe Walker. "To sit there and watch this insulting travesty of the original was a nightmare", says Tucker. "It was the only occasion when I rejoiced in a show's failure."[31]

The satirical revue *Wait a Minim!* (a "minim" is a half note) opened in Johannesburg on 17 January 1962 in a small theatre in a YMCA. Leon Gluckman had built this entertainment around the talents of two multi-instrumentalist brothers, Andrew and Paul Tracey, whose father Dr. Hugh Tracey was an acknowledged expert on African music. Gluckman soon learned that, however versatile they may have been, they were not seasoned thespians, so he rounded out his cast by adding six more performers, including actor and comedian Kendrew Lascelles and English-born folk-singer Jeremy Taylor, who would provide most of the original songs. The revue, which Percy Tucker describes as "a *mélange* of music, mime, song, satire, dance and general craziness"[32] was, at first, a sleeper. It was only when Jeremy Taylor made a hit recording of one of the songs, "Ag, Pleez Daddy" that the show took off. It ran for seventeen weeks in Johannesburg before mounting a national tour. "At that time, we had no censor to pass on scripts", Gluckman told Rex Reed in 1966. "For every person in the government we angered, we pleased ten more. We always played to integrated houses. The blacks loved it as much as the whites... We didn't hide from anything."[33]

A sequel, *Minim Bili* (Nguni for "two") opened in April 1963, followed by *Minim Export*, which combined the best of the two. It was this version that transferred with its all white cast to the Fortune Theatre in London's West End on April 10, 1964 under its original title, *Wait a Minim*. The *Times* wrote: "Following the disappointments of *King Kong* and *The Blood Knot* [a play by Athol Fugard, also staged by Gluckman] one has learned to be wary of shows that arrive from South Africa loaded with the honours of their own country and heralded by the organs of British liberal opinion". Nevertheless, they concluded that *Wait a Minim* was "much the best of the lot"[34]. It played in London for two years before moving on to New York, where it enjoyed a run of 456 performances at the John Golden Theatre beginning in March, 1966. Stanley Kauffman wrote in the *New York Times*: "although it is sometimes unfunny and its topical satire is weak, *Wait a Minum* has a congenial spirit."[35] An excerpt from the revue was performed on the popular *Ed Sullivan Show*.

187

In the early 1970s, composer Bertha Egnos was approached by American singer Eartha Kitt who was performing in South Africa and wanted to use some African music. She didn't use the songs that Egnos offered to her, but in 1973 they appeared on a concept album called *The Warrior*. This was later turned into the musical *Ipi-Tombi*, (sometimes called *Ipi Ntombi*, a corruption of the Zulu "iphi intombi", "where is the girl?") which told the story of a young black man who leaves his family to work in the mines of Johannesburg. The lyrics were by her daughter, Gail Lakier. It opened initially in Perth, Western Australia, where the backer disappeared with their money. Back home in Johannesburg, Brian Brooke, whom Percy Tucker describes as "a man of immense charm, urbanity and good looks"[36], presented it in his own theatre, where it opened 31 March 1974, and played for three years. With a white creative team and an all-black cast, it was required to play before segregated audiences. Again, Percy Tucker's Computicket handled the box office. "It was impossible to run a colour check at the Computicket terminals, nor did we wish to. In addition, every visitor to Johannesburg rushed to buy tickets, and many locals didn't bother to check which performances were designated for which racial group. The result was a chaotic, illegal and thoroughly amicable breaking of the colour bar which, surprisingly, was ignored by the authorities."[37]

On 19 November 1975 it opened at Her Majesty's Theatre in London. *The Times* described it as, "all ulating leaps, steatopygous flourishes, and tableaux of warriors framed in russet skybroth silhouette... an evening of exotic escape."[38] The *Sunday Times* called it a "thrilling production, presented with a verve, an *éclat*, a technical brilliance, a richness of voice in the singing, an excitement and a precision in the dancing which I do not believe that even the best American musical could rival. It is a riot of colour and movement, yet it is as controlled as the changing of the Guard. Every member of the huge cast is superb."[39] It ran for about four months. It would later tour Europe, the U.S. and Canada. In New York, it was greeted by anti-apartheid protests when it opened at the Harkness Theatre on 12 January 1977. *Time* magazine wrote that the dances "illustrate how close to nature some Africans apparently still are. The gestures, the rhythms and the sounds indicate an unbroken totemic relationship with animals... This is all done with an agility, grace and energy that is breathtaking."[40] It closed on 13 February. In 1981 it returned to London for a one-month run at the Cambridge Theatre, and it has been revived many times, in revised forms, on its home turf. According to Mbongeni Ngema's biographer Laura Jones, these shows "were aimed at white audiences, with almost no appeal to the black communities in South Africa".[41]

In 1971, Welcome Msomi, founder of the Zulu Dance Theatre collaborated with Professor Elizabeth Sneddon of Natal University on a Zulu adaptation of *Macbeth* called *Umabatha*. This was invited to London's Aldwych Theatre in 1972 as part of a World Theatre Season organised by Sir Peter Daubeny (1921-75). The *Times* reported, "The effect is as stunning visually as it is to listen to: a mass of moving skins and weapons transforming separate members into a single indomitable animal, bent on celebration, joy, or killing, but unstoppable no matter what its objective."[42]

Kwa Zulu, another London export, began life as *Isintu*, created by Cocky Thlotothlamaje for Phoenix Players. Canadian producer Clarence Wilson redeveloped it as *Meropa* ("drums") and toured it to Japan and the Far East. Then it was restaged and expanded by Joan Brickhill-Burke and opened in Johannesburg on 3 December 1974 where it ran for three months. Finally, it was brought to the New London Theatre, where the title was changed to *Kwazulu*. (The earlier title was thought too similar to the name of Aristotle Onnasis' sister, Merop.) *The Times'* Irving Wardle said, "If the London stage must carry advertisements for South Africa, the job could hardly be done more plausibly than it is in this production... *Kwazulu* depicts the homelands as a tribal paradise where nothing disturbs the rhythm of man and nature and the only cloud in the sky is that of approaching locusts. The picture is unreal, but there is no denying that an atmosphere of unfaked happiness comes across."[43]

Two women who had toured in *Ipi Tombi*, Todd Twala and Thembi Nyandeni, formed their own dance company called *Baobab* (after an African tree that grows robustly in spite of difficult conditions). This eventually evolved into *Umoja*, a show that opened at London's Shaftesbury Theatre on 15 November 2001. The *Daily Mail* found it "totally irresistible", while the *Times* said it "exudes a sincere populist commerciality that is hard not to like", and the *Guardian* called it "A breath of fresh air".

Umoja was forced to close on 6 February 2002 because of noise complaints from neighbouring flats. It returned in the summer to the Queens Theatre for a two-month run, and was back in London again the following year at the New London.

This was not the last time *Umoja* would find itself in trouble. A five-month Canadian tour was curtailed because of complaints from the promoter of irresponsible behaviour by cast members. "Many people come to watch this show because they want to learn more about Africa", co-creator Thembi Nyandeni told South Africa's *Saturday Argus*, "and it is embarrassing when these cast members are falling down drunk on stage — they are an embarrassment to our entire nation."[44]

Kat and the Kings told the story of a mixed-race singer in 1950s Capetown, loosely based on the memoirs of Salie Daniels (who appeared as narrator), with book and lyrics by David Kramer (1951-) and music by Taliep Petersen (1950-2006). It opened in London in 1998 where it won the Laurence Olivier award for Best Musical, then transferred to the Cort Theatre (the same Broadway house where *Sarafina!* had moved a decade earlier) the following year. While the *New York Times*

189

praised the cast's talent, "Yet for all their innate appeal and exuberant energy, there is a sense that they are as confined as genies in bottles, hemmed in by the formulaic cartoonishness of the show in which they appear. And by the evening's end, their exertion in trying to turn period pastiche songs into showstoppers is so visible that you find yourself sweating in sympathy. Talent of this caliber should never have to go begging."[45] Sadly, Petersen was murdered by burglars in 2006.

More recently, it is *Impempe Yomlingo*, an African re-interpretation of Mozart's *The Magic Flute* that has impressed London audiences. It was an Englishman living in Capetown, Mark Dornford-May, who assembled a cast drawn from the townships, schooled, not in opera but in church singing. The music was adapted for an all percussion ensemble, including specially designed marimbas and African drums. It was two South African expatriates, Eric Abraham and David Lan who backed the project. Lan was the artistic director of London's Young Vic, and Abraham a film producer whose credits included *Birthday Girl* (starring Nicole Kidman) and the television series *Dalziel and Pascoe*. The Queen of the Night was played by the director's wife, Pauline Malefane.

The *Independent* declared, "This updating of *The Magic Flute* to South Africa offers such a miraculous glimpse into a possible musical future that it's hard to watch without a lump in the throat. It speaks directly out of the townships, yet it's entirely true to Mozart."[46] It transferred to the Duke of York in February 2008 for a strictly limited two-month engagement. Then it toured to the Tokyo International Forum.

It's that "possible musical future" that I'll be watching for.

"Down South American Way" – Musical Theatre in Latin America

Whenever the English speaking musical theatre has attempted to represent South America on stage, it has veered from the kitsch stereotype of Carmen Miranda to the faux sentimentality of a Jackie-Kennedy-with-claws called *Evita*. Neither image would appear to square with how Latinos see themselves. Given the cultural vibrancy of Brazil, Argentina and Chile, this seems inexplicable. Each one of those countries has a long musical theatre heritage of its own.

The commercial theatres of Buenos Aires line Corrientes Avenue, with their own traditions dating back to the late eighteenth century, brought over by Spanish and Italian immigrants. One of the earliest was a *sainete* (lyric farce) entitled *El amor de la estanciera* ("The Love of the Rancher's Daughter", ca. 1787). The Argentineans also developed their own localised form of the Zarzuela, called the Zarzuela Criolla that lasted in popularity from the 1880s until the 1920s.

Some describe the Tango as the "anthem of the proletariat". It has been a popular feature of the English-speaking musical theatre since the 1950s, and has been celebrated in several Broadway revues, including *Tango Argentino*. What many people probably don't know is that it has come full circle: the musical theatre is where the Tango first attained popularity.

Tango is a cocktail of European and African music and dance forms brought to Argentina and Uruguay by immigrants in the nineteenth century. Some say that it is related to the Flamenco. Buenos Aires' earliest Tango, "Tomá, matte, che" by Santiago Ramos was first heard in a play called *El gaucho de Buenos Aires* at the Teatro de la Victoria in 1857. However, the real history of Argentine musical comedy begins in 1897, when the Zarzuela *Justicia Criolla* with a libretto by Ezequiel Soria (1873-1936) and music by Basque-born Antonio Reynoso Compuesto (1869-1912) opened at the Teatro Olimpico on 28 September. It featured the famous Tango "Soy al rubio Pichinango".

After that followed a number of shows which integrated the Tango into their plots. "Many of the most famous Tangos were part of musical comedies," says Pablo Gorlero, a journalist with *La Nacion* and the author of *Historia de la Comedia Musical en la Argentina*, a comprehensive history of Argentine musical theatre. "In general, people don't know about that. But many famous Tangos like 'Los amores con las crisis', 'La muchachada del Centro', 'Adiós, Pampa mía' or 'Se dice de mí' are a little piece of a musical play. The particularity of many of those Tangos (such as the milongas[1]) is that each of them reflects a little story or situation."

In 1926 came the first show in Buenos Aires to call itself a musical comedy, *Judía*, a romantic mystery set in Russia and starring Iris Marga, which opened at the Teatro Porteña on 8 July. The book and lyrics were by Ivo Pelay and the music by Ermanno Andolfi. That began a wave of shows with Tango, milonga, valss and fox trot as the principal rhytms.

Composers and authors worked together to try to forge a distinct Argentine identity in the musical theatre, but over time these were eclipsed by the imports from Broadway and the West End. However, from the 1920s through to the early 1960s, Corrientes Avenue was illuminated by up to fifty home-grown productions a year which drew on many traditions – Zarzuela, music hall, café-concert, revue, variety shows, operetta and foreign musicals.

One of the founding fathers of the Argentine musical was the playwright Ivo Pelay (1893-1959) who wrote *La canción de los barrios* ("Song of the Streets", 1925). His musicals, many written with the composer Francisco Canaro (1888-1964), helped to popularise the Tango. Canaro's 1932 hit *La muchachada del Centro* ("The girl in the middle") ran for over nine hundred performances in two years at the National theatre. In 1957 he celebrated his Golden Tango jubilee with a spectacle at the Alvear Palace Hotel, *Tangolandia*.

Some of the other key figures of this time include composer and onetime actor Enrique Santos Discépolo (1901-51) whose Tango hits included "Que vachache" and "Esta noche me emborracho". Within days of its first performance, the latter song earned him notoriety for its lyrics: the title means "Tonight I'm getting drunk".

Así se ama en Sudamérica ("That's love in South America") which opened 29 March 1950 at the Teatro Presidente Alvear with a book and lyrics by Sixto Rios Pondal (1907-68) and Carlos Olivari (1902-55) and music by Bert Rosé and the Brothers Ábalos poked fun at foreign stereotypes of Latin America. Other titles from this period included *El otro yo de Marcela* ("The other face of Marcela"), *Luna de miel para tres* ("Honeymoon for three"), *Yo llevo el Tango en el alma* ("I've the Tango in my soul"), *La cumparsita*, *Rascacielos* ("Skyscraper") and *El Tango en París* ("Tango in Paris").

Buenos Aires even attracted expatriates. Turkish-born French composer Paul Misraki (1908-98), who worked with such legendary singers as Sarah Vaughan and Josephine Baker, was a refugee from the German occupation of France in 1943 when he wrote *Si Eva se hubiese vestido* ("If Eva would be dressed") with Olivari and Pondal. It opened at the Teatro Astral on 7 July 1944.

However, in 1956, an American invasion began with an Argentine production of *Plain and Fancy* ("Simple y Maravilloso"), a Broadway hit from 1955 set in an Amish community with a book by Joseph Stein and Will Glickman and a score by Albert Hague

(1920-2001) and lyrics by Arnold B. Horwitt, translated by Christopher Cooke Cotton and Gaiza Guillermo Paz. (Hague later became familiar to a younger audience is his role as music teacher Professor Shorofsky in the film and television series *Fame*.) This was followed over the years by *My Fair Lady, Kiss Me Kate, Fiddler on the Roof, Hello, Dolly!* and many others.

A few Argentine writers and composers were able to respond to this challenge with independent work. Composer Astor Piazzolla (1921-92), whose "Tango opera" *Maria de Buenos Aires* with a libretto by Horacio Ferrer premiered on 8 May 1968 at the Planeta, was a Tango moderniser. Piazzolla had spent part of his youth in New York City, where he was exposed to both jazz and classical music. "He was a great innovator", says percussionist and artists' manager Guillermo Masutti. "Rhythmically he broke the **1-2-3-4, 1-2-3-4** etc... He wrote putting accents in some weak moments of the bars... in a sort of jazzy oriented rhythm, although he couldn't evade... accenting the first beat of each bar, such as jazz music has: jazz can evade falling on the 'one', Tango can't."[2] In 1954 he moved to Paris to study under Nadia Boulanger. According to his memoirs, the legendary teacher looked at his manuscripts and told him, "It's very well written... Here you are like Stravinsky, like Bartók, like Ravel, but you know what happens? I can't find Piazzolla in this." Then she began to grill him about his private life. "I was ashamed to tell her that I was a Tango musician", he says. "Finally I said, 'I play in a *night club*'. I didn't want to say *cabaret*... Finally, I confessed and she asked me to play some bars of a Tango of my own. She suddenly opened her eyes, took my hand and told me, 'You idiot, *that's* Piazzolla!'"[3] (However, while Piazzolla is one of Argentina's greatest composers, and he did write one "tango opera", according to Masutti, "he was not a musical theatre composer".)

Like the European musicals, the Argentine scene suffered a loss of momentum under Fascism. The 1970s, during the military rule, marked a dark period in Argentine history, and the theatre suffered for it. *Hair*'s run was suspended shortly after opening, and the theatre where *Jesus Christ Superstar* was to open, the Teatro Argentino was firebombed. New forms of alternative theatre began to spring up, including the café-concert, a form of cabaret. Pablo Gorlero describes it as "a small bar with a small stage, and a solo number. The same actor/actress made differents characters and little plays, generally with songs between them. The most notorius stars of the café-concert was: Nacha Guevara (1940-), Enrique Pinti(1939-), Carlos Perciavalle, Edda Díaz, Antonio Gasalla (1941-), Cecilia Rossetto and 'La' Pavlovsky."[4] There were other variations on this type of cabaret show. "Our 'varieté' is the synonym of vaudeville or burlesque or variety, in Europe and North America. The Revista Porteña was an adaptation of the brilliant French revue. I think they are siblings of the musical comedy."

By 1976, mainstream musicals with social or political comment were banned, until the restoration of democracy in the mid 1980s. "In the 80's the Argentinian musicals were about the freedom, the modernity, the oppresion," says Gorlero. One of the results of the period of censorship was that Argentine theatre was cut off from much of its heritage. "A Berlin Wall was felt in Argentina on those years."

When people in the English speaking world think of musical theatre in Argentina, they probably will mention *Evita*, unaware that the Andrew Lloyd Webber – Tim Rice tuner has never been professionally staged there. Not that the subject is taboo – there are several Argentine-written shows about their notorious former first lady. It seems that Buenos Aires audiences prefer to see their leaders with their own eyes rather than through foreign ones. "We considered Lloyd Webber's *Evita* as a fake history", says Gorlero. According to him, when Tim Rice came to Buenos Aires, he spoke only to the upper class people who hated Peronism. "He didn't [do any] historical research about Evita."

Eva, el gran musical argentino opened at the Maipo Theatre in 1986 with a score by Alberto Favero and a libretto by Pedro Orgambide, in collaboration with director and star Nacha Guevara, a veteran of Buenos Aires café-concerts, with a cast of twenty-one. Another unrelated version of Eva Perón's life appeared three years later: *Evita – Tango Popular Opera* (also known as *Evita - Volveré y seré millones* – "Evita - I'll come back and shall be millions") was written by composers Roberto Pansera and Domingo Federico with librettist Miguel Jubany.

Cuban-born lyricist José "Pepe" Cibrián Campoy's first musical, *Universexus* with music by Oscar Lopez Ruiz was first presented at the Teatro Municipal Sarmiento on 22 June 1971. His breakthrough came seven years later when he was inspired to write *Aquí No Podemos Hacerlo!* ("You Can't Do That Here") after seeing *A Chorus Line* in London. It opened on 6 October 1978 after six months of workshops. Although they received a fifteen-minute standing ovation on opening night, the audiences were small until Daniel Lopez, critic for *La Opinion*, proclaimed it "the first major Argentine musical". The music was by Luis Maria Serra, and the choreography by Ana Itelman, with Cibrián directing a cast that included Graciela Pal. His greatest successes would come after meeting a one-time piano salesman who called himself Angel Mahler.

Angel Pititto was born in Buenos Aires in 1960, and studied piano with Evi Swillinger and orchestration with Manolo Juárez. He adopted the surname of the noted Austrian composer Gustav Mahler as his stage name. In 1982, he met Cibrián, and together they wrote *Dracula*, a pop opera based on the Bram Stoker novel. It originally opened at Luna Park Arena in Buenos Aires on 29 August 1991. Australian composer and TV producer Peter Pinne saw a production in October 1997. "The show is very good, with accessible music, spectacular costumes, a large physical production, and in this version, the most wonderful voices... The set was mainly scaffolding, on several trucks, which were mounted on castors and moved around the stage to form various locales... I'm surprised no-one has translated it ... a la *Les Miz* because it has the same potential." It has toured nationally four times, as well as to Chile, Brazil, Uruguay and

Barcelona, Spain. Their other works together have included *El Jorobado de Paris* ("The Hunchback of Paris") (1993) and *Caligula* (2002).

La Fiaca ("lazy") with book and lyrics by Ricardo Talesnik and music by Gabriel Goldman was based on Talesnik's 1967 satirical play of the same name that was also made into a film by Fernando Ayala in 1969. The story concerns a worker who, bored by his daily routine, decides one day not to come in to work. He is declared "lazy", but is having what we would now understand to be a nervous breakdown. The musical was directed by Valeria Ambrosio. *Clarin*'s Olga Cosentino wrote that the music "speeds up the drama... to get a dramatic synthesis [at] times more potent than dialogue. And the music brings colour and volume to the description of a city that is both home and prison lair."[5]

Dracula
Photo courtesy of Angel Mahler

Playing the protagonist's wife was a young woman named Elena Roger who would soon come to international attention when Andrew Lloyd Webber cast her in the title role in his revival of *Evita*, directed by Michael Grandage. Two years later, she won an Olivier award for her portrayal of *Piaf* at the Donmar Warehouse, a role that she repeated in 2009 at the Teatro Liceo in Buenos Aires and in Madrid in 2010. She began her career in 1995 in *El Jorobado de Paris II* ("The Hunchback of Paris II") and *Dracula*, both by Cibrian and Mahler. Other credits included playing Bess (Houdini's wife) in *Houdini, una ilusion musical* (2005) at the Metropolitan Theatre with book, music and lyrics by Gonzalo Demaria, and in the Argentine versions of *Les Misérables*, *Nine*, *Saturday Night Fever* and *Beauty and the Beast*. In 2003 she toured Europe in *Tango por Dos*.

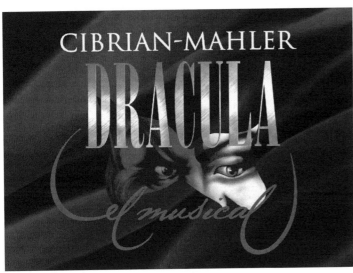

Peter Pinne spent eight years in Santiago, Chile during the 1990s, where he was overseeing adaptations of Australian soap operas. A musical theatre writer himself, he managed to take in some of the local offerings. "The emphasis on classical music is huge. Fifty percent of the stock in any record store was classical. You would get into a taxi and find the drivers listening to classical music, and even my local supermarket had a string quartet playing in the foyer at Christmas. Opera is very popular, and some of the top singers in the world appear there. On the popular music front, they have a lot of rock bands, and cover bands (they play a lot of Beatles), and of course tours of Latin American pop stars. Buenos Aires is similar. They love opera. But I did see some shows like the Casino de Paris type of show there, headed by a local comic. They love farce, as do Peru. In Lima there is always some hugely popular farce playing with local comics, most are known from TV, and they love dressing up in drag. So do the Argentinean performers."

La Pergola de las Flores ("The Pergola of Flowers") with music and lyrics by Francisco Flores del Campo and book by Isidora Aguirre opened at the Teatro de Ensayo at the Catholic University of Chile in April, 1960. The story was based on a true incident in which flower sellers appealed to the public to help them save the Pergola de San Francisco in the flower market of Mapocho in Santiago in 1929. It was written to commemorate the sesquicentennial of Chilean independence. Peter Pinne saw a revival in 1996. "The story gave ample scope for some stylish costumes, and the odd – if rather incongruous in the setting – Charleston routine… There was far too much book, not helped by expansive physical business, but the music was pleasant, particularly a first act duet by the young lovers."

Brazil has a long musical history and has exported many popular songs to the English speaking world. Now it is one of the world's fastest growing economies. As Reed Johnson wrote in the *Los Angeles Times*, "Perhaps in a country where irresistible rhythms are always pulsing somewhere and the interplay of tanned bodies along the Copacabana beach can seem as carefully choreographed as a Jerome Robbins ballet, the notion of people breaking into spontaneous song and dance doesn't appear all that far-fetched."[6] Like Argentina, some of this music started out in the musical theatre or the "teatro de revista" (cabaret revues).

196

On 13 June 1930, a revue called *É do Outro Mundo* opened at the Teatro Recreio in Rio de Janeiro. The music was by Ary Barroso (1903-64), the lyrics by noted cartoonist and illustrator José "J." Carlos (1884-1950), and the book by Margarida Max. Although it was well received critically, audiences didn't really take to it, and it closed within a matter of days. It would have been forgotten, except that a young samba composer named Lamartine Bablo saw the show and fell in love with one of Barroso's melodies, "Esse Mulato Val Sê Meu", although he detested Carlos' lyric. Evidently without the authors' permission, he wrote his own lyric with a new title, "No Ranch Fundo", which he presented on a radio show with Bando de Tangarás. It was first recorded in 1931 by Elisina Coelho, and went on to become a standard. Bablo and Barroso wrote many more hits together. On the other hand, José Carlos never forgave what he considered to be Barroso's betrayal.

Another song by Barosso would achieve even greater international fame. "Aquarela do Brasil" ("Watercolour of Brazil") also first appeared in a stage musical, *Entra na Faixa* with book by Luis Iglesias which opened on 10 June 1939 in Rio. Like "No Ranch Fundo", it was not an immediate hit. In fact it was only after it was included in a Walt Disney animated film *Saludos Amigos* that it became popular, becoming the first Brazilian song to be played over a million times on American radio in a recording by Xaviar Cugat. It even formed the basis for the 1985 Terry Gilliam film, *Brazil*.

Another leading Brazilian samba composer was Noel Rosa (1910-37), whose 1935 operettas *O barbeiro de Niterói* ("The barber of Niterói") and *Ladrão de Galinhas* ("Hen thief") written in collaboration with Arnald Gluckman were musical parodies of Rossini. He also contributed a number of songs to "chanchada"s, Brazil's own form of movie musical.

"Chanchada" was a somewhat derisive term coined by journalists to describe these cheaply made films. (Although the quality improved, the name stuck.) Radio stars were employed to tell backstage stories in a revue or carnival setting. One such film, *Alô, alô, Brasil!* (1935) starred Carmen Miranda. The military dictatorship that ruled for twenty years from 1965 – 1985 put a stop to the teatro de revista, and the chanchada declined in popularity. As in Argentina and Chile, it was on the fringe where those with the courage to stand up to the authorities flourished. Once democracy was restored, the public's appetite for light entertainment returned.

Like Argentina, Brazil has been dominated in recent years by the major Anglo/American blockbusters, mostly presented by the Mexican entertainment giant La Corporacion Interamericana de Entretenimiento. But they have also developed a few shows of their own.

Opera do Malandro, a salsa and jazz reworking by Chico Buarque of Weill and Brecht's *Threepenny Opera* (itself a reworking of *The Beggar's Opera*) first opened in

1978, during the country's twenty year military dictatorship. (Buarque was an outspoken critic of the regime.) It was revived in a hit production in 2004.

South American Way, produced and directed by Miguel Falabella (1957-) in 2001 from a script by Falabella and Maria Carmen Borbosa, tells of Carmen Miranda's rise from the slums of Rio to Hollywood stardom. Although she has been the heroine of transvestites throughout the world, her image has not always been so popular on her home turf. "Lots of people here still think she was nothing but a caricature"[7], Falabella told the *New York Times*' Larry Rohter. For one thing, she was born in Portugal, and never did become a Brazilian citizen. But worst of all, Hollywood imposed a kind of Pan-American image on her that was more Mexican than Brazilian. "Brazilians don't always value their own culture," actor and singer Tuca Andrada told *Newsweek International*'s Mac Margolis. "What's gratifying is discovering just how much Brazilians like Brazil."[8] The show ran for two years in Brazil and toured to Buenos Aires. It won a Shell Prize in 2002.

Although Brazil and Argentina have successfully exported both their music and their cinema (*Black Orpheus*, *City of God*, *The Official Story*, *Nine Queens*, *The Motorcycle Diaries*), no Latin American musical has successfully penetrated the English speaking market – so far.

Peru can, however, lay claim to one of the most popular Latin American "show tunes" of all time – although it is not generally known as such. "El Cóndor Pasa" ("The Condor Goes by") is the title song from a Zarzuela with music by ethnomusicologist Daniel Alomía Robles and libretto by Julio Baudouin. Set in a mine in Cerro de Pasco, *El Cóndor Pasa* tells of the struggle between the native workers and their European bosses. The condor is used as a metaphor for freedom. It premiered at Teatro Mazzi located in Lima's Plaza Italia in 1913 and was performed over 3,000 times.[9] When Simon and Garfunkel recorded a version of the show's namesake finale in 1970, it was incorrectly credited as an eighteenth century Andean folk song. Shortly afterwards, film maker Armando Robles Godoy – the composer's son – successfully sued to assert his father's copyright,[10] and subsequent reissues of the recording have corrected the error.

"The Theatre Is Alive" – Musical Theatre in Asia

Forbidden City. Rose of Versailles. Magnificat. Lunatic. Beauty World. These are all the titles of hit musicals from Asia that you have probably never heard of. On the other hand, when I searched online for "Asian musicals", the list that came through included only *The King and I, Flower Drum Song, South Pacific, Miss Saigon, Pacific Overtures* and *Bombay Dreams.* Just to clarify, with the possible qualified exception of the last one, these are *not* "Asian musicals". These are Western fantastical notions, an exotic vision of Otherness. No, I want to talk about musicals that were created in Asia, by (for the most part) Asians and for an Asian audience.

This is one part of the world where musical theatre is in its ascendancy. Companies in Korea, Japan and China are investing in the development of new works – both local and foreign. The Philippines has long had a great reputation for its performers, including Lea Salonga. Even Singapore, long considered a cultural wasteland, is trying to get in on the "act".

The Asian country with the longest tradition of staging Western-style musicals is Japan. Although the Kabuki Theatre was founded by a woman – Izumo-no-Okuni – in the early seventeenth century, it was soon determined by those in charge that this was a fast-lane to prostitution, and so from 1629 until 1890, actual females were banned from the stage, and their parts in the Kabuki played by "onnagata", or male actors with a female form. These artistes sometimes carried this pretence into their private lives.

In 1913, railway and department store magnate Ichizo Kobayashi (1873-1957) conceived of a plan to present all-female musical performances in the emerging spa-town of Takarazuka, near Osaka, as a way of boosting passenger revenues on his Hankyu Railway. An academy was established where young recruits from affluent families were drilled with militaristic discipline. All of this was intended to prepare them to be "good wives" and "wise mothers" in accordance with then-government policy. Ironically, this rather conservative ideology unwittingly gave birth to a form that has been embraced by radical feminists.

It was after the Takarazuka Grand Theatre was completed in 1924 that the show began to assume its revue format. "There was a dramatic change in the physical appearance of its performers on stage, from childish 'school play' participants to sexually alluring young women,"[1] says Leonie Stickland, who wrote her doctoral thesis on the Takarazuka Revue at Murdoch University in Australia in 2004. Takarazuka staged the first ever Moulin Rouge-style revue in Japan, *Mon Paris*, on 1 September 1927. They toured Europe, China and North America in the years immediately before World War II at the behest of the Japanese government in an attempt to improve Japan's image with the Western powers. They were also co-opted by the government to promote "Japanization" in the occupied Far East during the war. (Although Kobayashi was a minor minister in the wartime government, he was acquitted by the Allies of any wrongdoing.)

The Takarazuka company has five troupes: Hana (flower), Tsuki (moon), Yuki (snow), Hoshi (star) and Sora (cosmos).   In a variation on the traditional kabuki form, all roles are played by women; the actors who play men are known as otokoyaku (male role) and those who play women are called musumeyaku (daughter's role). The acting style fuses Japanese elements such as kabuki with western techniques.

Their fan base is overwhelmingly female, and some can become quite obsessive. In fact, the management has always encouraged a kind of platonic-romantic fantasy, although they deny that it is overtly homoerotic. Opinion is divided as to suggestions of lesbianism. Some argue that the otokoyaku defy gender stereotyping by, in effect, showing women in positions of power. In any case, the otokoyaku do not attempt to become fully masculine – rather, they represent highly idealised representations of man and woman. Jennifer Robertson, an American cultural anthropologist who has studied the revue in detail writes, "Whereas Kobayashi sought to use the actor as a vehicle for introducing the spectacular artistry of the theater into the home, some Takarisiennes and their fans used the theater as a starting point for an opposing strategy, which included the rejection of gender roles associated with the patriarchal household."[2] Dr. Stickland, who teaches at the University of Western Australia and has acted as a translator for the Revue, says that "Takarazuka is a shared fantasy of not only fans, but of the performers, too, who 'live' the dream of portraying beautiful people in their everyday work, and even perpetuate this fantasy after the curtain is down, in an environment considerably removed from regular society."[3] Amon Miyamoto (1958-), whose critically acclaimed minimalist revival of *Pacific Overtures* was remounted in English on Broadway, regards the Takarazuka as "kitsch". He says that the Japanese "love foreigners, but not *real* foreigners, more imaginary. Ladies dream about men like that... It's a fantasy for them." He believes that real men frighten them.

The repertoire of Takarazuka is a mixture of Western musicals such as *Flower Drum Song, Oklahoma!* and *Grand Hotel*, as well as their own adaptations of classic novels, such as Edith Wharton's *The Age of Innocence* or Leo Tolstoy's *War and Peace*, and some original stories, mostly with foreign and exotic settings. The company have also adapted works from Japanese fiction, including *Osaka Samurai*, based on a short story by Ryōtarō Shiba.

Kiri no Mirano ("Milan Wrapped in a Fog") is a tale of political intrigue set in Italy under Austrian rule in the 1850s with a book by Yukihoro Shibata and music by Kohji Nishimura and Shinichi Kuratomi, produced in 2005. *Higher than the Sky of Paris* (2006) with music by Yuko Yishida is based on *Flowered Port* by Kazuo Kikuta, and tells of love and larceny set against the backdrop of the building of the Eiffel Tower.

Canadian-born choreographer Paddy Stone was the first of many Western artists brought over since the 1960s to try to raise their standards, which had declined from the pre-war period. In 2006, American composer Frank Wildhorn (1958-) worked with librettist Shuichiro Kolke on *Never Say Goodbye* (2006), set in the Spanish Civil War. Tommy Tune, the original Broadway choreographer of *Grand Hotel* created a revue, *Broadway Boys*, for them to perform in tandem with it in 1993. "I saw *Grand Hotel* and its attendant revue in Tokyo," says British director Jeremy Sams, "and have never forgotten it – the sheer numbers and the faultless routines – kind of like synchronised swimming on stage. But, no connection with real emotion"[4], an opinion that Miyamoto shares.

Sams found Takarazuka to be "deeply puritanical. No one kisses for real. At one point a girl took her stockings off, to reveal another pair of stockings underneath (oddly quite sexy!)... Also, the 'negro' bartenders had their faces painted red to show 'otherness'."

As with *Grand Hotel*, many of Takarazuka's shows are accompanied by a pre-or-post-show revue. For example, their 2008 revue *Miroirs* ("Endless Dreams of the Mirrors") was created by director Satoru Nakamura and choreographers Risa Wakao, Satoshi Hirasawa, Anju and Yumino Miori to accompany the Snow Troupe's production of *Je T'aime*. Using both original music and popular standards such as "Johnny Angel", "Night and Day" and "The Way We Were", the show explores the power of mirrors, including the story of Snow White.

"Takarazuka has always seemed to be a very obvious dialogue between Western and Japanese cultures", says Ben Whaley in his blog *A White Boy in Japan*. "This dialogue is by no means confined to the stage; it permeates nearly every aspect of modern Japanese culture."[5]

Long before Disney began to adapt their animated features for the stage, Takarazuka was adapting works from their Manga (comic book) and Anime (animation) traditions. Takarazuka has, in turn, influenced the anime tradition. Leading animator Osamu Tezuka grew up in Takarazuka and his mother was friendly with many of the troupe members.

Berusaiyu no bara ("The Rose of Versailles") was a 1974 adaptation by Shinji Oeda (with music by Irie Kaouru, Hirao Masaaki, Kuratomi Shinchi, Terada Takio, Kawasaki Tsuneo and Yoshida Yuuko) of a 1972 comic book by Riyoko Ikeda about a young woman named Oscar who is raised as a boy. (Although she has a masculine name and dresses in male clothing, it is common knowledge among those who know her that she is in actuality a woman. In fact, she inspires a fashion for cross-dressing.) She grows up to be Marie Antoinette's personal guard, but becomes disenchanted with what she sees and ultimately joins the revolution.

The success of *Rose of Versailles* prompted Takarazuka to commission new scripts, which emphasised different sub-plots of the original story. Some dwelled on the romance between Marie Antoinette and her lover the Swedish Count Axel von Fersen. Others concentrated on the relationship between Oscar and her servant and best friend André Grandier. More recent versions have developed side stories about some minor characters, including Victor-Clément de Girodelle, the man whom Oscar is intended to join in an arranged marriage. (When the Revue adapted *Gone With the Wind*, they also created a "Scarlett version" and a "Rhett version".)

In total, the various Takarazuka versions of *Rose of Versailles* have been seen by some four million people. The same story also formed the basis for Jacques Demy's 1979 English-language film *Lady Oscar*. An anime television series appeared in the same year.

The Viennese musical *Elisabeth*, with book and lyrics by Michael Kunze and music by Sylvester Levay, has been performed several times by Takarazuka, and also in a more conventional version by the Toho Company. In fact, Maki Ichiro, the otokoyaku who played the androgynous male lead in the Takarazuka production, was later cast in the (female) title role in the Toho version. "When you get used to the strange fact that all characters are played by woman you find that the production works quite well"[6], says Kunze. "The audiences obviously love the Takarazuka version of *Elisabeth*. As a Japanese production, I prefer the one of the Toho Company." In fact, the two companies are affiliated: both were founded by Kobayashi and are now part of the Hankyu Hanshin Toho Group, which includes the famous Toho film studios, makers of *Godzilla* and the Tokyo run of *Les Misérables*.

With playwright Kazuo Kikuta (1908-73) as its head, the theatrical division of Toho introduced open ended runs in the 1950s, presenting both indigenous Japanese musicals such as *Morugan Oyuki* ("Oyuki Morgan") about a Geisha who marries into the J.P. Morgan family, as well as imported musicals like *My Fair Lady* in 1963[7], the first major production of a Broadway musical in Japan. He also wrote the book for *Scarlett*, a musical version of *Gone With the Wind*, with a score by Harold Rome and direction by Joe Layton. (This was later presented in London as *Gone with the Wind* with an English book by Horton Foote.) Kikuta is credited by some for revolutionising the presentation of musical theatre in Japan.[8]

Of course, there are other major players in the Japanese market. Shiki ("Four Seasons") Theatre Company was founded in 1953 by artistic director Keita Asari, and like Takarazuka, they provide a training regime for their actors. Their original shows have included *Yume Kara Samete Yume* ("A Dream Within a Dream") based on a novel by Jirō Akagawa, and *Yuta to Fushigina Nakama-tachi* ("Yuta's Enchanting Friends") based on a novel by Miura Tetsuo. They have also presented Japanese adaptations of West End and Broadway shows such as *Cats*, *A Chorus Line* and *Wicked*, as well as *Anne of Green Gables - The Musical* from Canada and *Le Passe Muraille* from France (produced on Broadway as *Amour*). When *Anne* opened in Tokyo, its composer, the late Norman Campbell told me, "There was no strangeness. Everyone thought we should react to a Japanese girl wearing red pigtails, but it was perfectly natural... The cast was excellent, all of them being good musicians and having great schooling in theatrical arts."[9]

Their first original musical was *The Emperor's New Clothes* in 1964, presented as part of the first Nissay Masterpiece Theatre, a programme sponsored by the Nissay cultural foundation to bring first class theatre to school children. Their first mainstage original show, *Ri Koran* premiered in Tokyo in 1991, then toured four cities in China in 1992 as part of celebrations of the twentieth anniversary of restoring diplomatic relations. *Ikoku-No-Oka*, presented in 2001, dealt with post-war prisoners in Siberia, and *Southern Cross* (2004) told the story of innocent Japanese soldiers accused of war crimes. *Ri Koran* and *Southern Cross*, together with *Foreign Hill* make up the *Showa Trilogy*. Shiki Theatre Company employs more than a thousand people with over 3,000 performances a year.

In 1969, a young student named Yutaka Higashi (1945-2000) left Waseda University with a plan to form a company of actors called the Tokyo Kid Brothers to present his own musicals. One of their first shows, *The Golden Bat*, with book and lyrics by Higashi and music by Itsuro Shimoda came to New York's La MaMa Experimental Theatre Club (where *Godspell* was originally developed) in 1970, then transferred to the Sheridan Square Playhouse. A second show, *The Moon is East, The Sun is West* toured Europe, and they returned to La MaMa with *Coney Island Play* and *The City*.

A decade later, *Shiro*, with book and lyrics by Higashi and music by Takashi Yoshimatsu told the story of a group of teenagers who travel back in time to 1623 and the great Shimbara Revolt, the greatest peasant uprising in Japanese history. *New York Times* correspondent Henry Scott-Stokes describes Higashi's work as "the right mixture of blatant sentimentality and deliberate *kitsch*. It's an echo of the old Kabuki tradition. There is lots of colour, noise, action – and tears, with elaborate tableaux and gorgeous costumes adjusted on stage by kuroko (black-clad stage hands)... If all this sounds risky, the entire show is a gamble befitting the theatre, a great throw of the dice. No one else in Japan but Mr. Higashi would risk the spectacle of fully armoured samurai trundling about the stage in horned hats to music from a tiny rock combo, reinforced by the magical *shakuhachi*, or bamboo flute."[10] Mel Gussow in the *New York Times* wrote, "*Shiro* is sumptuous in its design but in other respects it is a mixed blessing... The confrontation between contemporary street kids and medieval warriors is a promising idea, but the issue is confused in the telling. The dialogue is in long bursts of Japanese, followed by an often indecipherable bullet of English."[11] He added that Yoshimatsu's score "has an exotic Japanese flavor". Following its New York engagement in 1981, it transferred to the Kennedy Center in Washington, D.C., then toured the U.S. and Canada.

There are many other small companies creating original Japanese works. Musical-za, led by book writer Toru Hamanaka and composer Hideya Yamaguchi presented *New Yorkers* in 2003. The script resets *War and Peace* in New York at the time of the World Trade Centre attack. *Site*, produced in 2008 and directed by Toshiaki Takemoto, is about a community of people who withdraw from society into a world of cyberspace chat rooms. Eventually one lonely young woman arranges to meet some of her "pen-pals" only to discover that one of them is her own mother.

Another show that takes an intriguing twist on a Western classic is *Romeo & Juliet in Summer Night* produced by Arts Sphere Theatre with a book by Kazunori Tamano that combines two Shakespeare plays into one. *Blackout on Broadway* performed by Life Company with book by Hisao Kabuki and music by Mitsutaka Tajiri, is a true story about a Japanese diplomat in Lithuania named Chiune Sugihara (1900-86) who saved more than 6,000 Jews in World War II by signing their transit visas to Japanese territory.

Totemo Ghost (2006) has a book by Yoshikazu Yokoyama – artistic director of STEPS (Stage, Theatre, Entertainment, Performance and Show), with music by Shigeru Yahata. It tells the story of a young designer who dies in a car accident, and then comes back as a ghost and falls in love with a young man who can only see her after midnight. *I Love Botchan* (2007) based on a novel by Souseki Natsume with music by Motoki Funayama, is about a young teacher in rural Japan, while *Boy Be* with book by Yoshikazu Yokoyama and music by Shigeru Yahata is about a scientist who builds a robot to replace the son he lost.

Amon Miyamoto collaborated with the noted Singapore composer Dick Lee on *Hong Kong Rhapsody* (1993), which tells the story of a Japanese photographer covering the Tian-an-men massacre. He delivers a letter from a dying man to his daughter in Hong Kong. The inspiration came when, as a student in London, Miyamoto saw the massacre on the news. When he and a friend went to a pub in Leicester Square, he was mistaken for Chinese. Until that time, he considered London and New York, rather than China, to be his neighbours. "I have a confidence about the Japanese culture, but I didn't have a confidence about another Asian culture" he told me. "So I went back to Japan and did research about China where this happened. And in Japan, they said, 'Don't talk about that'. It's so forbidden, because Japan and China still have a distance. Politically they don't really get on." At first, Lee was reluctant to get involved. "It's so dangerous for him." However, he was anxious to explore the crossover between Western and Eastern music, and he agreed to do it.

Miyamoto is often cited as Japan's leading director of musicals, and is the founding artistic director of the Kanagawa Arts Theatre in Yokohama which opened at the beginning of 2011. His production of *Pacific Overtures* (for which he was nominated for a Tony award) has played in New York in both its Japanese and English versions.

(Kanagawa is the setting for the opening scene of *Pacific Overtures*.) His other Sondheim productions include Japanese versions of *Sweeney Todd* and *A Little Night Music*. His production of *The Fantasticks* played in London's West End in 2010. He cites directors Peter Brook, Robert LePage and Simon McBurney among his influences.

Amon's parents ran a coffee shop across from the Embujo Theatre in the Shambashi area of Tokyo. His mother had been a dancer, entertaining American troops after World War II, but she gave it up when she married his father, who didn't approve of the "showbiz" lifestyle. Still, she encouraged young Amon in his love of musicals, and coached him as he worked out his own dance routines. At one point, as a teenager, he stayed at home, refusing to go to school, and shut himself in his room with his beloved cast albums. (Small wonder that, many years later, he should identify himself with the Man in Chair character in *The Drowsy Chaperone*.) "At the time, I'm looking – why I grow up. How can I live from now? I wanted an answer." A production of *The Fantasticks* was a major influence, because "I was the same age as [its ingenues] Matt and Luisa, and so trying to find 'How can I grow up? What is my future?' That's the kind of guy I was." Tom Jones, who wrote the book and lyrics for that show, cites Peter Brook's book *The Empty Space* as a major influence, and Amon followed in the same footsteps. "I fell in love with Peter Brook's *The Empty Space*, and this is my most important thing at the moment, because what is real for me is always looking for something. It has to touch the heart. One record [he listened to was] *A Little Night Music*, and 'Send in the Clowns' made me so cry. And when I read *Empty Space*, this is for real. I decided to myself, I want to be a director some day. I can communicate more with people. How I can live honestly to myself. That's why I choose this theatre."

"In Japan, I think audiences are a little bit getting lazy. They sit waiting – what is next? – like a film. They don't want to use imagination. The theatre is alive. Audiences and casts are connected with creation. We are not animals, right? Human beings can make a creation with each other. This is a great moment for me – why I like theatre." He told Hideo Nakamura of *Chopsticks New York*, "We Japanese are people who appreciate the spirit behind things, in my opinion. We are people living in a culture that treasures things, no matter how small they are. I think that's what we can let the world know."[12]

Japan also has an intriguing collective community theatre movement. Gekidan Furusato Caravan is a touring company established in 1983 that performs original musicals about modern Japanese life written by its artistic director Katsuhiko Ishizuka. Some of their shows have traveled to Korea and the U.S. *Jishin Kaminari Kaji Oyaji* ("Earthquake Thunder Fire Father") (2007), with music by Tateo Teramoto was about volunteer firemen.

Another show that travelled internationally was *Bunna* (2001) produced by Theatre Project Shizuoka, based on the book *Come Down from the Tree, Bunna* by Tsutomu Minakami. It tells a story about a frog and his spiritual journey, learning of the interdependence of all living beings. It travelled to Birmingham for the Japan 2001 Festival.

Japan also imports musicals from other Asian markets, including Korea, Singapore and India. *Muthu* was an Indian musical that was exported to Japan by Indian Productions and Min-On Japan based on the film *Muthu, Dancing Maharaja*. "In the end of the show, all the audience stood up and most of them started to dance with the music," say Hiroko and Yoshihisa Honda, Japan correspondents to *Musical Stages*. "Both of us stood up without any hesitation and were very surprised to see young and old people were equally happy to dance with the performers. As you can imagine, the costumes were very exotic and beautiful."[13]

Of course, India has its own well established, vibrant tradition of film musicals. It is easy to see why Andrew Lloyd Webber was so anxious to draw on this, especially with a large Indian Diaspora in Britain. According to Indian journalist Mihir Bose, "Songs had been part of Indian films since the days of the talkies, reflecting the enormous part music, song and dance play in Indian daily life."[14] The tradition of Hindi musicals can be traced back to Sanskrit "natya", or dance-dramas, and to later Indian folk traditions and Parsi theatre. Elaborate and colourful dance numbers feature in many Hindi films, with leading actors usually lip-synching to recordings of professional singers. This form became especially popular after India achieved its independence in 1947. However, since classical Indian music is largely improvised, some Western conventions – such as music notation – had to be adopted in order to make filming practical.

Bose explains, "The Bombay film song had become the Indian song, with a song for every situation – romance, laughter, sadness, cabarets, eroticism – important in a country where the censor did not allow kissing on the screen… The songs lived on long after the films had been forgotten and Indian movie-goers had made it clear that a film without song was not worth going to."[15] While the films were influenced by the early Hollywood musicals, they departed from them in several important ways. "Indian filmmakers, while enhancing the elements of fantasy so pervasive in Indian popular films, used song and music as a natural mode of articulation in a given situation in their films", say K. Moti Gokulsing, K. Gokulsing and Wimal Dissanayake in their book *Indian Popular Cinema: A Narrative of Popular Change*. "There is a strong Indian tradition of narrating mythology, history, fairy stories and so on through song and dance… Whereas Hollywood filmmakers strove to conceal the constructed nature of their work so that the realistic narrative was wholly dominant, Indian filmmakers made no attempt to conceal the fact that what was shown on the screen was a creation, an illusion, a fiction. However, they demonstrated how this creation intersected with people's day to day lives in complex and interesting ways."[16] In turn, Australian director Baz Luhrmann says that Hindi musicals inspired his film *Moulin Rouge*.[17]

Only occasionally does the Bollywood form interact with its Western counterpart. In India, Disney's *High School Musical* was promoted through a series of

"My School Rocks" dance competitions, which produced some interesting localised results. "They are moving beyond those American-oriented movements and meanings to produce cohesive, hybrid, original dances,"[18] says Kristin Rudisill, Assistant Professor of Popular Culture at Bowling State University in Ohio. "This contest is not about careful viewing or even careful imitation of *High School Musical*, but about bringing Indian kids' own experiences and cultural capital to this American product and claiming it through their bodies and movement." The competitions were so popular that Disney repeated the idea in Malaysia, Singapore and Taiwan. (Although not noted as a breeding ground for musicals, even Taiwan came up with *The Chess King* in the early 1980s, produced by composer-turned-impresario Hsu Po-yun's International New Aspect Educational and Cultural Foundation.)

Adapting this form to the West End stage proved to be a daunting challenge. Producer Andrew Lloyd Webber began by approaching noted Indian film director Shekhar Kapur, who suggested the composer A. R. Rahman, a Bollywood legend who had scored the Oscar nominated *Lagaan*. Then he hired comedienne Meera Syal to write the book, and Don Black – the only non-Asian on the creative team – to do lyrics. Here the cultural gap was felt. Rahman, who had never seen a stage musical, was accustomed to improvising his music on synthesisers in a recording studio. "Getting full-length songs out of him was very difficult", Black told his biographer James Inverne. "It was a long, laborious job to get actual shapes of songs that could be right for the West End and Broadway. And I had to remember the whole time to tread that delicate line, getting the theatricality we needed and yet keeping Rahman's own distinctive voice."[19] *Bombay Dreams* enjoyed a modestly successful London run at the Apollo Victoria Theatre, although it disappeared quickly on Broadway.

The Philippines has been noted for the quality of its musical theatre talent ever since Lea Salonga won the title role in *Miss Saigon*. (In fact, Cameron Mackintosh found much of his cast there.) Most successful of the indigenous musical writers is Ryan Cayabyab (1954-), a pop singer who has also crossed over into the classical world as a composer, arranger and conductor of the now-defunct San Miguel Philharmonic Orchestra. His musicals have included *Noli Me Tangere* (1994, libretto by Bienvenido Lumbera) and *El Filibusterismo* (1996, libretto by Jovi Miroy) both based on novels by Filipino patriot Dr. Jose Rizal (1861-96), which toured Japan and Malaysia in the 1990s. Other works for the theatre include *Magnificat* and *Katy* (with a libretto by Jose Javier Reyes).

A New York-based company called Broadway Asia International with extensive involvement in Chinese performing arts brought a show called *Reel to Real, the Movies Musical* to the 2010 Edinburgh Fringe Festival. The multi-million pound show with a cast of twelve but a backstage crew of 32 used cutting edge projection technology to allow its live actors to interact with characters from classic Warner Brothers, MGM and 20th Century Fox movie musicals. The show, which was performed in English, used interpolated songs drawn from the catalogues of Rodgers and Hammerstein, Stephen

Sondheim, Frank Loesser, Irving Berlin and others. It was originally commissioned to open the Huairou Theatre in a suburb of Beijing. "There's a huge renaissance in Mainland China right now in terms of incorporating culture into the development of the socio-economic system", producer Simone Genatt Haft told *The Stage*. "It's a shift in perspective from when they were a country where culture was primarily for the purposes of propaganda."[20] Their next project, a contemporary adaptation of the traditional Kunqu opera *The Peony Pavilion*, by a team of Broadway artists, opened in Beijing in January 2012.

Broadway Asia has been involved in China since the government opened the market up to foreigners in 2005. Their productions have included *The Sound of Music*, *Cinderella*, *42nd Street*, *West Side Story*, *Cookin'* and *Hairspray*. They have also worked with the Shanghai Conservatory of Music on a student production of *Carousel* and the Shanghai Dramatic Arts Centre to train local performers. With the latter, they co-produced the first Mandarin language production of the off-Broadway hit musical, *I Love You, You're Perfect, Now Change* starring a Chinese pop star named Lin Yu-lin. In the last ten years, Broadway Asia has toured shows in thirty-five cities throughout Mainland China. Gennatt told me they "have always focused on a two-way cultural bridge, bringing the best of Broadway to Asia and developing new shows with Asian artists."[21]

Similarly, Nederlander Worldwide Entertainment, who presented *Aïda* in Beijing in 2008, has worked with both Central Academy of Drama and Peking University to develop localised adaptations of Broadway shows, including a Mandarin version of *Fame*.

In the past decade, musicals have become very big business in Korea. In 1998 a Korean musical crossed the Atlantic for a run at New York's Lincoln Center. *The Last Empress*, with music by Kim Hee Gab and lyrics by Lee Moon Roel, tells the story of Queen Min, wife of King Kojong, the late-nineteenth century monarch who fought a futile struggle to maintain Korea's independence from Japan. (Min was eventually assassinated.) Director Yun Ho Jin explains, "The form is Western-style, the sets are Western, but the songs carry a lot of Korean rhythm and emotion." The show premiered in Seoul on December 30 1995, and was brought to New York three years later.

"The Korean musical is going to boom," said the show's American-educated musical director Kolleen Park at the time. "We are the frontiersmen. That's why we shed tears and blood. We've been working on this show for seven years. The musical is here to stay."

Between 2000 and 2002, musical grosses in Korea jumped from US$30 million to over $110 million, or roughly half of all live performing arts takings. By 2006 the figures had nearly doubled again. This has made the country's moribund film industry sit up and take notice. "These days, audiences are responding much better to musicals than films," says Kim Mi-hee of film company Sidus FNH. "The musical industry has huge possibilities insofar as it attracts talent and money."[22] Goh Jung-min of the Samsung Economic Research Institute says, "The musicals sector is slowly becoming one of the areas with the brightest prospects."[23] More than a thousand musicals were produced in Korea in 2005.

At first, the beneficiaries of this new market were the usual suspects – *Phantom of the Opera*, *Mamma Mia!* and *Miss Saigon*. Then things took a rather unique turn, as film producers began to adapt their own catalogues to the musical stage, and a number of investment funds have been created to back new ventures.

One of these "movicals", *Nae maeumui punggeum* ("The Harmonium in My Memory") is based on a 1999 film of the same name, which in turn was based on a novel called *Female Student* about a sixteen year old girl who falls in love with her teacher in rural 1960s Korea.

Another recent movie-to-stage adaptation was *200 Pound Beauty*, about a singer who undergoes plastic surgery to lose weight, in order to improve her career prospects. The show combined some songs heard in the original film with a score by American composer Tim Acito. It opened in Seoul in January 2009 at Chungmu Art Hall.

Comedian Baek Jae-hyun created an adaptation of Neil Simon's *The Good Doctor* called *Lunatic* that has been seen by more than 600,000 people since its debut in 2004. For his follow-up creation, *Skywalk*, he is aiming even higher. "With the experience and know-how I gained doing *Lunatic*, I hope to make the show popular across Korea first, and ultimately on Broadway"[24], he told Han Aran of Korea.net. Another musical of his, *Steam-Family*, about the Korean martial art Taekwondo enjoyed an off-Broadway run in October 2008.

Some Korean musicals tackle serious subjects. Jung Sung San's *Yoduk Story* is set in a North Korean prison camp, featuring song titles such as "If I Could Walk Freely" and "All I Want Is Rice." Faced with resistance to his difficult subject matter, Jung at one point borrowed money to finance the show from a loan shark, putting up his kidney as collateral. "Even a dark and tragic story can be beautiful," he told *Los Angeles Times*' Barbara Demick. "It will make them realize what happy lives they have here".[25] Jung defected from the North in the early 1990s, after being imprisoned for listening to South Korean radio. His father, a highly placed civil servant, was later executed.

Korean producers have begun to look beyond their own domestic market, exporting both homegrown and Korean productions of Broadway and West End shows. "It shows the growth of the Korean musical that a Korean troupe is staging a Broadway musical hit in our native language in Japan, a nation which is so proud of its long performing arts history", says Eric Song of Shownote, whose production of *Hedwig and the Angry Inch* toured in 2006. They have also sent home-grown works there. *Winter*

Sonata based on a Korean TV drama with music by Kim Kyong Suk, toured to Sapporo, Tokyo and Osaka.

All of this is very remarkable for a country that, until the twentieth century, had no indoor theatres. Only after a strong merchant class began to emerge at the end of the nineteenth century was there a demand for this type of entertainment. This led to an indigenous Korean form of music-theatre called Ch'anggŭk, or "singing play", with roots in an earlier tradition of P'ansori, or dramatic narrative singing, which dates from the late seventeenth century. In the latter, a solo singer is accompanied by a round drum called a puk. Originally the performances would take place outdoors, in a market or a green. The Ch'anggŭk expanded on this by distributing the parts among a number of singers, adding sets and a larger ensemble of traditional instruments, performed in a theatre. However, P'ansori purists looked on Ch'anggŭk as a dilution of their form, and with its short history, it has struggled to firmly establish itself. "I wouldn't say that ch'anggŭk has influenced Western-style musicals in Korea as far as I know," says Dr. Andrew Killick, senior lecturer in ethnomusicology at the University of Sheffield, "though the reverse is certainly true and ch'anggŭk itself often tries to combine traditional Korean music with elements of modern Western musical theatre. In fact, some recent productions have been advertised as 'musicals with traditional music'."[26] When asked if there was any potential to use ch'anggŭk in modern musicals, he replied "I don't think that's very likely except for occasional scenes of 'diagetic' [source music] P'ansori singing in musicals with a historical Korean setting."[27]

Singapore, on the other hand, is a country with virtually no musical theatre tradition. However, it is so full of contradictions – an Asian country that speaks English, for a start – that it is perhaps not so surprising that they should want to sing and dance. Its name translates as "lion city", although lions have never been native to this city state of just under five million people. Originally a Malay fishing village, the East India Company founded it as a British trading fort in 1819. It has four official languages: English, Mandarin, Tamil and Malay, of which Mandarin Chinese form the largest ethnic group. The working language is English, which everybody learns in school. Since gaining independence in 1965, the city-state has concentrated on economic development, and until the late 1980s, paid scant attention to the arts. That has now changed, and the government is actively promoting it as a "Renaissance" city.

"I used to go to pantomimes when I was a kid, because I grew up in colonial Singapore with a very colonial grandmother", says composer Dick Lee (1956-). "My father used to work with a lot of British and Dutch people in Shell Petroleum, so my upbringing was pretty Western."

It was in 1988 that Lee premiered what is considered to be the first major native Singaporean musical. *Beauty World*, with a book by Michael Chiang, tells the story of a young woman who returns to Singapore and a cabaret called Beauty World in the period after World War II in search of her family. The title refers to an actual amusement park and market that began during the Japanese occupation and continued until the 1970s which had areas for performance as well as for gambling. Its initial production by Theatreworks ran for eleven sold-out performances, seen by nearly 10,000 people. It has been revived three times and toured Japan. There have also been student productions abroad, one at the University of Chicago in 2006, and another at King's College London in 2009.

Malaysian-born actress Claire Wong was in the original production in 1988. "Before that I was doing a lot of Western plays, where locals would go up on stage and use blonde wigs and speak with an English accent, because they were playing these white characters," she told the Kuala Lumpur *Star*. "*Beauty World* was, in fact, one of the first early plays created and told by people who were close to us – who were us. It was the first time I went on stage and spoke normally as a local person would. It was a very exciting period."[28]

"*Beauty World*'s success, with its secrets, cabaret girls and themes of rape and Japanese love, has been popularised by Singaporeans because it is something to which they can relate", says Dr. Aaron Hales of the University of Western Australia. "As such, Chiang and Lee have written about these themes using history, humour and song that draws upon clichéd Singaporean characters reminiscent of the 1950s and 1960s..."[29] Although *Beauty World*'s music is largely the Latin-based pop that was popular in Singapore in the late 1950s, it is also influenced by Cantonese melodrama, and uses such localised Asian entertainment forms as *getai* ("song-stage") and *gamelan* (a type of performance associated with the Hungry Ghost Festival), both of which featured in the real Beauty World park.

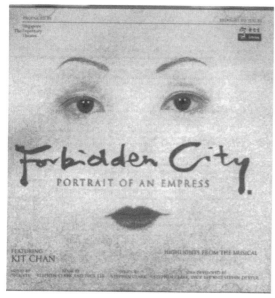

"*Beauty World*, intended for tourist consumption and composed with Western techniques, has actually used Asian music genres that are either specific or geographically related to Singapore itself", says Dr. Hales. "It is interesting to note that in his pursuit of creating a West End or Broadway-styled musical, my analysis suggests that Lee has, whether it be a conscious or unintentional choice, done so using musical composition structures and performance genres very much rooted in Southeast Asia and Singapore itself."[30]

Forbidden City (2002) has been, to date, Lee's – and Singapore's – biggest success. Chosen to open the Esplanade Theatres, it tells the story of China's last empress through the eyes of an American woman who has been hired to paint her portrait. It has been revived three times since opening in 2002. "Everything that I'm doing, I feel that I'm laying some kind of foundation", Lee says.

"Being Asian working in a Western medium, I'm always faced with this issue of East meets West… There's a true, very real sense of fusion from Singapore, because we speak English… It does confuse us writers because … I am Chinese doing things in English in a Western medium using mainly Western influences and yet being Asian". As a result, even his perceptions of Asia are westernised. "All my references have been from *Madame Butterfly* to *Turandot*. All the big, major interpretations of Asia I've seen have been from the West… All of us in the arts are trying to find our own voice."

Lee is seventh generation Peranakan Chinese, a minority group whose ancestors settled on the Malay Peninsula and became assimilated into Malay culture, and his first language is English. "My relatives all speak Malay… The irony is that eighty-percent of our population is Chinese, so there is the problem in terms of racial harmony. The Malays were outnumbered by us Chinese. A few thousand of us Peranakans were in between. We were once the bridge, but we ended up being more British than anything else. The new Singapore has got a lot more tradition infused from the different ethnic groups because so many more immigrants came in. Most of the Singaporeans you see are second generation. They are still very Chinese. They bring a strong Chinese culture, which is why there are many pop stars from Singapore in the Chinese market. This coupled with the way the colonial past mixed with this new thing, I think that's creating

Forbidden City: Hossan Leong and Sebastian Tan.
Photo Sealey Brand courtesy Singapore repertory Theatre

something very interesting."

While Lee has been a pioneer, and is so far the most successful writer of Singaporean musicals, there are others who are trying to develop new work. Another Singapore musical that has travelled to Malaysia, Thailand and China was *Chang and Eng* (about the original "Siamese" twins) which received its world premiere in 1997 at the Festival of Asian Performing Arts, with book by Ming Wong and music and lyrics by Malaysian-born Ken Low, the director of the brand management division of the Singapore Tourism Board. It starred Robin Goh as Chang, Sing Seng Kwang as Eng and Selena Tan as their mother Nok. *Malaysian Business* magazine wrote, "The depth and myriad emotions that the audience experienced just from watching the musical is testament to the level of talent and expertise involved in the Asian production."[31] The cast included a mixture of Singaporean, Thai, Filipino, Malaysian and Australian talent (including one-time *Neighbours* star Nathalie Basingthwaite). The director, from Thailand, was Ekachai Uekrongtham. After playing in Malaysia, Thailand and Beijing, China, it was revived in Singapore in 2001.

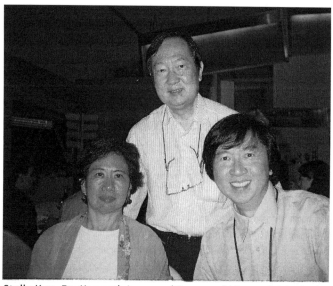

Stella Kon, Dr. Kenneth Lyen and Desmond Moey of Musical Theatre Limited

"Singapore is at the crossroads between the Far East and the West", says Dr. Kenneth Lyen, a noted paediatrician, composer and vice-president of Musical Theatre Limited, a development group for original Singapore musicals. "Our musical theatre influences are from England and the USA on the one hand, China and Japan on the other, and perhaps to a lesser extent, Southeast Asia and India." Lyen studied medicine in England in the 1970s, where in his free time he saw shows like *A Chorus Line*. He became hooked.

Beginning in October 2004, Musical Theatre Limited has been running a programme called "Beat By Beat" to "incubate" new musicals, by presenting them in a no-frills environment as part of the Singapore Festival of the Arts fringe. Seven playwrights were teamed with seven composers, and assigned mentors. In February 2005, a director was assigned to each team. In April, performers were brought in, and each musical was read in front of all the participants. According to Lyen, "a community of collaborators, producers, directors and actors was created." These shows were presented in front of an audience in June 2005, as part of *Five Foot Broadway*, in collaboration with the United Artistes Network and the Next Stage Performing Arts

Academy. "The general public's response was overwhelmingly positive", says Lyen. "Not only did we have full houses every night, but we received a heavy demand for tickets, and eventually had a waiting list of 150 members of the public who were unable to get tickets." In August 2005, Creative Community Singapore became involved. Since that time they have staged 22 new musicals. The mentoring programme has also been bolstered. Only shows that receive a positive dramaturgical report go on to the next stage. While they have yet to produce any world beating successes, it is still early days, and they know they have a long way to go. Part of their aim is to create training programmes and workshops for composers, lyricists and book writers.

Unlike Lee, Dr. Lyen doesn't feel the "dislocation between East and West". Like the majority of Singaporeans, he is second generation Chinese. "We embrace both Eastern and Western cultures quite naturally. We lapse into English and Chinese with ease, and hardly notice anything out of the ordinary... most Singaporeans, especially those who are more recent immigrants, retain their Chinese cultural heritage, whereas the Peranakans who are a much older vintage, have almost totally forgotten their Chinese culture. They cannot even speak Chinese. This makes them feel culturally dislocated. It is observed that many prominent personalities in the performing arts are Peranakans (a far greater proportion than expected given their relatively small population size), and I have often wondered if it is because of their sense of dislocation that makes them feel like 'outsiders'. The theory is that artists tend to be people who do not fit in with their society or culture."

Esplanade Theatres on the Bay

Until the *Report of the Advisory Council on Culture and the Arts* recognised the importance of cultural investment in 1989, Singapore had been a virtual wasteland. "Countries all over the world are recognising the positive impact of the arts on the economy"[32], wrote the report's author, Ong Teng Cheong, then the country's second Deputy Prime Minister. Lyen believes that the arts and the creative industries are vital to Singapore's continued prosperity. "Government policy has a great influence on the arts. The Government suddenly realised that in order to get brilliant people to come and live in Singapore, they have to diversify. They have to tolerate different religions, different viewpoints, and so now suddenly they've woken up and they now want to have musical theatre as one of the many art forms." According to William Peterson, who helped establish a theatre programme at the National University of Singapore, "No cultural terrain in Singapore has received more conscious engineering on the part of the government or prominent individuals in the arts community than the Singaporean Musical."[33] In recent years, the Singapore government has invested some S$600 million in developing the Esplanade, a complex of theatres, concert hall and a performing arts library that opened in October 2002 with Dick Lee's *Forbidden City*, co-produced with Singapore Repertory Theatre. Since then, a major casino and entertainment complex has opened at Marina Bay Sands, where BASE Entertainment Asia staged a smash hit production of *The Lion King*. Thien Kwee Eng, Executive Director of the Economic Development Board hopes that producers "can find in Singapore world-class performing venues, as well as forge collaborations with our creative talent and theatre groups."[34]

Lily Kong, Associate Professor in the Department of Geography at the National University of Singapore says, "I will suggest that, despite the rhetoric about the importance of the arts in developing a 'gracious society', the major motivation behind cultural policy is economic; indeed, often, the economic works through the socio-cultural. Certainly, despite fears about the potential threat to the development of 'Singaporean' artistic and cultural forms posed by cultural development policies which appear to privilege foreign talents over local ones, such presumed challenges to the construction of a 'Singaporean idiom' are dismissed by the state whereas in other arenas, it has been vigorous in efforts to construct a 'nation' and build national identity."[35] Between 2005 and 2010, government investment in the arts rose by 82%, with the hope that the arts will contribute 6% of gross domestic product by 2012. "If they want vibrancy," says Dr. Lyen, "they've got to pay for it."

Lee adds, "Singapore is striving to be a global city. Singapore has been criticised for its stringent, old-fashioned ways and they need to open up. They realise that, but they don't quite know how to do it... You can't just let loose. Personally, I think some kind of governance is good, because we don't really know where to go. Being born and bred in Singapore, I cannot try and replicate Western values the way I'd like. I think it would be chaotic. It has to come one step at a time."

For some people, those "stringent, old-fashioned ways" have been a stumbling block to the musical's progress. If musical theatre developed alongside democracy, then how does it fare in a place where democracy is still quite constrained? While, since obtaining full independence from Britain in the 1960s, Singapore has become one of the most prosperous countries in Asia, it is looked on by many Westerners as being highly authoritarian. The U.S. based Freedom House classes it as "partly free". Homosexuality is frowned upon. Party political films are banned. Although it regards itself as a parliamentary democracy, ever since home rule was established it has been ruled exclusively by the People's Action Party, and is effectively a one-party state.

"The rise of musical theatre requires a democracy, and also economic well-being," says Lyen. "Our government, which has been very successful economically, has been less successful in terms of the arts, in part because of their fear of the Communist element, and also civil unrest due to racial conflict. Censorship was very heavy. Shows were not allowed to have any racial or ethnic conflict in it, nor could they have anything to do with overt politics – especially left-wing politics – and gay movement, same-sex relationships were also frowned upon… All we could do was write romantic comedies. You run out of ideas after a while. This really deterred a lot of people from writing." About *Beauty World*, Dr. Aaron Hales of the University of Western Australia says, "The fact that Chiang and Lee are able to write about contentious issues such as race and class within Singapore is a testament to the genre of the musical. Practitioners of the arts, for fear of censorship, generally avoid issues of race within their representations, as such subject matter is heavily scrutinised by the government."[36]

Librettist Stella Kon, Musical Theatre Limited's chairperson, told me of a rather blatant example of censorship in a play called *Trial*, in which Socrates is on trial in Singapore: "It came back with one line cut. The line was where a student gets up and shouts, 'There is no freedom of speech in Singapore!' You're not allowed to say there is no freedom of speech in Singapore!" The play went on, minus that one line. "It was crafted such that everything was said between the lines." Lyen adds, "We write fairy tales, we write folk tales, but actually we are writing about Singapore. So when we write [in] *The Magic Paintbrush* [2000, with music by Lyen and book and lyrics by Brian Seward] about the dictatorial emperor, it is actually about Singapore… We defy the government in our own very subtle way, and they don't seem to have noticed."

(Singapore's neighbour Malaysia also suffers from censorship. "No musicals that have elements of dissent or put the government in a bad light are allowed," says librettist Teng Ky-Gan. "Ever." More about that later.)

Although things in Singapore have been liberalised in recent years, the legacy of repression has resulted in a kind of arrested development. Aaron Hales says, "I would argue it is impossible to sustain and expand culture if it is illegal to comment upon almost every cultural aspect of society in which you live."[37] "If we were allowed, we could have explored all these issues, the controversies and the emotional depth," says Dr. Lyen. "We could have produced really world-class plays and musicals… One of the problems I find now with the younger generation of writers is that they don't want to tackle these subjects. They shy away from them, which to me is a tragedy… To me, the best writers are the rebels."

Aaron Hales wrote his doctoral thesis on the influence of censorship on Singapore's indigenous musical theatre. In it, he discusses three musicals by Dick Lee: *Beauty World* (1988), *Mortal Sins* (1995) and *Forbidden City* (2002). Hales argues that it is *Mortal Sins*, one of Lee's least known works, which is most interesting. The book by Michael Chiang is openly critical of Singapore's censorship regime. "*Mortal Sins* – intended as a popular product for Singaporean and tourist consumption – articulates the conservative ideology within the island nation. The musical was far too confronting for Singaporean audiences – it was not a comedy with light-hearted music. Instead, its narrative was serious, tackling the serious problems that underpin Singapore, such as censorship and suggestions of corruption in the civil service – themes that are generally located in 'niche' theatre representations and not large scale musical theatre representations."[38] It played for a week to full houses, but has never been revived, and Lee doesn't even include it in the biography on his website.

However, Lee claims that he has not suffered from censorship. "They used to censor local works but now most theatre companies practice self-censorship. They trust us. I'm with the Singapore Repertory Theatre, so I know we don't have to submit our scripts anymore." Dr. Lyen adds, "Funnily enough, when you are immersed in the Singapore system, you are less consciously aware about the effects of censorship... And to be fair to the Singapore government, the days of heavy censorship is largely over, and nowadays there is considerable freedom of expression... with the one proviso that if you are seeking Government funding for a controversial show, you may sometimes find yourself inexplicably unfunded."

Singapore also lacks a sufficient pool of trained actors, musicians, technicians, directors and choreographers. "We had to more or less start from scratch," says Lyen. "Singapore is quite dated in its content", says Amanda Colliver, an Australian-born singing teacher at the LaSalle College of the Arts, "but you have cultural things that you don't want to leave behind in the name of Western progression, and I think that's a very challenging mixture." However, according to Colliver, Singapore has yet to develop triple-threats – actors who also sing and dance with equal proficiency. "The level is quite low here, but the potential is here."[39] Dr. Lyen says, "We do have good performers here, but you can count them on one hand. We often import a lot of singers. The Philippines is blessed with quite a large talent pool... We are training our directors, we are training our singers, choreographers, dancers, the whole lot. It's a team effort."

Dick Lee has frequently worked with British and American collaborators. "I had been in Japan for about five or six years, and I'd done three musicals in Japan. The Japanese tradition for theatre and musicals is so strong. It's so professional, so developed. When I was considering doing a musical in Singapore, I wanted the same standards. The Singapore Repertory Theatre was an offshoot of a theatre group called Stars – the American community theatre in Singapore. The man who ran it, Tony Petito, when he came to see me, I got the sense that he wanted to have a very high standard, and that meant bringing in and collaborating with people from Broadway and the West End." His first show written this way was *Sing to the Dawn* (1996), with London based South African-born director Steven Dexter (1962-), who had previously staged *Little Shop of Horrors* for SRT. "Tony Petito wanted the musical to be properly constructed with the right production values that a musical should have." He brought in lyricist Anthony Drewe (*Honk!, Mary Poppins, Betty Blue Eyes*), with whom he would also work on *A Twist of Fate* the following year. A few years later, he teamed up with Dexter again, along with lyricist Stephen Clark (*Martin Guerre, Zorro, Love Story*) to write *Forbidden City* for the opening of the Esplanade Centre in 2002.

Dr. Lyen feels that more could be done to develop Singapore's own writing talent. "Dick Lee realizes that book writing and lyric writing is relatively weak here in Singapore, and so he collaborates with English book writers and lyricists. While it gives him instant credibility and brings his works up to international standard via the express stream, it raises a few thorny questions... The look and feel of his musicals are very British. Indeed, you would not realise they are from Singapore, despite the fact that the subject matter is Asian... His works are not really representative of Singapore in language and 'soul'... Having said that, Dick Lee deserves a place in the hall of fame of Singapore musical theatre writers."

Although Singapore speaks English, it has its own unique dialect known as Singlish, a pidgin English which borrows words from Malay, Hokkien, Tamil, Cantonese and other south-east Asian languages. Singlish has always been frowned on by the government, who want to promote Standard English. "We do it when we're talking to our friends and our children and our neighbours," says Dr. Lyen. "It's colloquial English spoken, and some of the songs, especially songs written by Dick Lee, contain a lot of Singlish. Some of the words, like the word 'kiasu' is actually a Hokkien term." It refers to fear of failure, in which you modify your behaviour so you do things that are not necessarily socially acceptable. For example, at a buffet, you take more than you need because you are afraid that when you come back later the food will be gone. "We do borrow a lot of phrases from other dialects – Malay, Chinese, Indian... In a sense this has affected our theatre because it's less able to travel. If people cannot understand lyrics in Singlish, it is less likely that these shows will travel overseas." To illustrate, he says, "It is relatively cheap to employ a rickshaw puller, it is therefore a 'cheap buy', meaning an inexpensive purchase, but 'cheebye' is also a Hokkien very fowl word. Your grandmother will kill you if you use that word."

Some Singlish was employed in *Beauty World*, but Dick Lee felt that the results were mixed. "There's a very fine line between it sounding comical and a bit over-the-top. Even with Singlish-speaking Singaporean actors, when they do Singlish on stage, it sounds forced. I don't know why, they can't speak naturally. They're only just now starting to do that... [The audiences] don't laugh anymore. Now a lot of theatre has gone very natural." Dr. Lyen adds, "When Dick Lee's *Beauty World* came out in 1988, it was chocker-block full of Singlish. Only Singaporeans could understand it. But that was fine because only Singaporeans watched it... Therefore we are caught in this awful dilemma – should we write for an international audience with the hope that our shows can travel abroad? Or should we write something that reflects our culture?... You can see why musical theatre has trouble finding its own voice here in Singapore because of our conflicted use of English."

For Dr. Lyen and his group, developing a strong sense of Singapore identity is important. "We are in the business of discovering and nurturing new talent, and to carve out a unique Singapore voice, influenced by but different from Broadway and

West End", says Dr. Lyen. "Indeed we have a lot of young raw talent. My job now is to find a way to help them develop further, and if necessary, to invite people from Broadway and the West End to help in this process. Our mission at Musical Theatre Ltd is not only to build up our creative team and performers, but we are also trying to increase our audience size. Our core objective is to get people writing, and we do 'demo' staged readings. Also we are actively involved in community and school musicals."

Although most Singapore musicals have been in English, there has been a recent trend toward shows in Mandarin. "Everything seems to have come together over the past three years", Goh Boon Teck, chief Artistic Director of the Toy Factory told the *New York Times*' Sonia Kolesnikov-Jessop in 2010. "The few Mandarin musicals that have been put on so far have done well at the box office."[40] These have included *December Rains*, with a book by Liang Wern Fook and songs by Liang and Jimmy Ye, first presented by Toy Factory Productions in 1996, and revived at the Esplanade Centre in 2010. It tells the story of an idealistic young woman who falls for a political activist in 1950s Singapore. "Such familiarities have a stronger pull"[41], says J. P. Nathan, director of programming at the Esplanade. Other Toy Factory musicals have included Raymond To Kwok-Wai's *Shanghai Blues* (2007).

It is the stated aim of the Singapore government to develop a "renaissance" city, but they face a number of obstacles. "In a nation built upon the necessity for financial success", asks Aaron Hales, "where is the space for artistic failure if every artistic product has to be considered an economic miracle?"[42] Dr. Hales does not believe that shows like *Forbidden City*, which seem to him tailored to gain official approbation, are the answer. "*Forbidden City* is a safe, reliable spectacle – highly colonialist – with clichéd depictions of Western music and imagery. It is colourful and bright and contains stereotypical Chinese costumes for colonial viewing. The production adheres to all the stage conventions for a European and American audience. At the same time, Singaporean audiences appreciated these themes and the musical sold out repeatedly. It is the perfect production for the selling of an Asian stereotype." But, says Hales, it "defines everything wrong with the Singaporean arts – all of Singapore is removed from the narrative… The local Singaporean public does not endorse works that challenge the audience and push theatrical boundaries in Singapore. Therefore, no 'endorsed' musical theatre product from Singapore is going to make a mark on the global arts scene."[43]

Dick Lee counters, "Nowadays the problem we're facing is sponsorship. A musical costs so much to stage. You have to sell so many tickets at such high prices to recover, which is why *Beauty World* could only be staged [in revival] because it had been staged three times before. But to do a new show with a new title would be – I wouldn't even take that risk. Not now."

Broken Bridges
Photo courtesy Teng Ky-gan

Like its neighbour, Malaysia has a nascent musical theatre culture. Playwright and lyricist Teng Ky-gan (1982-) began in 2006 by collaborating with composer Lim Chuang Yik on *Broken Bridges* about a young man who returns to his home town of Ipoh (Teng and Lim's home town) in the 1950s. "He comes home with bright ideas," says Teng, "but the people of the town hate him for bringing change."

The following year the same team created *Tunku*, a historical epic. However, censorship in Malaysia is even more restrictive than in its neighbour. "I'm surprised it got through," says Teng. "It was about a racial riot in 1969. The official government version [of history] is that the opposition started the riot. My musical showed the government starting the riot (to cut the very long story short). I was surprised it escaped banning, but my guess is that the person who read it couldn't read English very well, especially if it's in verse form... If you keep your lines ironic or sarcastic, they usually can't see further than what is written. Many political plays have been let through this way." Like Dick Lee, Teng's first language is English. Just as Singapore has "Singlish", so Malaysia has its own native form of pidgin English called Manglish. Teng's ethnic background is Chinese, which makes him part of a minority in this Islamic, Malay dominated country.

According to Teng, the government encourages musicals that advance its own agenda. "Anti west/ anti colonialism/ anti Jew musicals or musicals with these elements are a big favourite. Stories of Malay rebels slaughtering evil white colonizers are also big."

The official performing arts centre in Kuala Lumpur is the Istana Budaya ("Palace of Culture") which presents classical music, opera and musical theatre. One Malaysian musical that was presented there to great success was *Puteri Gunung Ledang* (2006) with music by Dick Lee and book by Adlin Aman Ramlie, Saw Teong Hin and Zahim Al-Bakri based on a 2004 Malaysian film of the same name. It also travelled to Singapore's Esplanade Centre.

Singapore and Malaysia are both at the beginning stages of developing a musical theatre culture. I believe they could benefit from the guidance of visiting foreign artists, but only if those artists are sensitive to the local idiom. While they do have a few composers with potential, they have yet to develop world-class lyricists and book writers. However, a teacher who wants merely to impose West End and Broadway values would not benefit them, unless they can also help to nurture their own nascent voices. The principles of good lyric writing can surely be adapted to Singlish and Manglish. They have a long road ahead of them. With the right nurturing – and some master classes – who knows?

New Musicals: "You Have to Kiss a Lot of Frogs"

In the mid-1970s, I had a conversation with Jennings Lang (1915-96), who was then a vice-president of Universal Pictures. We were talking about who we thought might advance the musical into the twenty-first century. I mentioned Andrew Lloyd Webber and Tim Rice to the man whom, a few years previously, had green-lit the film version of *Jesus Christ Superstar*. He shook his head. "One hit wonders", he said. Lang was not alone in this assessment; Richard Kislan's book *The Musical*, published in 1980, doesn't even mention Lloyd Webber by name, and dismisses his potential impact on musical theatre by saying, "Not surprisingly, the rock opera frenzy initiated by *Tommy* and *Jesus Christ Superstar* declined simultaneously with the popularity of those productions."[1] (And *Evita* had already been running for a couple of years when he said this.) Critic Mark Steyn writes, "To Broadway folk, Lloyd Webber was just one of many writers who had emerged in the peace and love era, turned out one rock musical and then disappeared."[2]

Yet, three decades later, Lloyd Webber and his contemporaries are equally dismissive of the next generation. "There is a great misconception in the heart of the musical theatre industry that the world is littered with Cole Porters and Irving Berlins", says lyricist Don Black. "It is not. They are not out there and Andrew Lloyd Webber is always saying he wishes he had more competition from younger people. There is not a bunch of new people writing."[3] His fellow lyricist Sir Tim Rice concurs. "Where is a single young team or young writer writing fresh new musicals that are successful? I can't think of one."[4] But when somebody complained to American director Harold Prince that "there are no composers anymore", he replied, "That's nonsense! There are not enough serious, creative producers."[5] By way of contrast, in the late fifties-early sixties, Frank Loesser actively nurtured the careers of Meredith Willson, Jerry Herman, Adler and Ross and many others.

"I think that the majority of producers are incredibly complacent about new work", says Georgina Bexon, former Executive Director of Mercury Musical Developments. "They think the really hot musical is just going to land on their desks. They don't accept the challenge of going out and searching." "For my mind", says Chris Grady of Musical Theatre Matters, "we have to do a lot of development work first to see that there is cream to rise to the surface." In other words, you have to feed and milk the cow.

Sir Cameron Mackintosh maintains, "There have never been that many really good musicals… We can all probably agree on the top dozen, but then we'd all have a huge argy-bargy about the next 20. And that's about all there is."[6] Of the many musicals he receives from unknown writers, "Ninety percent are terrible. They're

222

untalented and shouldn't write musicals… There's also a group of people out there who are talented, who can write terrific songs, good lyrics. But only rarely do you find people who can write a good *musical*… *What you write about* is as important as what you've written… A lot of these scripts – there is no reason for people to see these shows."

Not all of us see the half-empty glass. The real misconception is that you can always spot a diamond in the rough. Few people who heard "We're Six Little Nieces of Our Uncle Sam" back in 1917 thought to remember the name of the composer – somebody called George Gershwin. Writers do not appear out of the woodwork like magic. They must be trained and nurtured. Even *My Fair Lady* was not an obvious hit in its developmental stage – when Lerner and Loewe auditioned their score for Mary Martin, she reportedly said, "These dear boys have lost their talent!"[7] And they weren't alone – Rex Harrison was not initially won over by the score either.[8] Mackintosh concedes, "Most of what we look back on now as the great classics of musical theatre were basically shows that everyone else in the theatre thought was [sic] going to be crap and thrown out of town. I mean, *Romeo and Juliet* with street gangs?"

"Nowadays the terrible thing is that young people don't get a chance to be heard," said Stephen Sondheim in 1973. "And therefore they get discouraged and say, 'Screw it,' and they start writing stuff for movies, or they try to start a rock group. It's awful. A terrible shame – nobody gets a chance to learn what he's doing."[9] Things have not improved since then.

In the U.S., where the development of new musicals has always been taken more seriously, there is a trend toward workshopping at universities. Tracey Moore, who played Emma Goldman in the national tour of *Ragtime*, is now the head of the Musical Theatre program at Western Kentucky University. "Spending so much time in the presence of musical theatre writers in my career as a musical theatre performer meant that many become close friends, so it was a natural consequence that I would start a new musical development series at my university, twenty years later," she wrote in *Studies in Musical Theatre*. "I call it 'Before Broadway'. And mine is not the only one. I've noticed a surprising groundswell of new musical performances – in small schools like mine and in Banner Elk, North Carolina, and in larger ones like Penn State, Yale and Northwestern. University theatre programmes have become a new, safe place for writers, a place where they can make mistakes and learn from them – in front of an audience."[10] Oklahoma City University's Bass School of Music started a similar program, "OCU Stripped", in 2006.

However, outside the U.S., new musicals are not being so widely supported. In 2003, the British parliament's Culture, Media and Sport Committee held a series of hearings into the state of funding for musical theatre development in the UK. This coincided with a funding crisis that had engulfed both the Bridewell Theatre and the

National Youth Music Theatre. The transcripts of these hearings were published in 2005, and they make interesting reading.

"We should be asking ourselves why there are so few brand new musicals by British writers in the West End", said the written submission from Mercury Musical Developments, "and to answer that question, one has to look behind the successful gloss of West End musical theatre at the structure that lies behind it, or, rather, the lack of any kind of funded structure. It is easy to conclude that, because of the success of certain West End musicals, plenty of money is floating around the industry. Unfortunately, however, this income is returned to private investors ('angels') and to the producers as profit (once costs are recouped) and is not being fed back into the grass roots level of development, to the very area where it is most needed. West End producers can and will happily continue to stage revivals and pop shows but these shows say little about the world we live in and are doing little to advance an art form which is the most popular live art form in the world. We need to create a proper structure for new musicals to be developed and flourish." [11] Some progress has been made in this direction – beginning in 2011, Arts Council England has given grants to Mercury as well as to two other development groups, Perfect Pitch and Musical Theatre Matters.

There are a number of helpful organisations in different countries aiming to create an environment conducive to the creation of new musicals. In New York, there are musical theatre workshops started by both ASCAP and BMI, and the Tisch School of the Arts at New York University has a training programme for musical theatre writers. London has both Mercury Musical Developments and Musical Theatre Matters. (I should say, at this point, that both Don Black and Tim Rice have, in the past, supported some of these organisations.) Toronto has had Script Lab (dormant at time of writing) which ran courses based on the Lehman Engel Workshops, as well as the new Canadian Musical Theatre Project at Sheridan College. In Australia, Melbourne's Magnormos Theatre runs the Annual OzMade Musicals Festival, while the Pratt Foundation funds a prize for the best Australian-written musical. In Singapore, Musical Theatre Limited has their "incubation" programme. In Fredericia, Denmark, there is a programme called Uterus run by Søren Møller, which develops two to six shows per year, a third of which are aimed at the international market.

Yet, when I participated in a series called Musical Futures at Greenwich Theatre (London) in 2005, there was nary a West End producer to be found in the audience. It seems that the only way that new work can be produced is if the writer has the wherewithal to mount it himself. (And unless you're Adam Guettel and your grandfather was Richard Rodgers and you have a trust fund to live off of...) Only in the US are there well-funded workshops to develop new writers. And guess what? They're finding them.

Chris Grady complains, "We don't have a network of theatres yet that are funded or supported to do musical theatre… The writer needs to see it up on its feet so that they can see what works and they can see what doesn't." London's Bridewell Theatre had hoped to fill this void, but the funding crisis forced them out of their venue in 2005. Although the Arts Council England has begun to take musical theatre seriously, it is not treated as a separate form from either music or drama, and the higher development costs for musicals have discouraged most regional theatres from taking them on.

In Denmark, Uterus does not have that problem. "Uterus is mainly government money", says Søren Møller. "I give credit to the Danish Ministry of Culture for being brave with that, but actually it's the only sane thing to do. Musical theatre is the stage art that brings in the most audience. It's the most viewed art form, and it's the only art form that doesn't have development at all." As the principal of the Danish Musical Theatre Academy, he knew he was in the best position to move this idea forward. "I realised that, us being the only musical theatre institution in the country, we should do something about that. Having taken that initiative, they've only backed us from the beginning, and that's great."

Some of the shows developed through Uterus have included *Steam*, a musical reworking of *A Midsummer Nights' Dream*, re-set in New York in the 1950s. The music and lyrics are by Helle Hansen, with book by Mads Abeløe and Thomas Bay Pedersen, all Danish, based on an idea by American-born Tim Zimmermann, who is based in Germany. It played the Edinburgh Fringe in 2008. "We already have American producer interest in that", Møller says, "so that definitely has a future in the States. It's very intended as an off-Broadway sort of thing."

Møller explains, "There are three phases that you go through when you submit. Anyone from anywhere in the world can submit work. Having done that, when you get selected, which happens from both us that run the centre and we have a committee of external readers – a producer, two musical directors, a composer and a lyricist that read and give feedback which we of course listen to, but ultimately we take the decision. Getting selected, you get a three week workshop. There's a pre-phase to that where we give feedback to the writers where we say what we see is lacking or how this would benefit most from a workshop would be to hire such-and-such. Hopefully they agree to that. We've had projects where we've had to stop at that phase. Sometimes a composer or a writer does not really want their work developed or doesn't want the feedback, and I completely respect an artist's right to say, 'I don't want that.' We give, I think, very constructive critique upon the work, very caring and nurturing critique, but we will say what we see the problem is. Maybe we don't know, and then we will call somebody – maybe abroad – and say, 'this work has this problem – do you know a really good arranger for this style?' It could be an arranger, it could be a dramaturge or it could be a director. Having agreed upon what we are going to do, we will then cast it as we would cast a professional show. You will have either a pianist, a combo or a full orchestra, depending on what the piece needed and where the focus should lie. Then they dive into that three week workshop of development. Mid-way through that three-week period, we will sit down and find out whether we will take it to phase two, which is a showcase. So we might actually do a three-week workshop and not showcase it. We will still invite a few business people to come and watch a reading or whatever at the end, but we will not do the showcase if we do not think that the work is ready for it. It doesn't mean we've killed it – we might have to take it back and do another pre-phase and say this needs further development." Uterus pays the full development cost, in exchange for 1.5% of the show's future royalties.

The correct conditions for the nurture of talent need to be in place. Canadian journalist and cultural commentator Gladwell writes, "The sense of possibility so necessary for success comes not just from inside us or our parents. It comes from our time: from the particular opportunities that our particular place in history presents us with."[12] Writers need to achieve a critical mass – an environment in which the more peers achieving success, the better – to prosper in. It is common for people in the theatre to jokingly say that they hope their colleague's show is a flop, but it really doesn't work that way. One of the lessons that I learned from my research for *Broadway North* was that the more people who are writing good, successful musicals there are, the easier it becomes for the rest of us. Success breeds success. Not only does it make it easier to raise financing, but also the artists inspire each other. (In the pop music world, it was after John Lennon heard the Beach Boys' pioneering *Pet Sounds* album that he and the other Beatles set to work on *Sergeant Pepper's Lonely Hearts Club Band*.)

They also need to be allowed to fail. While many critics will complain about a string of flops, the fact is that you have to kiss a lot of frogs to find the one that will turn into a handsome prince. Approximately one show in six on Broadway is successful, and that doesn't include the 99% that don't make it that far. That's how it has always been. In the so-called "golden age", the ratio of flops was just as high, but there was so much more product being turned out that more hits were created.

Minimising the risk is the function of workshops and try-outs. Beginning in 1961, Broadway maestro Lehman Engel, who began his career as musical director of Marc Blitzstein's *The Cradle Will Rock* in 1936, established a workshop in New York under the auspices of Broadcast Music, Inc. to teach the craft of writing for the musical theatre. While Engel was not known as a composer of musicals himself, he had waved his baton in front of enough of them – including *L'il Abner*, and *Destry Rides Again*, among many others – to have developed a few theories about what makes them tick. Members of his New York workshop went on to create hits like *A Chorus Line*, *Nine* and *Little Shop of Horrors*. Eventually, more workshops were established in Nashville, Los Angeles and Toronto. (Leslie Arden, from the Toronto workshops, was also a student of Stephen Sondheim. When her *The House of Martin Guerre*, produced in Chicago and Toronto in 1996, was compared with the bigger and more famous Boublil-Schönberg *Martin*

Guerre, it prompted American author Tom Shea to opine, "smaller is better".[13]) After Lehman died in 1982, the workshops carried on, led by former pupils. In Toronto, Jim Betts taught them, first through the Guild of Canadian Musical Theatre Writers, and later through Script Lab. The New York workshops were led for a time by *Nine* composer Maury Yeston, and in Los Angeles, the current artistic director of the workshop is John Sparks.

"It's a bastard art," says *Annie* composer Charles Strouse (1928-) "and there are those who want to make it into some kind of a lady. I think the workshops, all of the workshops — and I started one [for ASCAP] — I'm not sure they do any good. But on the other hand, I don't know what the alternative is."[14]

An example of the advice Engel would give can be heard in this anonymous account by one of his students from the New York workshop's newsletter: "'To make 'em cry, write optimistically... because self-pity only makes 'em laugh. Learn to find comedy in pathos; tragedy in optimism. Remember, we weep for those who do not weep for themselves'... Lehman discussed the dramatic device of what he called 'misplaced optimism,' comparing two songs from *Porgy And Bess*: 'We cry more at 'Oh Lord, I'm On My Way' than we do at 'My Man's Gone Now'. [In the latter] we just hope she hits the high notes.' Lehman also had cautionary advice on the subject: 'Beware of adding sentiment to sentiment. Just adding *music* is adding sentiment.' Finally, he insisted that, 'Genuine emotion is not corny,' and on at least one occasion admonished a writer that '[The] ending [of your song] is straight from a can of Niblets.'"[15]

I joined the workshops in Toronto in 1983, one year after Engel died. At the time, they were being carried on by the Guild of Canadian Musical Theatre Writers, an organisation that aimed "to encourage and promote the development of composers, lyricists and librettists in musical theatre across Canada". When I was researching my book *Broadway North: The Dream of a Canadian Musical* Theatre, I spoke to four of my former colleagues – David Warrack, Nelles Van Loon, Jim Betts and Susan Cluff – about their memories of the man.

Toronto composer and musical director David Warrack took part in both the Toronto and New York workshops. "They were an inspiration", he told me. Jim Betts adds, "He brought a great enthusiasm about musical theatre to those of us who met with him over the years. It was wonderful hearing him talk about what was going on in NYC, getting caught up on the latest shows, learning about who was writing what, etc. He gave those of us in Toronto a feeling of being a part of the greater musical theatre community."

"Indeed, the uncompromising nature of his personality put a lot of people off", says Warrack. "After one of the showcases in which [Martin] Short was a performer, Marty informed me in no uncertain terms that he would never do it again, because of the way Lehman treated him. Fair enough. But I saw Lehman in so many different circumstances that I believe it gave me some perspective on his mercurial moods." Another Toronto participant, Nelles Van Loon, says "In my view, Lehman was a great teacher and great teachers have a way of being dogmatic, not just out of arrogance, but because they have earned their stripes and acquired their convictions through many years of study."

"At the root of it all," Warrack explains, "was his insistence on the highest professional standards and his immense love for the theatre. He positively glowed with that elfish smile on his face when he encountered a magnificent song, or scene, or performance. It wasn't easy to get him there, but anybody who did received tremendous encouragement."

Engel's advice wasn't always correct. Susan Cluff remembers, "He told us not to worry about getting the rights to source material, which, in at least one writer's case, was not good advice. Lehman felt that if you wrote a good show that you or the producer would be able to [obtain] the rights." Nor were his assessments of shows always universally accepted. He claimed that, during the so-called "golden age" of the Broadway musical, only one show – *Bye Bye Birdie* – with an original book (as opposed to an adaptation) had been an enduring hit. Yet, he cites *Brigadoon* as one of the all-time greats. And what of *Finian's Rainbow*? And *The Music Man*? None of those shows were based on existing material. And I'm sure that many producers – and even authors – would have balked at his suggestion that "On the Street Where You Live" should be cut from *My Fair Lady*.[16]

"I would also say that Lehman's students taught each other a great deal," says Van Loon. "I can remember Jim Betts saying it was quite possible for one person to write book, music and lyrics, or I might never have tried it." (This runs counter to one of Broadway's unwritten "rules". "It is too much for one person to carry," says Tom Jones, book writer and lyricist of *The Fantasticks*. "And it is too much to expect of one person's talents."[17]) "So," Van Loon continues, "the disciples … have altered the principles in various ways, but for my money, Lehman had an (almost) unerring instinct for what was at the guts of a show."

In November 2006, Script Lab presented its first ever Festival of Canadian Musical Theatre in Toronto. The festival included songs from established Canadian hits such as *The Drowsy Chaperone* and *Billy Bishop Goes to War*, as well as a reading of *Turvey* by Don Harron and Norman and Elaine Campbell, the creators of *Anne of Green Gables - The Musical*. Although I wasn't there for the festival, one of my songs – "Something in the Air" (from *Perfect Timing*) was included in a showcase of new writing. Still, as in London, it has been difficult to get the industry to back indigenous musicals, and a subsequent Festival had to be cancelled when a sponsor withdrew. Still, Toronto has managed to foster such talents as Neil Bartram and Brian Hill, whose *The Story of My Life* played – briefly – on Broadway.

228

A "Graduate Musical Theatre Writing Program" was established at New York University's Tisch School of the Arts in 1981, the only programme of its kind in the world. Its founding mentors included Jule Styne, Leonard Bernstein, Lee Adams, Sheldon Harnick and Arthur Laurents. The early instructors included Betty Comden and Adolph Green, Stephen Sondheim and Richard Maltby Jr. One of the first students was George C. Wolfe (*Jelly's Last Jam*, *Bring in da Noise, Bring in da Funk*). Under the leadership of Deena Rosenberg, a curriculum evolved until, after 1991, a permanent faculty was assembled, all drawn from the professional theatre community. In 1996, Sarah Schlesinger, author of *The Ballad of Little Jo* replaced Rosenberg as programme head.

The admissions process is extremely competitive. "We don't want people who aren't ready to collaborate", Schlesinger told playwright and journalist Lee Davis. "The one thing they have to have in common is the desire to be a collaborative artist." [18]

For the first year, they concentrate on the basics of structure and craft. "We use the past to inform the present", says Schlesinger. They learn by doing, writing simple songs and scenes, culminating in a twenty minute musical and seeing it performed by professional guest artists. In the second year, the focus is on developing a finished "thesis" piece, which is critiqued at each stage of its development. The students now come from all over the world – Europe and Asia. "It's a big world out there."

In recent years, London's Theatre Royal Stratford East has initiated a programme to develop musicals specifically for their ethnically diverse audience. One of their first successes was *The Big Life*, a version of Shakespeare's *Love's Labours Lost* transposed to Britain's Caribbean immigrant community of the 1950s. The book and lyrics were by Paul Sirett and the music by Paul Joseph. The *Independent*'s Adam Scott wrote, "The emergence of a strong, original-book musical into the London stage wilderness of cut-and-paste, back-catalogue plundering was always going to be welcomed. That when it arrived it would be as joyous an affair as Paul Sirett and Paul Joseph's *The Big Life* is more than the jaded musical theatre-goer could have dared hope for... Amid the fun, the social comment laced through the evening gains power from its understatement. The racist hostility the characters endure is met with a confusion and pain that Sirett's clear lyrics convey without rancour. Indeed, for all the show's verve and exuberance, every element - from performers, band, laughs and social comment to the economical and witty set - is perfectly balanced in an irresistible whole."[19]

Founded by Joan Littlewood as Theatre Workshop in 1953, the theatre has always nurtured working class writers and composers, including Lionel Bart, whose *Fings Ain't Wot They Used T'Be* opened there on 17 February 1959, then transferred to the Garrick for a two-year run. Three years later, *Oh, What a Lovely War!* transferred to both the West End and Broadway and was made into a film. More recent successes have included *Five Guys Named Moe*.

"We did more black, Caribbean and South Asian new work than any other theatre in the country," says current Artistic Director Kerry Michael, who was then Associate Director. "That was all because the area was changing, and those immigrants were now finding themselves in East London. All that kind of work had a popular, accessible feel to it, and often used comedy and music to kind of tap into an audience that connected with them."

In 1996, then-Artistic Director Philip Hedley initiated a development programme for "urban musicals", drawing on East End hip-hop and Asian music. He felt the theatre was "well-placed to achieve this, with its famous history in musical theatre and its deep roots in its own urban community."[20] He brought over two professors from the Tisch School. Beginning in 1999, Fred Carl and Robert Lee came over for an annual four-week summer workshop, working with writers who would have had neither the funds nor the academic standing for the NYU course. Hedley "began a process of developing the Urban Musical, while not excluding or disparaging the creation of new musicals in the classic Broadway tradition."

How adaptable is the classic Broadway model to new cultural environments? John Sparks says, "I think that the Lehman Engel style workshop could work in any cultural setting, because it emphasises how the craft of the writing affects the communication in the theatre," he said. "In other words, whatever one is trying to communicate, at whatever level of theatrical abstraction, a writer must remember that the words and music are a means to an end – therefore, the music and lyrics must work together in a way that clearly communicates to the audience at which the piece is aimed."

"The variations in rap fascinate me", Hedley told Tim Saward. "I am no expert in rap, but even I could see how easily blank verse raps. Just as Shakespeare would vary the blank verse or just do half a line for some emotional reason, or he would suddenly rhyme two lines and give you a couplet for good reason, that rap had all its rules and had its grammar and so on. The youngsters listening to it understood what was going on, and I was of that generation where it's all terribly loud and I can't understand the words, and they can perfectly understand them. Their ears are trained for it."[21]

This plan has been met with some resistance by advocates of the "classic Broadway tradition", who feel that hip-hop is not "theatre music". Interestingly, however, Stephen Sondheim disagrees. "Of all the forms of contemporary pop music", he writes, "rap is the closest to traditional musical theatre (its roots are in vaudeville), both in its vamp-heavy rhythmic drive and in its verbal playfulness."[22] The nearest thing to a mainstream success with a hip-hop influence has been *In the Heights* by Latino composer-lyricist Lin-Manuel Miranda (1980-), which opened on Broadway in 2008 and was nominated for thirteen Tony Awards. Of Miranda's work on *In The Heights* Sondheim says, "Rap is a natural language for him and he is a master of the form, but enough of a traditionalist to know the way he can utilize its theatrical potential."

Many critics complain that few recent musicals deal with contemporary issues – but this criticism is not new. Most of Rodgers and Hammerstein's (and all of Lerner and Loewe's) works are set either in the past or in a fantasy locale. Rodgers and Hammerstein's only real success with a then-contemporary time period – *South Pacific* – had an exotic setting.

Critic Mark Steyn, a musical theatre specialist who also doubles as a conservative political commentator, dismisses rap and hip-hop out of hand. "Rap is the logical consequence of promoting social over musical content: the reduction of the tune to a banal stationary backing track, the debasement of lyric-writing to a formless pneumatic laundry list of half-baked hoodlum exhibitionism."[23] On the other hand, it could be argued that William Walton and Edith Sitwell's 1921 "entertainment" *Façade* was an early form of rap.

In 2003, Stratford East was given permission to do a hip-hop adaptation by DJ Excalibah and MC Skolla of *The Boys from Syracuse* called *Da Boyz*. For *British Theatre Guide*'s Jackie Fletcher, it was an "invigorating blend of dance, song and comedy".[24] "That was for a very specific kind of audience who completely got it", says Michael, although some clearly didn't: "My review of *Da Boyz* could be condensed to 'Worst Fears Confirmed'", wrote Rhoda Koenig in *The Independent*. "The men are portrayed as either fools or hustlers, the women as robots or sluts, and the exquisite waltzes, punchy duets, and impish comedy numbers either altered by simple perversity (in 'This Can't Be Love,' for instance, by failing to resolve a chord) or, more often, bludgeoned and broken by constant pounding and thumping … *Da Boyz* has more in common with a pop concert or a TV variety show than a musical. The libretto has been slashed to the barest minimum, and is literally sidelined onto large screens flanking the stage on which the actors, behind the scenes, mug their way through brief comic bits. The mood of the music, either angry or glumly earnest, is not up to conveying more than a limited number of emotions, and rather unpleasant ones at that."[25]

Attempts to bring contemporary popular music into the theatre since the time of *Hair* have been fraught, and success has been rare. The reasons are partly economic – the young people to whom the music would appeal can't afford Broadway and West End ticket prices. There are also practical reasons. When it can take a decade to get a show on, following trends can be pretty futile. But it may also be that few pop writers have taken the care to learn the craft of writing for the theatre. This is where Stratford East feel they have an edge. "I think that rap and hip-hop are more easily accessible to musical theatre by far than rock and roll", Hedley told Saward.

"They [the Tisch instructors] talk about principles as opposed to rules," says Michael. "But the nature of the kind of students who went to the Tisch school were being filtered because they had to pay to do that course. You get a certain kind of person who can afford to do that, and another kind of person, for whatever reason, falls by the wayside. What we were able to do here was give them a whole raft of kinds of artists who they weren't particularly working with in America. That's what excited them in terms of coming over here every summer and doing the course. What we did was put them in a room and talked about collaboration and partnership and how musicals aren't written, they're rewritten, and also why does this story need music for the story to be told."

By 2004, over a hundred writers had been through the programme: 60% of them were black, 20% Asian and the rest were white. "It is greatly to the advantage of the originality of British pop music that this mixing of styles of music from different racial backgrounds happens more readily in London than in, say, New York," says Hedley. "There is an advantage too that no country has the particular mix of cultures that Britain has from its colonial history, and so the contemporary musicals developed in Britain will by definition be different from those developed in the USA."

"We did a piece by Jonzi D (a black, British hip-hop artist) called *Aeroplane Man* which was a dance musical", says Kerry Michael. "He goes back to find who he is as a hip-hop artist and he goes from London to America to find if that's where he belongs. Then he goes back to Jamaica, to Jamaican influences on hip-hop, and then from Jamaica he goes to Africa. From the gum-boots to reggae to hip-hop, there are links there in terms of the musical form. That's how he worked out what he was about." Jonzi D explains, "For once I heard a culture that actually celebrated this environment and used it creatively. I enjoy the fact that we use walls and pavements as our arenas of expression. That's cool. That makes a bit more sense to me than going to dance school and wearing tights… Can you imagine how embarrassing it is when you tell your friends what you are up to? As far as I am concerned, classical ballet was a bit camp for me, and hip-hop culture is a truer way of expressing myself."[26]

"Hip-hop is so broad now", says Michael. "You have British hip-hop, French hip-hop, R&B, R&B jazz. When you look at the spectrum of where hip-hop spans, it's quite broad. It's just about tuning your ears to the complexity. I think hip-hop is far more complicated, far more broad than Sondheim is. If anything, Sondheim's the same thing for two and a half hours."

Hedley contends, "There are comparatively few black and Asian writers and composers concentrating on musical theatre, partly because they can see so few role models to encourage them to do so." Michael continues, "They're bringing their music, they're bringing their words, they're bringing their stories. The basic challenge we have with all that is the structure of two-hour story telling. A 'well-made play' has a Western model to it. That's how we perceive something to be good or bad in this part of the world. What we want to do is kind of break free from that." Michael is carrying forward Hedley's legacy, although they have had to discontinue the summer Tisch programme due to withdrawal of funding.

Whether the hip-hop musical is the wave of the future, or just one faction in a many-faceted new way of looking at musicals remains to be seen. What is clear is that there are people in different parts of the world working to develop new and unique forms.

In Singapore, Dr. Kenneth Lyen of Musical Theatre Limited observes, "Our globalisation is an inadvertent one in that the traditional Chinese, Indian and Malay dramas do not follow the traditional Aristotelian three act structure. It is a little bit more meandering. It's good and bad – it's good in that it's more Asian and has a slightly mystic quality, but it's bad in that it doesn't have the dramatic tension which most Western theatre has – developing, complications and final resolution."

"I believe and I hope that musical theatre can become part of the present culture," says Søren Møller. "At a certain period in time, it seemed like musical theatre had become a musical style of its own, and I actually don't think that is the case. I do believe that musical theatre is a stage art form that contains a million different musical genres beneath it. So I am very much about trying to stay true to the genre that you're writing in, and I don't want to develop one kind of musical genre. I really want it to be different. We are all under the influence of everything that's run through the water until this very day."

I believe that the potential exists to combine the expertise and craft of the classic Broadway musicals with indigenous forms.   "How any particular audience hears and simultaneously understands songs in the context of their culture is certainly a factor in shaping the craft of song writing for that culture", says John Sparks. "In the theatre, regardless of cultural differences, one thing remains the same – it is not like listening to music in other forms because there are competing elements. Sets, costumes, movement, aspects of character, linguistic anomalies... the song in the theatre must cut through all the competition and communicate directly to the audience with no need to process the information. The audience must be able to understand it without thinking about it. If, however, you are in a culture where the music and words are not part of the drama, but more of a decoration, more like scenery than content, then of course, that craft would not be so important. The American musical does have impact in other cultures, first by being performed in translation, and ultimately by imitation. But as other cultures adopt and adapt the form, it changes and becomes suitable to the culture borrowing the style. This is how European operetta morphed into the American musical in the first place, being infused with jazz and variety, taking bits from African American music styles, from vaudeville and other influences that were at the time rather uniquely American."

At Stratford East, they are aiming to reinvent the form. "But I don't know whether we'll call it a musical", says Kerry Michael. "Is *Cirque du Soleil* a musical? In our terms it's not, but from other points of view they're doing as many of the common traits you'd find in a more conventional musical. It's just that we have to think about what we mean by the word 'musical' and how we define what a musical is. As far as I'm concerned, it's just something that fuses music, lyric and word. So a pantomime's a musical as much as *West Side Story* is."

Finale: Are We Up For It?

If I had known when I was starting out as a musical writer in the early 1980s just how difficult a road it was going to be, I might very well have given up. I say this because I am actually grateful that I didn't know then what I know now. On the other hand, when Stephen Schwartz told me back then that I showed "enormous promise", that kept me going through many a dark night. I say this not to blow my own horn, but to stress the importance of *nurture*. (Now, through his ASCAP and Disney workshops, Schwartz has similarly encouraged hundreds of other promising writers.)

When I hear course leaders telling their students to lower their expectations, something inside me rebels. Like the students in the opening scene of the original Broadway version of *Merrily We Roll Along*, I want to scream, "Give us a break, Mr. Shepard!" Not that I'm naïve about the reality behind the musical theatre business, but I would never discourage anybody with talent from aiming for the Big Brass Ring. After all, nobody chooses to write musicals for a living unless they're at least a little bit delusional. As the noted Basque writer and poet Miguel de Unamuno (1864-1936) said, "Only he who attempts the absurd is capable of achieving the impossible." You can never hit higher than you aim.

However, thinking "outside of the box" dictates that we must consider the possibility that the exact whereabouts of that brass ring may have changed. "I can categorically state that myriad musicals are being developed in America with no thought of Broadway", says John Sparks, Artistic Director of the Academy of New Musical Theatre in Los Angeles and the Theatre Building Chicago. Stephen Sondheim certainly believes that Broadway – and the commercial theatre – is in terminal decline. "There is an anodyne homogeneity that governs Broadway musicals, so I don't see many. There's nothing wrong with having a lot of commercial crap as long as you have something else. You want a supermarket. Unfortunately, nearly everything on Broadway is commercial crap. The same is true of the West End. When I scan what's on, my heart sinks into my boots."[1] But, says lyricist and director Richard Maltby Jr., "All it takes is one new voice with talent and a fresh vision and a hot sense of entertaining people."[2]

The musical is in a strange place in the western theatre right now. It is the most popular theatrical art, yet even with the cinematic success of *Chicago*, *Mamma Mia!!* and *Sweeny Todd*, it is "uncool". "In the old days," Sir Tim Rice says, "musical shows that you wax nostalgic about, were aiming for a very middle class, elitist type of audience. Now musicals are for anybody. Everybody's got their record player, their radio, their CD. The sort of music most people want is not the very sophisticated, twee, *Anything Goes* type of musical. They want raw chunks of emotion in three-minute slabs and they want it now and they want it hard. That's very hard for people brought up on the rather privileged diet of forties and fifties musicals to take." He adds, "I happen to come from a very cushy background, to have been brought up on those musicals, to like them very much, but I also love and enjoy more emotionally, if I'm honest, a great Mick Jagger performance."[3]

Film and theatre producer Scott Rudin (1958-) says, "Why would musical theater be the only culture that resists newness? It doesn't make sense. Bands become successes on [social networking site] tumblr. Where's the tumblr of musical theater? [The problem is] older people are willing to pay for it, and they're the same audience that's not going to want something new. It's a self-fulfilling prophecy. I'd rather go see our future than most musicals. The theater is simply not democratized in any way, and other art forms are. And that's even more true of musicals."[4] Since the musical theatre came into being alongside democracy, does this mean it is no longer a viable cultural expression? The economics of the musical are such that creators need to aim for longevity in a way that film makers and pop songwriters don't. A musical that is part of a passing trend will not be likely to have a long shelf life.

The musical falls into that awkward slot called "middle-brow", meaning it is neither fish nor fowl. It does not meet the mandated criteria for "high art", nor does it appeal to the lowest common denominator, and so it slips between the cracks. Hence, so far as the mass media is concerned, it does not exist – *High School Musical*, *Smash* and *Glee* notwithstanding.

"For some reason, unfathomable to me, musicals are a much maligned form," says Arden Ryshpan, Executive Director of Canadian Actors' Equity Association. "People complain that they are maudlin, but I suspect that it is because they found themselves swept up in the emotion of the music. Folks scoff at the notion of characters suddenly breaking into song, rather than seeing the musical numbers as a way of telling us more about a character than dialogue ever could, or in some circumstances, actually advancing the plot."[5]

For some, musicals are inspiring – a barometer of the human spirit. Ian Bradley, a Presbyterian theologian writes that "Nostalgia, retreat from reality and sheer simple uncomplicated entertainment value, as well as massive commercial calculation and hype, all undoubtedly play their part in the continuing appeal of musicals but perhaps they also speak to that deeper sense of yearning which is part of the human condition, particularly in times like our own where so much seems frightening, uncertain and hopeless."[6]

I should say at this point that I love musicals for what they are capable of being, not for what they necessarily are. Most of what Broadway and the West End are turning out right now is admittedly pretty banal. But then I hear a score like *Grey Gardens* (2006, music by Scott Frankel, lyrics by Michael Korie) and I feel hopeful for the future.

If the development of the musical coincided with the emergence of democracy, then what will happen as new democracies emerge? Chris Grady of Musical Theatre Matters asks, "Should we in the developed-musical-theatre-world then be looking at the composers and markets coming through in the wake of the Arab Spring? ... Is the North Korean musical theatre market the next one to keep an eye on?"[7]

As the arts become more polarised, it is the middle ground that invariably loses out. In my native country, the Canadian Broadcasting Corporation has revamped its English network radio format. Classical music has been cut back. "Indie" rock is in. They have disbanded the last of their once-proud local orchestras, and what passes for "arts" programming is somewhat redolent of the MTV generation. What little interest they do show in musical theatre is strictly after the fact news reporting, and even that can be pretty weak-kneed. As for nurturing of musical theatre, there is none.

It has not always been this way. Time was when CBC Radio actually commissioned original musicals. One of them, *Rockaybye Hamlet*, even made it to Broadway. (Well, for a few performances, anyway.) But alas, those days are well behind us. The CBC national network (as opposed to regional and local programming) resembles a geek who longs to be part of the "in-crowd". Although he will never be "cool", he shamelessly courts popularity at the expense of both his integrity and his real identity. So even though Canadian musicals have never been so successful on the international scene (*The Drowsy Chaperone*, *Evil Dead*), the CBC all but ignores them because they are "un-cool" in the view of the "yuppie-puppies" who are now in charge.[8] In 2009, in an episode of their flagship daily "arts" show *Q*, host Jian Gomeshi (for whom I otherwise have great respect) interviewed an American journalist about the current state of Broadway, without ever mentioning the Canadian musical – *The Story of My Life* – that had opened on the Great White Way that very week. They are more interested either in "indie" rock bands, or in what one senior network executive once described to me as the "tinkling and banging" of the avant garde. This same network's television counterpart, run by a former Hollywood producer, proudly announced that they were adding American game show *Jeopardy* to their prime-time schedule, at the same time as they cancelled a major performing arts showcase series. Non-Canadian musical theatre did get a bit of a boost when they carried Andrew Lloyd Webber's "reality" talent search *How Do You Solve a Problem Like Maria?* They even tried to cash in – after the fact, of course – on the success of *The Drowsy Chaperone* with a proposed dramatic recreation of that show's original stag-night incarnation, but the creators said "uh, no". (To be fair, *North by Northwest*, a highly-regarded regional arts program out of Vancouver, did do a feature on Canadian musicals in 2011, to which I was a contributor.)

This is not a problem unique to Canada, never mind the CBC. In Britain, where the BBC's *Culture Show* occupies a similar jejune turf to *Q*, *The Stage* complains of "a palpable dumbing down" in arts journalism. "Now the squeeze is on space and the demand is going to be for more glamour-based coverage to compete with the consumer-led material arts editors are going to be obliged to schedule. Arts

237

correspondents will be appointed for their 'compatibility' with the wishes of news desks, not for their knowledge and judgement of the cultural sector or for their skill with concise prose, but for their aptitude for getting alongside stars and their agents."[9]

As has been discussed previously in this book, we have a similar problem with funding agencies. Only in the U.S. (and more recently, Britain) is musical theatre taken seriously. However, there are encouraging signs. While development programmes for writers and composers are thin on the ground, musical theatre courses for performers are a growth industry. From Buenos Aires to Singapore, schools are cropping up to train singers and dancers for all the cloned musicals that New York and London can supply. Some of these schools are taking a proactively internationalist stance. The Musical Theatre Educators Alliance has members from across North America, Europe and Australia.

I have shown that there are people in many different countries struggling to create indigenous musical theatre. These people are facing many of the same problems, and often finding very creative solutions to them. In several places, there are organised workshops to develop new, indigenous work. It seems to me that the next step would be to borrow a page from the Musical Theatre Educators Alliance and to form an international network. While Mercury Musical Developments in the UK has fraternal relations with the Academy of New Musical Theatre and the National Alliance of Musical Theatre Producers in the U.S., I believe it would be useful to expand that group to include Sheridan College's Canadian Music Theatre Project, OzMade Musicals in Australia, Uterus in Denmark and Musical Theatre Limited in Singapore. For example, all could learn from the kind of showcases that Aaron Joyner produces for OzMade. They could also benefit from the expertise of the Academy of New Musical Theatre and the Lehman Engel workshops. Musical Theatre Limited have expressed the desire to bring in outside mentors to help to develop their own writers. Such an alliance could facilitate this.

The next step would be an International Festival of Musical Theatre. While this was tried to some extend with the Global Search for New Musicals in Cardiff, I believe it should be truly internationalised and hosted by a different country each year.

I have already seen that shows from Austria (*Elisabeth*) and Canada (*Anne of Green Gables*) have been very successful in Japan without having been Broadway hits. Likewise, *Evil Dead* has triumphed in Korea. Toronto has transferred two shows from Australia, via London (*Dirty Dancing, Priscilla Queen of the Desert*). Perhaps soon a show will move directly between Canada and Australia. Maybe we'll even have international co-productions. (We've had them for years in the non-musical theatre.)

Let's reclaim that middle ground by reaching out to a populist audience and then raising their aspirations without pandering, just as Mozart and Schikaneder did with *The Magic Flute*. Let's become as aware of the international community in musical theatre as we are in cinema and world music. That way, we can re-invigorate the musical. Who knows – we may even make it cool again.

Bibliography:

Appignanesi, Lisa, *The Cabaret*, Yale University Press, New Haven, CT, 2004

Arundell, Dennis , *The Story of Sadler's Wells,* David & Charles, London, 1978.

Atkey, Mel, *Broadway North: The Dream of a Canadian Musical Theatre*, Natural Heritage Books, Toronto, 2006.

Baillie, Joan Parkhill, *Look at the Record: An Album of Toronto's Lyric Theatres 1825-1984*, Mosaic Press, Oakville, ON, 1985.

Baker, Richard Anthony, *British Music Hall – An Illustrated History*, Sutton Publishing, Stroud, Gloucestershire, 2005

Bawtree, Michael, *The New Singing Theatre*, Oxford University Press, New York, 1991.

Behr, Edward, *Thank Heaven for Little Girls – The True Story of Maurice Chevalier's Life and Times*, Hutchinson, London, 1993

Berton, Pierre, *Hollywood's Canada: The Americanization of Our National Image*, McClelland and Stewart, Toronto, 1975.

Bradley, Ian, *You've Got to Have a Dream: The Message of the Musical*, SCM Press, London, 2004.

Brett, David, *Piaf – A Passionate Life*, Robson Books, London, 1998

Cabaret Berlin – Revue, Kabarett and Film Music Between the Wars, (Lori Münz, Editorial Director) Ear Books, Hamburg, 2005.

Castle, Charles, *The Folies-Bergère*, Methuen, London, 1982.

Cate, Phillip Dennis and Shaw, Mary, *The Spirit of Montmartre – Cabarets, Humor, and the Avant-Garde, 1875-1905*, Jane Voorhees Zimmerli Art Museum, New Brunswick, NJ, 1996

Cherlin Michael, Filipowicz, Halina and Rudolph, Richard L., *The Great Tradition and Its Legacy – The Evolution of Dramatic and Musical Theater in Austria and Central Europe*, Berghan Books, New York, 2003.

Clements, Jonathan and McCarthy, Helen, *The Anime Encyclopedia – A Guide to Japanese Animation Since 1917*, Stone Bridge Press, Berkeley, California, 2001.

Collerick, George, *Romanticism and Melody*, Juventus, London, 1995.

Collerick, George, *From the Italian Girl to Cabaret*, Juventus, London, 1998

Damase, Jacques, *Les Folies du Music-Hall*, Anthony Blond Ltd., London, 1962

Drabinsky, Garth (with de Villiers, Marq) *Closer to the Sun*, McLelland and Stewart, Toronto, 1995.

Druxman, Michael B., *The Musical From Broadway to Hollywood*, A.S. Barnes and Company, Cranbury, NJ, 1980.

Engel, Lehman, *The American Musical Theater*, Collier Books, New York, 1975

Engel, Lehman, *The Making of a Musical*, MacMillan Publishing Company, New York, 1977

Engel, Lehman, *Words With Music*, Schirmer Books, New York, 1981.

Freund, Philip, *Oriental Theatre*, Peter Owen Publishers, London, 2005

Gänzl, Kurt, *Musicals*, Carlton Books, London, 2001.

Gänzl, Kurt, *The Musical – A Concise History*, Northeastern University Press, Boston, MA, 1997.

Goodall, Howard, *Big Bangs – The Story of Five Discoveries That Changed Musical History*, Chatto & Windus, London, 2000.

Gorlero, Pablo, *Historia de la comedia musical en la Argentina : desde sus comienzos hasta 1979*, N. H. Oliveri, Buenos Aires, 2004.

Harcourt, Peter, *Fantasy and Folly – The Lost World of New Zealand Musicals 1880-1940*, Steele Roberts, Wellington, 2002

Harron, Don, *Anne of Green Gables the Musical – 101 Things You Didn't Know*, White Knight Books, Toronto, 2008.

Hirsch, Foster, *Kurt Weill on Stage – From Berlin to Broadway*, Limelight Editions, New York, 2003.

Holloway, Peter, *Contemporary Australian Drama*, Currency Press, Sydney, 1987.

Honolka, Kurt, *Papageno – Emanuel Schikaneder, Man of the Theater in Mozart's Time*, Amadeus Press, Portland, Oregon, 1990.

House of Commons Culture, Media and Sport Committee, *Theatre – Fifth Report of Session 2004-05 Vol. III Oral and Written Evidence*, The Stationery Office Ltd., London, 2005

Inverne, James, *Wrestling with Elephants – The Authorised Biography of Don Black*, Sanctuary Books, London, 2003.

Jackson, Arthur, *The Best Musicals*, Crown Publishers, New York, 1977.

Jackson, Jeffrey H., *Making Jazz French*, Duke University Press, Durham, North Carolina, 2003

Jenkins, John and Linz, Rainer, *Arias – Recent Australian Music Theatre*, Red House Editions, Melbourne, 1997

Johnston, Peter Wyllie, *From the Melburnian*, Ellikon Publishing, Fitzroy, Victoria, 2011

Jones, Tom, *Making Musicals*, Limelight Editions, New York, 1998.

Kennedy, Michael and Joyce, *Oxford Concise Dictionary of Music*, Oxford University Press, Oxford, 2007

Kislan, Richard, *The Musical: A Look at the American Musical Theatre*, Prentice-Hall Inc., Engelwood Cliffs, NJ , 1980.

Knapp, Raymond, *The American Musical and the Formation of National Identity*, Princeton University Press, Princeton, NJ, 2005.

Lahr, John, *Automatic Vaudeville*, Alfred A. Knopf, New York, 1984.

Lamb, Andrew, *150 Years of Popular Musical Theatre*, Yale University Press, New Haven, CT, 2000.

Larkin, Colin, *The Virgin Encyclopædia of Stage and Film Musicals*, Virgin Books, London, 1999.

Lerner, Alan Jay, *The Musical Theatre: A Celebration*, McGraw Hill, New York, 1986.

Leibovitz, Liel and Miller, Matthew, *Lili Marlene – The Soldiers' Song of World War II*, W.W. Norton & Co., New York, 2009.

Lindfors, Bernth, (editor) *Africans on Stage: Studies in Ethnological Show Business*, University of Indiana Press, Bloomington, 1999.

Mandelbaum, Ken, *Not Since Carrie: 40 Years of Broadway Musical Flops*, St. Martin's Press, New York, 1991

Mariel, Pierre (translated by Peter Munk) *Paris Revue*, Neville Spearman, London, 1962

McBride, Jason and Wilcox, Alana, *UTOpia – Towards a New Toronto*, Coach House Books, Toronto, 2005.

Mellers, Wilfred, *Music in a New Found Land – Themes and Developments in the History of American Music*, Alfred A. Knopf, New York, 1964.

Moore, Mavor, *Reinventing Myself*, Stoddart, Toronto, 1994.

Mordden, Ethan, *Open a New Window – The Broadway Musical in the 1960s*, Pagrave, New York, 2001.

Most, Andrea, *Making Americans – Jews and the Broadway Musical*, Harvard University Press, Cambridge, Mass, 2004.

Previn, André, *No Minor Chords*, Doubleday, New York, 1991.

Raymond, Jack, *Show Music on Record*, Washington, DC, 1998.

Robertson, Jennifer, *Takarazuka – Sexual Politics and Popular Culture in Modern Japan*, University of California Press, Berkeley, 1998.

Salys, Rimgaila, *Laughing Matters: The Musical Comedy Films of Grigorii Aleksandrov*, Intellect, Bristol, 2009.

Samuels, Edmond, *If the Cap Fits*, Modern Literature Co., Sydney, 1972.

Schneider, Jason, *Whispering Pines – The Northern Roots of American Music from Hank Snow to The Band*, ECW Press, Toronto, 2009.

Secrest, Meryle, *Somewhere for Me: A Biography of Richard Rodgers*, Bloomsbury, London, 2001.

Steyn, Mark, *Broadway Babies Say Goodnight*, Faber & Faber, London, 1997.

Stickland, Leonie, *Gender Gymnastics: Performing and Consuming Japan's Takarazuka Revue*, Trans Pacific Press, Melbourne, 2008

Struble, John Warthen, *History of American Classical Music*, Checkmark Books / Facts on File, New York, 1995.

Tait, Viola, *A Family of Brothers – The Taits and J.C. Williamson; a Theatre History*, William Heinemann, Melbourne, 1971.

Traubner, Richard, *Operetta: A Theatrical History*, Routledge, New York, 2003.

Trevin, J.C., *Peter Brook – A Biography*, Macdonald, London, 1971.

Tucker, Percy, *Just the Ticket!*, Jonathan Ball Publishers, Johannesburg, 1997

Vermette, Margaret, *The Musical World of Boublil and Schönberg*, Applause Theatre and Cinema Books, New York, 2006.

Whitcomb, Ian, *After the Ball – Pop Music from Rag to Rock*, Limelight Editions, New York, 1972/1989.

Whitehouse, Edmund, *London Lights – A History of West End Musicals*, This England Books, Cheltenham, Gloucestershire, 2005.

Wright, Adrian, *Tanner's Worth of Tunes – Rediscovering the Post-War British Musical*, Boydell Press, Woodbridge, Suffolk, 2011.

Discography:

N.B. Many cast recordings are independently produced and do not have catalogue numbers or record labels.
N.B. While books are listed by author, videos and recordings (which have many creators) are listed by title.

Anne of Green Gables Charlottetown Festival Cast Music by Norman Campbell Book by Don Harron Lyrics by Don Harron, Norman Campbell, Elaine Campbell, Mavor Moore Attic ACDM1225

Amour Broadway cast album Music by Michel Legrand English Lyrics by Jeremy Sams Original French Lyrics by Didier Van Cauwelaert 2002 Sh-K-Boom CD 4003-2

Aqui No Podemos Hacerlo!, Music by Luis M. Serra, Lyrics by Pepe Cibrián Campoy, Teatro Nacional Cervantes 1994 Argentine Cast CD 672

Belle Époque, La – The Songs of Reynaldo Hahn Susan Graham Sony Classical CD SK 60168

Berlin Cabaret Songs, (English Version) Uta Lemper, 1997 London 452 849-2

Berlin Cabaret Songs, (German Version) Uta Lemper, 1996 Decca 452 601-2

Best That We Can Be Various composers Musical Theatre Limited 2008 CD

Big Bang Music and Lyrics by Kenneth Lyen and Desmond Moey 1995 Rainbow Music/Serenip Productions

Billy Bishop Goes to War 20th Anniversary Recording Book, Music and Lyrics by John Gray 1999 CD

Boy from Oz, The Music and Lyrics by Peter Allen (& others) Book by Nick Enright 1998 EMI 7243 4 95660 2 6

Bunch of Ratbags, A Music and Lyrics by Peter Pinne, Book and Lyrics by Don Battye 2005 RNBW033

Chang & Eng, Music and Lyrics by Ken Low, Action Theatre, 2000

Cheminds de l'amour, Les Jean Stilwell, CBC Records MVCD 1135

Ciske de Rat, Music by Henny Vrienten, Book and Lyrics by *André* Breedland and Maurice Wijnen, 2007, Universal CD 1751114

Como in la Gran Cuidad ("Like it is in the Big City") Music and Lyrics by Pancho Flores, Book by Herman Letelier, 1971 LP EMI SLDC-41002

Cyrano de Musical, Music by Ad Van Dijk, Lyrics by Koen Van Dijk, Original cast 1992 CD DICD 3797

Dracula Music by Angel Mahler, Lyrics by Pepe Cibrián Campoy 1992 CD Luna Park CD-9791

Driegroschenoper, Die Berlin 1930 1929-30, Telefunken Legacy 0927 42663 2

Drowsy Chaperone, The Broadway Cast recording Music by Greg Morrison Lyrics by Lisa Lanbert, Book by Bob Martin and Don McKellar Ghostlight CD 7915584411-2

Elisabeth Music by Sylvester Levay, Lyrics by Michael Kunze Vienna cast 2004 Hit Squad

El Alma Secreta de las Cosas ("The Secret of the Soul and things") Music and lyrics by Juan del Barrio, Argentina, 1993, CD Ciclo-3-50043

El Jorobado de Paris ("The Hunchback of Paris") Music by Angel Mahler, Lyrics by Pepe Cibrián Campoy, 1993 CD 669/2

El Locos de Asis ("The Madman of Assiswi"), Music by Martin Bianchedi, Book and lyrics by Manuel Gonzalez Gil, 1985

El retrato de Dorian Gray, Citlalixayotl / Carbalho, Mexico 1997.

En Nu Naar Bed Original Cast, 1970 Phillips LP 8410046

Evil Dead – The Musical Music by Frank Cipola, Christopher Bond, Melissa Morris, George Reinblatt, Book and Lyrics by George Reinblatt Time Life M19407

Evita – Tango Popular Opera, Roberto Pansera, Miguel Jubany and Domingo Federico, Argentina 1989 CD Music Hall MH 10.021-2

Field of Stars: Songs of the Canadian Musical Theatre, Betts, Jim (editor) Northern River Music, Toronto, 2005.

Five Foot Broadway Various Composers Musical Theatre Limited CD

Fledermaus, Die Metropolitan Opera Music by Johann Strauss Book by Garson Kanin Lyrics by Howard Dietz CD PACO 030

Forbidden City Music by Dick Lee, Lyrics by Stephen Clark, Book by Stephen Clark and Dick Lee 2006 Singapore repertory Theatre

Foxtrot Music by Harry Bannink, Lyrics by Annie M.G. Schmidt 2004 CD: Brommerpech PCD 505039 2

French Operetta Arias Susan Graham Erato Disques CD 0927-42106-2

Gitano – Zarzuela Arias, Placido Domingo (conductor) Rolando Villazón (tenor) 2007 CD Virgin Classics LC 7873

Ha'penny Bridge, The, Book, Music and Lyrics by Alastair McGuckian. Original cast 2005

Hatpin, The Original Cast Recording Music by Peter Rutherford, Book and Lyrics by James Millar CD NGP01 9 369999 007645

Hired Man, The Music and Lyrics by Howard Goodall, Book by Melvyn Bragg TER CD CDTER2 1189

Ipi Ntombi Music by Bertha Egnos, Book and Lyrics by Gail 7 Lucille Lakier CDSGP0577

Irma la Douce Music by Marguerite Monnot, Book and Lyrics by Alexandre Breffort, 1967 Paris cast, VEGA CD 465 826-2

Irma la Douce Music by Marguerite Monnot, English Book and Lyrics by Monty Norman, David Heneker and Julian More, London Cast, SEPIA CD 1120

Irma la Douce Music by Marguerite Monnot, English Book and Lyrics by Monty Norman, David Heneker and Julian More, Broadway Cast Sony Broadway CD SK 48018

Joe de Musical, Music by Ad Van Dijk, Lyrics by Koen Van Dijk, Original cast CD, Endemol ENCD 7111

Kabarett Jean Stilwell CBC Records MVCD 1162

Kat and the Kings, West End Cast Book, Music and Lyrics by David Kramer and Taliep Petersen First Night CD CASTCD 67

King Kong Music by Todd Matshikiza, Lyrics by Pat Williams Book by Harry Bloom CDZAC 51 R

La Pergola De Las Flores, ("The Pergola of Flowers") Chilean musical comedy with music by Pancho Flores, lyrics by Isidora Aquirre, Presented by "Teatro de la Universidad

Catolica de Chile" with Ana Gonzalez, Silvia Piñeiro, Carmen Barros, Hector Noguera and original cast. Phillips LP 630 500 issued in 1960.

Lapin Agile, Au – Le doyen des cabarets de Montmartre EPM CD 980122

Lola Montez Music by Peter Stannard, Lyrics by Peter Benjamin, Book by Alan Burke Bayview CD RNBW003

Magic Flute, The (Impempe Yonlingo) Original Cast recording Young Vic Production CD

Magic Paintbrush, The Music by Kenneth Lyen, Lyrics by Brian Seward

Mama es una Estrella ("My Mother is a Star") Music by Angel Mahler, Book and Lyrics by Jorge Mazzini 1997 CD-675

Marguerite Original London Cast recording Music by Michel Legrand Lyrics by Herbert Kretzmer, Original French Lyrics by Alain Boublil, Book by Alain Boublil, Claude-Michel Schönberg and Jonathan Kent First Night CAST CD102

Morphium und Widerstand Music by Mischa Spoliansky Klein aber Kunst CD KK-003/4

Musicals from the Land of Oz Various composers Bavview CD RNBW012

Opérettes Marseillaises Music by Vincent Scotto Universal CD 476 2107

Phi-Phi Music by Henri Christiné Book and Lyrics by Albert Willemetz and Fabien Sollar Universal CD 465 886-2

Re:mix Music by Dick Lee, Book by Dick Lee, Cheek and Paul Tan Singapore repertory Theatre 2002 Teflon Music CD YM-REMIX003/EA70099

Rob Roy Book, Music and Lyrics by David Warrack 2006 WPRR-1

Sentimental Bloke, The ABC Television Production Music by Albert Arlen, Book and Lyrics by Nancy Brown and Lloyd Thomson LP

Sideshow Alley Original Australian Cast recording Music by Paul Keelan, Book and Lyrics by Gary Young CD

Spend, Spend, Spend Music by Steve Brown, Book and Lyrics by Steve Brown and Justin Greene 2000 Garforth Records GAR001

Strike! Music and Lyrics by Danny Schur Book by Danny Schur and Rick Chafe 2006 CD

Toi, C'est Moi, Music by Moises Simons, Book by Henri Duvernois, Lyrics by Albert Willemetz, Marcel Bertal, André Mouezy-Eon, Louis Malbon and Robert Chamfleury. Les Brigands CD Tourdillon

Tristan Book, Music and Lyrics by Jay Turvey and Paul Sportelli 2007 JPCD04

Twist of Fate, A Music by Dick Lee, Lyrics by Anthony Drewe, Book by Steven Dexter and Tony Petito 1997 Singapore repertory Theatre

Ute Lemper Sings Kurt Weill, 1988 Decca CD 425 204-2

Veronique Music by André Messager, Book and Lyrics by Albert Vanloo and Georges Duval CD EMI Classics 7243 5 74073 2 3

Videography:

Amandla! A revolution in Four-Part Harmony Directed by Lee Hirsch 2002 Artisan DVD

Billy Bishop Goes to War Directed by Barbara Willis Sweete Brightspark Productions DVD BSPK779

Blue Angel, The ("Der blaue Engel") Directed by Josef Von Sternberg, Music by Friedrich Holländer 1930 Ufa Kino International DVD

Bran Nue Dae – a film about the musical by Jimmy Chi and Kuckles Directed by Tom Zubrycki, Bran Nue Dae Productions Aboriginal Corp., Broome, Western Australia, 1991.

Broadway – The American Musical Directed by Michael Kantor 2004 Granada DVD

Chasing the Tango High, Written and Directed by Shel Piercy, Infinity Filmed Entertainment, 2006

"Drowsy Chaperone, The", *Working in the Theatre*, American Theater Wing, City University Television, April 2006

French Can-Can Directed by Jean Renoir, Music by Georges Van Parys 1954 DVD The Criterion Collection

Keating! The Musical Directed by Neil Armfield, Book, Music and Lyrics by Casey Bennetto 2008 Australian Broadcasting Corp. DVD

Not on the Lips ("Pas sur la Bouche") Directed by Alain Resnais, Music by Maurice Yvain, Book and Lyrics by André Barde 2003 Wellspring DVD FLV5452

Oh Rosalinda! ("Die Fledermaus") Music by Johann Strauss Lyrics by Dennis Arundel Directed by Michael Powell and Emeric Pressburger

Rose of Versailles: Girodelle side story Written and directed by Shinji Ueda, plus *Miroirs* ("Endless Dreams of the Mirrors") Book by Nakamura Satoru, Music by Nishimura Kouji, Kuratomi Shinichi, Kai Masato and Nakao TarouTakarazuka Snow Troupe, 2008 DVD TCAD-216

Sarafina! Directed by Darrell James Roodt, Book, Music and Lyrics by Mbongeni Ngema, Additional Music and Lyrics by Hugh Masekela DVD Buena Vista 26283

Umbrellas of Cherbourg, The ("Les parapluies de Cherbourg") Directed by Jacques Demy, Music by Michel Legrand (DVD includes documentary *The World of Jacques Demy*) 1963 Optimum Releasing DVD

Voices of Sarafina! Directed by Nigel Noble Music by Mbongeni Ngema and Hugh Masekela New Yorker Video 1988 NYY 58091

Interviews

Georgina Bexon, London, 4 November 2008
Peter Cousens, Sydney, 14 November 2008
René Driessen, Arnhem, 12 May 2009
Julian Forsyth, London, 27 October 2009
Chris Grady, London, 31 October, 2008
Peter Wyllie Johnston, Melbourne, 17 November 2008
Aaron Joyner, Melbourne, 18 November 2008
Dick Lee, London, 2 December 2008
Kenneth Lyen, Stella Kon, Desmond Moey, Singapore, 11 November 2008
Kerry Michael, London, 27 October 2008
Amon Miyamoto (with Yuriri Naka, interpreter), London, 7 June 2010
Søren Møller, Hamburg, 12 September 2009
Tony Sheldon and Ray Kolle, Sydney, 13 November 2008

Mel Atkey

Mel Atkey has been writing musicals ever since he was in high school in his native Vancouver. He was a finalist for the Musical of the Year competition in Aarhus, Denmark, and his work has been short-listed for the Vivian Ellis Prize, the Quest for New Musicals, the Ken Hill Prize and Musical Stairs. His first musical, *Shikara*, was produced on radio in Canada. A single was released by singer Janice Jaud of one of the songs, "Far Away", and received airplay across Canada and the U.S.

Mel spent two years as a theatre critic in Vancouver before moving to Toronto to pursue his career as a musical theatre writer. He was commissioned to write songs for CBC Radio, and was a member of the Guild of Canadian Musical Theatre Writers' Lehman Engel Workshop. He was a director of the Cabaret and Musical Theatre Alliance until he moved to London in 1991. He made his New York debut in April 2001 with an off-off-Broadway showcase of *O Pioneers!* with book by Robert Sickinger. This show was then a finalist for "Stages 2002" at the New Tuners theatre in Chicago. Their second musical, *A Little Princess* was presented at Wings Theatre in New York in 2003, and his two character musical *Perfect Timing*, for which he wrote the book as well as music and lyrics, was showcased in 2005 to great acclaim as part of Greenwich Theatre (London)'s Musical Futures series. He wrote the opening number for Janie Dee's critically acclaimed one-woman show.

His two previous books, *When We Both Got to Heaven* and *Broadway North: The Dream of a Canadian Musical Theatre* were published by Natural Heritage Books in 2002 and 2006 respectively. Hehas also lectured internationally on the subject of musical theatre.

www.melatkey.com

Abbey Theatre 130
ABC Music Hall...67
Abeløe, Mads..225
Abraham, Eric 190
Academy of New Musical Theatre..........235, 238
Accident Waiting to Happen, An 138
Achard, Marcel 67
Achilles in Heels 49
Acito, Tim...209
Actors' Benevolent Fund 172
Adams, Arthur 156
Adams, Lee 229
Adelaide Cabaret Festival 175
Adelaide Festival Centre................................166
Adelaide Festival Theatre 165
Adiós, Pampa mía' 191
Adler, Gusti..52
Adler, Richard 222
Aeroplane Man 232
Aeschylus...51
After the Fair..106
Ag, Pleez Daddy 187
Age of Innocence, The...................................200
Aguirre, Isidora 196
Ahmanson Theatre 141, 143
Aida...125, 208
Alamein Concerto 163
Albery, Donald 69
Aldolpho 138
Aldwych Theatre 188
Aleichem, Sholem 106
Aleksandrov, Grigorii 25
Alhambra..66
Ali Baba and the Forty Thieves 155
Alibert, Henri 63
All Het Up...170
All I Want Is Rice 209
Allan, Anne 149
Allen, Peter 167, 245
Alô, alô, Brasil!...197
Alvear Palace Hotel..192
Always (film)...127
Amadeus (film) 19
Ambrosio, Valeria 195
American in Paris, An................................66, 78
American Psycho 134
American Theater Wing.............................138, 250
Americana 90
An Over-rated World (With Seven
   Underwhelming Wonders)......................141
Andersen, Hans Christian 103

Anderson, David Cameron................................48
Anderson, Lale 46
Andersson, Benny 129
Andolfi, Ermanno...192
Andrada, Tuca..198
Andrews, William...105
Angel (Sarah McLaughlin song) 48
Anna and the King of Siam 101
Anne of Green Gables – The Musical 5, 13, 15,
   98, 99, 108, 111, 134, 143, 166, 203, 228,
   238
Anne with an E..98
Annie Get Your Gun 24, 72, 157, 161
Ant & Dec Show, The 121
Anyone Can Whistle.......................................91
Anything Goes......................................158, 235
Apollinaire, Guillaume 38
Apollo Victoria Theatre..................................207
Appignanesi, Lisa 36, 40, 47
April in Paris 82
Aquarela do Brasil 197
Aqui No Podemos Hacerlo! 194, 245
Aragon, Joseph 151
Aran, Han 209
Archer, Robyn 49, 164, 174
Arden, Leslie 226
Arlen, Albert 163
Arlen, Harold...82, 248
Armfield, Neil...175, 250
Armiger, Martin 166
Arms and the Man 31
Armstrong, Gillian..153
Armstrong, Louis.......................................54, 65
Arts Club Theatre 151
Arts Council England.............................224, 225
Arts Sphere Theatre.......................................204
As We Stumble Along 141
Asari, Keita 202
ASCAP 88, 224, 227, 235
Asche, Oscar 155
Así se ama en Sudamérica 192
Askey, Arthur 160
Aspects of Love 125
Astaire, Fred 76
Astoria Theatre 120
At the Bullfight..147
At the Silver Swan 160
Athenaeum Theatre (Melbourne) 154, 175
Atkinson, Brooks...........................12, 113, 120
Attlee, Clement...117
Au Pays du Soleil..63

Aufricht, Ernst Josef..54
Auric, Georges 37
Austral, Florence..159
Australia Council...169
Australian Broadcasting Commission
    Australian Broadcasting Corporation.*See, See*
Australian Broadcasting Corporation 153
Australian Elizabethan Theatre Trust 162
Avec les anges 69
Axel an der Himmelstür 32, 55
Ayala, Fernando...195
Ayer, Nat D. 61
Aymé, Marcel 76
Aznavour, Charles 14
Aznavour, Charles 56
Aznavour, Charles 57
Bablo, Lamartine 197
Bacharach, Burt 89
Bäckers, Heinrich Bolten- 50
Badura-Skoda, Eva 19
Baek Jae-hyun..209
Baker Street 65, 137
Baker, Josephine...................39, 63, 66, 67, 192
Baker's Wife, The 63
Bakker, Piet...128
Balanchine, George 52, 82
Balcovske, Sandra 139
Ball, Michael 94
Ballad Of Angel's Alley, The 164
Ballad of Little Jo, The..................................229
Ballad of Mack the Knife, The..........................54
Bancks, J.C. 160
Banff Centre 148
Bannink, Harry 47, 126, 127, 128, 247
Baobab
    Umoja..*See*
Bar Mitzvah Boy 99
Barbican Theatre 77
Barbieri, Francisco Asenjo 24
Barcelona...171
Barde, André...................................58, 64, 250
Barratts of Wimpole Street, The....................164
Barrie, J. M..113
Barroso, Ary 197
Barry, Jeff...89, 92
Bart, Lionel.....................14, 24, 117-119, 229
Bartók, Béla 193
Bartram, Neil 145, 228
Basingthwaite, Nathalie...................................213
Bat Out of Hell 125
Battersea Arts Centre 43
Battle, Hinton 144
Battye, Don...165, 245

Baudouin, Julio 198
Bäuerle, Adolf 28
Bearde, Chris...162
Beaufort, John 180
Beaumont, Binky..69
Beauty and the Beast................................33, 195
Beauty World 199, 210, 211, 216, 218, 219
Because...69
Beethoven, Ludwig von 28
Beggar's Opera, The 11, 23, 54, 71, 197
Beguelin, Chad 143
Behr, Edward 62
Behrens, Jergen 46
Being Erica 109, 134
Belasco, David 82
Benatzky, Ralph 31-33, 51, 55
Benedix, Roderich 29
Benjamin, Peter 162, 248
Bennett, Robert Russell 67
Bennett, Tony 133
Bennetto, Casey 175
Beresford, Bruce 153
Berger, Michel 77
Berkoff, Steven 12
Berlin, Irving...............9, 20, 81, 88, 208, 222
Bernard P. Jacobs Theatre 131
Bernardi, Herschel 72
Bernauer, Rudolf..31
Bernhardt, Ian..183
Bernhardt, Sarah..157
Bernicat, Firmin 59
Bernstein, Leonard 9, 12, 22, 33, 81, 89, 106,
    120, 229
Berry, Chuck...89
Bertal, Marcel 65, 249
Bertaut, Jules 60
Berton, Pierre 98
Berusaiyu no bara
    Rose of Versailles ....*See*
Bet Your Life 160
Betjeman, John 130
Betts, Jim 93, 148, 151, 227, 228
Betty Blue Eyes.....................................122, 217
Bexon, Georgina 222, 252
Beyond Eden 150
Biberti, Robert 43
Big Life, The..229
Billington, Michael 43, 75, 122, 176
Billy Bishop Goes to War.109, 136, 228, 245, 250
Birch, John Youlin 157
Birkenhead, Susan 143
Birnie, Peter 151
Birthday Girl..190

255

Bittersweet 24
Bitter-Sweet 22
Bizet, Georges................................21, 57
Black Crook, The 14
Black Orpheus..198
Black Swan Theatre Company 174
Black, Don 99, 172, 207, 222, 224, 242
Blackadder..120
Blackout on Broadway................................204
Blair, Ron 165
Blakemore, Michael................................155
Blanche, Francis..73
Blank, Larry 107, 130, 141
Bless the Bride 24
Blitz 118
Blitzstein, Marc................45, 54, 81, 226
Blitzstein, Marc..67
Blood Knot, The..187
Bloodless 151
Bloom, Harry..........................183, 186, 247
Bloom, Orlando 183
Blue Angel, The 41, 43
Blue Mountain Melody 160
Blye, Alan 162
Blythe, Alecky 122
BMI 10, 88, 224, 226
Boat that Rocked, The 91
Bogdanovich, Peter 66
Bolton, Guy 160
Bombay Dreams 199, 207
Bonbonnière 55
Bond, Christopher..........................144, 246
Bond, Grahame 165
Bootz, Erwin..43
Borbosa, Maria Carmen............................198
Born to be Wild 132
Borovansky Ballet 157
Bose, Mihir 206
Bosom Buddies 136
Bosom Friends 136
Boublil, Alain.....56, 57, 75, 76, 77, 226, 244, 248
Boughton, Kathryn 107
Boulanger, Nadia 67, 74, 193
Bourgeois Bleibt Bourgeois................................41
Bourgeoise Gentilhomme 41
Bowness, Gordon 139
Boy Be 204
Boy Friend, The 100
Boy from Oz, The 154, 167, 168
Boy's Own McBeth......................................165
Boyer, Charles..41
Boyer, Jean 65
Boyett, Bob..140

Boys from Syracuse, The 231
Braden, Bernard... 155
Bradley, Ian.................................121, 236
Bran Nue Dae..................................174, 175, 250
Brantley, Ben 127, 141, 145
Brazil (film).. 197
Bread and Butter 147
Breaker Morant 153
Brebner, Morwyn 146
Brecht, Bertolt . 41, 44, 45, 48, 53, 54, 55, 83, 91,
    112, 125, 147, 164, 197
Brecht< Bertolt 51
Breedland, André............................128, 245
Breffort, Alexandre 68, 69, 70, 72, 73, 247
Brel, Jacques 14, 39, 48, 56, 57, 70, 77, 78, 97
Brentano, Felix.. 52
Brice, Fanny 61, 65, 67
Brickhill-Burke, Joan 189
Bride's Lament................................139, 141
Bridewell Theatre 171, 223, 225
Brigadoon 82, 103, 110, 228
Bring in da Noise, Bring in da Funk 229
Brink, Jos.. 127
Bristol Hippodrome 122
British Broadcasting Corporation 42, 91, 100,
    177, 237
Broadway Asia International 207
Broadway at Bedtime 13, 153
Broadway Boys 201
Broadway North: The Dream of a Canadian
    Musical Theatre 13
Broken Bridges 220
Brook, Sir Peter.................70, 73, 182, 205, 244
Brooke, Brian 188
Brooks, Daniel 139
Brooks, Shelton.. 98
Brother, Can You Spare a Dime? 90
Brothers Ábalos 192
Broussolle, Jean 65
Brown, Jason Robert.................................. 171
Brown, Nancy 163, 164, 248
Brown, Steve..120, 248
Bruant, Aristide...37, 41
Bruce, Lenny.. 47
Buarque, Chico.. 197
Bucchino, John.. 47
Buchanan, P.J.. 153
Buddy – the Buddy Holly Story...............149, 150
Bunch of Ratbags, A.. 165
Bunna.. 205
Buntes Theatre
    Überbrettl ....See
Bunyan, Mark 49

Bunyan, Paul..133
Burke, Alan 162, 248
Burnett, Jim 165
Busch, Charles 167
Busoni, Ferruccio 53
Busoni, Ferrucio 82
Buzzard Song 97
Bye Bye Birdie 71, 92, 95, 228
Cabaret 40, 99, 110
Cabaret Chez Gilles...68
Cabaret des Assassins
    Lapin Agile ....*See*
Cabaret Grössenwahn 41
Caesar, Irving 55
Caird, John 77
Caligula 195
Calloway, Ann Hampton 48
Calvi, Gerard 73
Cambridge Theatre 122, 188
Camelot 82
Campbell, Elaine 5, 98, 134, 228, 245
Campbell, Norman......13, 98, 108, 134-136, 203,
    228, 245
Canada Rocks – A Celebration 149
Canadian Broadcasting Corporation 49, 133, 134,
    139, 147, 148, 150, 162, 237, 245, 247, 253
Canadian Music Theatre Project 151, 238
Canadian Musical Theatre Project.................224
Canadian Stage Company 145, 146
Canaro, Francisco 192
Can-Can 57, 72, 110, 250
Candide 33, 91
Cantabile..43
Capilano University 148
Carden, George...162
Carl, Carl 29
Carl, Fred 230
Carlos, José "J."...197
Carltheater...29, 33
Carmen 14, 21, 22, 57, 248
Carmen Jones...22
Carmichael, Hoagy..88
Caroline..165
Carousel 101, 110, 208
Carré Theatre...125
Carroll, Garnet H..164
Carter, Wilf 133
Carver, Brent 145, 151
Casey, Warren 114
Casiono-Montparnasse.....................................74
Cats..8, 33, 96, 125
Cats,..202
Cattrall, Kim 176

Cave of the Golden Calf 46
Cayabyab, Ryan..207
Cedar Tree, The..160
Central Academy of Drama............................208
Central Park Tango 152
Chagal, Marc...106
Chakiris, George..75
Chamfleury, Robert 65, 249
Chang and Eng..213
Chapman, Christopher.......................................99
Chapman, John 71
Charell, Erik 32
Charles, Hugh..185
Charlottetown Festival 98, 99, 109, 134, 149,
    151, 161, 245
Charnin, Martin 100
Chase, Will 145
Chat Noir...................................35, 36, 37, 38, 39, 57
Chat Noir (Berlin) 40
Cherlin, Michael 26
Chess 129
Chess King, The 207
Chevalier, Maurice......56, 62, 63, 64, 67, 76, 240
Chez Fischer 37
Chez Fyscher 65
Chi, Jimmy...174, 250
Chiang, Michael 210, 216
Chicago 69, 106, 235
Chocolate Soldier, The 31
Chocolate Soldier, The 51
Chocolate Soldier, The 82
Chorus Line, A 33, 93, 96, 125, 213, 226
Christie, Craig..171
Christie, Dinah 49
Christiné, Henri 14, 48, 60, 61, 62, 63, 248
Chu Chin Chow 155
Chungmu Art Hall 209
Churchill, Sir Winston 46, 117
Chute, B.J. 113
Ciboulette 58, 62
Cibrián Campoy, Pepe....................194, 245, 246
Cinderella, ...208
Cipolla, Frank 144
Circus 25
Cirque du Soleil 233
Ciske de Rat 128, 129, 131, 245
Citadel Theatre 142
City of God 198
City, The 203
Clair, René 65
Clark, Professor Manning 166
Clark, Stephen....................................217, 247
Clarke, Elizabeth 133

Clarke, Kevin 51
Clarke, Terrence 166
Clarke, Terry 165
Cleese, John 94
Cluff, Susan 227, 228
Cocciante, Richard 77
Cochran, C.B. 61
Cocteau, Jean 37
Coelho, Elisina 197
Cohan, George M..................................80, 129
Cohen, Leonard 93
Cold Feet 139
Cole, Allen 147, 148
Cole, Stephen 106
Coleman, Cy 99
Coleman, Ross 177
Colerick, George 19, 22, 26, 53
Collet, Henri 37
Collin, Erich 43
Collits, Pierce 159
Collits' Inn 15, 158, 159, 160, 174
Colliver, Amanda 217
Colman, Charles..165
Comden, Betty 229
Come Down from the Tree, Bunna 205
Come from Away 152
Comedian Harmonists, The 43, 44
Comedy Theatre (Melbourne)........154, 164, 166
Comme de Bien Entendu..................................65
Company......................78, 93, 125, 151, 171, 172
Complainte de la Butte.......................37, 65, 78
Comte, Charles 11, 18, 37, 39, 41, 56, 57
Comte, Louis 11, 57
Coney Island Play 203
Consider Yourself..77
Constantine, Eddie 67
Conversation Piece 24
Conyers, Will...................153, 154, 168, 177
Cook, Peter 41, 46
Cookin' 208
Copland, Aaron..................................81, 113
Coppin, George...157
Cork Opera House 130
Cork, Adam 122
Corporacion Interamericana de Entretenimiento
....197
Corrugation Road 174
Cort Theatre 181, 189
Cosentino, Olga 195
Cottesloe Theatre 122
Cotton, Christopher Cooke........................193
Coulter, John..13
Coups de roulis...62

Coups de Roulis 58
Courthouse Theatre......................................146
Cousens, Peter 170, 173, 252
Coveney, Michael 100, 118, 176
Cowan, Ron...122
Coward, Noël 90, 101, 117, 119, 135
Coward, Sir Noël.....................................23, 24
Coward, Sir Noël 22
Cox, Christopher 101
Cradle Will Rock, The 81, 226
Craig, Phil 64
Crawford, Michael 125
Creative Community Singapore 214
Crémieux, Hector 21
Crew, Robert 138
Croft, Martin 170
Crombie, Jonathan..138
Crooked Mile, The 119
Crosby, Bing 107
Cryer, Gretchen 98
Cugat, Xaviar 197
Culture Show 237
Cup of Tea, A Bex and a Good Lie Down, A.... 162
Cushman, Robert 145, 146, 147
Cuvillier, Charles 58
Cycowski,,Roman 43
Cyrano...127, 128
d'Albert, Eugene 82
D'Oyly Carte Opera Company 157
Da Boyz 231
Da Kink in My Hair 148
Dahl, Roald..49, 122
Dallas, Lorna 48
Dalton, Karen C. C. 39
Daly's Theatre 31
Dalziel and Pascoe 190
Dancap Productions......................................142
Dance of the Vampires 33, 125
Daniels, Salie 189
Danish Musical Theatre Academy 225
Dante, Ron 92
Darewski, Herman 61
Das Gefängnis..29
Das Pensionat 29
Daubeny, Sir Peter 188
David,Hal...89
Davis, Lee 229
Day in Hollywood / A Night in the Ukraine, A.. 93
Days of Hope...120
de Crane, John 126
De dader heeft het gedaan 127
De Garis, Jack 155, 156
de Jongh, Nicholas 176

258

De Mounties 47
de Munk, Danny 128
de Sivry Charles 37
de Tourdonette, Vincent 148
Debussy, Claude 36, 56, 60, 78
December Rains 219
Dédé 62
Delerue, Georges 56
Delysia, Alice..160
Demaria, Gonzalo 195
Demick, Barbara 209
Demy, Jacques 74, 75, 202, 251
Demy< Jacques 75
Deneuve, Catherine......................................75
Dennis, C.J. 163
Der Rosenkavalier 51
Deréal, Colette..68
Desert Song..51
Destry Rides Again 41, 226
Deutsch, Diana...9
Deutsch, Leon Benoit- 64
Deutsches Theater..................................52, 53
Dexter, Steven 217, 249
Dhéry, Robert 73
Dhlamini, Ezekiel "King Kong" 184
Diamond, Dick 164
Diamond, I.A.L. 72
Díaz, Edda 193
Dick, William 165
Dickens, Charles...118
Dickson, Barbara..121
Die Csárdásfürstin...32
Die Distel 46
Die Dreigroschenoper
    Threepenny Opera....................................54
    Threepenny Opera, The ....*See*
Die Fledermaus 22, 30, 32, 52, 82, 250
Die Hölle 31, 45
Diesel Playhouse..144
Dietrich, Marlene.....................39, 40, 41, 42, 43
Dietz, Howard 30
Diggers..159
Dimba, Peter...182
Dingo, Ernie 175
Dirty Dancing 149, 150, 238
Discépolo, Enrique Santos 192
Dis-Donc..72
Dissanayake, Wimal.....................................206
DJ Excalibah 231
Dollar Princess, The
    Die Dollarprinzessin ....*See*
Dollar Princess, The 31
Domingo Placido...24

Dominus, Susan 139
Don Quijote...24
Donan, Stanley...74
Donizetti, Gaetano...................................20, 21
Donizetti, Gaetano..29
Donlon, Denise 148
Donmar Warehouse 195
Donnelly, John 183
Donovan, Jason..176
Dorgelès, Roland 38
Dorléac, Françoise 75
Dorn, Egon 46
Dornford-May, Mark......................................190
Dos Passos, John 51
D'Oyly Carte, Richard 59
Dr. Who 164
Dracula 194, 195
Drainie, John 135
Dranem 64
Dreiser, Theodore 51
Dresselhuys, Mary 126
Drewe, Anthony.....................121, 122, 217, 249
Dreyfus, George 166
Dreyfuss, Max 82
Driessen, René 47
Drowsy Chaperone, The .8, 14, 94, 100, 105, 135-
    148, 205, 228, 237,
Drylips Ought to Move to Kapuskasing 150
Dublin Theatre Festival 130
Due South 98, 134
Duffy, Rosemary 169
Duke of York Theatre 190
Duke, Vernon 82
Dumas, Alexandre..76
DuMaurier, Daphne 125
Dumbells, The 141
Dunayevsky, Isaak Osipovich 25
Dupuy, René 68
Durey, Louis 37
Duval, Georges......................................59, 249
Duvernois, Henri....................................65, 249
Dvořák, Antonin.....................................55, 82
É do Outro Mundo 197
Easy Rider 91
Ebb, Fred......................................69, 99, 110
Ebersole, Christine 140
Ebinger, Blandine..41
Ed Mirvish Theatre..144
Ed Sullivan Show 187
Eddy, Nelson 98
Edge, Simon 176
Edinburgh Fringe 207, 225
Edinburgh Fringe Festival 207

Edison, Thomas...57
Edmonton, Dennis.......................................132
Edwards, Gale.............167, 168, 171, 177
Eenens, Paul.....................................128, 129
Egnos, Bertha.....................................188, 247
Einstein, Albert...38
Eisenstein, Sergei..25
El amor de la estanciera.......................191
El barberillo de Lavapiés.......................24
El Cóndor Pasa.................................25, 198
El Cóndor Pasa"...25
El Diablo en el poder................................24
El Filibusterismo.....................................207
El gaucho de Buenos Aires...................191
El Jorobado de Paris.....................195, 246
El Manisero
     Peanut Vendor, The.............................*See*
El otro yo de Marcela.............................192
El Tango en París....................................192
Eleven Executioners....................................40
Elgar, Edward...9
Elgin Theatre.......................................142, 144
Elisabeth.....................33, 124, 202, 238
Ellington, Duke.......................65, 90, 186
Elliot, Cathy...151
Elliot, Stephan...175
Ellis, Sarah T..113
Ellis, Vivian...........24, 64, 84, 117, 121, 253
Elmer Gantry..121
Embujo Theatre...205
Emerald Hill Theatre..................................165
Emigrants, The...129
Emperor's New Clothes...............171, 203
En Nu Naar Bed....................125, 126, 246
     And Now to Bed.................................*See*
Eng, Thien Kwee...215
Engel, Lehman . 10, 12, 23, 58, 73, 81, 93, 94, 97,
     101, 110, 113, 151, 161, 224, 226, 227, 230,
     238, 253, 286
Enoch, Wesley...175
Enright, Nick...........164, 165, 167, 245
Ensemble Theatre.......................................166
Entra na Faixa..197
Erdöd, Count Ferdinand Palffy von...........28, 29
Es liegt in der Luft....................................42
Esplanade Centre..........211, 215, 217, 219, 220
Esse Mulato Val Sê Meu............................197
Esta noche me emborracho.......................192
Establishment Club.......................................46
Eternal Road, The.....................................53
Eureka...168
Eurobeat...171
Eva, el gran musical argentino.......104, 194

Evil Dead – the Musical.............................144
Evil Dead -- The Musical..143, 144, 237, 238, 246
Evita.........69, 104, 125, 191, 194, 195, 222, 246
Evita – Tango Popular Opera.................194, 246
Evita - Volveré y seré millones.............104, 194
Expresso Bongo.................................69, 119
Expresso-Bongo..92
Eyre, Sir Richard..122
Eysler, Edmund...31
Eysler, Edmund...33
Faith, Percy..133
Falabella, Miguel...198
Fall, Leo...31
Fall, Leo...31
Fall, Leo...33
Fall, Leo...35
Falling in Love Again....................................41
Falling Slowly..131
Fame...193, 208
Fancy Dress...141
Fantasticks, The...............................205, 228
Farago, Peter...77
Farnon, Robert.....................................133, 134
Fauré, Jean-Baptiste....................................56
Favero, Alberto..194
*Fearless Vampire Killers (or, "Pardon Me But
     Your Teeth are in my Neck")*, The............125
Federico, Domingo...............................194, 246
Feingold, Michael.......................................105
Female Student...209
Fenwick, John...135
Feore, Donna...130
Ferré, Léo...39
Ferrer, Horacio..193
Festival of Asian Performing Arts.............213
Festival of Canadian Musical Theatre...........228
Feuersnot..39
Feur, Cy...100
Feydeau, Georges...58
*FFF*155
Fiddler on the Roof.......13, 72, 96, 105, 182, 193
Fidelio...28
Fields, Dorothy..99
Filichia, Peter...146
Fings Ain't Wot They Used T'Be.............118, 229
Finian's Rainbow.......................................228
Finkle, David..170
Firefly..82
Fireweeds: Women of the Yukon...............151
Five Foot Broadway.........................213, 246
Flash Jim Vaux..165
Flashpoint..134
Flatley, Michael..129

260

Fledermaus (cabaret) 46
Fletcher, Jackie 231
Fletcher, Mark 170
Flores del Campo, Francisco 196
Flory, Régine 64
Flower Drum Song 199, 200
Flowered Port 200
Floyd Collins 172
Fly, Robin, Fly...124
Flynn, Patrick 165
Foil, David 21
Folies-Bergère.. 11, 50, 57, 58, 59, 61, 62, 66, 67, 78, 240
Follies 125
Follies of the Day 67
Fontaine, Robert..99
Fonteyn, Margot..158
Foote, Horton 113, 202
Forbidden City. 199, 211, 215, 216, 217, 219, 247
Ford, Anne Kerry 47
Ford, Nancy 98
Foreign Hill 203
Forever Plaid 144, 145
Forsyth, Julian 43
Forsyth, Marguerite 43
Fortune Theatre...187
Forty-Second Street 208
Four Seasons Opera House...........................144
Fox, Maxine 114
Foxtrot 127, 128
Francisquita, Doña..24
François-les-Bas-Bleus 59
Frankel, Scott...236
Franklin, Benjamin 102
Frau Luna 50, 55
Free Wind, The 25
Freedman, Bill..135, 136
Freihaus-Theater auf der Wieden 19
French Cancan 65, 66
French Can-Can..37
Friml, Rudolph 82, 97, 98
Fringe of Toronto Festival....................137, 138
From a Prison Cell' 71
From A to Z 160
From Russia With Love 118
Frommermann, Harry...43
Fronz, Oskar..33
Frühling 31
Fugard, Athol 187
Fulford, Robert 132, 135
Fulton Theatre..64
Funayama, Motoki...204
Funny Girl..158

Funny Thing Happened on the Way to the Forum, A...59, 137
Furth, George..151, 172
Furtwängler, Wilhelm 50
Gabin, Jean..37, 66
Gaiety Theatre 23
Gandhi (film) 179
Gänzl, Kurt 8, 26, 52, 57, 62, 63, 74, 77, 119, 120, 124, 186, 286
Garber, Victor..148
Garfunkel, Art 25
Garland, Judy 65
Garrick Gaieties 82
Gasalla, Antonio...193
Gate Theatre (Charing Cross, london) 160
Gates, Henry Louis Jr. 39
Gay, John 11, 23, 54
Gay, Noel 23
Gehry, Frank 132
Geistinger, Marie 29, 30
Gekidan Furusato Caravan...........................205
Gélinas, Gratien 119, 134
Genatt Haft, Simone 208
Genée, Richard 22, 29
George Ignatief Theatre 138
George, Bruce 164
Gerard, Frédéric "Frédé" 38
Gerard, Jeremy 127
Gershwin, George 9, 13, 42, 53, 64, 78, 82, 88-91, 223
Gershwin, Ira 23, 83, 97
Get Up and Boogie...124
Gets, Malcolm...145
Gevisser, Mark 181
Gielguid Theatre 75
Gigi 57
Gilbert, Robert 43
Gilbert, Sir William Schwenk....11, 22, 23, 31, 79, 83, 117, 131
Gill, André 38
Gilliam, Terry 197
Gingold, Hermione..160
Ginzler, Robert..71
Gipsy Princess, The
Die Csárdásfürstin 32
Girl from Utah, The 80
Girlfriends 120
Glee...236
Glickman, Will 192
Global Search for New Musicals 238
Glory of the Railwaymen 25
Glow-Worm 50
Gluckman, Arnold 197

Gluckman, Leon 184, 187
Godspell 182, 203
Godzilla 202
Goebbels, Joseph 46, 50
Goetz, E. Ray 61
Goffin, Gerry 89
Goh Boon Teck 219
Goh Jung-min 209
Goh, Robin 213
Gokulsing, K. 206
Gokulsing, K. Moti 206
Goldberg, Whoopi 181
Golden Bat, The 203
Golden Dawn 32
Golden Valley, The 25
Golderich, Arthur 184
Goldman, Gabriel 195
Goldoni, Carlo 166
Goldwyn, Samuel 103
Gomeshi, Jian 237
Gone With the Wind 202
Gontier, Robert 152
Good Doctor, The 209
Goodall, Howard 9, 12, 89, 120, 121, 247
Goodbye for Now 78
Goodbye to Berlin 40
Goodeve, Piper 99
Goodman, Benny 42
Goodspeed Opera House 99
Gordon, Maggie May 168
Gorlero, Pablo 191, 193
Gorney, Jay 90
Goulet, Robert 99, 148
Grady, Chris 222, 225, 237, 252
Grainer, Ron 164
Grand Hotel 200, 201
Grandage, Michael 195
Granowsky, Andrew 41
Grant, Bruce 178
Grant, Mark N. 93
Grappelli, Stéphane 38
Grattan, Harry 64
Gray, John 109, 136, 245
Grease 114
Greco, Juliette 68
Green, Adolph 229
Greene, Justin 120, 248
Greenwell, Peter 119
Greenwich Theatre 224, 253
Greenwich, Ellie 92
Greenwillow 113
Greer, Germaine 168

Grey Gardens 236
Grey, Clifford 61, 160
Greyeyes, Michael 150
Gribble, Harry Wagstaffe 61
Griffiths, Rudyard 132
Groovy Kind of Love 92
Grosses Schauspielhaus 51, 55
Grossmith, George 31, 83
Grossmith, George Jr. 31
Grotowski, Jerzy 182
Grudeff, Marian 137, 138
Grünbaum, Fritz 31, 46
Guerrero, Jacinto 24
Guettel, Adam 151, 224
Guettell, Adam 172
Guevara, Nacha 193, 194
Guild of Canadian Musical Theatre Writers.... 12, 227, 253
Guiraud, Ernest 21
Guitry, Sacha 58, 62, 74
Gurr, Thomas Stuart 158
Gussow, Mel 203
Guttman, Arthur H. 61
Guy Named Joe, A 127
Guys and Dolls 55, 69, 72, 95, 96, 113
Gypsy 71
H.M. Tennent Ltd. 69
H.M.S. Pinafore 23
Ha'penny Bridge 130, 247
Habbema, Eddy 127
Hackney Empire 181
Hague, Albert 192
Hahn, Phil 140
Hahn, Reynaldo 58, 62, 63, 245
Hair 92, 94, 165, 193, 231
Hairspray 141, 142, 149, 208
Hales, Dr. Aaron 211, 216, 219
Halévy, Fromental 20, 21
Halévy, Ludovic 20, 21, 22, 29
Haley, Bill 88
Half a Sixpence 119
Hamanaka, Toru 204
Hamilton, Barbara 143
Hammerstein, Oscar II . 15, 22, 32, 52, 84, 91, 97, 101, 120, 166, 207, 231
Hampton, Christopher 125
Hampton, Wilborn 181
Handel, George Frideric 43
Hans Christian Andersen 103
Hansard, Glen 131
Hansel and Gretel 53
Hansen, Helle 225
Hansen, Max 32

262

Happy End....................................55, 112
Happy Guys...25
Happy Time, The.................................99
Harbach, Otto.......................................32
Harbach, Otto.......................................97
Harburg, E.Y. "Yip"..........................82, 90
Harcourt, Peter....................................157
Harkness Theatre.................................188
Harmonists, The..................................43
Harnick, Sheldon.............29, 75, 127, 229
Harrison, George..................................117
Harrison, Rex...................................101, 223
Harron, Don.............98, 134, 135, 143, 228, 245
Harron, Martha.....................................134
Harron, Mary..134
Hart, Lorenz......................................32, 92
Hart, Moss...103
Harvey, Michael Maurice.....................168
Hasenclever, Walter.............................41
Hatpin, The....................................170, 171
Hauptmann, Elisabeth......................54, 55
Hayes, Nancye................................158, 168
Hays, Matthew......................................142
Heawood, John......................................69
Hedley, Philip.................92, 174, 230
Hedley, Phillip...............230, 231, 232
Hedwig and the Angry Inch.................209
Heerlijk duurt het Langst....................126
Hein, David...152
Held, Anna..67
Hello, Dolly!................29, 96, 154, 193
Helpmann, Sir Robert.........................155
Helta, Jenő...62
Hemmingway, Ernest.............................51
Henderson, Bill....................................150
Heneker, David.........24, 69, 73, 119, 247
Henry, Marc..46
Her Majesty's Theatre.....................100, 188
Her Majesty's Theatre (Brisbane)...........162
Her Majesty's Theatre (Melbourne).......154, 157
Her Majesty's Theatre (Sydney)........157, 167
Herbert, Victor...............................81, 129
Herman, Jerry................................88, 222
Hermans, Toon......................................46
Hervé..20
Hesterberg, Trude................................42
Heuberger, Richard...............................30
Hey, Sourpuss.....................................138
Higashi, Yutaka....................................203
High School Musical.....................206, 236
Higher than the Sky of Paris................200
Highway, Thomson...............................150
Highwayman, The..............160, 161, 174

Hill, Alfred..156
Hill, Brian......................................145, 228
Hillman, Jessica...................................105
Hindemith, Paul....................................42
Hirasawa, Satoshi................................201
Hired Man, The.............................120, 121
Hirsch, Foster.......................................53
His Majesty's Theatre (London)
  Her Majesty's Theatre...........................*See*
Hitchings, Henry...................................122
Hitler, Adolph. 32, 41, 42, 46, 50, 53, 55, 86, 114,
  124
HMS Pinafore..................................79, 83
Hobson, Harold.....................................70
Hoile, Christopher................................147
Holländer, Felix....................................41
Holländer, Friederich.............................51
Holländer, Friedrich 14, 35, 41, 42, 45, 46, 50, 51,
  53, 110, 250
Holländer, Victor...................................42
Holländer< Friedrich..................41, 42, 55, 84
Holly, Buddy..88
Holmes à Court, Janet..........................174
Holmes, Eda...146
Home and Beauty...............................42
Honda, Hiroko.......................................206
Honda, Yoshihisa...................................206
Honegger, Arthur....................................78
Hong Kong Rhapsody...........................204
Honk!..121, 217
Honneger, Arthur..........................37, 61, 64
Honolka, Kurt..27
Honolka, Kurt..29
Hood, Basil..31
Hope, Bob.......................................94, 107
Hopper, Dennis......................................91
Hornez, André..65
Horwitt, Arnold B...................................193
Hossein, Robert.....................................77
Hot Jazz Club of France...........................38
Houdini, una ilusion musical................195
House of Martin Guerre, The................226
How Do You Solve a Problem Like Maria?.....237
Howes, Sally Ann...................................160
Hsu Po-yun...207
Huairou Theatre....................................208
Hui, Melissa..150
Hull House Theatre................................114
Hummingbird Centre
  Sony Centre...*See*
Humperdinck, Engelbert..........................53
Humphries, Barry..................................162
Hunchback Of Notre Dame, The.............125

Hydropathes 36
Hylton, Jack..185, 186
Hymne à l'Amour 67
I Am a Camera 40
I Can't Touch You with Words 147
I Do I Do in the Sky.................................139
I Go to Rio 167
I Love Botchan 204
I Love the Night Life................................176
I Love You, You're Perfect, Now Change.173, 208
I Remember Love..139, 141
I Will Wait for You 74, 75
I'll Never Smile Again 133
I'm Alan Partridge..................................121
I'm Calm' 137
I'm Getting My Act Together and Taking it on the Road..98
Ibsen, Henrik..155
Ichiro, Maki...202
If I Could Walk Freely.................................209
If I Ever Fall in Love Again 119
Iglesias, Luis 197
Ikeda, Riyoko 201
Ikoku-No-Oka...203
Il a Raison..69
Im weissen Rössl
   White Horse Inn, The .... *See*
Impempe Yomlingo....................................190
Imperial Theatre (St. John, NB)......................136
Improbable Frequency............................130, 131
In the Heights 230
Indian Love Call......................................97
Indian Productions....................................206
International New Aspect Educational and Cultural Foundation 207
Into The Woods......................................125
Inverne, James 207
Ipi-Tombi...188
Irglová, Markéta 131
Irma la Douce 69, 70, 71, 73, 77, 247
Irma La Douce....................57, 68, 69, 74, 124
Is Australia Really Necessary? 161
Isherwood, Charles................................131, 177
Isherwood, Christopher................................40
Isintu
   Kwa Zulu... *See*
Istana Budaya 220
It's a Wonderful Life 121
It's an Over-rated World (With Seven Underwhelming Wonders)......................138
Itelman, Ana 194
Ives, Charles...80
Ives, David 125

J'ai deux amours 63
Jackman, Hugh.........................158, 166, 167
Jackson, Frederick.................................... 64
Jackson, Jeffrey....................................36, 37, 60
Jacobs, Jim 114
Jacobsen, Amber....................................... 150
Jacobson, Leopold 31
Japan 2001 Festival................................... 206
Jardin de Paris 67
Jarre, Maurice 56
Je T'aime 201
Jelavich, Peter.......................................39, 40
Jelly's Last Jam 229
Jenbach, Bela 32
Jessel, Raymond....................................... 65
Jessell, Ray.. 137
Jessop, Sonia Kolesnikov- 219
Jesus Christ Superstar .77, 94, 119, 148, 193, 222
Jewison, Norman 106, 149
Jishin Kaminari Kaji Oyaji 205
Joe 127
Joe Starts Again 170
Johann-Strauss-Theater...............................32, 33
John Golden Theatre 187
John, Alan 166
Johnny Angel.. 201
Johnson, Laurie 118
Johnson, Melody 147
Johnson, Reed 196
Johnston, Dr. Peter Wyllie 154, 155, 159, 160, 161, 163, 164, 165, 166, 173, 174, 252
Jones, Arnold Wayne 108
Jones, Chris 114
Jones, Laura 182, 188
Jones, Tom 91, 112, 113, 205, 228
Jonzi D.. 232
Joplin, Scott 93
Jorgensen, Peter 151
Joseph and the Amazing Technicolor Dreamcoat 96, 176
Joseph Papp Public Theater........................... 75
Joseph Papp Public Theatre........................... 75
Joseph, Paul 229
Jouy, Jules 38
Joyner, Aaron..111, 169, 172, 173, 176, 238, 252
Jubany, Miguel......................................194, 246
Judía.. 192
Jugar con fuego 24
Julia, Raul 45
Jung Sung San 209
Jungr, Barb 49
Just a Kiss 64
Just for Laughs 144

Just So	121
Justicia Criolla	191
Kabarett der Komiker	42
Kabuki, Hisao	204
Kálmán, Emmerich	31, 33, 51
Kanagawa Arts Theatre	204
Kander, John	71, 99, 110
Kander,John	110
Kanin, Garson	30
Kaouru, Irie	201
Kaplan, Jonathan	146
Kapur, Shekhar	207
Karastamatis, John	138
Karczag, Wilhelm	30, 32
Karloff, Boris	101
Kärntnertortheater	18
Kat and the Kings	189, 247
Katharina Knie	43
Katy	207
Kauffman, Stanley	187
Kaye, Danny	103
Keane, Edmund	89
Keating	49, 96, 175, 250
Keelan, Paul	168, 248
Kelly, Conor	130
Kelly, Dennis	122
Kelly, Gene	75
Kelly, Veronica	175
Kennedy, Jackie	191
Kente, Gibson	183
Kerby, Paul	52
Kern, Jerome	13, 31, 80-83
Kerr, Deborah	75
Kerr, Walter	71
Kesten, Hermann	41
Khalek, Hisham Abdel	106
Khan, Hazrat Inayat	9
Kidman, Nicole	190
Kikuta, Kazuo	200, 202
Killick, Dr. Andrew	210
Kim Hee Gab	208
Kim Kyong Suk	210
Kim Mi-hee	209
Kindred Spirits	136
King and I, The	30, 75, 101-103, 110, 111, 199
King Kong	184, 185, 186, 187, 247
King, Carole	89
King, David	166
King's Theatre (Melbourne)	156, 161
Kingston Mines Theatre	114
Kingston, Claude	155, 156
Kipling, Rudyard	121
Kiri no Mirano	200
Kirk's Gallery	165
Kislan, Richard	23
Kislan, Richard	54, 82, 83, 222
Kiss Me Kate	193
Kiss of the Spider Woman	33, 125
Kitt, Eartha	188
Kleines Theater	55
Knapp, Raymond	79, 105, 112, 113
Kneebone, Tom	49
Knickerbocker Holiday	83
Kobayashi, Ichizo	199, 200, 202
Koenig, Rhoda	231
Kolke, Shuichiro	201
Kolle, Ray	153, 252
Kon, Stella	111, 216, 252
Kong, Lily	215
Kookaburra	153, 154, 170, 171, 172, 173
Kopit, Arthur	11
Korda, Alexander	42
Korie, Michael	236
Korngold, Erich Wolfgang	52
Kostelanetz, André	81
Kraft Durch Freude	33
Kramer, David	189, 247
Krane, David	106
Kretzmer, Herbert	77, 129, 248
Kristina	129
Kubelik, Jan	82
Kuchwara, Michael	141, 146
Kuhn, Jeffrey	145
Kunze, Dr. Michael	33, 68, 124, 125, 202, 246
Kunze, Michael	33
Kuratomi, Shinichi	200
Kwa Zulu	189
Kwazulu	
Kwa Zulu	*See*
L'Amour Masque	58
L'Amour Masqué	63
L'Attaché d'ambassade	30
L'il Abner	226
L'Impasse de la Fidélité	72
La Basoche	59
La Belle de Cadix	74
La belle Hélène	58
La Belle Hélène	22, 51
La canción de los barrios	192
La cumparsita, Rascacielos	192
La Femme du Boulanger	63
La Fiaca	195
La Goualante du Pauvre Jean	67
La Grande-Duchesse de Gérolstein	21, 58
La Grosse Valise	73
La MaMa Experimental Theatre Club	203

La muchachada del Centro 191, 192
La muchachada del Centro' 191
La P'tite Lili 67
La Pergola de las Flores 196
La Périchole 58
La Petite Functionnaire 58
La Plume de ma Tante 73
La Route Fleurie 74
La Strada..118
La Vie Parisienne.......................................22
Labiche, Eugène Marin 58
Ladrão de Galinhas 197
Lady in the Dark.......................................83
Lady Oscar 202
Lafayette, Maximillien de 35
Lagaan..207
Là-Haut 64
Lahr, John 93
Lai, Francis 56
Lakier, Gail 188
Lamb, Andrew 51, 55, 62, 74, 80
Lambert, Catherine..................................174
Lambert, Lisa ..136, 137, 138, 139, 140, 142, 143
Lamond, Toni 158
Lamoureux, Robert....................................67
Lan, David 190
Landon, Margaret....................................101
Landor Theatre 49
lang, k. d. 133
Langdon, Harry 158
Lapin Agile 37, 38, 39
Larsen, Anika 130
LaSalle College of the Arts 217
Lascelles, Kendrew 187
Last Empress, The 208
Latimer, Jeffrey......................................144
Lauder, Sir Harry 103
Laurence, Margaret 134
Laurents, Arthur 229
Lawrence, Gertrude.................................101
Lay, Evelyn 61
Layton, Joe 202
Le Chef Grotesque 137
Le Mariage aux lanternes 29
Le Merliton 37, 41
Le Passe Muraille
    Amour ....See
Le Passe-Muraille......................................76
Le Réveillon 22, 29
Leander, Zarah...................................32, 55
Learn Everything
    Open the Window.............................See
Lee Moon Roel..208

Lee, Dick. 204, 210, 214, 215, 216, 217, 218, 219, 220, 247, 248, 249, 252
Lee, Robert 230
Lee, S.G. 136
Lees, Gene 82
Left Luggage 128
Legrand, Michel .14, 68, 74-76, 78, 245, 248, 251
Legrand, Raymond 68
Lehár, Franz 22, 30-33, 51
Lehrer, Tom 89
Leibovitz, Liel 42
Leip, Hans 46
Lemon, Jack 72
Leningrad State Musical Comedy Theatre.......25
Lennon, John..............................88, 117, 226
Lenya, Lotte 40, 54, 91
Leon, Ruth..77
Léon, Victor..30
Leonowens, Anna 101
LePage, Robert.......................................205
Lerner, Alan Jay 10, 11, 21, 23, 29, 31, 81, 82, 90, 94, 103, 119, 179, 223, 231, 242, 286
Lerner, Sammy..41
Les Aventures du Roi Pausole 64
Les Belles et le gitan................................74
Les Belles Soeurs 151
Les Brigandes 58
Les Chasseurs d'images 65
Les Demoiselles de Rochefort 75, 76
Les Fridolinades 134
Les Harengs Terribles 68
Les Million 65
Les Misérables ...8, 12, 33, 56, 77, 78, 94, 96, 99, 103, 127, 128, 130, 131, 170, 171, 194, 195, 202
Les mômes de la clouche..............................63
Les P'tites Michu 59
Les Six 37
Leschnikoff, Aspurach...............................43
Lessing Theatre 41
Letterman, David 112
Levay, Sylvester 33, 124, 202, 246
Leveux, David...106
Liang Wern Fook 219
Lichtenberg, George 72
Light in the Piazza, The 151
Likes of Us, The 119
Lilac Time 159
Liliom 101
Lillie, Beatrice 82
Lim Chuang Yik......................................220
Lin Yu-lin 208
Lincke, Paul 50, 53, 55

266

Lincoln Center................72, 105, 180, 182, 208
Lincoln, Abraham................81, 102
Lind, Jenny................29
Linder, Cec................155
Lindfors, Bernth................186
Lion King, The................58, 125, 183, 215
Lion of the East................183
Lion, Margo................42, 43
Lipman, Daniel................122
Litchfield, Neil................170
Little Mercy's First Murder................146
Little Night Music, A................34, 205
Little People................77
Little Shop of Horrors................125, 217, 226
Little Women................172
Littlewood, Joan................164, 229
Livermore, Reg................165
Living Doll................117
Lloyd Webber, Andrew 90, 91, 94, 100, 104, 118, 119, 120, 125, 148, 150, 172, 194, 195, 206, 207, 222, 237
Lock Up Your Daughters................118
Loesser, Frank.... 29, 41, 48, 55, 82, 88, 103, 112, 113, 208, 222
Loewe, Edmund................82
Loewe, Frederick................31, 82, 103, 223, 231
Lola Montez................162, 163, 248
London Pavilion................61
London Road,................122
London, Jack................51
Lonsdale, Freddie................60
Look Back in Anger................90
Lopez Ruiz, Oscar................194
Lopez, Daniel................194
Lopez, Francis................74, 124
Lord of the Rings................142
Lorenzo's Oil................165
Los amores con las crisis'................191
Los diamantes de la corona................24
Lotherington, Dean................170
Louÿ, Pierre................64
Love is Always Lovely in the End................141
Love is Blue................70
Love Story................120, 217
Love's Labours Lost................229
Low, Ken................213, 245
Lowe, Ruth................133
Lubbock, Mark................21
Lucas, Craig................151
Lucille Lortel Theatre................98
Luhrman, Baz................65
Luhrmann, Baz................206
Lully, Jean-Baptiste de................20

Lulu................65
Lumbera, Bienvenido................207
Lumière Brothers................57
Luna de miel para tres................192
Luna Park Arena................194
Lunatic................199, 209
Lund, Alan................143
Lyen, Dr. Kenneth ..213, 214, 215, 216, 217, 218, 219, 233, 245, 248, 252
Lyric Stage................108
Lyric Theatre................70, 164
Lyric Theatre Hammersmith................54
Lysistrata................50
Macbeth................188
MacDonald, Jeanette................98
Macdonoughy, Glen................61
Machin, Antonio................65
Mack the Knife
    Ballad of Mack the Knife, The................*See*
Mack, Paul................140
MacKenzie, David................99
Mackintosh, Cameron................27
Mackintosh, Sir Cameron 56, 77, 96, 100, 121, 207, 222
Maclaine, Shirley................72
Mac-Nab, Maurice................37
Mad About the Boy"................24
Mad Dogs and Englishmen"................24
Madame Arthur................127
Madame Butterfly................212
Madame Pompadour................51
Maen, Norman................75
Maggie May................118
Magic Flute, The................11, 14, 18, 19, 28, 190, 238
Magic Paintbrush, The................216
Magnificat................199, 207
Magnormos Productions................111, 169, 170, 224
Magnormos Theatre................111, 224
Mahler, Angel................194, 195, 246, 248
Mahomed, Ismail................183
Maid in the Mountains................60
Maid of the Mountains, The................159
Maipo Theatre................194
Make Me an Offer................119
Makeba, Miriam................181, 184
Makeham, Paul................174
Malefane, Pauline................190
Maltby, Richard Jr.................100, 145, 229, 235
Mame................135
Mamma Mia!................125, 129, 150, 209, 235
Man of La Mancha................57, 97
Manana, the Jazz Prophet................183
Mandela, Nelson................181

Manheim, Ralph 45
Manitoba Theatre Centre 147
Mankowitz, Wolf 119
Mann, Thomas 146
Manning Clark's History of Australia – the
   Musical 166
Mantovani 163
Margolis, Mac 198
Marguerite 75, 76
Maria de Buenos Aires 193
Maria Severa 146
Marie Antoinette 125
Marigold 160
Marischka, Hubert 32
Marishka, Ernst 52
Market Theatre of Johannesburg 180
Marquis Theatre 136, 141
Martell, Julie 146
Martin Guerre 217, 227
Martin, Bob.... 136, 137, 138, 139, 140, 142, 143,
   144, 246
Martin, Mary 223
Martin, Steve 38
Mary Bryant 166
Mary Poppins 121, 217
Masaaki, Hirao 201
Masakela, Hugh 180, 184
Masquerade 127
Massary, Fritzi 51
Massey Hall 144
Masteroff, Joe 110
Masutti, Guillermo 193
Matchmaker, The 29
Matilda 49, 122
Matshikiza, Todd 184, 247
Matsui, Rumi 105
Maubon, Louis 65
Maugham, Somerset 42
Maurice Ravel 9
Max Havelaar 127
Max Reimer 142
Max, Margarida 197
Maxwell, Jackie 146
May, Elaine 47
Mayer, Louis B. 98
MC Skolla 231
McAnuff, Des 148
McArthur, Colin 103
McBroom, Amanda 47
McBurney, Simon 205
McCartney, Sir Paul 88, 117
McClain, John 71
McCollum, Kevin 140

McCracken, Hugh 92
McGuckian, Alastair 130, 247
McGuickan, Garrett 130
McIntosh, Hugh D. 155
McKellar, Don .136, 137, 138, 140, 142, 143, 246
McKelllar, John 161
McLaughlin, Sarah 48
McLuhan, Marshall 8
McPherson, Jim 168
Meat Loaf 125
Meehan, John Jr. 52
Meehan, Thomas 143
Meilhac, Henri 21, 29, 30
Meilhac, Henri 22
Melba, Nellie 159
Melbourne Repertory Theatre 157
Melbourne Theatre Company 165
Mellers, Wilfred 18
Mellers, Wilfred 79
Mellers, Wilfred 286
Melville, Alan 160
Melville, Herman 79
Menopause – The Musical 168
Menuhin, Yehudi 52
Menzies, Robert 164
Mercer, Johnny 53
Mercure 37
Mercury Musical Developments......92, 222, 224,
   238
Mérimée, Prosper 21
Mermaid Theatre 118
Meropa
   Kwa Zulu ....*See*
Merrick, David 71, 99
Merrily We Roll Along 235
Merry Widow 51
Merry Widow, The
   Die Lustige Witwe ....*See*
Merry Widow, The 30, 32, 82
Mersey Dotes 89
Message from a Nightingale 139
Messager, André 32, 58, 59, 60, 62, 63, 249
Mestral, Marie-Claude 73
Metropol Theater 41
Metropolitan Opera..............22, 30, 81, 246
Metropolitan Theatre 195
Michael, Kerry.............230, 231, 232, 233, 252
Michel, Keith 70
Michell, Keith 70, 155
Midler, Bette 177
Midsummer Nights' Dream, A 51
Mikado, The 83
Milhaud, Darius 37

Millar, James.............................170, 247
Millar, Ronald 164
Miller, Matthew..........................42
Miller, Roy 140
Milord 67
Mimi, or A Poisoner's Comedy.............147
Minakami, Tsutomu........................205
Minchin, Tim..............................49, 122
Minelli, Liza 12
Minervini, Rina 180
Ming Wong 213
Mini, Vuyusile 182
Minim Bili 187
Minim Export 187
Minnie Moustache.........................65
Minogue, Kylie............................153
Min-On Japan 206
Minskoff Theatre 125
Minsky's 143
Miori, Yumino.............................201
Miracle, The 51
Miranda, Carmen..................67, 191, 197, 198
Miranda, Lin-Manuel 230
Mirande, Yves 63
Miroirs 201, 250
Miroy, Jovi 207
Mirvish Productions.................139, 142, 150
Mishima, Yukio 104
Misraki, Paul 192
Miss Saigon.................57, 75, 199, 207, 209
Mistinguett 61, 66
Mitzi E. Newhouse Theatre 180
Miyamoto, Amon.....96, 104, 105, 142, 200, 201, 204, 252
Moberg, Vilhelm...........................129
Mofokeng, Jerry...........................181
Molina, Alfred............................106
Møller, Søren 111, 224, 225, 233, 252
Molnár, Ferenc 101
Mon Homme 61, 65, 67
  My Man ....*See*
Mon Paris................................199
Moncrieff, Gladys 159, 160
Mongkut, King 101, 103
Monk, Varney 158, 159, 160
Monnot, Marguerite..............14, 48, 67-73, 247
Monsieur Beaucaire.......................60
Montaner, Rita 65
Montgomery, Lucy Maude 99
Monty Python's Flying Circus.............94
Moody, Ron 118
Moon is East, The Sun is West, The 203
Moore, Mavor ..98, 119, 134, 135, 143, 149, 245

Moore, Tracey 223
Moorish Maid, A 157
Mordden, Ethan...........................80, 146
More, Julian 69, 73, 119, 247
Morel, Steven 138
Morgan, Paul 32
Morley, Sheridan 77
Morrison, Greg 136, 138, 142, 246
Mortal Sins..............................216
Morugan Oyuki 202
Mosman Town Hall........................159
Motley theatre
  Überbrettl ....*See*
Motorcycle Diaries, The 198
Mouezy-Eon, André.....................65, 249
Moulin de la Chanson 63
Moulin Rouge 11, 37, 57, 65, 66, 199
Moulin Rouge (film) 206
Moulin, Jean-Pierre 73
Mozart (Kunze/Levay) 125
Mozart (musical play) 18, 19, 26, 28, 58, 63, 242, 286
Mozart, Leopold 27
Mozart, Leopold ...11, 12, 18-21, 27, 52, 89, 120, 190, 238
Mr. Bean 120
Mr. Cinders 24
Mrs. Pretty and the Premier 157
Msomi, Welcome..........................188
Murphy, Colin 130
Murphy, Frank 165
Murphy, Gareth 56
Murray Anderson's Almanac 160
Music Box Theatre 76
Music Man, The 112, 113, 228
Musical Futures 224, 253
Musical Theatre Educators Alliance............238
Musical Theatre Limited 213, 216, 224, 233, 238, 245, 246
Musical Theatre Matters 222, 224, 237
Musical-za 204
Mussorgsky, Modeste......................25
Muthu 206
Muthu, Dancing Maharaja 206
My American Cousin 109
My Beautiful Mother 181
My Brilliant Career.......................153
My Fair Lady 10, 24, 31, 82, 96, 97, 103, 112, 126, 158, 193, 202, 223, 228
My Man 56, 61, 65, 67
My Man's Gone Now 227
My Yiddishe Momma.......................181
Nae maeumui punggeum 209

Nakamura, Hideo..205
Nakamura, Satoru..201
Nallon, Steve..103
Nash, N. Richard 99, 112, 113
Nassour, Ellis..125
Nathan, J. P. 219
National Alliance for Musical Theatre's Festival
    of New Musicals 140
National Alliance of Musical Theatre Producers
   238
National Arts Centre 142
National Arts Festival (Grahamstown) 183
National Institute of Dramatic Art.........158, 166
National Theatre............104, 105, 121, 122, 286
National Theatre (Buenos Aires) 192
National University of Singapore...........214, 215
National Youth Music Theatre......................224
Natsume, Souseki 204
Natzler, Leopold 31
Natzler, Sigmund 31
Necessary Angel Theatre Company...............139
Ned Kelly 165
Nederlander Worldwide Entertainment 208
Neighbours 153, 213
Neil Simon Theatre 127, 148
Nelson, Rudloph...42
Nelson, Rudolph...40
Nestroy, Johann...29
Never Say Goodbye...................................201
Neville, John 70
New London Theatre 189
New Theatre 135
New Theatre (Melbourne)............................164
New Tivoli Theatre.......................................159
New World Stage 144
New York Musical Theatre Festival 170
New York Theatre Workshop 131
New Yorkers 204
Newman, Bill..158
Newman, John..158
Newton, Sir Isaac 14
Next Stage Performing Arts Academy 214
Next to Normal 94
Ngema, Mbongeni . 179, 180, 181, 182, 183, 188,
    250, 251
Nicholaw, Casey......................140, 141, 143
Nichols, Mike 47
Nicholson, Viv 120
Nielsen, Carl...111
Night and Day 201
Night of the Hunter....................................106
Night They Raided Minsky's, The...............143
Nightcap 162

Nimrod Theatre 165
Nine.....................................106, 195, 226, 227
Nine Queens..198
Nishimura, Kohji 200
Nissay Masterpiece Theatre 203
Nixon, Marni 75
Nkosi Sikelel' iAfrika..................................186
No No Nanette..............................56, 58, 62
No No, Nanette..158
No Ranch Fundo 197
Noli Me Tangere 207
Norman, Monty 69, 73, 119, 247
Norris, Rufus 122
North by Northwest (Radio show) 237
Norton, Frederic 155
Not the Nine o'Clock News 120
Notorious Betty Page, The 134
Nôtre Dame de Paris 77
Nottingham Rep...184
Novello Theatre.....................................141, 171
Novello, Ivor 23, 24, 84, 117, 122
Nunn, Sir Trevor.......................................43, 77
Nyandeni, Thembi..189
O barbeiro de Niterói.................................197
Ô mon bel inconnu 63
O' Callaghan, Patricia...................................130
O'Connor, Caroline 158, 170
O'May, John 154
Oates, Jennifer 103
Oberlin, Karen 47
Octagon Theatre (Perth)...............................174
OCU Stripped 223
Oeda, Shinji 201
Offenbach, Jacques. 11, 20-23, 29, 32, 35, 37, 51,
    57, 58, 67, 76-78
Official Story, The.......................................198
Oh Lord, I'm On My Way' 227
Oh, What a Lovely War! 229
Oklahoma! 21, 24, 28, 52, 84, 110, 200
Okuni, Izumo-no- 199
Old Vic..89, 184
Olivari, Carlos 192
Oliver! 14, 77, 96, 118, 119, 120
Oller, Joseph 66
On connaît la chanson 64
On the Street Where You Live 94, 103, 228
Once 131
Once in a Blue Moon (CD) 153
One Hundred Ten in the Shade 112, 113
One Kiss 64
Ong Teng Cheong 214
Only Girl, The 41
Onnasis, Aristotle...189

Open a New Window 136, 243
Open the Window 135, 136
Opera Ball 30
Opéra Comique...59
Opéra Comique (London) 23
Opera do Malandro 197
Opéra-Comique 20, 21, 60, 63, 73
Oresteia 51
Orgambide, Pedro 194
Orlando Rourke..166
Orpheus in the Haymarket............................21
Orpheus in the Underworld......11, 20, 21, 51, 57
Orr, William 161
Osaka Samurai..200
Osbourne, Charles 83
Osbourne, John...90, 91
Othello 89
Our Lady of the Camelias..............................76
Our Language of Love 69
Ouzounian, Richard130, 139, 140, 142, 146, 147, 148, 177
Oyama, David 104
Oz Showbiz Cares 172
OzMade Musicals 153, 169, 224, 238
Pabst, G.W. 54
Pacific 231 64
Pacific Overtures............104, 142, 199, 200, 204
Paget, Clive 171
Pagnol, Marcel...63
Paige, Elaine 141
Pajama Game, The 158
Pal Joey 72
Pal, Graciela 194
Palace Theatre 160, 176
Palace Theatre (New York) 177
Palace Theatre (Sydney) 161
Palais des Sports 77
Palmer, John...166
Palmer, Robert...180
Pam Ann 49
Pan y toros 24
Panasonic Theatre 144, 151, 152
Pansera, Roberto 194, 246
Panter, Howard 13
Paparelli, P.J..114
Papp, Joseph..45
Parade 37
Parade Theatre 166
Pardon Miss Westcott 163
Parès, Phillipe 65
Paris in the Rain 78
Paris Olympia 66
Paris Opéra 21, 60, 62

Park, Kolleen 208
Park, Sam 130
Parker, Ross 73
Parlor Match, A 67
Pas sur la Bouche 58, 64, 250
Pasadena Playhouse 184
Passionnément 58, 62
Patachou 72
Patel, Dr. Aniruddh 9
Patrick Street Productions 151
Patterson, Vincent 110
Paulsen, Harald 42, 54
Pavillion Theatre 70
Paviot, Paul 73
Pavlovsky, 'La' 193
Paz, Gaiza Guillermo 193
Pedersen, Thomas Bay 225
Pélagie 147
Pelay, Ivo...192
Pelléas et Mélisande 60
Peony Pavilion, The 208
Perciavalle, Carlos 193
Perfect Pitch 224
Perfect Timing 228
Perfect, Eddie 175
Perkins, Rachel 175
Perón, Eva..104, 194
Perón, Juan 104
Perryman, Jill 154, 158, 167
Persephone Theatre.....................................147
Pet Sounds 226
Peters, Bernadette......................................100
Petersen, Taliep 189, 247
Peterson, Eric..136
Peterson, William 214
Petito, Tony 217, 249
Phantom 11
Phantom of the Opera ..8, 96, 119, 125, 144, 209
Phillip Street Revues 161, 165, 171
Phillip Street Theatre 161
Phillips, Nicky...152
Phi-Phi.................57, 60, 61, 62, 69, 73, 78, 248
Phoenix Players 189
Phoenix Theatre...75
Piaf, Edith 39, 48, 56, 57, 63, 66, 67, 68, 195, 240
Piazzolla, Astor...193
Pibulsonggram, Nitya...................................101
Picadilly Theatre 121
Picasso at the Lapin Agile 38
Picasso, Pablo 38
Pickwick 118, 119
Picnic at Hanging Rock 153
Pimootewin (The Journey), ...150

271

Pinne, Peter 153, 165, 194, 196, 245
Pinsent, Gordon 109
Pinti, Enrique 193
Pippin 171
Pitre, Louise 129, 150, 151
Place To Stand, A 99
Plain and Fancy 192
Plamondon, Luc 77
Planché, John Robinson 21
Players Theatre 100
Playhouse Theatre (Brisbane) 168
Playhouse Theatre (Canberra) 163
Plummer, Christopher 155
Plymouth Theater 71
Plymouth Theatre 160
Pokorny, Alois 29
Pokorny, Franz 29
Polanski, Roman 125
Pondal, Sixto Rios 192
Popp, André 70
Porgy and Bess 91, 97
Porgy And Bess 227
Porter, Cole.. 61, 72, 78, 88, 89, 90, 93, 101, 126,
222
Poulenc, Francis 37, 78
Pratt Prize 168, 170, 224
Pratt, Jeanne 168
Pratt, Richard 168
Preston, Mary 162
Previn, André 9, 72, 94, 286
Priestly, J.B. 90, 91
Primrose 83
Prince Ananius 81
Prince, Harold 104, 151, 222
Princes Theatre
    Shaftesbury Theatre .... *See*
Princes Theatre (Manchester) 64
Princess of Wales Theatre 130, 144, 177
Princess Theatre 80, 159, 160, 166
Princess Theatre (Melbourne) 154, 157
Printemps, Yvonne 56, 61, 63
Priscilla -- Queen of the Dessert 14
Priscilla Queen of the Desert 177, 238
Priscilla, Queen of the Desert 150, 175
Prisoner Cell Block H 165
Producers, The 94, 142
Prokofiev, Sergei 9
Puteri Gunung Ledang 220
Pygmalion 31, 42
Q 237
Quast, Philip 158
Quatre Jours à Paris 74
Que vachache 192

Queens Theatre 189
Quinson, Gustave 58, 64
Radic, Leonard 165
Raffenaud, François 74
Ragtime 223
Rahman, A. R. 207
Raimi, Sam 144
Raimund Theater 33
Raimund, Ferdinand 33
Rainmaker, The 99, 113
Ramlie, Adlin Aman 220
Ramos, Santiago 191
Randall, Carl 161
Rattigan, Terrence 90, 117
Ravel, Maurice 56, 78, 193
Really Useful Group 172
Rebecca 33, 125
Red Dwarf 120
Red, White and Boogie 165
Reddy, Helen 158
Reds 78
Reed, Rex 187
Reedy River 164
Reel to Real, the Movies Musical 207
Reeves, David 166
Reeves, Peter 127
Regent Theatre (Melbourne) 154
Reid, Bill 150
Reid, Caroline 49
Reinblatt, George 144, 246
Reindhardt, Max 55
Reinhardt, Django 38
Reinhardt, Gottfried 51, 52
Reinhardt, Max 14, 27, 31, 40-42, 51-53, 55
Relâche 37
Renard, Colette 68, 70, 73
Renoir, Jean 37, 65, 66, 78, 250
Rent 12, 94, 130
Resnais, Alain 64, 250
Revue '60 162
Revue Nègre, La 39
Reyes, Jose Javier 207
Reynoso Compuesto, Antonio 191
Rez Sisters, The 150
Rhapsody in Blue 53
Rhapsody in Blue' 88
*Rhapsody on Songs of the People of the Soviet
    Union* 25
Ri Koran 203
Ricci, Nino 152
Rice, Emma 75
Rice, Sir Tim . 69, 78, 91, 104, 119, 129, 194, 222,
224, 235

Rich, Frank 180
Richard, Cliff 117
Rimsky-Korsakov, Nikolai 25
Ring of Fire 149
Riordan, Arthur 130
Rise and Fall of the City of Mahagonny, The ...53, 54
Ritchard, Cyril 155, 160
Riveira, Chita 95
Riverdance 104, 129, 130
Riviera Girl, The
    Die Csárdásfürstin 32
Rivoli 138
Rizal, Dr. Jose 207
Road to Qatar, The 107, 108
Robert and Elizabeth 164
Roberts, Nick 147
Robertson, Jennifer 200
Robertson, Malcolm 157
Robertson, Robbie 133
Robertson, Tim 166
Robitschek, Kurt 42
Robles Godoy, Armando 198
Robles, Daniel Alomía 25
Robles, Daniel Alomía 198
Rock Around the Clock 88, 92
Rock Island 112
Rockaybye Hamlet 237
Rockin' with the Cave Men 117
Rocky Horror Show, The 144
Rodgers, John 175
Rodgers, Richard...... 15, 20, 83, 84, 91, 101, 102, 110, 113, 120, 166, 207, 224, 231, 243
Roger, Elena 195
Rogers, Ginger 76, 135
Rohter, Larry 198
Rolls, Ernest C. 157
Romberg, Sigmund 51, 82, 83
Rome, Harold 73, 202
Romeo & Juliet in Summer Night 204
Romeo and Juliet 223
Romeril, John 166
Ronnie Scott's 46
Roodt, Daryl James 181
Rooney, David 146
Roosevelt< Franlin Delano 102
Rosa, Noel 197
Rosalinda 52
Rose Marie.... 56, 58,63, 64, 82, 97, 98, 103, 159, 160
Rose of Versailles 111, 199, 201, 202, 250
Rosé, Bert 192
Rose, Billy 88

Rosenbaum, Jonathan 76
Rosenbaum, Thane 106
Rosenberg, Deena 229
Rosenkavalier 43
Rosenthal, Jack 99
Rosenwax, Nathalie 159
Ross, Adrian 31
Ross, Jerry 222
Ross, Michael 130
Ross, Peter 172
Rossetto, Cecilia 193
Rossini, Gioachino 20
Rossini, Gioachino 197
Rostand, Edmond 127
Rothenberg, David 8
Roud, Richard 72
Roundabout Theatre 105
Roux, Michel 68
Rowan and Martin's Laugh-in 134, 162
Rowdyman, The 109
Roy Thomson Hall 144
Royal Alexandra Theatre 97, 144
Royal Canadian Air Farce 49
Royal Opera House 60
Royal Shakespeare Company 77, 122
Royal Winnipeg Ballet 147
Rubinoff, Michael 99, 152
Ruddell, Bruce 150
Rudin, Scott 236
Rudisill, Kristin 207
Rufelle, Frances 94
Rufen Sie Herrn Plim!
    Send for Mr. Plim ....*See*
Runyon, Damon 69, 113
Rush, Geoffrey 142, 175
Russell, Jenna 120
Rutherford, Peter 170, 247
Ryshpan, Arden 236
Sahl, Mort 47
Saint-Saëns, Camille 59
Salad Days 137
Salis, Rodolphe 36
Salis, Rodolphe 38
Salonga, Lea 199, 207
Salten, Felix 31
Salten, Felix 45
Saludos Amigos 197
Salys, Rimgaila 25
Sams, Jeremy 76, 78, 201, 245, 286
Samuels, Edmond 160
Sanders, Frank 127
Sankoff, Irene 152

Sarafina! .. 14, 179, 180, 181, 182, 183, 186, 189, 250, 251
Sarvil, René 63
Satie, Eric 37, 78
Saturday Girl 163
Saturday Night Fever 195
Savage, Lilly 165
Savary, Jérôme 73
Savoy Theatre 160
Saw Teong Hin 220
Saward, Tim 230, 231
Schall und Rauch
     Sound and Smoke ....*See*
Schiffer, Marcellus 42, 44
Schikaneder, ...19, 27-30, 238
Schlesinger, Sarah 9, 229
Schmidt, Annie M. G. 47, 126, 128
Schmidt, Harvey 91, 112, 113
Schönberg, Claude-Michel 57, 75, 76, 77, 226, 244, 248
School for Scandal 43
Schrödinger, Erwin 130
Schultze, Norbert 46
Schur, Danny 147, 148, 248
Schütz, Adolph 32
Schwartz, Arthur 82
Schwartz, Roberta Freund 112
Schwartz, Stephen 63, 69, 171, 235
Scott, Allan 177
Scott, Sir Walter 103
Scotto, Vincent ... 22, 35, 48, 61, 63, 74, 124, 248
Scott-Stokes, Henry 203
Script Lab 93, 224, 227, 228
Scrooge 118
SCTV 49
Se dice de mí 191
Seal, Elizabeth 69, 70
Second City 49, 139, 143
Secrest, Meryle 81
Senczuk, John 168
Send for Mr. Plim 43, 44
Send in the Clowns 205
Sentimental Bloke, The 15, 163
Serban, Andrei 75
Sergeant Pepper's Lonely Hearts Club Band ...226
Serra, Luis Maria 194
Serrano, José 24
Seven Little Australians 166
Seventeen Seventy-six 108
Seventeen-Seventy-six 79
Seventy-six Trombones' 113
Seward, Brian 216, 248
Seymour Centre (Sydney) 154, 170

Shaffer, Paul 112
Shaftesbury Theatre (original) 64, 189
Shall We Dance? 30
Shane Warne – The Musical 175
Shanghai Blues 219
Shanghai Conservatory of Music 208
Shanghai Dramatic Arts Centre 208
Shaw Festival 146
Shaw, George Bernard 31
Shaw, George Bernard 42
Shaw, George Bernard 129
Shea, Tom 74, 227
Sheldon, Tony 158, 161, 163, 165, 167, 170, 175, 176, 177, 252
Shenton, Mark 123, 172
Sheridan College 148, 151, 224, 238
Sheridan Square Playhouse 203
Sheridan, Richard Brinsley 43
Sherman, Richard M. 122
Sherman, Robert B. 122
Shiba, Ryōtarō 200
Shibata, Yukihoro 200
Shiki Theatre Company 136, 202, 203
Shimoda, Itsuro 203
Shinchi, Kuratomi 201
Shippey, Dr. Theo 179
Shiro 203
Short, Martin 227
Show Boat 84
Show Off 139
Showa Trilogy 203
Showboat 160
Shubert Organization 61
Shuttleworth, Ian 121
Si Eva se hubiese vestido 192
Sibande, Gert 183
Sickinger, Robert 114
Sideshow Alley 168, 169, 172, 173, 248
Sidus FNH 209
Signature Theatre 99
Sikalo 183
Sikov, Ed 72
Silk Stockings 126
Silver Lake, The 53
Simon, Paul 25, 89
Simons, Marlise 127
Simons, Moisés 61, 65
Simplicissimus 46
Simplicius 30
Simpson, Professor Michael 183
Sing Seng Kwang 213
Sing to the Dawn 217
Singapore Festival of the Arts 213

Singapore Repertory Theatre 215, 217
Singh, Anant 181
Singin' in the Rain 74, 76
Sirett, Paul 229
Site 204
Sitwell, Edith 231
Sklar, Matthew 143
Skywalk 209
Slings and Arrows 143
Smash 236
Smith, Harry B. 67
Smith, Janet 151
Smits, Sebastiaan 128
Sneddon, Professor Elizabeth 188
Snip en Snap 47
Snow, Hank 133, 243
Society of Cavaliers 28
Sollar, Fabien 61, 248
Some Like It Hot 92
Someone is Waiting 78
Something in the Air 228
Somewhere in the World 145
Son p'tit frère 58, 64
Sondheim, Stephen 10, 12, 22, 29, 34, 59, 64, 69,
        78, 90, 91, 93-95, 104, 112, 151, 171, 172,
        205, 208, 223, 226, 229, 230, 232, 235, 286
Song and Dance 100
Song, Eric 209
Songs for a New World 171
Songs of a Sentimental Bloke 163
Sonneveld, Wim 46, 126
Sons of France 71
Sontonga, Enoch 186
Sony Centre 144
Sorcerer, The 23
Soria, Ezequiel 191
Sothart, Herbert 97
Sound and Smoke 41, 42
Sound and Smoke, ...51
Sound of Music, The 113, 114, 142, 150, 166, 208
Sousa, John Phillip 112, 113
South American Way 198
South Pacific 102, 110, 111, 199, 231
Southern Cross 203
Soy al rubio Pichinango 191
Spamalot 140
Sparks, John 11, 227, 230, 233, 235
Sparks, John ....
Spend, Spend, Spend 120, 248
Spicer, David 173
Spielberg, Steven 109, 121, 127
Spitting Image 121
Spoli Mills 43

Spoliansky, Mischa 14, 35, 42-45, 51, 53, 55, 110,
        248
Sportelli, Paul 146, 249
Spring Awakening 94
        original play 40
Spring Thaw 15, 49, 134, 137, 143, 161
St. Lawrence Centre 144, 150
Stage Entertainment 128
Stamp, Terrence 176
Stan Stange 31
Stannard, Peter 162, 248
Star is Born, A 65
Starr, Ringo 117
Stars 217
State Theatre of South Australia 166
Stavisky 64
Steam 225
Steam-Family 209
Steele, Tommy 117
Stein, Joseph 63, 96, 192
Stein, Leo 30, 32
Steiner, Maximilian 29
Steinman, Jim 33, 125
STEPS 204
Stevens, Cat 186
Stevens, Ray 92
Stewart, Kris 170
Stewart, Sandy 49
Steyn, Mark 222, 231
Stickland, Dr. Leonie 199, 200, 244
Stiles, George 121, 122
Stoker, Bram 194
Stoll Moss Theatres 174
Stolz, Robert 31, 51
Stone, Paddy 47, 126, 201
Stone, Peter 8
Stoneham, Reginald 155
Stoppard, Sir Tom 131
Story of My Life, The 145, 228, 237
Strampfer, Friedrich 29
Stratford Festival 130, 148
Straus, Oscar 31, 39, 40, 46, 51, 82
Strauss, Adele 52
Strauss, Johann 52
Strauss, Johann Jr. 22, 29, 32, 52
Strauss, Richard 39, 43, 50, 51
Strauss, Johann Jr. 22, 23
Stravinsky, Igor 193
Strike! 147, 248
Strindberg, August 46
Strindberg, Frida 46
Strouse, Charles 67, 88, 143, 227
Struble, John Warthen 81

Stuart, Connie 126
Stuart, Conny 126
Styne, Jule 99, 229
Sugar, Sugar 91, 92, 95
Sugihara, Chiune 204
Sullivan, Sir Arthur Seymour.... 11, 22, 23, 31, 50, 83, 117, 131
Summer of '42 76
Summer Rain 166
Sunset Boulevard 125
Sunshine Club, The 175
Suppé, Franz von 29, 33
Surabaya Johnny 55
Suskin, Steven 129
Sweeney Todd 170, 205
Sweet And Low 160
Sweet Charity 158
Sweeter And Lower 160
Sweetest And Lowest 160
Swillinger, Evi 194
Syal, Meera 207
Sydney Theatre Company 166
Sydow, Max von 129
Synge, J. M. 113
Ta Bouche 58, 63
Taillefere, Germaine 37
Tait, E. J. 157
Tait, Frank 157
Tait, John 157
Tait, Nevin 157
Taitte, Lawson 108
Tajiri, Mitsutaka 204
Takarazuka Grand Theatre 199
Takarazuka Revue.. 111, 126, 199, 200, 201, 202, 243, 244
Takemoto, Toshiaki 204
Takio, Terada 201
Tales of Hoffman 21, 57
Tales of Hoffmann 51
Talesnik, Ricardo 195
Talking Stick, The 151
Tallis, Sir George 157
Tamano, Kazunori 204
Tan, Selena 213
Tango Argentino 191
Tango por Dos 195
Tangolandia 192
Tapu 156, 157
Tarkington, Booth 60
Tarnow, Toby 135
Tarragon Theatre 146, 147
Tatárjárás 31
Taubman, Howard 71

Tautou, Audrey 64
Taylor, Jeremy 187
Taylor, Samuel A. 99
Taylor, Tiki 158
Teatro Argentino 193
Teatro Astral 192
Teatro de Ensayo 196
Teatro de la Victoria 191
Teatro Liceo 195
Teatro Mazzi 198
Teatro Municipal Sarmiento 194
Teatro Olimpico 191
Teatro Porteña 192
Teatro Presidente Alvear 192
Teatro Recreio 197
Teatro Smart 72
Tell Me on a Sunday.........................100, 172
Teng Ky-gan 214, 216, 220
Teng Ky-Gan 216
Tennant, Neil 12
Tenterfield Saddler 167
Tetsuo, Miura 202
Tezuka, Osamu 201
That Haircut Doesn't Suit You, Mr. Green 137
That's a Crime 69
The Boys in the Back Room 41
The Chocolate Soldier
    Der tapfere Soldat ....See
The Merry Widow 22
The Point (Dublin venue) 130
The Production Company 168
The Ragtime Pipes of Pan 61
The Song of the Young Sentry
    Lili Marlene ....See
The Way We Were 201
Theater am Gärtnerplatz 43
Theater am Schiffbauerdamm 54
Theater an der Wien.... 26, 28, 29, 30, 31, 32, 33, 45, 124
Theater and der Wien..................................30
Theater auf der Wieden 28
Theater der Stadt..72
Theater zum lieben Augustin 45
Théâtre Comte
    Theatre Bouffes-Parisiens ....See
    Théâtre des Bouffes-Parisiens................See
Théâtre Danou 65
Théâtre Daunou 58, 64
Théâtre de l'Athénée 68
Théâtre de la Gaîté-Lyrique 65
Théâtre de la Michodière 58
Théâtre des Ambassadeurs 72

276

Théâtre des Bouffes-Parisiens . 20, 57, 58, 59, 60, 61, 64, 65
Théâtre des Bouffes-Parisiens 11, 57, 76
Théâtre des Capicines....................................58
Théâtre des Capucines 65
Théâtre des Nouveautés 64
Théâtre des Variétés......................................58
Théâtre du Châtelet..65
Théâtre Edouard VII.......................................58
Théâtre Gramont..68
Théâtre Marigny...58
Théâtre Mogador..58
Théâtre Mogador..63, 97
Théâtre Montparnesse 75
Théâtre Nouveautés..58
Theatre Passe Muraille 139
Theatre Project Shizuoka...............................205
Theatre Royal (Sydney).........................160, 171
Theatre Royal Drury Lane 64, 97
Theatre Royal Stratford East ...92, 118, 174, 229, 231, 233
Theatre Royal, Sydney 72
Theatre Twenty 151
Theatre Workshop...................................164, 229
Theatreworks...98, 211
There is Only One Paris for That'...................71
There'll Always Be an England.......................185
There's a Bluebird on Your Windowsill 133
Thespis..23
They Didn't Believe Me 80
They're in Love..160
This Can't Be Love..231
This Hour Has Seven Days..............................49
Thlotothlamaje, Cocky 189
Thomas Crown Affair, The 76
Thompson, Fred...61
Thomson, Lloyd 163, 248
Thorburn, Sandy..137
Thoroughly Modern Millie 176
Thousand Islands Playhouse..........................137
Three Little Fishies (Boop Boop Diddum) 89
Three Musketeers...128
Threepenny Opera 41, 42, 45, 54, 125, 197
Thring, F.W. 159, 160
Tiffany, John 131
Timlin, John 166
Tinchant, Albert..37
Tingel-Tangel 41, 46
Tisch School of the Arts 9, 224, 229, 230, 231, 286
Tisch School of the Arts' Graduate Musical Theatre Writing Program 9
To Kill a Mockingbird 179

To Kwok-Wai, Raymond..............................219
Toho Company...202
Toi c'est moi..65
Tokyo International Forum 190
Tokyo Kid Brothers 203
Toledo Surprise 141
Toller, Ernst...41
Tolstoy, Leo...200
Tomá, matte, che..191
Tommy...222
Totemo Ghost 204
Touchstone Theatre......................................151
Toulouse-Lautrec, Henri de 66
Toy Factory...219
Tracey, Andrew..187
Tracey, Dr. Hugh..187
Tracey, Paul..187
Tranzac Club...144
Traubner, Richard....................................35, 63
Travers, P.L. 121
Treacher, Arthur 61
Treemonisha 93
Tremblay, Michel 151
Trenet, Charles..39, 56
Trennet, Charles...14
Très Très Snob 71
Tretchikoff, Julie Jackson-...........................156
Trial 216
Trial By Jury 23
Tricycle Theatre 121
Tristan..146, 249
Trois Gymnopédies 78
Trotha, Gatti- 31
Trudeau, Pierre..98
Tsedu, Mpho..183
Tsuneo, Kawasaki 201
Tucholsky, Kurt..40
Tucker, Percy 180, 183, 184, 185, 187, 188
Tucker, Sophie...181
Tune, Tommy..201
Tunku...220
Turandot...212
Turner, Ethel..166
Turvey..228
Turvey, Jay..146, 249
Twain, Mark..81, 153
Twala, Todd...189
Twang!! 118
Twist of Fate, A 217
Two Hundred Pound Beauty 209
Two Pianos, Four Hands 148
Überbrettl 39
Uekrongtham, Ekachai...................................213

277

Uhre, Mark 146
Ullmann, Liv 129
Ulvaeus, Björn 129
Umabatha 188
Umbrellas of Cherbourg, The 74, 75, 77
Umoja 189
Unamuno, Miguel de 235
Underhill, Jeff 164
Une Femme par Jour 65
Union of Southern African Artists..................183
Union Theatre Repertory Company 162
United Artistes Network 213
Unity Theatre............................117, 164
Universal Amphitheatre 48
Universexus............................194
University of Ballarat 158
Uterus 111, 151, 224, 225, 226, 238
Valetti, Rosa 41
Valse Millieu 69, 71
Van Cauwelaert, Didier..................76, 245
Van de Graaff, Janet 138
van den Ende, Joop....................127
Van den Ende, Joop....................128
van Dijk, Ad 127
van Dijk, Bill 127
van Dijk, Koen 127
Van Loon, Nelles....................227, 228
van Parys, Georges 78
Van Parys, Georges....................37, 61, 65, 250
Vancouver Playhouse 142
Vanishing, The 128
Vanloo, Albert............................59, 249
Variations 100
Varney, Alphonse 58
Vaughan, Sarah............................192
Veber, Serge 65
Venetian Twins, The 166
Veronique 57, 249
Véronique............................59
Victor/Victoria 126
Victoria 42
Vilsmaier, Joseph 43
Vincy, Raymond 74
Violettes impériales............................63
Vives, Amadeu 24
Vluchten kan niet meer" 126
Volksoper............................33
von Trapp, Baron Georg 114
Vosburgh, Dick............................93
Vrienten, Henny............................128, 245
Wada, Emi 105
Wagner, Richard 43
Wainwright, Rufus 65

Waissman, Ken 114
Wait a Minim!............................187
Wakao, Risa 201
Walk a Little Faster............................82
Walker, Joe 187
Walker, Oliver............................185
Wallace, Shani 70
Walsh, Enda 131
Walsh, Michael 117
Walt Disney Company 72, 122, 197, 201, 206, 207, 235
Walton, William 231
Waltz Dream............................51
War and Peace............................200, 204
Wardle, Irving 189
Warrack, David 227, 228, 248
Warrior, The............................188
Washington, George............................102
Wat een planeet............................127
Watermill Theatre 121
Watson, Don 166
Watts, Matt 138, 139
Watts, Richard Jr............................71
We Will Rock You............................149
We'll Meet Again 185
We're Six Little Nieces of Our Uncle Sam 223
We're the Only Tulips on the Track Team 137
Weaver, Harry............................70
Webb, Clifton 61
Webb, Marti 100
Webber, Christopher 24
Wedekind, Frank............................40
Weidman, John 104
Weigl, Hans 32
Weill, Kurt ...12, 14, 41, 44, 45, 48, 50, 51, 53-55, 82-84, 89, 91, 110, 112, 120, 125, 147, 164, 197, 241, 249
Weir, Peter............................153
Welch, Elisabeth 119
Welles, Orson 81
Wenn die beste Freundin 42
West Side Story..................74, 77, 186, 208, 234
West Yorkshire Playhouse 121
Western Australia Academy of Performing Arts 166
Western Australian Academy of Performing Arts 158
Whaley, Ben 201
Wharton, Edith 200
Whelan, Bill 129
Whelan, Christie 171
When I Say My Say 136
Whitcomb, Ian 89

White Horse Inn, The
  Im Weissen Rössl ....*See*
White Horse Inn, The 55
White Jacket, The 79
White Rabbit Productions 147
White, Onna 71
Whiteman, Paul 53
Whitfield, Sarah 123
Whiting, Steven Moore 37
Why Can't the English? 103
Wicked 125, 202
Wie lernt man Liebe? 43
Wiener Bürgertheater 33
Wiener Frauen and *Der Rastelbinder* 30
Wiener Stadttheater 33
Wijnen, Maurice 128, 245
Wilde Brühne 42
Wilde, Oscar 129
Wildeblood, Peter 119
Wilder, Billy 72
Wilder, Thornton 29
Wildhorn, Frank 201
Wilhelm, Kaiser 50
Wilkinson, Colm 151
Willard, Kathy 135
Willemetz, Albert... 48, 61, 62, 63, 64, 65, 67, 74, 248, 249
Willett, John 45
Williams, Pat 184, 247
Williamson, J.C....... 156, 157, 158, 159, 160, 161, 164, 244
Willner, A. M. 31
Willson, Meredith 88, 112, 222
Wilson, Angus 186
Wilson, Brian 88
Wilson, Clarence 189
Wilson, Julie 160
Wilson, Lambert 64
Wilson, Sandra (film director) 109
Wilson, Sandy 100
Wine, Toni 92
Winter Garden Theatre 139, 140, 142
Winter Garden, Theatre 144
Winter Sonata 210
Witwatersrand University Great Hall 184
Wiz, The 125, 128

Wodehouse, P.G. 80
Wolfe, George C. 229
Wolzogen, Ernst Von 39, 40
Wong, Claire 211
Words, The 136
Working in the Theatre 138, 139, 140, 250
Wortman, Laura Farrell- 104
Wright, Adrian 119, 120
Wright, Katey 151
Wrong Son, The 147
Xanadu 130
Ya Got Trouble 112
Yahata, Shigeru 204
Yamaguchi, Hideya 204
Yarnell, Bruce 72
Ye, Jimmy 219
Yeldham, Peter 166
Yes 58
Yeston, Maury 8, 11, 12
Yishida, Yuko 200
Yoduk Story 209
Yokoyama, Yoshikazu 204
Yoshimatsu, Takashi 203
You Could Drive a Person Crazy 171
Youmanns, Vincent 82
Young Vic 190, 248
Young, Gary 168, 248
Young, Josh 148
Young, Neil 137
Yume Kara Samete Yume 202
Yun Ho Jin 208
Yuta to Fushigina Nakama-tachi 202
Yuuko, Yoshida 201
Yvain, Maurice 58, 61, 63, 64, 65, 67, 250
Zahim Al-Bakri 220
Zakaria, Fareed 10
Ziegfeld, Florenz 27, 61, 67
Zimmermann, Tim 225
Zitterbarth, Bartholomäus 28
Zorro 217
Zuckmayer, Carl 43
Zulu Dance Theatre 188
Zulu, Lindewe 182
Zuma, Dr. Nkosazana 183
Zwar, Charles 160, 161
Zwei Krawatten 43

Endnotes

Preface: A Search for Signs of Life

[1] Kurt Gänzl, *The Musical – A Concise History*, Northeastern University Press, Boston, 1997, p. xi.

[2] Scott Brown, "How Can Musical Theater be Saved?", Vulture.com, 24 May 2012, accessed 21 July 2012.

[3] See "The Musical Comedy Book" in *Dramatists' Guild Quarterly*, Vol. 25 No. 4, Winter 1988, p.8.

[4] Marshall McLuhan, *The Gutenberg Galaxy* Routledge & Kegan Paul, London, 1962, p.31

[5] David Rothenberg, "More than Words", *The Guardian and Observer Guides to Performing Part 2: Singing*, May 2009.

[6] H. I. Khan, *The Music of Life*, Omega Publications, Santa Fe, New Mexico, 1983, p. 335-6.

[7] NYU Tisch School of the Arts Graduate Musical Theatre Writing Program course prospectus (no date indicated).

[8] *New Scientist*, issue 2681, 11 November 2008, p. 17

[9] Goodall, *Big Bangs*, Chatto & Windus, London, 2000, p. 224.

[10] André Previn, *No Minor Chords*, Doubleday, New York, 1991, p. 101.

[11] "Great Composers Scored on Language", *The Guardian*, London, 20 November 2004.

[12] From a platform talk given at the National Theatre, London, 1 June 1993, interviewed by Jeremy Sams. *Platform Papers 5: Musicals... and Sondheim*, Royal National Theatre Publications department.

[13] Fareed Zakaria, "The Rise of the Rest", *Newsweek*, 12 May 2008.

[14] Alan Jay Lerner, *The Musical Theatre: A Celebration*, McGraw-Hill Book Company, New York, 1986, p. 236.

[15] Lehman Engel, *Words With Music*, Schirmer Books, New York, 1981, p.6.

[16] Neil Tennant, "Out of Tune", *The Spectator*, 17 December 2011

[17] Nick Curtis, "Why I'm Bringing Brando to the West End", *Evening Standard*, London, 10 August 2007.

[18] Lehman Engel, *The American Musical Theater*, Collier Books, New York, 1975, pp. x-xi,

[19] John Coulter, "The Canadian Theatre and the Irish Exemplar", *Theatre Arts Monthly*, July 1936, p. 505-506.

[20] Alistair Smith, "ATG to work with regional reps to find new British musicals", *The Stage*, 15 September 2011

[21] The term "scientist" was coined in 1833 by English polymath William Whewell (1794-1866).

European Musical Comedy (Oops, I Mean Operetta)

[1] Wilfred Mellers, *Music in a New Found Land: Themes and Developments in the History of American Music*, Faber and Faber, London, 1987, p. 447.

[2] Letter of 30 January 1768 quoted in *The Letters of Mozart and his Family*, vol. 1 ed. And translated Emily Anderson, MacMillan and Co., London, 1938, p. 118.

[3] George Collerick, *From The Italian Girl to Cabaret*, Juventus, London, 1995, p.38.

[4] Exchange of letters dated 11 December 1780 and 16 December 1780 between Leopold Mozart and his song Wolfgang, cited in E.M. Batley, *A Preface to the Magic Flute*, Dennis Dobson, London, 1969, p.99.

[5] Eva Badura-Skoda, "The Viennese Singspiel, Haydn and Mozart", from Michael Cherlin, Halina Filipowicz, Richard L. Rudolph, *The Great Tradition and Its Legacy*, Berghahn Books, New York, 2003, p.177

[6] Peter Grammond, *Offenbach*, Omnibus Press, London, 1980, p. 42.

[7] Grammond, ibid, p.8.

[8] *The Tomahawk*, 24 August 1867, p. 174-175.

[9] Grammond, ibid, pp 140-41.

[10] Mark Lubbock, "The Music of 'Musicals'", *The Musical Times*, Vol. 98, No. 1375 (Sep., 1957), pp. 483-485.

[11] Lerner, p. 19.

[12] David Foil, *Carmen*, Black Dog & Leventhal Publishers, New York, 1996, p.24.

[13] Joan Peyser, Bernstein – A Biography, Billboard Books, New York, 1998, p.334.

[14] *Oxford Concise Dictionary of Music*, Fifth Edition, Michael Kennedy and Joyce Bourne Kennedy, eds., Oxford University Press, Oxford, 2007

[15] George Colerick, *Romanticism and Melody*, Juventus, London, 1995, p. 63.

[16] Stephen Sondheim, *Finishing the Hat*, Virgin Books, London, 2010, p. 332.

[17] Engel, *The American Musical Theater*, p. 137.

[18] Richard Kislan, *The Musical*, Prentice-Hall Inc., Englewood Cliffs, NJ, 1980, p. 94.

[19] House of Commons Culture, Media and Sport Committee, Fifth Report of Session 2004-05, The Stationery Office, London, 2005, Ev85.

[20] http://www.zarzuela.net/com/vives.htm, accessed 22 April 2010.

[21] Rimgaila Salys, *Laughing Matters – The Musical Comedy Films of Grigorii Alexsandrov*, Intellect, Bristol, 2009, p.7

[22] Richard Taylor and Ian Christie, eds. "Party Cinema Conference Resolution: The Results of Cinema Construction in the USSR and the Tasks of Soviet Cinema", *The Film Factory, Russian and Soviet Cinema in Documents 1896-1939*, Routledge, London, 1994, pp. 211-12.

Musicals for the Masses: Emanuel Schikaneder and the Theater an der Wien

[1] Email to author dated 9 July 2010.

[2] Michael Cherlin, "Conflict and Crossroads in Viennese Music", *The Great Tradition and Its Legacy*, Berghahn Books, New York, 2003, pp. 141-142..

[3] Colerick, *Romanticismm and Melody*, p.63.

[4] Kurt Honolka, *Papageno – Emanuel Schikaneder Man of the Theater in Mozart's Time*, Translated by Jane Mary Wilde, Amadeus Press, Portland, Oregon, 1990, pp 7-8.

[5] Honolka, p.95.

[6] Adolf Bäuerle, *Memoiren*, Wien, 1858, Vol. 1, p. 112, cited in Kurt Homolka, p. 187.

[7] Honolka, p. 207.

[8] While *The Magic Flute* and *The Merry Widow* are popularly known in the English-speaking world by their translated names, people seem happy to refer to *Die Fledermaus* by its German title, perhaps because producers knew that if they called it *The Winged Rodent*, box office queues would evaporate like a puddle in a heat wave. Similarly, Cameron Mackintosh resisted any temptation to call *Les Misérables* "The Wretched".

[9] *New York Times*, 7 July 1909.

[10] Lerner, p.42.

Cabaret: From "le Chat Noir" to the Algonquin Room

[1] Richard Traubner, *Operetta: A Theatrical History*, Routledge, 2003, p.10.

[2] Maximillien de Lafayette, *Entertainment Divas, Cabaret, Jazz Then and Now*, iUniverse, Lincoln, NE, 2006, p.47.

[3] This is a point where even "facts" become subjective. The Hydropathes existed from at least 1878, and the Lapin Agile – in its previous incarnation as "Cabaret des Assassins" – had been in business since 1860.

[4] Jeffrey H. Jackson, *Making Jazz French*, Duke University Press, Durham, 2003, p. 35.

[5] Lisa Appignanesi, *The Cabaret*, Yale University Press, New Haven, CT, 2004, p. 1-2.

[6] Jackson, ibid, p. 118.

[7] Philip Dennis Cate and Mary Shaw, editors, *The Spirit of Montmartre*, Rutgers, new Brunswick, NJ, 1996, p. 190.

[8] Henry Louis Gates Jr. and Karen C. C. Dalton, *Josephine Baker and La Revue Nègre*, Harry N. Abrams, Inc., New York, 1998, p.7.

[9] Ute Lemper *Blue Angels and Pirate Jennys* BBC Radio 4, 25 February 2006

[10] Cited in Colerick, *From the Italian Girl to Cabaret*, p.67.

[11] Peter Jelavich, *Berlin Cabaret*, Harvard University Press, Cambridge, MA, 1993, p.61

[12] Christopehr Isherwood, *Goodbye to Berlin*, Hogarth Press, London, 1939, p.38.

[13] Cited in Jelavich, p.96.

[14] Appignanesi, p.187.

[15] Cited by Jon Stewart, *Rolling Stone*, 29 September 2011

[16] Davies, Cecil William, *The Plays of Ernst Toller: A revaluation*, Routledge, New York, 1996, p. 355.

[17] Liel Leibovitz and Matthew Miller, *Lili Marlene – The Soldier's Song of World War II*, W. W. Norton & Co., New York, 2009, p.45.

[18] Michael Billington, "Life and soul of the cabaret", *The Guardian*, London, 31 August 1999.

[19] Liner notes to the 1976 New York Shakespeare Festival cast recording of *Threepenny Opera*, CBS Records PS 34326.

[20] Roger Boyes, "Life is a cabaret in Kohl twilight zone", *The Times*, London, 29 August 1998.

[21] Sandy Stewart, *Here's Looking at Us*, CBC Enterprises, Toronto, 1986, p. 160.

[22] Barb Jungr, "Thriving Cabaret Scene Down Under", *The Stage*, London, 4 October 2007.

Give My Regards to Friedrichstrasse

[1] Furtwangler was the subject of the Ron Harwood play *Taking Sides*.

[2] *Deutschen Allgemeine Zeitung*, 11 April 1933.

[3] Cited by Wolf Lepenies in "Die Nationalsozialisten und die Kultur", *Berliner Morgenpost*, 18 May 2008.

[4] Andrew Lamb, *150 Years of Popular Musical Theatre*, Yale University Press, New Haven, CT, 2000, p.226.

[5] Radio interview conducted by William H. Marshall, Assistant District Director of Immigration and Naturalization at Ellis Island on the NBC Blue Network, 9 March 1941. Weill-Lenya Research Center, Ser.122/3

[6] Email to author dated 18 November 2009.

[7] Gottfried Reinhardt, *The Genius – A Memoir of Max Reinhardt*, Alfred A. Knopf, New York, 1979, pp. 68-69.

[8] Email to author dated 14 July 2010.

[9] Yehudi Menuhin, *Unfinished Journey*, MacDonald & Jane's, London, 1977, cited in Reinhardt, *Genius*.

[10] "Light-Opera Boom", *Time*, 9 November 1942.

[11] Reinhardt, p. 74.

[12] Gusti Adler, *Max Reinhardt*, Festungsverlag, Salzburg, 1964, p. 43, cited in Michael Patterson, "Populism versus Elitism, *The Great Tradition and Its Legacy*, Berghahn Books, New York, 2003, p. 73.

[13] Esther Slevogt, "A hard-nosed Utopian", *signandsight.com*, 25 January 2006, originally published in German in *Die Tageszeitung*, 28 December 2005.

[14] Colerick, *From The Italian Girl to Cabaret*, p.70.

[15] Foster Hirsch, *Kurt Weill on Stage*, Limelight Editions, New York, 2002, p. 18.

[16] John Willett, translator, *Brecht on Brecht*, Methuen, London, 1964, p.131-2, cited in Michael Bawtree, *The New Singing Theatre*, Oxford University Press, New York, 1991, p.60.

[17] Richard Kislan, *The Musical – A Look at the American Musical Theater*, Pretice-Hall, Englewood Cliffs, NJ, 1980, p.192

[18] Lamb, ibid.

Paris: Where Musicals Were Born, and Where they Go to Die

[1] Margaret Vermette, *The Musical World of Boublil and Schönberg*, Applause Theatre and Cinema Books, New York, 2006, p.20.

[2] Sheridan Morley and Ruth Leon, *Hey Mr. Producer*, Back Stage Books, New York, 1998, p.102.

[3] Gareth Murphy, "Parisian Radar"!, *The Journal of Music*, Galway, Vol. 1 No. 1, April 2009, p. 36.

[4] "New Plays in Manhattan", *Time*, New York, 18 March 1929.

[5] Email to the author dated 25 June 2008.

[6] Engel, *Words With Music*, p.143.

[7] Stephen Sondheim, *Finishing the Hat*, Virgin Books, London, 2010, p.80.

[8] Jules Bertaut, *Paris: 1870-1935*, translated by R. Millar, Eyre and Spottiswoode, London, 1936, p. 256.

[9] Jeffrrey H. Jaclson, *Making Jazz French*, Duke University Press, Durham, NC, 2003, p.2.

[10] Société des Auteurs, Compositeurs et Éditeurs de Musique

[11] Confédération Internationale des Société d'Auteurs et Compositeurs

[12] "Five New Productions Next Week", *The Times*, London, 28 August 1919, p. 8.

[13] "E. Ray Goetz Returns", *New York Times*, 3 May 1920.

[14] *The Daily Mirror*, London, 2 June 1922, p. 7.

[15] *The Daily Mirror*, London, 5 June 1922, p. 7.

[16] Edward Behr, *Thank Heaven for Little Girs – The True Story of Maurice Chevalier's Life and Times*, Hutchinson, London, 1993, p.96.

[17] Gänzl, *The Musical*, p. 163.

[18] Richard Traubner, *Operetta: A Theatrical History*, Routledge, 2003, p. 313.

[19] Cited in Jacques Damase, *Les Folies du Music-Hall*, Anthony Blond, London, 1962, p. 63.

[20] Kurt Gänzl, *Encyclopedia of the Musical Theatre*, Blackwell, Oxford, 1994, p.1292.

[21] Maurice Yvain, *Ma Belle Operette*, Editions de la Table Ronde, Paris, 1962, cited in www.cinemagia.ro accessed on 5 June 2008.

[22] Yvain, loc. Cit.

[23] *The Times*, London, 9 September 1926, p. 10.

[24] Peter Bogdanovich, introduction to the Criterion Collection DVD of *French Cancan*, 2004.

[25] Cited in Pierre Mariel, *Paris Revue*, translated by Peter Munk, Neville Spearman, london, 1962, p. 21.

[26] This has been a common practice. A quarter of a century later, the French working classes in *Les Misérables* spoke with a cockney, and in the Dutch version of *My Fair Lady*, Eliza Doolittle speaks with a Jordanees dialect (from the working class De Jordaan area of Amsterdam).

[27] Cited in Tom Vallance, David Heneker obituary, *The Independent*, London, 8 March 2001., and in Didier C. Deutsch's liner notes for the 1991 Original Broadway Cast CD of *Irma la Douce*, Sony Broadway SK 48018

[28] Ira Henry Freeman, "Comprenez-vous Irma?", *New York Times*, 25 September 1960.

[29] Peter Brook, *The Shifting Point*, Harper & Row, New York, 1987, p.37.

[30] Harold Hobson, "Irma Translated", *Sunday Times*, 20 July 1958.

[31] *Punch*, 23 July 1958.

[32] *The Times*, 18 July 1958, p.3.

[33] Philip Hope-Wallace, *Manchester Guardian*, 18 July 1958.

[34] *Obsevrer*, London, 20 July 1958.

[35] Harry Weaver, "What's Irma Got?", *Daily Herald*, 18 July 1958.

[36] Anthony Cookman, "Good, clean fun in the Place Pigalle", *The Tatler & Bystander*, 30 July 1958.

[37] Howard Taubman, "Place Pigalle Genially Satirized; 'Irma la Douce' Has Debut at Plymouth Gallic Musical Turns Vice Into Innocence", *New York Times*, 30 September 1960.

[38] *Time*, 10 October 1960.

[39] *Daily News*, New York, 30 September 1960.

[40] *Journal American* , New York, 30 September 1960.

[41] *New York Post*, 30 September 1960.

[42] *Herald-Tribune*, New York, 30 September 1960.

[43] Ed Sikov, *On Sunset Boulevard – The Life and Times of Billy Wilder*, Hyperion, New York, 1998, p. 470.

[44] Ibid, p.471.

[45] *The Guardian*, 14 February 1964.

[46] Katherine Knorr, "'Irma': Bravos for a Good Laugh", *New York Times*, 4 August 2009

[47] *La Dennière Heure*, 25 February, 1971, cited in the liner notes for the 1967 Paris revival cast CD, VEGA 826-2.

[48] *La Dennière Heure*, ibid.

[49] "New Revue in Manhattan", *Time*, 24 November 1958

[50] *Musical Stages*, Issue 45, Spring 2005, p.10.

[51] Gänzl, *Encyclopedia*, p. 890.

[52] Andrew Lamb, *150 Years of Popular Musical Theatre*, Yale University Press, New Haven, p.236

[53] Tom Shea, *Broadway's Most Wanted*, Brassey's Inc., Washington, D.C., 2004, p.157.

[54] Agnès Varda, *L'Univers de Jacques Demy*, Ciné Tamaris, 1995 (Distributed by Optimum Releasing with the DVD *The Umbrellas of Cherbourg*).

[55] Varda, ibid.

[56] *The Guardian*, London, 22 March 2011.

[57] *Variety*, 22 March 2011.

[58] Jonathan Rosenbaum, "Not the same old song and dance", *Chicago Reader*, 17 March 2000.

[59] Alan Riding, "The Real Paradox: Musical Comedy Made in France", *New York Times*, New York, October 20, 2002

[60] Ben Brantley, "A French Milquetoast's Talent Lights the Fuse of Mischief", *New York Times*, 21 October 2002.

[61] Behr, Edward. "*The Complete Book of Les Misérables*". Arcade Publishing, London, 1989, p.50

[62] Sheridan Morley and Ruth Leon, *Hey Mr. Producer!*, Back Stage Books, New York, 1998, p.91.

[63] Vermette, p.24

[64] Kurt Gänzl, *Musicals*, Carlton Books, London, 2001, p. 236.

[65] See Steve Swayne, *How Sondheim Found His Sound,* University of Michigan Press, Ann Arbor, 2005, p.22

Declaration of Independence

[1] Herman Melville (1819–1891), U.S. author. *White-Jacket* (1850), ch. 36, *The Writings of Herman Melville*, vol. 5, eds. Harrison Hayford, Hershel Parker, and G. Thomas Tanselle (1969).

[2] Wilfred Mellers, *Music in a New Found Land: Themes and Developments in the History of American Music*, Faber and Faber, London, 1987, p.3.

[3] Raymond Knapp, *The American Musical and the Formation of National Identity*, Princeton University Press, Princeton, NJ, 2005, pp 32-33.

[4] Mellers, ibid., p.39.

[5] Ethan Mordden, *Broadway Babies: The People Who Made the American Musical*, Oxford University Press, New York, 1983, p. 27.

[6] Lamb, p.152

[7] Engel, *The American Musical Theater*, p.8

[8] Meryle Secrest, *Leonard Bernstein – a Life*, Bloomsbury, London, 1995, p.52

[9] John Warthen Struble, *History of American Classical Music*, Checkmark Books / Facts on File, New York, 1995, p.188

[10] Lerner, p.44.

[11] Engel, Ibid.,p.7.

[12] Lerner, ibid., p.117.

[13] Kislan, p. 102.

[14] Gene Lees, *The Musical Worlds of Lerner and Loewe*, Robson Books, London, 1990, p. 11.

[15] Lerner, ibid., p.71.

[16] Kislan, ibid, p. 99-100.

[17] Charles Osbourne, *The Dictionary of Composers*, The Bodley Head, London, 1977, p.376.

[18] Foster Hirsch, *Kurt Weill on Stage*, Limelight Editions, New York, 2003, p. 352.

[19] Max Wilk, *They're Playing Our Song*, Atheueum, New York, 1973, pp 12-13.

[20] Wilk, ibid, p.88.

The New World(s)

The Rock 'n' Roll Syndrome

[1] http://news.bbc.co.uk/go/pr/fr/-/1/hi/entertainment/8297635.stm, accessed on 9 October 2009

[2] 1956 hearings of the Anti-Trust Subcommittee of the House Judiciary Committee, cited in Ian Whitcomb, *After the Ball*, Limelight Editions, New York, 1972/1989, p. 209.

[3] Howard Goodall, *Big Bangs*, p.206.

[4] Tom Lehrer, *An Evening Wasted with Tom Lehrer*, Reprise Records, 1959.

[5] Whitcomb, ibid, pp 211-212.

[6] Paul Simon, "George on my mind", *The Observer*, 6 September 1998, © New York Times Syndication.

[7] "Where the Old Vic belongs", *Tribune Magazine*, 1 October 1948.

[8] Alan Jay Lerner, preface to *Camelot*, Random House, New York, 1961.

[9] Mel Atkey, "An Epiphany", *Musical Stages*, Issue 25, October 2000, p. 14.

[10] Engel, *Words With Music*, p 127

[11] Mel Gussow, "Sondheim Scores With 'Company'", *New York Times*, 28 April 1970.

[12] Engel, ibid, pp. 129-30.

[13] Mark N. Grant, *The Rise and Fall of the Broadway Musical*, Northeastern University Press, Boston, 2004, p. 161.

[14] John Lahr, *Automatic Vaudeville*, Alfred A. Knopf, New York, 1984, p. 101-102

[15] "Leonard Cohen on Hallelujah", telegraph.co.uk, 19 December 2008, accessed on 11 June 2009.

[16] Previn, p. 63.

Universality Part 1: "Do They Understand This Show in America? It's So Japanese!"

[1] Cameron Mackintosh in letter to the author dated 18 July 2003, cited in Mel Atkey, *Broadway North: The Dream of a Canadian Musical Theatre*, Natural Heritage Books, Toronto, p.138.

[2] Cited in Peter Stone, Jerry Bock, Sheldon Harnick and Joseph Stein, "Landmark Symposium: Fiddler on the Roof", *Dramatists Guild Quarterly*, New York, 1983, Vol.20, No.1, p. 27

[3] Engel, *Words With Music*, p.4-5.

[4] Engel sent Ira Gershwin a 79 page text entitled *Porgy in Ankara* describing his experience.

[5] Max Wilk, *They're Playing Our Song*, Atheneum, New York, 1973, pp 91-92.

[6] Letter from Ira Gershwin to Lehman Engel dated 15 July 1969, courtesy of . Ira and Leonore Gershwin Trusts

[7] Pierre Berton, *Hollywood's Canada – The Americanization of Our National Identity*, McLelland and Stewart, Toronto, 1975, p. 234

[8] Ibid, p. 139

[9] Don Harron, *Anne of Green Gables The Musical – 101 Things You Didn't Know*, White Knight Books, Toronto, 2008, p. 133

[10] Ibid, p. 72

[11] Although for reasons that have never been satisfactorily justified, "Happy Birthday to You", written by Patty and Mildred Hill in 1893, is apparently still in copyright, even although it was published in 1912 and both authors are long since dead.

[12] "The Other Anne", Kate Goodloe, *Ottawa Citizen*, 5 May 2007

[13] "Warning Sent to New York's Anne", CBC News, 10 May, 2007, http://www.cbc.ca/arts/theatre/story/2007/05/10/newyork-anne.html

[14] James Inverne, *Wrestling With Elephants*, Sanctuary, London, 2003, p.121.

[15] Inverne, p. 143.

[16] Michael Coveney, *The Andrew Lloyd Webber Story*, Arrow Books, London, 2000

[17] Vida Hope, "*The Boy Friend* on Broadway", *Plays and Players*, Christmas 1954, p. 12.

18 Letter to Christopher Cox, *Boston Herald*, September 19, 1997.

[19] Cited in Meryle Secrest, *Somewhere for Me: A Biography of Richard Rodgers*, Bloomsbury, London, 2001, p. 287.

[20] Engel, *The American Musical Theater*, p. 49.

[21] Although given the fate of the National Film Board of Canada's Oscar winning documentary *If You Love This Planet* – which was branded "foreign government propaganda" by the Reagan adminsitration – (meaning that anybody viewing the film must give their names to the U.S. Justice Department) – you never know.

[22] *New York Herald-Tribune*, 25 March 1951

[23] In an email dated 12 August 2010, Peter Pinne told me, "Last year when I was in Thailand as a guest of the Thai Tourist Agency I actually asked about *The King and I* and they said that the movie had been screened there, the songs were sung there, and that nobody these days worried about the depiction of Thailand in it.

[24] Jared Brown, *Moss Hart – A Prince of the Theatre*, Back Stage Books, New York, 2006., p.295

[25] Steve Nallon, "The Britishness of the British Musical", published in *Musical Stages*, London, 2000 (no date or volume given)

[26] Jennifer Oates , "Brigadoon: Lerner and Loewe's Scotland", Studies in Musical Theatre, Vol. 3 No. 1, 2009, p. 91

[27] Colin McArthur, Braveheart, Brigadoon and the Scots: Distortions of Scotland in Hollywood Cinema, I.B. Taurus, London, 2003, pp 2-3.

[28] Laure Farrell-Wortman, "The Riverdance phenomenon and the development of Irish identity in the global era", *Studies in Musical Theatre*, Vol 4 No 3, pp. 317-318.

[29] Jean Graham-Jones, "'The truth is… My Soul is With You': Documenting a Tale of Two Evitas", Theatre Survey, May 2005, p. 76.

[30] Cited in Philip Freund, *Oriental Theatre*, Peter Owen, London, p. 745.

[31] Ben Brantley, "Genuinely Ugly Americans, as Viewed by the Japanese", *New York Times*, 11 July 2002

[32] *Village Voice*, New York, 16 July, 2002

[33] William Andrews, "From Broadway to Yokohama as Japanese theater gets a new home", CNN Asia, 8 February 2011, http://www.cnngo.com/tokyo/visit/broadway-yokohama-873802

[34] *Village Voice*, 30 November, 2004

[35] Lisa Lambert, Greg Morrison, "Message from a Nightingale", from *The Drowsy Chaperone*.

[36] Raymond Knapp, The American Musical and the Formation of National Identity, Princeton University Press, Princeton, NJ, 2005, p. 279-80

[37] Jessica Hillman, "Goyim on the Roof: embodying authenticity in Leveaux's Fiddler on the Roof", Studies in Musical Theatre, Portsmouth, Vol. 1 No. 1, p. 25

[38] "A Legacy Cut Loose", Thane Rosenbaum, *Los Angeles Times*, 15 February, 2004.

[39] Stephen Cole, "The Road to the Road to Qatar", *Dramatists Guild Quarterly*, November/December 2008

[40] Kathryn Boughton, "The Quiet Composer", *Litchfield County Times*, 12 June 2009.

[41] Lawson Taitte, "Autobiographical Road to Qatar proves a bubbly tour of creating a musical", *Dallas Morning News*, 11 October 2009

[42] *Dallas Voice*, 16 October 2009.

[43] Mel Atkey, *Broadway North: The Dream of a Canadian Musical Theatre*, Natural Heritage Books, Toronto, 2006, p17-18

Universality Part 2: A Sense of Time and Place

[1] Atkey, *Broadway North*, p. 14.

[2] Engel, *Words with Music*, p. 131.

[3] *Blue Angels and Pirate Jennys*, BBC Radio 4, 25 February 2006.

[4] Engel, ibid, p.263.

[5] Raymond Knapp, *The American Musical and the Formation of National Identity*, Princeton University Press, 2005, p. 144.

[6] Roberta Freund Schwartz, "Iowa Stubborn: Meredith Willson's musical characterization of his fellow Iowans", *Studies in Musical Theatre*, Volume Three, Number One, Intellect Ltd., Bristol, 2009, p. 31.

[7] Stephen Sondheim, *Look, I Made a Hat – Collected Lyrics (1981-2011)*, Virgin Nooks, London, 2011, p.309

[8] Ibid, p. 37.

[9] Engel, *Words with Music*, p. 247.

[10] Tom Jones, "The Making of 110 in the Shade", *Theatre Week*, 20 July 1992.

[11] Tom Jones, *Making Musicals*, Limelight Editions, New York, 1998, p. 112.

[12] "Never Will I Marry", from *Greenwillow*, music and lyrics by Frank Loesser, © Frank Music Corp.

[13] *New York Times*, 20 March 1960.

[14] *Time*, 21 March 1960.

[15] Sarah T. Ellis, "Establishing (and re-establishing) a sense of place: musical orientation in *The Sound of Music*", *Studies in Musical Theatre*, Vol. 3 No. 3, Intellect Ltd., 2009.

[16] Chris Jones, "Bring back our own, original R-rated 'Grease'", *Chicago Tribune*, 8 January 2009.

[17] Chris Jones, "Young, tough and heartfelt, it's the real 'Grease'", *Chicago Tribune*, 4 May 2011.

"Who Will Buy?" Lionel Bart and the Post-war British Musical

[1] Michael Walsh (with Mary Cronin), "Magician of the Musical", *Time*, New York, 18 January 1988.

[2] *The Stage*, London, 1 April 2010, p.5

[3] Ron Moody, *A Still Untitled (Not Quite) Autobiography*, JR Books, London, 2010, p.158.

[4] Ibid, p. 159.

[5] Michael Coveney, "Oliver!: The real story of Britain's greatest musical", *The Independent*, 9 January 2009.

[6] David Roper, *Bart!*, Pavillion Books, London, 1994, pp. 59-60.

[7] Liner notes from the original cast recording of *Passion Flower Hotel*, 1965. CBS BPG62598

[8] Adrian Wright, *A Tanner's Worth of Tune – Rediscovering the Post-War British Musical*, The Boydell Press, Woodbridge, 2010, p. 139.

[9] Ibid, p. 168.

[10] Gänzl, *The Musical*, p.341.

[11] Lerner, *The Musical Theatre*, p.225, 234.

[12] Kurt Gänzl, *The British Musical Theatre Vol. II*, Macmillan, London, 1986, p. 1127.

[13] Ian Bradley, *You've Got to Have a Dream – The Message of the Musical*, SCM Press, London, 2004, p. 190.

[14] Piers Ford, "Big Spender: Barbara Dickson", *Show Music*, Vol. 16, No.1, Spring 2000.

[15] *Evening Standard*, London, 14 April 2011

[16] *The Guardian*, 14 April 2011.

[17] George Stiles, "Don't Sing the Blues", *The Stage*, 8 October 2011.

[18] *The Times* 10th December 2010

[19] *The Independent*, 14 December 2010

[20] Henry Hitchings, *Evening Standard*, 10 Dec 2010

[21] "RSC already set to recoup on Matilda the Musical", *The Stage*, 12 January 2012.

[22] Sarah Whitfield, "Two different roads to new musicals in 2011 London: *London Road* and *Road Show*", *Studies in Musical Theatre*, Vol. 5 No. 3, pp309-310.

[23] *The Stage*, London, 21 April 2011.

Europopera

[1] Kurt Gänzl, *Musicals*, Carlton Books, London, 2001, p. 247.

[2] Nancy Rosati, "What's New on the Rialto? Interview with Michael Kunze of Dance of the Vampires", *Talkin' Broadway*, 27 October 2002.

[3] Ellis Nassour, "Michael Kunze: The Sondheim and Lloyd Webber of Europe", *Broadway Stars*, 5 December 2002.

[4] "Rialto gossip" is a New York expression for the showbiz grapevine. It may have originated with "News and Gossip of the Rialto", a column in the *New York Times*.

[5] *De Volkskrant*, 9 October 1998 (translated from Dutch for the author by René Driessen).

[6] Ibid

[7] Marliese simons, "THEATER: A Musical 'Cyrano': Can a Dutch hit sell on Broadway?", *New York Times*, 21 November 1993.

[8] Ben Brantley, "Cyrano's Flights Have Touched Down on West 52nd Street", *New York Times*, 22 November 1993.

[9] *Variety*, 22 November 1993.

[10] *Musical Stages*, Issue 60, Winter 2008/9, p. 21.

[11] *Variety*, 24 Sept 2009

[12] Michael Ross, "A Ha'penny for his thoughts", *The Sunday Times*, London, 12 June 2005.

[13] Patricia O' Callaghan, RTE. 15 June 2005.

[14] Colin Murphy, "Colin Murphy ventures upriver to check out the Ha'penny Bridge", *The Village*, Dublin, 1 July 2005.

[15] Richard Ouzounian, "Ha'penny Bridge Topples in Toronto", *Variety*, 20 February 2008.

[16] Richard Ouzounian, "Producer cancels North American premiere of Ha'penny Bridge", *Star*, Toronto, 21 February 2008.

[17] Charles Isherwood, "It's That Old Story: Spies, Physics and Gaelic", *New York Times*, 5 December 2008.

Canada – "Still Deciding What it Will Be"

[1] Robert Fulford, "Mary Pickford, Glenn Gould, Anne of Green Gables, and Captain Kirk: Canadians in the world's imagination" Lecture at The Hebrew University, Jerusalem, June 5, 1997

[2] Rudyard Griffiths, *Who We Are – A Citizen's Manifesto*, Douglas & McIntyre, Vancouver, 2009, pp. 148-49.

[3] Jason Schneider, *Whispering Pines – The Northern Roots of American Music... From Hank Snow to The Band*, ECW Press, Toronto, 2009, pp. 299-300.

[4] *The Times Magazine*, London, 27 November 2004, p. 13.

[5] Murray Ginsberg, *They Loved to Play – Memories of the Golden Age of Canadian Music*, East End Books, Toronto, 1998. p.116

[6] "In the Air", *Winnipeg Citizen*, July 14 1948, cited in Christian Riegel, *Challenging Territory: The Writing of Margaret Laurence*, University of Alberta Press, Edmonton, 1997, pp 204-205.

[7] Atkey, *Broadway North*, p.54.

[8] Harron, p. 16.

[9] Fulford, ibid.

[10] Atkey, p. 110.

[11] ibid, p. 112.

[12] ibid, p. 113.

[13] S.G. Lee, "Size Matters: A Consideration of the Canadian Musical", *Brock Review*, Vol. 12, No. 2, Brock University, 2012.

[14] Sandy Thorburn, "Who is the Drowsy Chaperone's Muse?", *Thousand Islands Theatre Programme*, 2009 (courtesy of Lisa Lambert and Sandy Thorburn)

[15] Ibid.

[16] "The Drowsy Chaperone", *Working in the Theatre*, American Theater Wing/City University Television, April 2006

[17] Susan Dominus, "In The Drowsy Chaperone, Bob Martin's Birthday [sic] present Became His Broadway Debut", *New York Times*, 30 April 2006.

[18] Gordon Bowness, "Musically fanatical", *Xtra!*, Toronto, 28 June 2001.

[19] *NOW*, 25 November 1999.

[20] Phil Hahn, "From the fringes to Broadway: The Drowsy Chaperone", *CTV.ca*, 7 June 2006 http://edmonton.ctv.ca/servlet/an/local/CTVNews/20060607/drowsy_chaperone_060607 accesed 30 July 2009

[21] *Associated Press*: 1 May 2006

[22] "'Drowsy Chaperone' a sleeping beauty", *New York Daily News*, May 1 2006

[23] "Nostalgic 'Drowsy Chaperone' Opens on Broadway", *New York Times*, May 1 2006

[24] *Star*, Toronto, 24 September 2007.

[25] Matthew Hays, "Can't Stop the Music", *Equity Quarterly*, Canadian Actors' Equity Association, Winter 2010, p.13.

[26] *Working in the Theatre*, ibid.

[27] *Downstage Center*, American Theater Wing/XM Satelite Radio, 2 June 2006.

[28] *Time Out Toronto*, Time Out Guides, London, 2007, p. 218.

[29] Email from Darcie Kennedy dated 20 April 2012.

[30] "Quaint musical demands we care", Robert Cushman *National Post*, Saturday, November 11, 2006

[31] Ben Brantley, "Male Bonding – It's a Wonderful Friendship", *New York Times*, February 20, 2009.

[32] *Variety*, February 20, 2009

[33] Michael Kuchwara, "Frienship Flowers in 'The Story of My Life'", *Associated Press*, February 20, 2009.

[34] Peter Filichia, "The Story on 'The Story of My Life'", Theatremania.com, February 23, 2009.

[35] Peter Filichia, email dated 24 February 2009, citing Ethan Mordden's *The Happiest Corpse I've Ever Seen : The Last 25 Years of the Broadway Musical* , Palgrave MacMillan, New York, 2004.
.

[36] Gary Smith, "The good and the gobblers of 2007", *Hamilton Spectator*, Hamilton, Ontario, December 29, 2007

[37] http://www.niagarafallsreview.ca/ArticleDisplayGenContent.aspx?e=3410, retrieved 22 November 2008.

[38] Richard Ouzounian, "Shaw's Tristan – Too Little, Too Late", *The Star*, Toronto, July 30, 2007.

[39] Jon Kaplan, "Ranney's Double Act", *Now*, Toronto, August 30, 2007.

[40] *Variety*, 9 August 2011.

[41] *The Star*, Toronto, 6 August 2011.

[42] *National Post*, 9 August 2011.

[43] Richard Ouzounian, "Mimi is wickedly, deadly delicious", *The Star*, Toronto, 24 September 2009.

[44] Robert Cushman, "The emancipation of Mimi is a success", *National Post*, 24 September 2009.

[45] *Eye Weekly*, Toronto, 29 September, 2009.

[46] Robert Enright CBC Manitoba 990 Radio review, May 27, 2005

[47] Morley Walker, *Winnipeg Free Press*, 28 May 2005.

[48] "Jesus Christ still a superstar 40 years on", *Evening Standard*, London, 23 March 2012.

[49] Richjard Ouzounian, "Jesus Christ superstar: Five reasons it flopped on Broadway", *Star*, Toronto, 20 June 2012.

[50] "Denise Donlon named to top job at CBC Radio", *CBC News*, 17 September 2008, www.cbc.ca/arts/media/story/2008/09/17/donlon-cbc.html.

[51] "CBC cancels shows, slashes 88 news jobs", http://www.cbc.ca/news/canada/story/2012/04/10/cbc-budget-programs.html, accessed 11 April 2012.

[52] Island Morning, *CBC-Radio*, 19 September 2012

[53] Email dated 6 May 2012.

[54] Norman Jewison, *This Terrible Business Has Been Good to Me*, Key Porter Books,Toronto, 2004, p.44.

[55] "West End Comes West", Kamal Al-Solaylee, *Globe and Mail*, Toronto, 14 December, 2006.

[56] www.cbc.ca.arts/theatre/story/2009/04/03/cree-opera.html accessed 20 May 2009.

[57] Peter Birnie, "Beyond Eden builds a beautiful bridge", *Vancouver Sun*, 25 January 2010.

[58] Janet Smith, "Theatre takes centre stage", *The Georgia Straight*, Vancouver, 21-28 June 2012.

[59] Sheridan College press release dated 4 April 2012.

[60] Quoted in Edward Keenan, "Making a Scene: A Bunch of Youngish Indie Rockers, Political Activists and Small Press Literati are Creating the Cultural History of Toronto", *UTOpia – Towards a New Toronto*, Edited by Jason McBride and Alana Wilcox, Coach House Books, Toronto, 2005, p.24.

Larrikins and Sentimental Blokes: Musicals Down Under

[61] Mark Twain, *Following the Equator*, American Publishing Company, New York, 1897, cited in Tim Flannery, *The Birth of Sydney*, William Heinemann, London, 2003, p. 321.

[62] *Broadway at Bedtime*, JOY-FM, Melbourne, 16 April, 2006.

[63] Except for the *Virgin Encyclopedia of Stage & Film Musicals*, which incorrectly declares he was "Austrian" – only one of many errors in that tome.

[64] Claude Kingston, *It Don't Seem a Day Too Much*, Rigby, Adelaide, 1971, p.73

[65] C.J. De Garis, *The Victories of Failure*, Modern Printing Company, Melbourne, 1925, p. 377.

[66] *The Herald*, Melbourne, 11 October 1920, cited in Frank Van Straten, "The Riddle of *FFF*, a forgotten Australian musical comedy", *Australasian Music Research*, No. 6, 2001, p. 116.

[67] Julie Jackson-Trechikoff, "Amateur operatics in Auckland: musical theatre's last frontier", *Studies in Musical Theatre*, Vol. 2 No. 2, Intellect, Bristol, 2008, p.196.

[68] Ibid, p.197.

[69] *New Zealand Times*, 17 February 1903.

[70] Peter Harcourt, *Fantasy and Folly*, Steele Roberts, Wellington, 2002.

[71] Cited in Viola Tait, *A Family of Brothers*, Heinemann, Melbourne, 1971, p.215.

[72] Malcolm Robertson, "The Australian Theatre: The Situation in the Seventies", *Biala*, Prahran College of Advanced Education, Vol. 1, 1977, No. 13.

[73] Cited in "It's Australian—and it's good! The Australian musical Collits' Inn", *National Library of Australia News*, December 2003 Volume XIV Number 3

[74] Edmond Samuels, *If the Cap Fits*, Modern Literature Co., Sydney, 1972, p. 74

[75] According to English theatre historian Philip L. Scowcroft, author of *British Light Music Composers*, some additional songs were contributed to the London production by musical director Percival Mackey.

[76] Ibid, p.90.

[77] Really Useful Theatres archives

[78] Letter from Peter Stannard, dated 11 May 2012.

[79] In *A Family of Brothers*, Viola Tait says it was in 1957.

[80] Viola Tait says it tried out at Sydney's Empire Theatre in front of an audience of fifty.

[81] Interview with Nancy Brown by Beryl Davis, 15 March 1989, Transcript, p. 39, National Library of Australia Oral History Collection, ORAL TRC 2426, cited in Margaret Marshall and Simon Platt, *Making a Song and Dance*, a booklet to accompany the exhibition of the same name at the Victorian Arts Centre, Melbourne, 2004.

[82] Robyn Archer, "The Politics of the Musical", *Australasian Drama Studies*, Vol. 1 No. 2, April 1983.

[83] *The Age*, Melbourne, 22 December 1958.

[84] Leonard Radic, "Local Novel Set to Music", *Age*, 16 May 1966.

[85] Jean Battersby, "Bright Musical from Australian Novel", *Canberra Times*, 7 June 1966.

[86] Clark Forbes, *Sun News–Pictorial*, January 1988

[87] Debbie Kruger, "Seven Little Australians Review", *Variety*, July 6, 1988.

[88] Robin Usher, "How to Stage an Epic", *The Age*, 13 September 2004.

[89] *Broadway at Bedtime*, ibid.

[90] *Talking Heads with Peter Thompson*, 13 August 2007, http://www.abc.net.au/talkingheads/txt/s2001093.htm

[91] "Musical a sure hit", *Courier-Mail*, Brisbane, January 12, 2007.

[92] Gary Young, "Creating an Australian musical freak show", *Arts Hub*, 2 february 2007, http://www.artshub.com.au/au/news.asp?sType=view&catId=1069&sc=&sId=152277 accessed 16 January 2008

[93] Bryce Hallett, "Knockout Aussie tale puts life back into musicals", *Herald-Sun*, Melbourne, February 5, 2007.

[94] Rosemary Duffy, *State of the Arts*, February 8, 2007

[95] OzMade Musicals 2008, 17 November 2008, Athanaeum Theatre, Melbourne.

[96] *Stage Whispers Performing Arts Magazine*, May-June 2008, Volume 17, Number 3.

[97] *Theatremania*, 21 September 2008.

[98] *Sydney Morning Herald*, 21 July 1007.

[99] *The Observer*, London, 22 July 2007.

[100] *The Stage*, London, 24 July 2007.

[101] Rosemary Neill, "Nobody can stop the music", *The Australian*, November 10, 2007.

[102] Diana Simmonds, "This Kookaburra Is Mort", http://www.stagenoise.com/newsdisplay.php?id=219, January 4th 2009

[103] David Spicer, "What Cooked Kookaburra?", *Stage Whispers*, March-April 2009 Vol. 18 No. 2, p. 52.

[104] Peter Cousens, "My biggest regret is not being able to carry on", *Sydney Morning Herald*, 2 June 2009.

[105] Bryce Hallett and Louise Schwartzkoff, "Troubled Kookaburra retreats into silence", *Sydney Morning Herald*, 5 March 2009.

[106] Makeham, Paul B, "Singing the landscape: 'Bran Nue Dae'". *Australasian Drama Studies*(28) (1996):pp. 117-132.

[107] J, Eccles, "Bran Nue Dae", *The West Australian*, 5 March 1991.

[108] Catherine Lambert, "Top Talent Tripped by Production", *Sunday Herald Sun,* 11 July 1993.

[109] Robyn Archer, "The music of survival, pride and indominability", http://www.australiacouncil.gov.au/__data/assets/pdf_file/0018/32382/04_aia_music.pdf accessed 28 April 2012.

[110] Veronica Kelly, "Shadows After the Sunshine", *The Australian*, December 1999.

[111] "Priscilla hits the West End", *Australian Times*, London, 17 March 2009, p.7.

[112] Ben Wardle, "Donovan a king among queens", *London News*, 24 March 2009, p.3.

[113] Martha de Lacey, "Carry on camping, Jase", *London Lite*, 24 March 2009, p.27.

[114] *Daily Express*, London, 24 March 2009.

[115] "Wild ride for Priscilla Queen of the Desert", *Evening Standard*, London, 24 March 2009.

[116] Michael Billington, "Priscilla: queen of the desert but not the Palace theatre", *The Guardian*, 24 March 2009, p. 9.

[117] *Independent*, London, 24 March 2009.

[118] *Spectator*, London, 28 March 2009, p. 9.

[119] *Variety*, 27 October 2010.

[120] Patrick Healy, "A Broadway Makeover for 'Priscilla' Queens", *New York Times*, 10 March 2011.

[121] Healy, ibid.

[122] *New York Times*, 21 March 2011.

[123] *Broadway at Bedtime*, ibid.

[124] *The Age*, Melbourne, 15 February 1958, p. 19

South Africa: "Freedom is Coming"

[1] Lerner, *The Musical Theatre*, p. 9.

[2] Robert Palmer, "A Musical Born of South African Prtoest", *New York Times*, October 25, 1987.

[3] Rina Minervini, "Life with Big Daddy Ngema", Time Out, *Sunday Star*, Johannesburg, June 14, 1987.

[4] Percy Tucker, *Just the Ticket!*, Jonathan Ball Publishers, Johannesburg, 1997, p.458.

[5] *Sunday Times*, Johannesburg, June 21, 1987.

[6] *New York Times*, October 26, 1987.

[7] *Christian Science Monitor,* Boston, October 28, 1987.

[8] Wilborn Hampton . "Cast of 'Sarafina!' Evokes Their Lives In South Africa", *New York Times*, March 13, 1988

[9] Mark Gevisser, "I should be paid a million rands", *Weekly Mail & Guardian*, March 8, 1996.

[10] Jerry Mofokeng, "Theatre and Change in South Africa", edited by Geoffrey W. Davis and Anne Fuchs, page 85, Harwood Academic Publishers, 1996

[11] Nigel Noble, *Voices of Sarafina!*, New Yorker Video, 1988

[12] Lee Hirsch, *Amandla! A revolution in Four Part Harmony*, Artisan Entertainment, 2003.

[13] Ibid.

[14] Laura Jones, *Nothing Except Ourselves –The Harsh Times and Bold Theater of South Africa's Mbongeni Ngema*, Viking, New York, 1994, p. 9.

[15] Jones, ibid, p. 128.

[16] John Donnelly, "On South African stage, learning song, dance, and history", *Boston Globe*, May 28, 2004

[17] *Mail & Guardian Online*, 19 August 2008. http://mg.co.za/article/2008-08-19-sarafina-iii-a-hot-potato accessed 13/04/2011.

[18] Ibid.

[19] Tucker, p. 158.

[20] Ibid., p.127.

[21] Todd Matshikiza, *Chocolates for My Wife*, Hodder & Stoughton, London, 1961, p.122-3

[22] Tucker, p. 129.

[23] Tucker, p. 132.

[24] , Matshikiza, p. 125.

[25] Angus Wilson, @South Africa – A Visit to My Mother's Land", *Reflections in a Writer's Eye*, Viking Penguin, New York, 1986, p. 72.

[26] *Times*, London, Feb 24, 1961.

[27] Bernth Lindfors, "Charles Dickens and the Zulus", *Africans on Stage: Studies in Ethnological Show Business*, Inadiana University Press, Bloomington, 1999, p. 78.

[28] "Cape Town Charge Against Author",*Times*, London, Feb 24 1961.

[29] Tucker, p.133.

[30] Tucker, p. 131.

[31] Tucker, p.134.

[32] Tucker, p. 161.

[33] Rex Reed, "Fun From South Africa", *New York Times*, March 20, 1966.

[34] *Times*, April 10, 1964.

[35] *New York Times*, March 8, 1966.

[36] Tucker, p.45.

[37] Tucker, p. 297.

[38] *Times*, London, 20 November 1975, p. 10.

[39] *Sunday Times*, 23 November 1975. P.35.

[40] *Time*, 24 January 1975, p. 35.

[41] Jones, ibid., p.68.

[42] *Times*, 4 April 1972, p. 6.

[43] Irving Wardle, "Unfaked Happiness", *The Times*, 25 July 1975, p.7.

[44] Terri-Liza Fortein, "Umoja cast gumbooted out of Canada", *Saturday Argus*, March 15, 2008.

[45] *New York Times*, August 20, 1999

[46] Michael Church, "Mozart magic meets African brilliance", *The Independent*, London, 4 February 2008

"Down South American Way" – Musical Theatre in Latin America

[1] Milonga was a precursor to the tango. It originated in the Rio de la Plata in the 1870s and is generally in 2/4 time.

[2] Email to the author from Guillermo Masutti dated 8 March 2010

[3] Astor Piazzolla, *A Memoir*, Natalio Gorin, Amadaeus, pp. 70-1.

[4] Email from Pablo Gorlero to the author dated 20 June 2009.

[5] *Clarin.com*, 19 May 2005 edant.clarin.com/diario/2005/05/19/espectaculos/c-1101.htm accessed and translated 26 June 2010.

[6] Read Johnson, "Brazil goes Broadway yet keeps its own beat", *Los Angeles Times*, 31 July 2005.

[7] Larry Rohter, "The Real Carmen Miranda Under the Crown of Fruit", *New York Times*, 13 December 2001.

[8] Mac Margolis, "Way, Way Off-Broadway; Brazilian producers are mastering the art of the musical", *Newsweek International*, 30 August 2004.

[9] Apuntes. *Historia de Huanuco, Revista antológica* N° 4, ago. 2000, pp. 15-23 "Daniel Alomía Robles en primera persona".

[10] *La República* Peru, Tuesday, April 13, 2004

"The Theatre Is Alive" – Musical Theatre in Asia

[1] Leonie Stickland, *Gender Gymnastics: Performers, Fans and Gender Issues in the Takarazuka Revue of Contemporary Japan,* Doctoral thesis at Murdoch University, 2004, p.72.

[2] Jennifer Robertson, *Takarazuka – Sexual Politics and Popular Culture in Modern Japan*, University of California Press, Berkeley, 1998, p.156

[3] Leonie Stickland, *Gender Gymnastics: Performing and Consuming Japan'' Takarazuka Revue*, Trans Pacific Press, Melbourne, 2008.

[4] Email from Jeremy Sams dated 5 October 2010.

[5] Ben Whaley, bwhaleyjapan.blogspot.com, accessed 31 May 2009.

[6] Email from Dr. Michael Kunze dated 15 June 2009.

[7] David Jortner, Keiko McDonald, Kevin J. Wetmore, Modern Japanese Theatre and Performance, Lexington Books, 2007, p.238

[8] Freund, p. 730

[9] Atkey, *Broadway North*, p. 113.

[10] Cited in Freund, pp. 733-4.

[11] Mel Gussow, "Stage: 'Japanesque' Samurai Musical", *New York Times*, 15 November 1981.

[12] *Chopsticks New York*, 1 April 2010, www.chopsticksny.com/people/2010/04/01 Accessed 19 June 2010.

[13] *Musical Stages*, Issue 31, Christmas 2001, p.7.

[14] Mihir Bose, *Bollywood – A History*, Tempus, Stroud, 2006, p. 226.

[15] Bose, ibid, p. 234.

[16] K. Moti Gokulsing, K. Gokulsing and Wimal Dissanayake, *Indian Popular Cinema: A Narrative of Popular Change*, Trentham Books, 2004, pp 98-99.

[17] "Baz Lurhman Talks Awards and *Moulin Rouge*", http://movies.about.com/library/weekly/aa030902a.htm.

[18] Rudisill, K. "'My School Rocks!' Dancing Disney's *High School Musical* in India", *Studies in Musical Theatre* Volume 3 Number 3, Intellect Ltd., pp. 253-271, 2009.

[19] James Inverne, *Wrestling with Elephants*, Sanctuary, London, 2003, p.191.

[20] Alistair Smith, "Multimillion pound Chinese musical is Ed Fringe first", *The Stage*, London, 15 July 2010.

[21] Email from Simone Genatt dated 28 September 2010.

[22] Han Sunhee, "Korean film industry tunes up stage musicals", *Variety*, 22 July 2008

[23] "S. Korean musicals market to nearly triple in 2-3 years.", *Asia Pulse*, 7 March 2006

[24] Han Aran, "Comedian-turned-musical director sets bar high", *Korea.net*, 10 July 2008 http://www.korea.net/news/News/NewsView.asp?serial_no=20080709001&part=113&SearchDay= accessed 30 December 2008.

[25] Barbara Demick, "Les Miserables' of North Korea", *Los Angeles Times*, 22 February 2006.

[26] Email dated 23 July 2009

[27] Email dated 3 August 2009.

[28] "The world's her stage", *The Star*, Kuala Lumpur, 1 September 2003.

[29] 29 Dr.Aaron Hales, *The State on Stage: A Socio-Political Critique of Singaporean Musical Theatre*, Doctoral Thesis, University of Western Australia School of Music and School of Social and Cultural Studies, September 2009, p. 79-80.

[30] Dr. Aaron Hales, p. 119

[31] S Y Chua, "A triumph for Asia", *Malaysian Business*, Kuala Lumpur, Mar 16, 2002

[32] Ong Teng Cheong, *Report of the Advisory Council on Culture and the Arts*, Government of Singapore, 1989, p.12.

[33] William Peterson, *Theatre and the Politics of Culture in Contemporary Singapore*, Wesleyan University Press, Middletown, CT, 2001, pp. 195-6.

[34] Katharine Ee, "Tip of the peninsula", *The Stage*, London, 3 November 2011.

[35] Lily Kong, "Cultural Policy In Singapore: Negotiating Economic And Socio-Cultural Agenda", Geoforum, For Special Issue on "Culture, Economy, Policy" 2000

[36] Dr. Hales, p. 70.

[37] Dr. Hales, p. 61.

[38] Dr. Hales, p. p. 147.

[39] *Front* Season 3, Episode 6, Arts Central TV, Singapore, broadcast 21 December 2007

[40] Sonia Kolesnikov-Jessop, "In Singapore, Musical Theater That Prefers Its Own Local Flavor", *New York Times*, 24 May 2010.

[41] Ibid.

[42] Dr. Hales, p. 230.

[43] Dr. Hales, pp. 253-4.

New Musicals: "You Have to Kiss a Lot of Frogs"

[1] Richard Kisland, *The Musical: A Look at the American Musical Theater*, Prentice Hall Inc., Englewood Cliffs, NJ, p.255

[2] Mark Steyn, *Broadway Babies Say Goodnight*, Faber and Faber, London, p. 163

[3] Mattthew Hemley, "Don Black Defends Lloyd Webber's TV Talent Shows", *The Stage*, London, 1 May 2008.

[4] Roger Foss, "Join the Parade", *What's On Stage*, London, September 2007

[5] "Kiss of the Spider Woman", *Working in the Theatre*, American Theatre Wing/ City University of New York, September 1993

[6] Robert Viagas, "Where in the World is Cameron Mackintosh?", *Show Music*, Vol. 15 No. 1, Spring 1999.

[7] Lees, p. 101.

[8] See Brown, *Moss Hart*, p. 338.

[9] Max Wilk, *They're Playing our Song*, Atheneum, New York, 1973, p. 237

[10] Tracey Moore, "The Out-of-Town tryout Goes Back to School", *Studies in Musical Theatre*, Vol. 3 No. 3, Intellect Ltd., 2010, p.304.

[11] House of Commons Culture, Media and Sport Committee, Theatre, Fifth Report of Session 2004-05 Volume III Oral and written evidence Ordered by The House of Commons to be printed 15 March 2005, HC 254-111 [Incorporating HC 1153-i, Session 2002-03] Published on 30 March 2005 by authority of the House of Commons London: The Stationery Office Limited

[12] Malcolm Gladwell, *Outliers – The Story of Success*, Allen Lane, London, 2008, p. 137

[13] Tom Shea, *Broadway's Most Wanted*, Brassey's, Washington, D.C., 2004, p.66.

[14] [14] Scott Brown, "How Can Musical Theater be Saved?", Vulture.com, 24 May 2012, accessed 21 July 2012

[15] "Lehman's Terms", BMI Lehman Engel Musical Theatre Workshop Newsletter Vol 3, No. 7 June/July, 2000

[16] see Engel, *Words With Music*, p.116.

[17] Tom Jones, *Making Musicals*, p. 89

[18] Lee Davis, "Two Days in Musical Theatre Paradise", *Show Music*, Vol. 15 No. 2, Summer 1999

[19] *The Independent*, London, 29 April 2004

[20] Philip Headley, "The Theatre Royal Stratford East's Musical Theatre Journey", *The Big Life* (published script), Oberon Books, London, 2004, p. 4.

[21] Episode 26, *Musical Talk*, 4 March 2008. (podcast)

[22] Sondheim, *Look, I Made a Hat*, p.xxi.

[23] Steyn, ibid., p. 226.

[24] http://www.britishtheatreguide.info/reviews/daboyz-rev.htm, accessed 1 April 2009

[25] *The Independent*, London, 9 May 2003.

[26] Charlotte Cripps, "Hip hop don't stop", *www.breakinconvention.com*, 27 April 2004 (accessed 1 April 2009)

Are We Up For It?

[1] "Sondheim decries modern Broadway", *The Times*, London, 6 March 2012.

[2] Email from Richard Maltby Jr. to the author, dated 15 August 2004.

[3] Platform talk given at the Royal National Theatre's Lyttelton Theatre, 24 May 1990, chaired by Mark Steyn. *Platform Papers 5. Musicals... and Sondheim*, RNT Publications Dept.,

[4] Scott Brown, "How Can Musical Theater be Saved?", Op. cit.

[5] *Equity Quarterly*, Canadian Actors' Equity Association, Winter 2010.

6 Bradley, p. 198.

7 Email to the author dated 9 April 2012.

8 This isn't new. The CBC cancelled *Don Messer's Jubilee* in the 1960s because, although it still attracted a reasonably large audience, it didn't appeal to the all-important "baby boomers".

9 Simon Tait, "The Writing's on the Wall", *The Stage*, London, February 26, 2009.